Film
Review
1984-5

Film Review 1984-5

INCLUDING VIDEO RELEASES

F. Maurice Speed

COLUMBUS BOOKS

LONDON

Copyright © 1984 F. Maurice Speed

First published in Great Britain in 1984 by Columbus Books
Devonshire House, 29 Elmfield Road, Bromley, Kent BR1 1LT

Designed by Fred Price

British Library Cataloguing in Publication Data
Film review.—1984–85
1. Moving-pictures—Periodicals
791.43′05   PN1993
ISBN 0-86287-168-9
ISBN 0-86287-169-7 Pbk

Printed and bound by Clark Constable,
Edinburgh, London, Melbourne

Contents

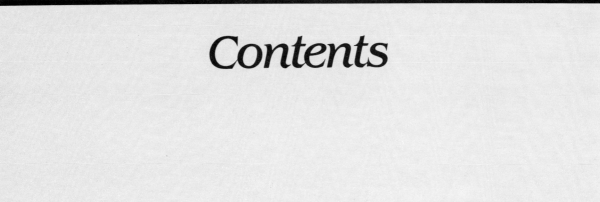

Introduction

F. MAURICE SPEED

Even after watching the ups and downs of the film world for 40 years, this is a strange and uneasy period for the Cinema. Every week one reads contrasting, confusing and often contradictory stories – today the Cinema is dying . . . tomorrow a boom in British studios is forecast. But the hard fact is that the introduction of the video-cassette has done the cinema of bricks-and-mortar no good at all, even if, as many think, it will prove a shot in the arm for film production in the long run. There is also the hard fact that cinemas in Britain are still closing. During 1983, the Rank Group put the shutters up at 11 of their houses and the ABC moved the projectors out of nine of theirs. Along with various other smaller managements abandoning the showing of films in some of their cinemas, selling out to bingo or whatever, the final result was that the total of screens (as apart from cinemas, in which there are now often two, three or in some cases even four mini-cinemas, or screens) was reduced from 1,528 to 1,439. And, as far as I can gather, closings have continued at a similar rate during 1984. According to the CEA (Cinema Exhibitors Association) there were only 1,304 screens operating in Britain at the end of February 1984.

It is particularly sad when the closing of a local cinema means that whole communities are. left without reasonably easy access to films, the nearest cinema being so far away that large numbers of potential regular, or even irregular, patrons lose the cinema-going habit altogether and rely entirely upon the small screen for their large-screen fare.

In contrast to this gloomy story there was the cheering news that if anything there has been a slight upturn in movie-going generally in Britain during 1984. One reasonably reliable estimate suggests that against 1982's all-time low of 64 million, some 71 million went to the cinema in Britain in 1983. But it would be foolish to get too hopeful about a trend which might easily be reversed.

Definitely heartening news, however, emanated from the British film studios, which have been considerably busier during 1984 than they were in 1983. There have been times this year when they have been almost bursting at the seams. And most uplifting of all has been the rising status – and commercial success abroad – of the British film, which has seldom if ever enjoyed such world-wide prestige as it does right now.

Internationally it is still the really big films, the so-called blockbusters (be they made in America, or here with American money) which bring the big blockbusting returns, making it more of a gamble than ever for the small producer, making a routine first feature film on a carefully worked out budget, to make a profit. Regretfully, so many of these often critically acclaimed movies fall by the wayside, either because they fail to gain the so badly needed circuit booking or, when they do, they fail to please a movie-going public weaned on the big budget spectacular. History has shown again and again that it is seldom the 'best' films that enjoy the greatest success; some real stinkers make a lot of entirely unjustified money, while a number of delightful, intelligent and artistic little movies end up as financial disasters.

The most successful movie of 1983, in terms of hard cash return, was George Lucas's third 'Star Wars' episode, *The Return of the Jedi*, which by the beginning of 1984 had already taken $165.5 million at the American and Canadian box-offices combined, since which time there has been a steady flow from all parts of the world into the Lucas coffers.

The only film to show any real competition to the Lucas movie was *Tootsie*, with a 1983 take of $94.5 million. Third place in the financial league went to *Trading Places* ($40.5 million), followed by (according to *Variety*) *War Games* ($36.5 million), *Staying Alive* ($33), *Octopussy* ($33), *Mr Mom* ($31.5), *48 Hours* ($30), *National Lampoon's Vacation* ($29.5), and *Risky Business* ($28.5). As a snide aside, I cannot help wondering how high, if anywhere, any of these movies would feature in a Critics' Circle list of 1983's 'best' movies?

My own list would probably include *Trading Places* (one of the best comedies of the period I thought) but the dire *Toy* certainly would not, even if it appears to have taken more money in America than did *Gandhi*. Nor would the awful *Porkys 2* get any vote of mine, even if it took $17.5 million across the Atlantic, against the mere $3.5 million which that marvellous British comedy *Educating Rita* appears to have accrued so far.

You may find it interesting to compare America's ten leading multi-million-dollar-making films with our own top ten, which were: *E.T. The Extra Terrestrial*, *The Return of the Jedi*, *Octopussy*, *Gandhi*, *Tootsie*, *Superman III*, *An Officer and a Gentleman*, *Staying Alive*, *Airplane II* and *Monty Python's Meaning of Life*. As a hint of the monies earned by these ten, *Octopussy* accrued more than £3 million and *Gandhi* achieved about a half million less.

Film production in 1984 began on a quite sensational note. During the first six months the major Hollywood companies launched 63 films (42 in the States and 21 abroad) as against 59 during the same period in the previous year. And this figure is all the more impressive when you realize that the latter number was already some 52 per cent up on the same period in 1982. (In fact *Variety* came up with an overall figure for the rise of American productions in the first half of 1984 of 41 per cent.)

Although British studios are busy, many of the movies being made here are American financed. But the boom may not last. If the present Finance Bill becomes law without amendment, it will effectively dissuade American companies

Directors at Work. Steven Spielberg's first success was a designed-for-TV movie, *Duel*, a marvellous compact and tense thriller, which when shown in the cinemas made a great impact. He then went on to make such blockbusting movies as *Jaws* and *Close Encounters of the Third Kind*. Currently at work on this year's Warner Bros release, *Twilight Zone – The Movie*, he is seen here behind the camera making his segment, which focusses on the rediscovery of childhood joys.

from coming here to set up shop and make their movies in our studios. The reason is complicated – simply put the Bill will mean artistes working in this country will have to pay full UK taxes, without being able to offset UK earnings against American tax bills. That it is a very real threat was illustrated by Pierre Spengler – the Salkinds' producer now working here on the company's *Santa Klaus* picture – who announced that if this clause in the Bill is not altered the company will be moving its future line-up of productions to Ireland, Hungary, or other countries where tax incentives are still offered. British production would almost certainly slump disastrously if all the welcome foreigners now working here, or planning to do so, turned to other countries. However, though the picture is gloomy, it may still change before the deadline, as it will be quite a while yet before the Bill reaches the statute book by which time various amendments, hopefully, will have been made.

So what are the current trends in the Cinema? What kind of new movies will dominate the screen in 1984–85? It certainly will not be the gore-and-guts thriller, as the audience for this kind of celluloid fare is diminishing. Against a 1982 peak of

these often highly repellent movies, 1983 saw the number on offer halved. Of the overall total of around 50 such movies released, all but three were the result of previous years' production and were presumably hurried into circulation from the shelf on the assumption that it must be now or never if they are to give their makers any sort of cash return. The trio of newly-mades were, by the way, *The Dead Zone*, *Christine* and *Amityville 3D*. There are a number of thrillers scheduled for 1984 production, but it looks as if they will be comparatively few and far between, and then less gorily sickening than many of their predecessors.

The rise and fall of the more lurid kind of spine-chiller is a very old, oft repeated, but seldom heeded, Hollywood story. Following the big success of one or two of these movies in the early 1980s, a whole gaggle of producers leapt on the bandwagon, churning out a succession of gory horrors which eventually disgusted and turned away even the most hardened fans of this kind of movie. The story has happened so regularly in the past, and will happen again no doubt in the future, as the rat-racers in the business try to earn the fast buck.

In contrast, science-fiction retains its hold on the audience, as demonstrated by the big success of films like *The Return of the Jedi*, *War Games*, *Superman II* and so on. And *E.T.* continues to coin in the money around the world.

A welcome statistic was the steady decrease in interest shown by the public in the hard-core pornographic picture, the producers of which are now turning to the video-cassette as a more likely path to riches. On average the makers of such movies reckon to get a $50,000 return from the new outlet, which with a further $50,000 from foreign sales still represents a pretty good profit. But even this bonanza may not last for long – at least in Britain, where the outcry against the so-called 'nasties' has reached a pitch of intensity that makes legislation seem only a matter of time.

What delights me is the success that comedy films have had recently. Films like *Tootsie*, *Trading Places* and *Risky Business* are all among the most popular movies of the period, proving that we need more laughter in the cinema. But sadly that old dependable the Western, with its international appeal, has suffered an eclipse beyond anything previously experienced. One has to turn to the small screen these days for this kind of cinema fare, where such films are proving once more their great general appeal.

Before I go any further I would like to get my annual list of complaints off my chest. Top of them comes a repeat of my main grumble last year, the question of foul language in the films. The needless and often mindless use of such words continues more or less unabated: one film critic actually counted the use of the four-letter word beginning with 'f' no less than 80 times in the re-make of *Scarface* (it was not used once, of course, in the original 1932 *Scarface*). This ludicrous and undefendable proliferation of such words is a reflection of the directors, screenwriters, producers and everyone involved and not only shows a lack of good taste, imagination and artistry, but is so utterly *boring*. If it is thought this sort of thing adds realism to a movie I would in riposte suggest that so would showing someone going to the toilet, but this, thank heavens, still appears to be unacceptable, and I can only recall this being shown on one occasion in a movie and that was not one I found particularly endearing.

While the occasional use of a swear word in context is

completely justifiable, nothing can excuse a continuous flow of such words, downgrading the English language and encouraging the young to think such expressions are obligatory for adulthood.

Another thing which regularly infuriates me in the cinema is shoddy, careless speaking and recording. Players are allowed, indeed, seem to be encouraged, to speak their lines with their mouths full, mumble or otherwise make them unintelligible. Speaking with their backs to the cameras and microphones is yet another fault. And there is nothing more exasperating than a conversation recorded against such high background noise – traffic, factory machines, aeroplanes or whatever – that it is virtually impossible to hear more than the occasional word. The same excuse that is often trotted out about adding 'realism' to a scene is nonsense. What is the use of dialogue if it is deliberately drowned? Many films and many players also give the lie to this: I don't think many lines were lost in *The Dresser*, in which it was a sheer delight to hear dialogue spoken fluently, (and recorded equally well) by players who revealed the elocution training which too many modern screen actors seem to lack – even one of this year's Oscar winners could have done with a few terms at RADA.

Directors at Work. Another of Hollywood's new crop of golden boy writer-directors, Francis Ford Coppola discusses a scene from his Warner Bros release *The Outsiders* with some of his young players (C. Thomas Howell, Matt Dillon and Ralph Macchio). After his great *Godfather* and *Apocalypse Now* successes, Coppola produced an awful flop with his *One from the Heart*, which, made in his own Zoetrope studios by his patented movie-making process, reputedly lost more than $20 million and was largely instrumental in forcing him to sell the studios.

Now back to finance. After a minor panic about rising production costs a little while ago, which led to all kinds of announcements about cost-cutting and budget pruning, the cost of movie-making is again steadily soaring. At a rough average the cost of the 150 movies now in various stages of planning, production and showing during 1984 will finally work out at well over the $11.5 million mark each (against 1983's 130 costing $9.7 million apiece). One reason for the increased cost has been the agreement between producers and players reached in July 1983 which was said would result in the take-home pay of the performers rising by about $60 million in the year. It took nearly two months of hard negotiations to reach this agreement, finalized in a 36-hour marathon in which both sides were more than anxious to avoid a repetition of the 10-week strike which occurred three years ago and proved a total disaster for all concerned with Hollywood movie-making.

Obviously the new budgets have been made with the assumption that after cinema release the films will earn large amounts from subsequent exposure on cable TV, television channels, home video and other subsidiary sources, for many of the productions appear to have little or no chance of making a profit from cinema release alone. An interesting comparison is that the cost of a film made for TV showing alone averages out at just over $2 million, with a series costing around the same for each hour's segment.

Two of the most expensive films to be screened during 1984 are likely to be *Greystoke* and *Cotton Club* (both costing about $30 million), with *Supergirl*, *A Woman for All Time*, *Ghost Busters*, *The Bounty* and *Rhinestone* all costing a little less. But even more expensive will be *Santa Klaus*, to be released at Christmas, which will have costs of about $50 million by the

time it is finally wrapped up. One reason why the film is costing so much, so the producers are reported as saying, is 'the expense of getting eight reindeer, a sleigh and the film's hero into the air!'

One company not addicted to this size of budget, however, is the busy Cannon Group. At the start of the year it began negotiations with the various unions trying to get them to agree to concessions so that a steady stream of first features could be made at around only $2.5 million each. It seems likely that the unions will agree (under certain circumstances) and if they do it will almost inevitably mean other producers doing the same, so leading to an increase in the overall number of movies made.

Although it has been a good year for British films, it is not a completely happy story. For instance, a number of movies made primarily for Channel 4 and partly financed by it have not had the initial cinema success that was hoped for, even when they have been critically acclaimed and have done well at their London launchings. Not winning any circuit interest, and obtaining too few provincial bookings, they are likely to wind up in the red. A good example is *Angel*, a very good Irish-made movie financially supported by Channel 4 and distributed by the BFI, which only took a mere £10,000 from the cinemas, nearly half of which was spent of pre-publicity. The highly acclaimed *Draughtsman's Contract* has earned little more than £350,000 from bookings so far, while *Heat and Dust*, James Ivory's classic film took around £200,000 during its 35-week premiere run at the Curzon, but earned considerably less than that when distributed to 145 cinemas out of town.

A big hurdle for TV-financed movies is that both the Rank and EMI circuits, many think quite rightly, adhere strictly to the rule that a film must have a three-year cinema life before it gets a showing on TV.

One of the year's big success stories again relates to the Cannon Group, now making a large number of movies and showing them in a large number of cinemas. Having bought the Classic cinema chain in 1982 for £7 million, within a few months they had made their investment highly profitable, raising the income from around £2 to £15 million. Now they plan to extend their 128 screens by about a further dozen. And of course they have quite recently also purchased the Rank-Tuschinski Dutch cinema chain, hoping to repeat the Classic story there. Yoran Globus and Menaham Golan, the men who run Cannon, have the right ideas about cinema-going. They say that a cinema must be a home from home, and they want all their cinemas to be comfortable, clean, friendly and well managed. To provide this they are prepared to spend large sums on renovation and improvement, accepting the maxim that to make money you must spend money.

Although 1984 seems likely to be a busier and better year than 1983 for British studios, this does not mean 1983 was a bad year for them. Despite the forebodings of the beginning of the year, they did pretty well, far above best expectations. Apart from Shepperton, where the promised *Boomerang* production did not show up, some two dozen films took varying space in the Pinewood, Elstree, Twickenham and other studios. And though most were American financed, six movies were wholly British (*Bullshot, Electric Dreams, The Cold Room, Slayground, Squaring the Circle* and the prestigious *The Dresser*). Any gaps were usually filled by American TV series, of which a number are regularly made over here.

An interesting studio story was the acquisition of the old Bray Studios, so long the home of those grand old Hammer Horrors, by the Samuelson Group who paid £100,000 for them in March 1984. It is not generally known that at over 11,000 square feet, Bray can boast one of the largest 'floors' in the UK.

Coincidentally Hammer Films announced a comeback with a 13-movie schedule made at least primarily for TV, under the label 'The Hammer House of Mystery and Suspense'. The first of these films will be called *Czechmate*, with *A Distant Scream* and *The Late Nancy Irving* to follow. The directors will include Peter Sasdy and John Hough, both of whom worked on previous Hammer productions, and Fox will be concerned in the package.

On the other side of the Atlantic, it was a year of smiles for the exhibitors. For the third year running the box office reached a new high with 1,173 billion tickets sold to movie-goers during 1983. The number of admissions was slightly down on 1982, but increased admission charges meant a rise in total receipts. During the period, the number of screens rose to nearly 19,000. The number of drive-ins (something which has never taken on in this country) fell quite markedly, but this was more than made up for by new cinema openings and by increasing the number of screens within existing cinemas.

As for other trans-Atlantic news, the first year of Columbia Pictures under Coca-Cola ownership saw profits outstripping all forecasts and hopes, adding $91 million to the parent company's profits. Gulf and Western, the conglomerate which now owns Paramount Pictures, also did very well from its celluloid subsidiary, which brought a higher return in 1983 than 1982, though after losses incurred by the TV division it had to show a $2 million loss on the entertainment side of the business. Warners did well, too, the motion picture division of the company showing an 82 per cent rise over 1982 figures.

After 30 years, it now seems certain that the Thatcher government will abolish the Eady Fund, the levy on cinemas whereby a percentage of takings goes to a fund to which producers can apply for part of their production cost. But everyone concerned agrees that it will have to be replaced in one way or another. One popular idea in the film world is that a similar levy should now be imposed on any TV company showing cinema films on its channels, a suggestion understandably not popular with the TV companies. Another idea is that a contribution should be made by the video-cassette industry.

One of the main beneficiaries from the Eady Fund has been the National Film Finance Company (another is The National Film and TV School) which has been getting a grant of £1.4 million a year. When the Fund was introduced it was intended for British producers only but in recent years, to constant criticism, overseas producers making films here have also been able to draw on it.

In Britain it now costs £50,000 to premiere a film in one of the London showcase cinemas, like the Odeon, Empire or Leicester Square Theatre, and a film needs to take more than £1 million at the box office before it can hope to break even. The danger of this is, of course, that the smaller films which cannot expect to do this sort of business, may not get any cinema release, but will be sold directly on completion to a television company, or to video and cable TV.

Satellite cable TV made its British debut on 16 January

1984, and now has some 10,000 subscribers situated in and around the Wiltshire town of Swindon. Named Sky Channel and operated by Satellite Television Ltd (a company in which the controversial Australian newspaper baron Richard Murdoch is involved) it already has subscribers in Norway, Finland and Switzerland. The initial schedule included films, repeats of favourite TV series (such as *Charlie's Angels*, etc) and American football matches.

A survey launched by one advertising agency concluded that by the end of 1984 one out of every three households in the country will be owning or renting a video recorder. And in another survey by the Consumers' Association, it was revealed that the British are the most persistent television viewers in Europe, the average viewing time being 3 hours a day. Only the Spanish, the Portuguese and the Greeks are slightly less addicted to TV. More serious French viewers only switch their set on for an average of two hours a day and, bottom of the league, Norway only watches for one hour a day.

Before leaving the British cinema scene, I would like to pay a warm and well earned tribute to that brave, dedicated, and mostly successful, delightful band of people who are running London's specialized cinemas. I am thinking of Romaine Hart (the Electric), the Engels (Artificial Eye Co, which runs the Lumière, Camden Plaza and Chelsea cinemas), David and Barbara Stone (the Gate cinemas) and Ivon Jarosy (the Academy). Charles and Kitty Cooper deserve similar praise, although it is sad that they have had to give up their Paris-Pullman and Finchley Phoenix cinemas. Without these stalwarts, and others, we would see far fewer fine films from abroad.

Last year I painted a rose-tinted picture of the French cinema, but quite recently, I have had a letter from an old friend across the Channel warning me that this year the picture has not been quite so bright. Apparently the big movies, both American and French, have continued to do extremely well, but attendance figures have levelled off and there are signs of a slight decline. The essentially French movies, the art or *auteur* productions, also seem to be failing a little in their appeal to the extent that some critics are already writing mournfully of their demise. Certainly a number of films highly valued by the critics made no impact on the gallic movie goers, though Truffaut's *Vivement Dimanche* and Philippe Labro's *The Crime* were both major financial and critical successes.

Not daunted by these portents, however, French producers continued to make more films on larger budgets during 1983 than they did in 1982. Among them are: Bertrand Blier's *My Buddy's Girl*, which did not seem to please very many people when it was shown; *Fort Saganne*, with the ubiquitous Gérard Départieu starring with Catherine Deneuve and Phillipe Noiret; Costa-Gavras's *Hanna K*; Claude Sautet's *Garçon*, starring the increasingly politically involved Yves Montand; and Francis Girod's *Tchao Pantin*, which has a starry triumvirate of Catherine Deneuve, Michel Serrault and Jean-Louis Trintignant.

In contrast to Britain, where the Arts have been hit quite severely by cash cuts, France's socialist government has upped the national spending on them by 15 per cent this year, and the film and audio-visual industry will actually be better off in 1984 by some 38 per cent over 1983.

But the smaller, specialized French cinemas are not happy. With four major circuits ready to pounce on any film which

seems to offer possibilities of success, the art cinemas find their choice of programme increasingly restricted. While in the past they could run, say, a Bergman film for a long and rewarding period, the circuits now snap up this kind of movie even though they may subsequently drop it like a hot potato if it does not prove to be the moneymaker they had expected it to be – by which time such films are of little help to the art houses. My gloomy Gallic friend even suggests that the situation is such that the art film will be dead within a few years and the cinemas that habitually depend on them will be finished.

Directors at Work. Franco Zeffirelli with his star singer Placido Domingo in the ITC release *La Traviata*. Magnificent in every department, with some stunningly artistic photography, imaginative settings and powerful vocal performances, this adaptation of the Verdi work is almost beyond question the finest operatic film ever made.

In France, as most places elsewhere, the video-cassette has been providing plenty of news. In particular there were some bold headlines when none other than that great favourite Jean-Paul Belmondo challenged in the courts the present ruling that a film could not be released on video. The film

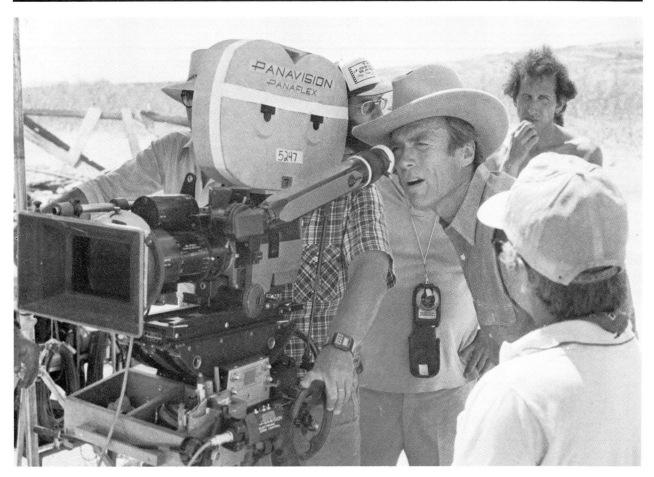

Directors at Work. Having made an extremely successful transition from the laconic star of Sergio Leone's 'Spaghetti Westerns' (as The Man With No Name in *A Few Dollars More, The Good, the Bad, and the Ugly*, etc) to director/star in the early 1970s, Clint Eastwood now combines starring roles with both the direction and production of movies made by his own company. He is seen here behind the cameras during the making of one of his more recent movies, the Warner Bros release *Honkytonk Man*.

which sparked off the row was Belmondo's own *La Marginal*, which his friend and business associate René Château wanted to transfer to video and sell in the shops. So far there has not been a judgment in the case, but it could have very important implications for the film industry in France.

In Canada producers are increasingly relying on pre-sold sales to television to raise their production money. In 1979, some 55 features were made and few if any had such arrangements. In 1983, only 17 features were completed and of the total only 6 were started without any firm contract for subsequent television exposure – and cash.

In Spain, the newly elected socialist government offered increased cash incentives for film production and a producer could get as much as a 75 per cent subsidy. To promote the showing of locally-made films, censorship was abolished and a quota introduced by which for every three foreign (dubbed) movies shown there must be one Spanish film on the programme.

In Italy, Renzo Rossellini, the president and managing director of Gaumont-Italia, stepped down (to be replaced by Mario Anniballi) complaining that his countrymen were becoming increasingly uninterested in locally-made films even when directed by such outstanding names as Tarkovsky, Olmi, Fellini, Wajda and Wertmuller. This meant the Americans were allowed to take up some 75 per cent of the screening time with their films in the Italian cinemas.

Figures indicate that movie-going in Italy declined by some 16 per cent during 1983 and showed little sign of revival in early 1984. Production figures were down, too, from a peak of about 250 movies annually a few years back to something like 100 planned for 1984. The soaring costs of production in Italy have not helped, just as the 20 per cent annual rise in seat prices has made it difficult for cinemas to keep their patrons. Luckily for the studios, at least some of the falling off in feature films has been offset by increasing American production for television, kicking off this year with a 13-episode series *The Gladiators*, and further series are in the pipeline, often with American players and made in English.

In Holland this year attendance figures actually rose by around 2 per cent, not much, maybe, but healthy when you compare this with similar statistics in other countries. The film industry is still very small, yet it is looking hopefully to the future. Certainly the movies unveiled at the Sorrento Festival were varied and often top-flight, ranging from cartoons to the *avante garde* features like *Naughty Boys*, and from documentaries to polished commecial thrillers such as the internationally released *The Lift*. Producers in Holland are becoming more ambitious and are obviously tailoring at least some of their productions to the American market.

Directors at Work. One of the crop of extremely promising new young British directors, Richard Lonoraine (right) discusses a scene with star Michael Palin during the filming of Handmade Films' *The Missionary*, The teaming proved highly successful and certainly launched former Monty Python performer Palin in a big way, for he not only wrote this amusing yet sometimes dramatic and moving film but also co-produced and wrote some of the best musical numbers.

In neighbouring Belgium, where annual production is around the dozen mark (in either French or Flemish), movie-goers still show a lack of interest in local product, preferring the more lavish American movies. This means that Belgian producers cannot hope to break even, let alone make a profit, unless they can get their films shown outside of the country.

Some extremely interesting facts about films in China were published in *Variety* in late 1983. With only one, the National, distributor and exhibition chain, the country has some 2,670 cinemas, and 118 film studios which, in 1982, produced 112 movies. China also has 38 TV stations and 246 relay stations serving the country's 200 million TV sets.

In the USSR, again according to *Variety* the cinema comes top of the entertainment league, with theatre and the ballet not far behind. There are 120 million movie goers, giving rise to a 4.25 billion yearly attendance figure. The cinemas are clean and offer fixed-time programmes, with nobody allowed to sit through a film again. The country's 39 studios produce about 150 films a year, each having a budget of about £¾ million. The studio workers (about one third of a million) are all employed on a permanent weekly basis.

In Japan, they are more lavish, Akira Kurosawa's *Ran* (based on Shakespeare's *King Lear*) costing nearly £9 million. The country also staged a big international film festival for the first time in the summer.

Greece makes some 50 films a year of which only about one third are good enough to have any hope of getting a showing outside their country of origin. Here, too, producers are finding it difficult to break even without getting export cash, and the government has stepped in with financial incentives to help Greek productions towards success in overseas markets.

In West Germany there was also a decline in film-going, the 1983 total over 1982 showing a fall of 11.8 per cent. Production, however, has been pretty steady.

News Clips...
Films continued to provide a major part of Britain's 1983 Christmas television entertainment. From Christmas Eve to Boxing Day 9 cinema and 2 special TV films were shown on ITV (34 between 17 and 30 December, plus 8 TV features); on Channel 4, the comparable figures were 9 and 31; on BBC 1, they were 10 and 27; and on BBC 2 30 and 32.

Another bite of the hand.... Touring Israel to promote the Cannon film about New York's Jewish community, *Over the Brooklyn Bridge*, star Elliott Gould is reported as saying: 'The innocence and the fascination of the film world ended some time back. Today the computers have taken over. They are taking away our work and our talent. Spielberg, for instance,

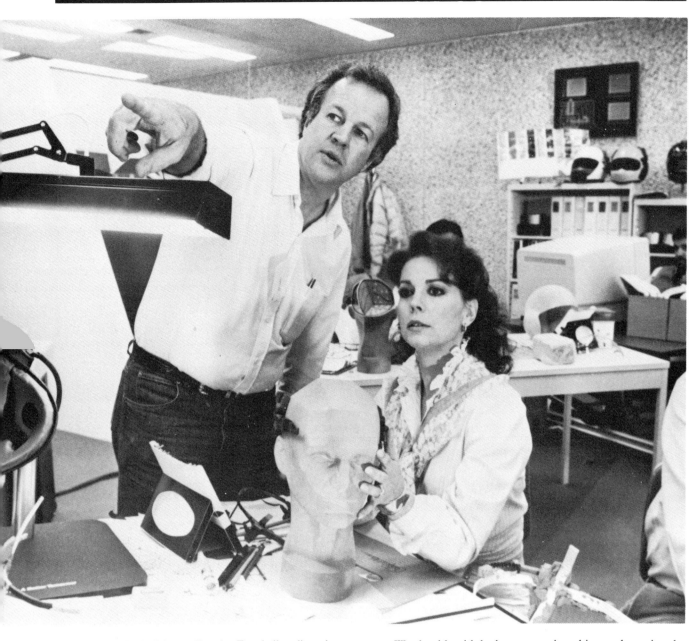

Directors at Work. Director Douglas Trumbull outlines the next scene to Natalie Wood in MGM/UA's *Brainstorm*, a film which had more than its fair share of production problems, including Miss Wood's sad and tragic death during the making of the movie.

is forced to keep repeating himself. Nobody wants to take risks, everyone wants to make millions and sell their soul.'

While it is next to impossible for a member of the public to get past the gates of a British film studio, in Munich they welcome you with open arms – and collecting boxes. The Bavarian studios offer guided tours *during production* for £2 a time. Passing through the sets at 6-minute intervals, these curious onlookers might be expected to interfere with production, but this has not been so, and up to 2,000 visitors (£4,000) a day are now going through with everyone quite happy about it. Will British studios copy?

We should, with luck, at some time this year be seeing the $10 million debut feature of United Artists using the 70mm-12 track multiphonic 3-D system. Seeing is believing. So often in the past promises of new 3-D systems have proved pie-in-the-sky, but this time the promise of a stero-space 3-D system looks as if it has reached the commercial stage.

The film that created some of the hottest controversy at the Cannes Festival this year was musician Giorgio Moroder's refashioned Fritz Lang silent masterpiece *Metropolis*, which took him 2½ years to produce (he tracked down every known negative to be sure the picture was as complete as Lang intended) and to which he has added a modern musical soundtrack. And in Paris in the spring, the Cinemathèque Française premiered André Antoine's Belgian production *L'Hirondelle et la Mesange – The Swallow and the Titmouse* which, made more than 60 years ago, has never previously had a cinema showing. The original was shelved when completed and the version now shown was assembled from an untidy mass of some six hours of 'rushes'.

The revival of interest in the silent movies appears to be gathering pace, notice the way they are now showing old movies on TV. And after the major, somewhat sensational success enjoyed by Abel Gance's *Napoleon* and Cuckor's *The Crowd*, Paramount came up with new versions of Pabst's *Pandora's Box* and *Diary of a Lost Girl* (1929), both starring Louise Brooks.

At the Disney Studios, where a tug-of-war for control of the company developed during 1984, an innovation in the production of animated features is likely to give them a greater chance of financial success in the future. Some 20 years ago the studio switched from the laborious and costly hand-copying method of production to the faster and far less expensive photo-copying process. Now, in 1984, there has been a similar revolutionary technical advance with the adoption of the Animation Photo Transfer process. Twice as fast, the new method is claimed to add clarity to the image and will save as much as half a million dollars on the production of an animated feature.

According to the inventor, Disney's animation director Ed Hannen, it will also give the producer a greater range of colour tones, too. It was first tried-out experimentally in *Mickey's Christmas Carol* and is being used for the first time in a feature film *The Black Cauldron*, due to be released in 1985.

An interesting move by the Disney company this year has been the formation of a new company called Touchstone

Directors at Work. Australian director George Miller is not conducting the orchestra – as it might appear from this shot – but is in fact giving instructions to his cast of the last and by far the best segment of the Warner Bros release *Twilight Zone – The Movie*. Miller is one of several Australian directors who has been tempted to take all his considerable talent to make movies in America.

Films. This will be responsible in future for releasing all the movies that have anything but the 'U' certificate which has been such a feature of Disney films in the past. It will mean that while the Disney label will continue to guarantee 'family fare' the company will be able to diversify into the production and release of adult movies, such as the highly successful 1984 comedy release *Splash*, which is all about a bachelor who falls in love with a mermaid (shades of Glynis Johns in *Miranda!*).

And the future . . .

The cinema has always survived its various trials and tribulations. It has suffered increasingly over the years from rival forms of entertainment; but TV did not, as went the gloomy prophecy, kill it off, in fact it has worked to the contrary. The crisis caused by the video-cassette will get worse before it gets better, and more cinemas in Britain will close in 1985, but in the long run I think we shall see the good, attractive cinemas holding their own. And that is also likely to happen worldwide.

Film production, as I have said, is booming right now and seems likely to continue to flourish in the foreseeable future. Employment in the industry is rising – and producers' cigars are getting longer and fatter. The British film after its stay in the doldrums seems to be reconquering America and finding favour all over the world, thanks to the reality of the stories and the brilliance of the technicians.

Personally I have found 1984 so far a good year – more often than in 1983, I have emerged from press shows happy, less often depressed and disgusted. We have been shown more and better films from abroad, thanks to the gallant effort of our specialist cinemas. And though there are still too many people in the business who would be better employed elsewhere, there is a lot of real talent in the industry and a reassuring number of enthusiastic and dedicated youngsters waiting for the chance to show off their ability.

The Big Picture on the Small Screen

ALAN WARNER IN HOLLYWOOD

Watching American television today, it is hard to imagine a time when made-for-TV movies did not exist, yet both the term and the commodity it describes are contemporary innovations, brought about partly by the small screen's enormous appetite for new material. Today's television and movie industries are hotbeds of talent, with actors and actresses, ideas and spin-offs bouncing back and forth between them. But the traditional film side still claims superiority over television which it considers to be a fledgling offshoot. More than ever, small-screen versions of ideas for movies are being made, sometimes even from predominantly unsuccessful big-screen productions (as with *Author, Author*), but usually with hit titles and concepts (as with *Blue Thunder* and *Nine to Five*). In the opposite direction, there is the much-troubled 1983 release *Twilight Zone – The Movie*, which was adapted from the much-revered Rod Serling series of the 1960s, while yet another extension of the *Star Trek* saga is being readied for release, some 15 years after the series was cancelled.

Around 30 years ago, the independent television station WOR-TV in New York began showcasing the old RKO Radio pictures under the overall title 'Million Dollar Movie', ironically ushered in each time by Max Steiner's majestic 'Tara's Theme' from *Gone with the Wind*. That was just the beginning, of course, and since that time, the floodgates have opened wide with every major studio selling its library of features over and over again.

One problem for viewers now is trying to detect the difference between a theatrical feature and a made-for-TV production, which, without the ready assistance of a TV guide or one of the TV movie books, can prove arduous, particularly as the networks and TV stations here in America promote and announce presentations under the same all-purpose 'Movie of the Week' headings. Similar confusion is also brought about by American TV-movies becoming theatrical releases in other countries, as with John Carpenter's 1979 telepic *Elvis* (starring Kurt Russell as Elvis Presley) which was re-titled *Elvis – The Movie* for Britain. *The Jericho Mile* (Michael Mann's 1979 film with Peter Strauss as the prisoner turned athlete), *Duel* (Steven Spielberg's celebrated 1971 melodrama pitting Dennis Weaver against a huge tanker truck on a deserted highway), and *Marilyn: The Untold Story*, the 1980 adaptation of Norman Mailer's Marilyn Monroe biography, starring Catherine Hicks and helmed by no less than three directors!

In a reversal of this operation, the same applies to some of the UK Channel 4 films, particularly *Experience Preferred But*

Kurt Russell as *Elvis* (John Carpenter, 1979).

Not Essential (Peter Duffell: 1982) which was advertised in the States by its distributor (The Samuel Goldwyn Company) as 'a delicious new comedy from the producer of *Chariots of Fire* and *Local Hero*', and also *P'Tang, Yang, Kipperbang* (Michael Apted: 1982), released in North America in early 1984 by MGM/UA Classics under the abbreviated title, *Kipperbang*.

TV movies, as we know them today, came into being in the early 1960s, but the budgets were relatively smaller then, and the scope of subject matter was equally confined. Television is, after all, automatically beamed right into the home, and the producers were ordered to play it safe. Conforming to recognized formulas did, nonetheless, result in some first-rate entertainment and, with Universal the foremost studio in the field, some regular and memorable series were spun off early TV features. *Fear is the Name of the Game* in 1966 (itself adapted from one of Alan Ladd's Paramount pot-boilers of the 1940s – *Chicago Deadline*) gave birth to *The Name of the Game*, and among the other weekly series to be launched off the back of early TV movies were *Ironside*, *Night Gallery*, *Marcus Welby MD* and *McCloud*, as well as a revival of the old *Dragnet* formula. Incidentally, the *Night Gallery* movie was divided into three Rod Serling playlets with Joan Crawford and Barry Sulivan being directed by the young Steven Spielberg.

This method of launching a series is as powerful a programming tool as ever, and the format is not always restricted to a single episode of movie length. For instance, Columbia has recently revived Micky Spillane's Mike Hammer character as a weekly hour-long series with Stacy Keach in the title role. *Murder Me, Murder You* was chosen as the TV movie try-out which was first aired here in April 1983. The series was then put into production and subsequently screened in January 1984, preceded by a further TV movie episode, *More than Murder*. In a reversal of the TV movie as pilot policy, the ultra-successful series *M*A*S*H* (which had originally been born out of Robert Altman's 1970 motion picture), terminated its small-screen tenure with a 2½-hour episode titled *Goodbye, Farewell and Amen*.

Another reason for the current demand for TV feature productions is that the three American networks (CBS, NBC and ABC) can no longer guarantee the large viewing figures that blockbuster ex-cinema movies used to ensure. This is due in part to the uninterrupted exposure that feature films have on the increasingly-popular cable and pay-TV stations, prior to their being sold to the commercial channels. Two cases in point show this development quite dramatically. The TV movie *Elvis* was premiered in early 1979 opposite the first free-TV (non-cable) showing of the award-winning *One Flew over the Cuckoo's Nest*, as well as a rebroadcast of the first half of the 1939 classic *Gone with the Wind*, which had always been considered a ratings winner, *Elvis* won. More recently, in February 1984, a critically-lambasted TV movie titled *My Mother's Secret Life*, starring Loni Anderson as a call girl, played very successfully against the network premieres of the 1981 Oscar winners, *On Golden Pond* and *Chariots of Fire*, the latter achieving very low figures.

As strange as it now seems, television once found difficulty in luring stars away from the silver screen, but the growth in importance of the TV movie has helped wipe out this stigma. Edward G. Robinson, Bette Davis and Barbara Stanwyck were among headliners who made early TV productions and,

Walter Brennan, Fred Astaire, Chill Wills, Andy Devine and Edgar Buchanan in *The Over-The-Hill Gang Rides Again* (George McCowan, 1970).

in the more recent past, the late Henry Fonda's final work before the camera was the telefilm *Summer Solstice*, directed in 1981 by Ralph Rosenbloom and co-starring Myrna Loy. A 1969 comedy-western, *The Over-The-Hill-Gang* (Jean Yarbrough) brought together a wonderful array of cowboy movie actors, including Pat O'Brien, Walter Brennan, Andy Devine, Chill Wills, and Edgar Buchanan. When a sequel was mounted under the title *The Over-The-Hill Gang Rides Again* (George McCowan: 1970), the same old-timers reappeared with the exception of Walter Brennan, but this time they were joined by Fred Astaire, in the only Western movie role of his illustrious career.

TV movies have crystallized around a number of themes which are shown fairly regularly. One popular subject is the biographical account of celebrity figures. Although Elizabeth Taylor was successful in preventing such a film of her own life, countless other personalities have been depicted, of which the following productions deserve prominent recognition:

Eleanor and Franklin (Daniel Petrie: 1976) Jane Alexander as Eleanor Roosevelt and Edward Herrmann as Franklin Roosevelt.

Evita Perón (Marvin J. Chomsky: 1981) with Faye Dunaway.

Haywire (Michael Tuchner: 1980) with Lee Remick as Margaret Sullavan, Jason Robards as Leland Hayward and Deborah Raffin as Brooke Hayward.

Jane Alexander and Edward Herrmann as the Roosevelts in *Eleanor and Franklin* (Daniel Petrie, 1976).

Little Gloria . . . Happy at Last (Waris Hussein: 1982) Bette Davis as Alice Gwynne Vanderbilt and introducing Lucy Gutteridge as Gloria Vanderbilt.
The Patricia Neal Story (Anthony Harvey, Anthony Page: 1981) Glenda Jackson as Patricia Neal and Dirk Bogarde as Roald Dahl.
A Woman Called Golda (Alan Gibson: 1982) with Ingrid Bergman in her final role, as Golda Meir.

These productions are, however, far above the many other docudramas which have tended to sensationalize their facts and to cast well-known performers in roles in which they appear less than totally suited. Among this latter breed have been Lynda Carter as Rita Hayworth, Ann Jillian as Mae West, Jaclyn Smith as Jacqueline Bouvier Kennedy and Cheryl Ladd as Grace Kelly. Two of the networks even mounted a race to beat each other to the screen with less than convincing dramatizations of the British Royal Family, and in particular, Prince Charles and Princess Diana, just as the media was caught up in the Royal Wedding fever of 1982.

An ongoing fascination for television remakes of legendary Hollywood movies has provided some interesting comparisons. Among the most rewarding of these were *The Letter* (John Erman: 1982) with Lee Remick in the role made famous by Bette Davis in 1940 of a suspected murderess, and *The Corn is Green* (George Cukor: 1978) in which Katharine Hepburn gloriously trod in the footsteps of another former Bette Davis characterization, this time being the middle-aged schoolteacher in a Welsh mining village. Other reworkings of much-loved classics have included: *All Quiet on the Western Front, Cat on a Hot Tin Roof, Dial M for Murder, Hunchback of Notre Dame, Ivanhoe, Johnny Belinda, Master of Ballantrae, The Miracle Worker, Of Mice and Men, Topper* and *Winchester '73*.

Several TV movies have also taken up where memorable vintage TV shows left off, bringing back favourite characters and formulas which had, in the recent past, lived on only in re-runs. Those brought back to small-screen life included Buddy Ebsen in *Return of the Beverly Hillbillies* (Robert Leeds: 1981), William Conrad in *Return of Frank Cannon* (Corey Allen: 1980), the *Leave it to Beaver* principals (minus Hugh Beaumont) in *Still the Beaver* (Steven H. Stern: 1983), plus the much-loved duo of Robert Vaughn as Napoleon Solo and David McCallum as Illya Kuryakin in *Return of the Man from U.N.C.L.E.* (Ray Austin: 1983) who, this time out, were aided by Patrick Macnee, erstwhile cast member of another small-screen favourite of yesteryear, *The Avengers*.

Controversial themes have been readily tackled over the past years, often with first-class results and high ratings. Vanessa Redgrave drew both protests and plaudits as a Jewish concentration-camp survivor in *Playing for Time* (Daniel Mann: 1980), Powers Boothe portrayed the fanatical religious leader in *Guyana Tragedy: The Story of Jim Jones* (William A. Graham: 1980), Mike Farrell starred in *Memorial Day* (Joseph Sargent: 1983), about a man struggling with personal memories of a Vietnam war tragedy, and Tommy Lee Jones took on the soul-searching role of convicted killer Gary Gilmore in *The Executioner's Song* (Lawrence Schiller: 1982), which Norman Mailer adapted from his own Pulitzer Prize-winning novel.

Two star-studded TV movies were rushed into production following the Israeli rescue mission in Uganda in July 1976; *Victory at Entebbe* (Marvin J. Chomsky) was first on the air that December, with *Raid on Entebbe* (Irvin Kershner) following in January 1977. In a similar swift move, *The People vs Jean Harris* (George Schaefer: 1981) made it to the screen within just a few months of the sensational trial it depicted, that of the woman (played superbly by Ellen Burstyn) charged with the murder of the author of the Scarsdale Diet. NBC caused headlines on their own by allowing *Special Bulletin* (Ed Zwick: 1983) on the air which, by means of a life-like news bulletin format reminiscent of the Orson Welles 1938 radio broadcast of *War of the Worlds*, unleashed imaginary coverage of a nuclear explosion. However, the real test of both the media and the public's resilience came on a Sunday evening in November 1983, when what felt like the entire American population held its breath for *The Day After* (Nicholas Meyer: 1983), the graphic and disturbing story of a fictional nuclear holocaust in a Kansas town. Press, radio and television ballyhoo was whipped up by political activities from all sides for several weeks before the broadcast, and the whole exercise must go down in history as one of the most eagerly awaited and pertinently-timed television events. What is certain is that, while it probably answered few questions, *The Day After* certainly provoked extensive examination of, and discussion about, one of the major threats to modern civilization and, for that reason alone, it more than warranted air time.

Anthony Hopkins, Elizabeth Taylor and Kirk Douglas in *Victory at Entebbe* (Marvin J. Chomsky, 1976).

Whereas one is regularly reading assessments of 'the best-loved movies of all time', the comparative youth of TV movies is such that they are rarely afforded any such examination. While no such critique is being attempted here, the reputation of certain productions (not otherwise listed here) prompts me to mention some notable entries from the more recent past: *Bill* (Anthony Page: 1981) with Mickey Rooney as a retarded adult; *Divorce Wars: A Love Story* (Donald Wrye: 1982) starring Tom Selleck as a divorce lawyer and Jane Curtin as his wife; *Drop-out Father* (Don Taylor: 1982) with Dick Van Dyke portraying a disillusioned advertising executive; *The Shadow Box* (Paul Newman: 1980) in which Joanne Woodward headlines in the story of terminally-ill patients and their families; *Skyward* (Ron Howard: 1980) starring Bette Davis as a 60-year-old woman pilot and Suzy Gilstrap as a 16-year-old determined to leave her wheelchair behind; and *Who Will Love my Children?* (John Erman: 1983) with Ann-Margret as a dying woman seeking homes for her ten children.

As the early TV movies gained in both stature and audience acceptance, it was inevitable that producers would become more ambitious and the initial airing in 1976 of the 12-hour adaptation of Irwin Shaw's powerful novel, *Rich Man, Poor Man*, directed by David Greene and Boris Sagal, ushered in a new extended form of TV movie-making which has since become known everywhere as the mini-series. Though it was not the very first small screen feature to exceed the two-hour format, *Rich Man, Poor Man* overshadowed its predecesors both in terms of its world-wide success and the fact that overnight it single-handedly created stars out of Peter Strauss and Nick Nolte. The second mini-series milestone was reached in early 1977 when David L. Wolper's 12-hour production of Alex Haley's *Roots* (directors: David Greene, Marvin J. Chomsky, Gilbert Moses and John Erman) was broadcast with phenomenal record-breaking results. This was followed just a few weeks later by an Easter screening of the six-and-a-half hour religious epic *Jesus of Nazareth*, which was brought to the small screen by Sir Lew Grade for ITV, with Franco Zeffirelli directing. This production is shown annually by NBC in its now-extended eight-hour version. Since the mid-1970s, the mini-series has become an increasingly regular part of American television's staple diet, spurred on by tremendous viewing audiences who have tuned in on four and five separate evenings to watch richly-mounted productions, most often adapted from successful novels.

Of the mini-series which have been produced, the following is a selective list of key productions, showing their individual directors and the commercial network running times:

Peter Graves, Polly Bergen and Robert Mitchum in *The Winds of War* (Dan Curtis, 1983).

Backstairs at the White House (Michael O'Herlihy, 1979)	9 hours
Blind Ambition (George Schaefer, 1979)	8 hours
The Blue and the Gray (Andrew V. McLaglen, 1982)	8 hours
Centennial (Virgil V. Vogel, Harry Falk, Paul Krasny, Bernard McEveety, 1978/9)	26½ hours
Chiefs (Jerry London: 1983)	6 hours
The Far Pavilions (Peter Duffell, 1984)	6 hours
George Washington (Buzz Kulik, 1984)	8 hours
From Here to Eternity (Buzz Kulik, 1979)	6 hours
Holocaust (Marvin J. Chomsky: 1978)	9½ hours
Ike (Melville Shavelson, Boris Sagal, 1979)	6 hours
Masada (Boris Sagal, 1981)	8 hours
Marco Polo (Giuliano Montaldo, 1982)	8 hours
Pearl (Hy Averback, 1978)	6 hours
Roots: The Next Generations (John Erman, George Stanford Brown, Charles S. Dubin, Lloyd Richards, 1979)	14 hours

79 Park Avenue (Paul Wendkos, 1977)	6 hours
Shogun (Jerry London, 1980)	12 hours
The Thorn Birds (Daryl Duke, 1983)	7 hours
Washington: Behind Closed Doors (Gary Nelson, 1977)	12½ hours
The Winds of War (Dan Curtis, 1983)	18 hours

(NB *The Far Pavilions* is the first mini-series to be produced for and premiered on a cable channel; running times of the remainder listed above are based on commercial time-slots, inclusive of advertising.)

The Nielsen ratings system, upon which the American television industry relies, places the first series of *Roots* as the most successful TV mini-series up to and including early 1984, with *The Thorn Birds* in second place and *The Winds of War* close behind in third. The increase in production costs is partly responsible for the mere six million dollar budget officially quoted for *Roots* in 1977, alongside Paramount and ABC Television's joint investment of some forty million dollars for *The Winds of War*.

While both TV movies and mini-series have come a long way in a short span of time, their exploitation fascinatingly draws much from the movie industry and, in some ways, from the cinema of the past. The on-screen trailers and print advertising (American networks pre-sell their key movies in newspapers and magazines) resort to the hard sell on many occasions. Sidney Sheldon's *Rage of Angels* (Buzz Kulik: 1983) is a typical example, with newspapers carrying an artist's composite of poignant scenes dominated by Jaclyn Smith's face and the adline: 'Men Rage To Have Her. To Own Her. To Destroy Her'. The award-winning *The Acorn People* (Joan Tewkesbury, 1981) also spelt out its subject matter in one hard-hitting sentence: 'Handicapped Kids Melt A Tough Guy's Heart'. One old-style movie tradition being used for TV is the blunt reference to other notable movies in which the stars have appeared; for instance, the promotion for *A Long Way Home* (Robert Markowitz: 1981) referred blatantly to Timothy Hutton as 'Academy Award Winner for *Ordinary People*'.

Today, with the American TV pie being split into so many competitive pieces, the networks no longer have the picture sewn up, but the 1983–4 season proved that the mini-series is currently one of the hottest weapons they have. Even cable companies are producing their own TV movies, such as *The Terry Fox Story* (Ralph L. Thomas for HBO Premiere Films: 1983), as well as buying first-run mini-series from abroad (as with *All The Rivers Run* from Australia) and repeat showings of previous commercial productions like *Centennial*.

Television finally has a movie industry of its own. It is discovering that, over a wide range of subject matter, it can take the viewer's interest to seemingly endless heights. Not that every TV movie is a winner by any means, but commendable contributions have been in regular supply including on one hand, *Adam* (Michael Tuchner: 1983), a modest but hard-hitting two-hour film, tackling the growing social problem of missing children and which, in its final moments, turned into a nationwide public service message. At the other end of the scale, it can produce a hit mini-series like *The Winds of War* on relatively the same budget as the theatrical features *Reds* and *Heaven's Gate* and come out with a product around five times the length of each.

Move over Oscar . . . Emmy is flexing its muscles!

Films Shown on Television

ALAN WARNER

Acceptable Levels (1983). This Channel 4 film, which got an initial screening at the 1983 London Film Festival, centres on a documentary unit who, while making a film in Ireland about the life of a Catholic girl living in West Belfast, witness the tragic killing of a child by a plastic bullet. Cast: Kay Adshead, Frances Barber, Michael Bruce, Peter Dean, Derek Halligan, Ian McElhinney, Andy Rashleigh, Patrick Higgins, Tracey Lynch, Sally McCaffery, Cormac McKenna, Dierdre Morgan, George Shane, Rosena Brown, Doyne Byrd, Clum Convey, Mark Elliott, Martine Emmett, Rio Fanning, Laura Gorman, Michael Gormley, Dave Hill, Paul Jesson, Trudi Kelly, Rose McAllister, Laurence McArow, Vera McCann, George Mooney, Rory Poland, Ian Redford, Colin Rix, Ian Ruskin. Dir: John Davies. No screenplay credit. Channel 4, 30 April 1984.

The Alpha Caper (1973). A furious probation officer (played by Henry Fonda) takes revenge on his employers who have forced him into retirement, by recruiting three of his star probationers for a multi-million-dollar robbery from a heavily-guarded convoy. The film was previously shown in British cinemas under the title *Inside Job*, and although the plot may be somewhat familiar it is extremely competently put across with exciting results. Rest of cast: Leonard Nimoy, James McEachin, Elena Verdugo, John Marley, Larry Hagman, Noah Beery, Tom Troupe, Woodrow Parfrey, Vic Tayback, Kenneth Tobey, Paul Kent, James B. Sikking, Paul Sorensen, Wally Taylor. Dir: Robert Michael Lewis. Pro: Aubrey Schenck. Screenplay: Elroy Schwartz. BBC, 14 September 1983.

The Ambush Murders (1982). Based on a true story about an American negro activist who, suspected of the murder of two Californian cops, spends two years waiting for his trial while his dedicated white lawyer and equally devoted wife work endlessly on his behalf. Cast: James Brolin, Dorian Harewood, Alfre Woodard, Robert Denison, Louis Giambalvo, Amy Madigan, John McLiam, Teddy Wilson, Marc Alaimo, John Calvin. Dir: Steven Hilliard Stern. Screenplay: Tony Kayden; based on the book about the case by Ben Bradlee Jr. ITV, 18 August 1983.

Angel City (1980). Shades of Steinbeck and *The Grapes of Wrath!* The *City* is the name of a forced labour camp in Florida in the bad old Depression days. Ralph Waite as the unfortunate victim crop picking for, and suffering from, black-hearted boss Mitchell Ryan. Rest of cast: Paul Winfield, Jennifer Warren, Jennifer Jason Leigh, Robert McNaughton, Red West, Rob Minor, Pauline Myers, Ken Renard, John David Allen, Joe A. Dorsey, Wallace Wilkinson, Sandra Dorsey. Dir: Philip Leacock. Screenplay: James Lee Barrett; from a novel by Patrick Smith. Channel 4, 19 June 1984.

Another Time, Another Place (1983). Though made with TV exposure firmly in mind, and part-financed by Channel 4, this World War II film set in the remote north of Scotland was premiered in the cinema and full details will be found in the 'Releases of the Year' feature. Channel 4, 10 November 1983.

Antonio & the Mayor (1974). The mayor, the boy and the bicycle; the mayor takes his position seriously in his remote village in Mexico, the boy is super-bright and somehow always getting the better of him, the bicycle is shining new and loved... all very charming and amusing. Cast: Gregory Sierra, Javier Marc, Diego Gonzales, Farnesio Bernal, Claudio Martinez, Aurora Clavell, Julio Medina. Dir: Jerry Thorpe. Screenplay: Howard Rodman. BBC, 2 January 1984.

Are You in the House Alone? (1978). A thriller based on Robert Peck's literary prizewinner, with Kathleen Beller as the pretty little college girl threatened by a mysterious telephone caller. Rest of cast: Blythe Danner, Tony Bill, Scott Colomby, Robin Matson, Tricia O'Neil, Dennis Quaid, Alan Fudge. Dir: Walter Grauman. Screenplay: Judith Parker; based on the book by Robert Peck. ITV, 28 January 1984.

The A-Team (1983). In this feature start to a new TV series, 'Hannibal Smith' (George Peppard) leads a team of mercenaries, made up mostly of ex-Vietnam veterans and a girl journalist, who set out to find and bring back the girl's male colleague, missing somewhere in Mexico. Rest of cast: Dwight Schultz, 'Mr T' (the brute fighter in the 'Rocky' movies), Tim Dunigan, Melinda Culea, Bill Lucking, William Windom, Jorge Zepeda, Sergio Calderon. Dir: Rod Holcomb. Screenplay: Stephen J. Cannell and Frank Lupo. ITV, 22 July 1983.

Battlestar Galactica – The Movie (1978). More spectacular adventures in space some time in the future. Having had their planet destroyed by some outer-space villains, the survivors join up with the spaceship Battlestar Galactica and seek peace and safety on the far away colony planet which happens to be our Earth. Cast: Lorne Greene,

21

Richard Hatch, Dirk Bendict, Maren Jensen, Herb Jefferson, Terry Carter, Jane Seymour, Noah Hathaway, Lew Ayres, John Colicos, Tony Schwartz, Ray Milland, Wilfrid Hyde White and some other star guests. Dir: Alan Levi. Screenplay: Glan A. Larson. ITV, 3 November 1983.

The Best Little Girl in the World (1981). The story of a girl whose jealousy of her elder sister leads to her contracting anorexia nervosa – in simple terms, acute loss of weight. Cast: Jennifer Jason Leigh, Charles Durning, Eva Marie Saint, Lisa Pelikan, Jason Miller, Melanie Mayron. Dir: Sam O'Steen. Screenplay: David Moessinger; Channel 4, 5 July 1983.

Better Late Than Never (1981). Better known as an actor, Richard Crenna directs this amusing story of a revolt against the all too strict regulations of an old people's home by a 'mob' led by Harry Gould. Rest of cast: Strother Martin, Tyne Daly, Harry Morgan, Donald Pleasence, Victor Buono, Lou Jacobi, Jeanette Nolan, Marjorie Bennett, Paula Trueman, Meg Wyllie, Larry Storch. Dir: Richard Crenna. Screenplay: John Carpenter and Greg Strangis. Channel 4, 29 May 1984.

The Biggest Bank Robbery (1980). A fair mixture of laughs and thrills in this London-set, Big Heist caper, with the late David Niven as the leader of the gang and Richard Jordan as the ex-con 'inside' man at the bank. Rest of cast: Oliver Tobias, Gloria Grahame, Elke Sommer, Richard Johnson, Joss Ackland. Dir: Ralph Thomas. Screenplay: Guy Elmes. ITV, 12 December 1983.

Billion Dollar Threat (1979). Fast-paced hokum, in the James Bond mould about top-flight American secret agent ordered to stop a super-villain who is planning to destroy the world! Cast: Dale Robinette, Ralph Bellamy, Keenan Wynn, Patrick Macnee, Robert W. Tessier, Beth Specht, Karen Specht, Ronnie Carol, Stephen Keep. Dir: Barry Shear. Screenplay: Jimmy Sangster. ITV, 25 August 1983.

The Blue Knight (1973). This was originally a four-hour mini-series about the last days on the beat of a retiring Los Angeles cop (outstandingly played by the late William Holden), written by ex-policeman Joseph Wambaugh. But the material was cut down to feature film size (100 mins) and as a result got a cinema showing. Rest of cast: Lee Remick, Joe Santos, Eileen Brennan, Emile Meyer, Sam Elliot, Ernest Esparza III, Anne Archer, Vic Tayback. Dir: Robert Butler. Screenplay: E. Jack Neuman; based on the book by Wambaugh. BBC, 11 June 1984.

Bounty Hunter (1981). Another exciting adventure of a modern-day American bounty hunter, but at least this one is based on fact. Here ex-US marine Stan Rivkin (played by Ron Liebman) has to bring to court a criminal who has jumped bail of $50,000! And he finally gets his man after a dramatic chase through New York. Rest of cast: Harry Morgan, Glen Scarpelli, Bo Rucker, Harold Gary. Dir: Harry Harris. Screenplay: Peter Lefcourt. ITV, 4 July 1983.

Call to Danger (1973). Peter Graves, as the head of 'Tac Force 10' of the USA's Department of Justice, carefully picks a highly specialized group to rescue a very important witness a group of villains has kidnapped to prevent giving evidence. Rest of cast: Diana Muldaur, John Anderson, Clu Gulager, Tina Louise, Stephen McNally, Ina Balin, Michael Ansara, Roy Jensen, William Jordan, Edward Bell, Paul Mantee. Dir: Tom Gries. Screenplay: Laurence Heath. ITV, 19 March 1984.

The Capture of Grizzly Adams (1981). A 'wilderness' adventure about an old hermit – Grizzly – who for long has been on the run from a false murder rap. But when he hears his young daughter is to be put into an orphanage he decides to brave a visit to town and that means a confrontation with the true villain and his cohorts. Cast: Dan Haggerty, Kim Darby, Noah Beery, Keenan Wynn, June Lockhart, Sydney Penny, Chuck Connors. Dir: Don Keeslar. Screenplay: Arthur Heinemann. ITV, 25 December 1983.

A Caribbean Mystery (1983). Helen Hayes, as Agatha Christie's amusing sleuth Miss Marples, finds plenty to keep her investigatively busy when some odd things happen in the hotel in the West Indies where she is supposed to be vacationing. Rest of cast: Barnard Hughes, Jameson Parker, Season Hubley, Swoosie Kurtz, Cassie Yates, Zakes Mokae, Stephen Macht, Beth Howland, Maurice Evans, Lynne Moody, George Innes, Brook Peters, Mike Preston, Bernard McDonald, Santos Morales, Sam Scarder, Cecil Smith. Dir: Robert Lewis. Screenplay: Sue Grafton and Steven Humphries. ITV 23 March 1984.

The Case for the Defence (1976). One of three TV feature films about an Australian lawyer called Case (played by John Hamblin). In this movie, Case defends a man accused of kidnapping and murder. Rest of cast: Judith Arthy, Luis Wishart, Edward Howell, David Whitford, Brian Niland, John Waters, Julie Dawson, John Benton. Dir: Alan Coleman. Screenplay: Ron McLean. ITV, 30 November 1983.

Charlie Muffin (1979). David Hemmings, as the second-drawer British agent, succeeds where his superior colleagues have failed in bringing in the much needed evidence that will convict the suspected head of a Soviet spy ring. Rest of cast: Sam Wanamaker, Jennie Linden, Pinkas Braun, Ian Richardson, Ralph Richardson, Shane Rimmer, Tony Mathews, Christopher Godwin, Norwich Duff, Rohan McCullough, Donald Churchill, Frederick Treves, Clive Revill, Philip Joseph, Reinhold Ilszewski, Marc Smith, Peter Banks, Ray Hassett, Rodney Lovick, Peter Jessup, Ron Bone, Paulina Darc. Dir: Jack Gold. Screenplay: Keith Waterhouse; based on a novel by Brian Freemantle. ITV, 31 August 1983.

The Child Stealer (1979). The familiar problem of divorced parents and their relationship with the children of the marriage. Here father Beau Bridges, already fed-up that he is only allowed to see his two young daughters once a week, becomes scared that his wife's remarriage might further sever his links with them, and so he works out a plan to circumvent such a possibility. Rest of cast: Blair Brown, Tracey Gold, Lauri Hendler, David Groh, Christina Raines, Eugene Roche, Phillip K. Allen, William Bryant, Alan Fudge, Lee Wallace, Robert Doqui, Arthur A. Rosenberg. Dir: Mel Damski. Pro: Hugh Benson. Screenplay: Sue Milburn. BBC, 8 October 1983.

Coffee, Tea or Me? (1973). Veteran Hollywood screenwriter Norman Panama directed this comedy story about an air hostess with two husbands (one in Los Angeles, the other in London) who she hopes will never meet. But of course they do. . . and which one is the father of her child? Cast: Karen Valentine, John Davison, Michael Anderson Jr, Louise Lasser, Lou Jacobi, Erica Hagen, George Colouris, Nora Marlowe. Dir: Norman Panama. Screenplay: Panama, Stanley Ralph Ross and Albert E. Lewin: from a story by Trudy Baker and Rachel Jones. BBC, 24 January 1984.

Conquest of the Earth (1980). Battlestar Galactica, in the spacelanes once more, takes up the thermo lances against those awful Cylons and their determination to wipe the Earth off the face of the space map. Cast: Kent McCord, Barry Van Dyke, Robyn Douglass, Lorne Greene, Patrick Stuart, Robbie Rist, John Colicos, Robert Reed, Wolfman Jack, William Daniels, Lara Parker, Pamela Susan Shoop, Fred Holliday, Peter Mark Richman, Roger Davis. Dir: Sidney Hayers, Sigmund Neufeld Jr and Barry Crane. Screenplay: Glen A. Larson. ITV, 7 May 1984.

The Corn is Green (1978). A special TV adaptation of the famous Emlyn Williams play, with the considerable advantage of Katharine Hepburn playing the teacher in a small Welsh mining community who finds a bright young lad and fights against all opposition to see he gets his chance at Oxford. Rest of cast: Ian Saynor, Bill Fraser, Patricia Hayes, Anna Massey, Artro Morris, Dorothea Philips, Toyah Willcox, Huw Richards. Dir: George Cukor. Screenplay: Ivan Davis. BBC, 6 May 1984.

The Country Girls (1983). The story of Irish Kate and friend Baba as they move from village school to convent education and then to their first taste of freedom in Dublin before making their way to London. Cast: Sam Neill, John Cavanagh, Niall Toibin, Maeve Germaine, Jill Doyle, John Olohan, Britta Smith, Patricia Martin, Des Nealon, Sheila Flitton, Anna Manahan, Agnes Bernelle, Patricia Jeffares, Vincent Smith, Tom Laidlaw, Sheila O'Sullivan, Lisa Cook, Joan Harpur, Grace O'Shaughnessy, Maleila Nolan, Laura Conway, Susan Ryan, Frank Melia, Paul Conway, Diedre Raftery, Jim Reed, Pat Power. Dir: Desmond Davis. Pro: Aida Young. Screenplay: Edna O'Brien; based on her own book. Channel 4, 24 November 1983.

Crime Club (1979). Private eye Paul Cord (Lloyd Bridges) investigates a car crash in which his pal's son is killed, in this pilot feature for a follow-up series. But surprisingly the series never came about despite the fact that the film was well made and shows more promise than the many series which actually got as far as production. Rest of cast: Victor Buono, Paul Burke, William Devane, David Hedison, Cloris Leachman, Belinda Montgomery, Barbara Rush, Martin Sheen, Mills Watson, Frank Marth. Dir: David Lowell Rich. Screenplay: Charles Larson. BBC, 21 February 1984.

The Dark Side of Innocence (1976). This was a feature showcase for what was hoped would be an American TV series about the strains and stresses within a typical US family. But the hope proved still-born! Cast: Joanna Pettet, Kim Hunter, Anne Archer, John Anderson, Lawrence Casey, Claudette Nevins, Robert Sampson. Dir: Jerry Thorpe. Pro: Philip Mandelker. Screenplay: Barbara Turner. BBC, 18 July 1983.

The Day After (1983). Sensational – and controversial – picture of the effects of a nuclear holocaust on a group of Kansas City residents; graphic, terrifying and starkly convincing – and not at all to the liking of those in power who would like to play down what would happen after the bomb has been dropped. Cast: Jason Robards, Jobeth Williams, Steven Guttenberg, John Cullum, John Lithgow, Bibi Besch, Lori Lethin, Amy Madigan, Jeff East, Georgann Johnson, William Allen Young, Calvin Jung. Dir: Nicholas Meyer. Screenplay: Edward Hume. ITV, 10 December 1983.

Deadly Encounter (1982). Larry ('JR') Hagman, veteran pilot with his own small helicopter line in Mexico, becomes involved with the heavy mob through his old girl-friend, Susan Anspach, in this airborne thriller. Rest of cast: James Gammon, Michael C. Gwynne, Jose Chavez, Jack Dunlap, John Graham, Arnold Jeffers, Hank Kendrick, Roger La Rue, Glenn Miller. Tom O'Vonnor. Dir: William A. Graham. Pro: Paul Cameron and Robert Boris. Screenplay: David J. Kinghorn and Robert Boris. BBC, 11 September 1983.

Deadman's Curve (1978). Richard Hatch and Bruce Davison, play Jan Berry and Dean Torrence in the true story of the American pop star duo whose speciality was the singing of songs glorifying California's sunny sands and surf in the 1950s and 1960s. Rest of cast: Pam Bellwood, Floy Dean, Denise Du Barry, Priscilla Cory, Kelly Ward, Wolfman Jack, Dick Clark, Mike Love, Bruce Johnston. Dir: Richard Compton. Pro: Roger Gimpel. Screenplay: Dalene Young; based on the story by Paul Moranty. BBC, 27 August 1983.

Dead Men Tell No Tales (1971). A case of mistaken identity, with sole car-crash survivor Christopher George, a photographer on a Spanish assignment, thought by hired killers to be a secret agent who is to be rubbed out at any price – a story never taken too seriously. Rest of cast: Judy Carne, Patricia Barry, Richard Anderson, Larry D. Mann, Kevin Hagen, John Shawlee, Fred Sadoff, Mike Lookinland, Richard O'Brien, Judith Hart, Lincoln Kilpatrick Jr, Eric Sinclair, Ella Edwards. Dir: Walter Grauman. Screenplay: Robert Dozier. ITV, 5 July 1983.

Divorce Laws (1982). Set in Seattle, a divorce lawyer suddenly finds his own marriage is breaking up – in this 'biter bitten' legal story – and several other lawyers are also involved. Welcome back Joan Bennett, one of the film's assets. Rest of cast: Tom Selleck, Jane Curtin, Candy Azzara, Mimi Rogers. Dir: Donald Wrye. Screenplay: Wrye and Linda Elstad. Channel 4, 24 April 1984.

Don't Go To Sleep (1982). Macabre thriller about a little girl who plans with her elder sister, killed in a car crash, to murder the other members of their family. Cast: Dennis Weaver, Valerie Harper, Robin Ignico, Kristin Cumming, Oliver Robins, Claudette Nevins, Ruth Gordon, Robert Webber, Marilyn Coleman, Tim Haldeman, Haven Earle Haley, Ned Wynn, Ross Porter. Dir:

23

Richard Lang. Screenplay: Ned Wynn. ITV, 7 January 1984.

The Family Rico (1972). Mafia figure Ben Gazzara is caught with divided loyalties when he is called in by his 'grand-father' bosses and told to liquidate his errant brother, Sal Mineo. Which will Ben put first, family or 'Family'? Rest of cast: Dane Clark, Leif Erickson, James Farentino, John Marley, John Randolph, Jo Van Fleet, Sian Barbara Allen, Michael Anderson. Dir: Paul Wendkoss. Pro: George Lemaire. Screenplay: David Karp; based on a Georges Simenon novel. BBC, 1 November 1983.

Farewell to Manzanar (1976). Well made TV movie, seen through the eyes of a Japanese family, about the plight of America's vast Japanese population after Pearl harbour, when some 100,000 were put into special camps across the US. Cast: Yuki Shumoda, Nobu McCarthy, Akemi Kikimura, Clyde Kusatu, Mako, Pat Morita, James Saito, Dor Takeshita, Frank Abe, Gretchen Corbett, Louis Frizzell, Vernon Kato, Kip Niven, Seth Sakai, Mitsu Yashima, Momo Yashima. Dir and Pro: John Korty. Screenplay: Korty, Jeanne Wakatsuki Houston and James D. Houston; based on their book. BBC, 7 January 1984.

Fast Friends (1979). Fascinating and daunting peep behind the American TV show cameras as divorcée Carrie Snodgrass tries to break into the 'Chat Show' world of US television. Rest of cast: Dick Shawn, Jed Allan, Vivian Blaine, Denise Dubarry, Tom Hallick, Elayne Heilveil, David Letterman. Dir: Stephen H. Stern. Pro. and Screenplay: Sandra Harmon. BBC, 26 September 1983.

Fire! (1977). A routine story, with typical Irwin Allen action, about a timber fire in Oregon country which spreads and ·spreads into a major disaster so that even the local jail sends the inmates out to help. Cast: Ernest Borgnine, Vera Miles, Patty Duke Astin, Alex Cord, Donna Mills, Lloyd Nolan, Neville Brand, Ty Hardin, Gene Evans, Erik Astrada, Michele Stacy, Patrick Culliton, James W. Gavin. Dir: Earl Bellamy. Screenplay: Norman Katlov and Arthur Weiss. BBC, 2 June 1984.

First Love – Secrets (1983). Four schoolgirls with a jinx on them – real or imaginary? Well directed by Gavin Millar, allied to first-rate performances by the girls. Cast: Helen Lindsay, John Horsley, Anna Campbell Jones, Daisy Cockburn, Rebecca Johnson, Lucy Goode, Richard Telan, Jane Briers, Judith Fellows, Georgine Anderson, Matyelok Gibbs, Cynthia Grenville, Elizabeth Choice, Michael Packer, Peter Scott Harrison, Craig Stokes, Robert Stagg. Paul Gamble, Sarah Bennett, Lisa Hawkins, Michelle Hooper, Dawn Andrews, Kelly Conway, Victoria Griffiths, Tara Rodway, Louise Howard, Lucinda Platt, Antonia Clanchy, Caroline Downer, Rosalind Archer, Katherine Franklin Adams, Jenifer Toksvig, Rachel Gassin, Vanessa Jeffcoat, Ann Roberts, Abalene Goul, Justine Page, Cipriana da Silva, Tina de Bono, Ann Mansard, Amelia Dipple, Lisa Mareca, Jacqui Cryer, Frances Geary. Dir: Gavin Millar. Pro: Chas. Griffin. Screenplay: Noella Smith. Channel 4, 1 January 1984.

First Love – Sharma and Beyond (1984). National Film School graduate Brian Gilbert's first, quite impressive, TV feature film; an ironic comedy about the romance that develops between a young English teacher (and science-fiction fan) and the daughter of his favourite author. Cast: Michael Maloney, Suzanne Burden, Robert Urquhart, Benjamin Whitrow, Tom Wilkinson, Antonia Pemberton, Bernice Stegers, Takashi Kawahara, Francisco Moralles, Katherine Best, Hugh Quarshie, Daniel Wozniak, Yashar Adem, Lufti Oguz, Sofia Walkiewicz, Swee Hoe Lim. Dir. & Screenplay: Brian Gilbert. Channel 4, 24 May 1984.

A Flame to the Phoenix (1983). Set in Poland in 1939, it tells the story of two Polish Army officers whose fine weekend in the country is rudely interrupted. It also suggests how the famous ENIGMA decoder was smuggled to the West just before the guns started to roar. Cast: Malcolm Jamieson, Benedict Taylor, Donald Bisset, Ann Firbank, David Haig, Frederick Treves, Lucy Hornack, Martin Oldfield, Constantine Gregory, Andrew Burt, Richard Ireson, Frances Barber, Paul Geoffrey, Stuart Richman, Robin Sachs, Vishanya Petulengro, Danny McCarthy, David Miller, Stefan Brochwicz-

Lewinsky, Will Tracey, David Calladine, Christine Moore, Gerry Cowan, John Rowe, Jonathan Oliver, Louis Hasler, Ian Bleasdale, David Riley, Michael Shevelew, Nigel Cartner. Dir: William Brayne. Screenplay: Murray Smith. Channel 4, 15 December 1983.

Flash Gordon (1981). A feature cartoon based on the famous American comic-strip character. And who exactly is Flash? This film sets out to give the answers. Dir: Gwen Wentzler. ITV, 22 December 1983.

Flood (1976). Another Irwin Allen all-action melodrama! The non-caring inhabitants of a small town beneath a big dam are taught an extremely watery lesson when the walls crumble and the river tumbles down their streets – engulfing quite a number of them in the process. Cast: Robert Culp, Martin Milner, Barbara Hershey, Richard Basehart, Carol Lynley, Roddy McDowall, Cameron Mitchell, Eric Olson, Teresa Wright, Francine York, Whit Bissell, Leif Garrett, Ann Doran, Elizabeth Rogers, James Griffith, Edna Helton, Gloria Stuart, Jack Collins. Dir: Earl Bellamy. Screenplay: Don Inglass. BBC 16 June 1984.

Fly Away Home (1981). Another Vietnam war film which shows how those fighting, and those left at home, were affected. Cast: Bruce Boxleitner, Tiana Alexandra, Michael Beck, Randy Frederick Brooks, Teri Copley, Brian Dennehy, Laura Johnson, Lynne Moody, Edward Winter, Olivia Cole, Louis Giambalvo, Kieu Chinh, Barry Jenner, Michael Fairman, Keye Luke, Duc Huy. Dir: Paul Krasny. Screenplay: Stirling Silliphant. Channel 4, 12 July 1983.

Frankenstein: The True Story (1973). Christopher Isherwood has his own and certainly interesting, ideas about the bad old Baron in this star-studded British TV thriller. Cast: Michael Sarrazin, James Mason, David McCallum, Leonard Whiting, Jane Seymour, Nicola Paget, Michael Wilding, Clarissa Kaye, Agnes Moorehead, Margaret Leighton, Ralph Richardson, John Gielgud, Tom Baker. Dir: Jack Smight. Pro: Hunt Stromberg Jr. Screenplay: Christopher Isherwood and Don Bachardy. BBC, 18 December 1983.

Fun and Games (1980). A film which explores the currently popular topic of sexual harassment at work, where women are offered promotion in exchange for sexual favours, by following one American woman's struggle to free herself from such a situation. Cast: Valerie Harper, Cliff de Young, Max Gail, Jobeth Williams. Dir: Alan Amithee. Pro: Lillian Gallo and Fay Kanin. Screenplay: David Smilow and Elizabeth Wilson. BBC, 10 October 1983.

Funny Business (1978). A compilation of Hollywood's famous laughter-makers at work, introduced by Walter Matthau. The stars include Laurel and Hardy, Bob Hope, The Marx Brothers and W.C. Field, etc. Dir and Screenplay: Richard Schickel. Channel 4, 9 July 1983.

Gemini Man (1976). A variation on the well-known H.G. Wells story about a man who found the secret of invisibility – in this case it is a secret agent who uses this power to thwart a group of saboteurs. The film was made as the pilot movie for a series (which did not run long), and has been screened in shortened form under the title *Code Name: Minus One*. But it has now been restored to its original length. Cast: Ben Murphy, Katherine Crawford, Richard Dysart, Dana Elcar, Paul Shenar, Robert Forward, Cheryl Miller, Len Wayland, Quinn Redeker. Dir: Alan Levi. Screenplay: Leslie Stevens. ITV, 28 December 1983.

Ghost Dance (1983). An *avant garde* British production, made partly in colour and partly in black-and-white, about a pretty young Parisienne who arrives in Britain and becomes involved with a philosopher who discusses ghosts, and a woman who teaches her to do the exercise of the title. Cast: Leonie Mellinger, Pascale Ogier, Robbie Coltrane, Jacques Derrida, John Annette. Dir and Screenplay: Ken McMullen. Channel 4, 14 May 1984.

The Ghost of Flight 401 (1977). An odd little tale, supposedly true, about a plane crash which occurred in the Everglades of Florida in December 1972. Ernest Borgnine, the seriously injured flight engineer, takes the blame upon himself. Many of the jumbo jet's passengers were killed as well as the captain and chief engineer, who reputedly returned as very helpful ghosts to avert a number of other near-disasters. Rest of cast: Gary Lockwood, Kim Basinger, Robert F. Lyons, Carol Rossen, Tina Chen, Beverly Todd. Dir: Steven Stern and Bob Rosenbaum. Screenplay: Robert Malcolm Young. ITV, 1 September 1983.

The Gift of Love (1978). An adaptation of the O. Henry story *The Gift of the Magi*, starring Marie Osmond in her first straight role as the poor little rich girl. Rest of cast: Timothy Bottoms, Sondra West, Robert Pierce, James Woods, Donald Moffat, June Lockhart, Bethel Leslie, Peggy Rea, David Wayne. Dir: Don Chaffey. Pro: Mitchell Brower. Screenplay: Carl Ledner. BBC, 2 July 1983.

Going Home – Shebbear (1982). An out-of-the-rut mixture of documentary, historical reconstruction and semi-autobiographical drama about life in a small Devonshire village community girt by sea and moor in the 1930s. Cast: Stefan Sillifant, Vanessa Pett, Matthew Rowe, Brigid Lynch-Blosse, Roger Booth, Brian Gwaspari, Victor Langley, Elizabeth Bradley, Catherine Terriss, Roger Kemp, Mary Wimbush, David Delve, Philip Manikum, Roger Bizley, Royston Tickner, Jonathan Adams, Ian Collier, Donald MacBride, Michael Goldie, Audrey Noble, Diana Katis, Bernard Taylor, Graham Blockey, Alan Coveney, Alastair Maydon, Emma Rogers, June Marlow, Christopher Andrew. Dir. Pro. and Screenplay John Pett. Ex Pro: Patsy Boughton.

Good and Bad at Games (1983). The revenge of a humiliated pupil is seen against the effect a public school education has on three of its recipients (or victims as the film sees them). Cast: Martyn Stanbridge, Anton Lesser, Laura Davenport, Dominic Jephcott, Frederick Alexander, Graham Seed, Ewan Stewart, Ceri Jackson, Philip Goodhew, Tristram Wymark, Rupert Graves. Dir: Jack Gold. Pro: Victor Glynn. Channel 4, 8 December 1983.

Green Eyes (1976). A film based on a true story about a black GI from Vietnam who finds life back in the US so depressing he returns to Saigon to search for his girlfriend and child he left behind. Cast: Paul Winfield, Rita Tushingham, Jonathan Lippe, Victoria Racimo-Lemi. Dir: John Erman. Pro: David Seltzer and Eugene Logan. Screenplay: David Seltzer. BBC, 3 October 1983.

A Gun in the House (1981). Another film based on the problem of the citizen faced with mindless violence and the right to hit back hard; here the attacker is a rapist, the defender, with gun, an ordinary suburban wife and mother faced with violence in her own home. Cast: Sally Struthers, David Ackroyd, Joel Bailey, Frank Koppala, Dick Anthony Williams, Dir: Ivan Nagy. Screenplay: Stephen Zito and James M. Miller. Channel 4, 26 July 1983.

Hanging by a Thread (1979). Stranded in a broken-down cable car waiting for rescue or, equally possible, death, a group of apparently close friends gradually reveal their true selves as old sores are opened and true feelings expressed, in this 185-minute, two-part TV feature film. Cast: Michael Sharrett, Burr DeBenning, Oliver Clark, Ted Gehring, Roger Perry, Lonny Chapman, Jacquelyn Hyde, Brendon Boone. Dir: Georg Fenady. Pro: Irwin Allen. Screenplay: Adrian Spies. BBC, 30 and 31 August 1983.

Hardcastle and McCormick (1983). This pilot movie for a new American crime detection series features the strange sleuthing team of a judge and an ex-convict, who is a racing driver with a prototype 'flyer' at hand. Only members of the cast named are Brian Keith as the unconventional judge and Daniel Hugh-Kelly as his young sidekick. Dir: Roger Young. No Pro or Scriptwriter named. ITV, 16 October 1983.

Hotel (1983). This feature-film prelude to a successful TV series is based on a 1967 cinema movie which in turn was born out of a successful novel by Arthur Hailey. Bette Davis stars as the hotel owner (the role played by Melvyn Douglass in the 1960s version) dealing with the problems of guests and staff who all provide plenty of colourful material. Rest of cast: James Brolin, Connie Sellecca, Shea Farrell, Nathan Cook, Heidi Bohay, Michael Spound, Morgana Fairchild, Stephanie Faracy, Jack Gilford, Shirley Jones, Lainie Kazan, Bill Macy, Eron Morna, Alejandro Rey, Pernell Roberts, Mel Torme.

Dir: Jerry London. Screenplay: Harry Oringer and John Furia; based on the book by Arthur Hailey. ITV, 24 November 1983.

The House on Garibaldi Street (1979). A dramatized documentary about the search for Nazi war criminal Adolf Eichmann by a determined band of Israelis in Argentina, and what occurs when they eventually track him down, living, as a Mr Clement, in a house in Garibaldi Street. Cast: Topol, Nick Mancuso, Janet Suzman, Martin Balsam, Leo McKern, Alfred Burke, Derren Nesbitt, Charles Gray, Edward Judd, John Bennett, John Cater, Wolf Kahler, Gareth Hunt, Maria Isbert, Richard Wren, Simon Shepherd, Fernando Hilbeck. Dir: Peter Collinson. Screenplay: Steve Shagan; from the book by Isser Harel. Channel 4, 19 July 1983.

The Hunted Lady (1977). Donna Mills plays a cop in Los Angeles who is framed for murder by a gang of criminals and is then pursued by their hitman. Rest of cast: Lawrence Casey, Andrew Duggan, Alan Feinstein, Geoffrey Lewis, Michael McGuire, Jenny O'Hara, Quinn Redeker, Robert Reed, Mario Roccuzzo, Will Sampson, Jess Walton, Richard Yniguez, Hank Brandt, Patti Cahoon. Dir: Richard Lang. Screenplay: William Robert Yates. ITV, 11 August 1983.

Image of Death (1977). A thriller from Australia about a girl who lives by her wits and who cannot resist the temptation to gain an old school friend's wealth by murder. Cast: Cathey Paine, Cheryl Waters, Sheila Helpmann, Doreen Harrop, Tony Bonner, Barry Pierce, Penne Hackforth-Jones, Leon Gregory, Queen Ashton, Brenda Senders, Graham Corry, Barry Creyton, Max Meldrum, Stuart Finch. Dir: Kevin Dobson. Screenplay: Bruce Wishart. ITV, 12 July 1983.

The Incredible Journey of Dr Meg Laurel (1979). Lindsay Wagner gives an impressive performance as a woman medic who takes her skills and humanity to a not entirely welcoming small community in a remote part of the Appalachian Mountains. Jane Wyman, as 'Granny Arrowroot' leads the opposition. Rest of cast: Dorothy McGuire, James Woods, Gary Lockwood, Andrew Duggan, Brock Peters, Kathy

Soucie, John Keilly. Dir: Guy Green. Pro: Paul Radin. Screenplay: Doug Schwartz, Michael Berk and Joseph Fineman. BBC, 15 August 1983.

The Incredible Rocky Mountain Race (1977). The story of Mark Twain and his rival Mike Fink in a not too serious race from their small Missouri town of St Joseph to the shores of the Pacific Ocean in 1861. Cast: Christopher Connelly, Forrest Tucker, Jack Kruschen, Mike Mazurki, Larry Storch, Bill Zuckert, Whit Bissell, Don Haggerty, Parley Baer. Dir: James L. Conway. Pro: Robert Stabler. Screenplay: David O'Marley and Thomas Chapman. BBC, 6 July 1983.

In for Treatment (1979). A Dutch made-for-TV movie which did well when shown at a number of Film Festivals, including those of Cannes, Los Angeles, Locarno and Edinburgh. Based on a stage play, it tells, in a rather restrained way, the story of a man who goes to hospital for a routine check-up to find far more wrong with him than he had bargained for, and he has to face up to the fact he is suffering from an incurable illness. Cast: Helmert Woudenberg, Olga Zuiderhoek, Frank Groothof, Shireen Strooker, Gerard Thoolen, Marja Kok, Daria Mohr, Cas Enklaar, Hans Van Ivan Wolffers. Dir: Erik Van Duylen. Screenplay: Marja Kok. Channel 4, 11 April 1984.

Institute for Revenge (1979). John Schroeder (played by Sam Groom) leads the do-gooders set-up of IFR and hatches a neat plan to recover money stolen from his old-age-pensioner clients by a wealthy con-man (played by George Hamilton). The film was screened as a pilot for a new TV series, which in fact was never made. Rest of cast: Lauren Hutton, Lane Binkley, T. J. McCavitt, Robert Coote, Ray Walston, Leslie Nielsen, Murray Salem, Dennis O'Flaherty, Robert Emhardt, Jane Karen, John Hillerman. Dir: Ken Annakin. Bill Driskill. Pro: Bill Driskill and Bert Gold. Screenplay: Bill Driskill. BBC, 15 November 1983.

The Intruder Within (1981). Neatly made, if familiar, 'monster' movie, an ocean-bed creature becomes a very unwelcome visitor to an isolated oil-

drilling platform in the cold seas of Antarctica. Cast: Chad Everett, Joseph Bottoms, Jennifer Warren, Rockne Tarkington, Lynda Mason Green, Paul Larson, James Hayden. Dir: Peter Carter. Screenplay: Ed Waters. ITV, 12 November 1983.

Invasion of Privacy (1982). After a broken marriage, Valerie Harper moves to a new town to start life over again, only to be sexually assaulted. And she quickly discovers that she will get no sympathy from the disapproving locals – apart from the sheriff, who finds her attractive. Rest of cast: Cliff de Young, Tammy Grimes, Carol Kane, Richard Masur, Jerry Orbach, Jeff Daniels, Peter Michael Goetz, Fred Coffin, J.C. Quinn, Jacqueline Brookes. Dir: Mel Damski. Screenplay: Elaine Mueller. Channel 4, 8 May 1984.

The Invisible Man (1975). Based on the H.G. Wells fantasy about a man who discovers the secret of invisibility, this original feature movie, which was the pilot for a short-lived TV series, tells the story of an American scientist who is anxious to keep the formula away from the military. Cast: David McCallum, Melinda Fee, Jackie Cooper, Henry Darrow, Alex Henteloff, Arch Johnson. Dir: Robert Michael Lewis. Screenplay: Steven Bocho. ITV, 30 December 1983.

Ishi, The Last of his Tribe (1979). The White Man's massacre of the Yahi Indians at the beginning of this century sets the scene for the story of the only survivor, in Dalton Trumbo's last screenplay. Cast: Dennis Weaver, Devon Ericson, Geno Silva, Joseph Running Fox, Lois Red Elk, Gregory Norman Cruz, Arliene Nofchissey Williams, Michael Medina, Patricia Ganera, Eddy Marquezm, Dennis Dimster, Wayne Hefley. Dir: Robert Ellis Miller. Pro: James F. Sommers. Screenplay: Dalton Trumbo; based on the book *Ishi in Two Worlds* by Tehodora Kroeber Quinn. BBC, 19 September 1983.

The Islander (1978). A mainland lawyer gives up his practice for a quiet life as a hotel keeper in Honolulu but soon finds that this new life is anything but peaceful when he becomes embroiled with ruthless mobsters, runaway witnesses and a senator suspected of attempted murder. This is yet another feature film pilot that was intended to herald a TV series. Cast: Dennis Weaver, Sharon Glass, Bernardette Peters, Peter Mark Richman, Ed Kaahea, Robert Vaughn, John S. Ragin, Zitto Kazann, Sheldon Leonard, Glen Cannon, George Wyner, John Fitzgibbon, Inny Young, Jimmy Borges. Dir: Paul Krasny. Pro. and Screenplay: Glen A. Larson. BBC, 18 August 1983.

The Jordan Chance (1978). Raymond Burr (having discarded his wheelchair from *Ironside*) plays a successful lawyer who was once wrongly sent to prison for a crime he did not commit and who is now dedicated to saving other innocent souls from his former fate. The film was screened as a showcase pilot for a TV series, but this never got off the ground. Rest of cast: James Canning, Jeannie Fitzsimmons, Ted Shackleford, Marie-Elena Cordero, George Dicenzo, John McIntire, Peter Haskell, Stella Stevens. Dir: Jules Irving. Pro: Ron Huggins. Screenplay: Stephen J. Cannell. BBC, 2 September 1983.

Just You and Me (1978). A film about the incident-filled cross-country journey from New York to Los Angeles undertaken by driver Charles Grodin in his new car, along with passenger Louise Lasser. Rest of cast: Julie Bovasso, Mark Syers, Tony di Benedetto, Marcella Lowery, David Thomas, Rosemary de Angelis, Jeff Eagle, James Borelli, Paul Fix, Kate Murtagh, Michael Aldredge. Dir: John Erman. Pro: William S. Gilmore Jr. Screenplay: Louis Lasser. BBC, 12 September 1983.

Katharine (1975). Fictional embroidery of the factual Patty Hearst case, with Sissy Spacek splendid as the spoiled heiress who is kidnapped and turns terrorist. Rest of cast: Art Carney, Henry Winkler, Jane Wyatt, Julie Kavner, Jenny Sullivan, Hector Elias, Mary Murphy, Rene Enriquez, Joe de Santis, Barbara Iley, Ann Noland. Dir and Screenplay: Jeremy Paul Kagan. Channel 4, 21 January 1984.

The Kid from Nowhere (1982). Actor Beau Bridges directs as well as playing the star role in this movie about an athletics coach who tries to convince selfless divorcee mother of a child with Downs Syndrome that she should let the boy take part in the special Olympics in Los Angeles. Rest of cast: Susan Saint James, Loretta Swit, Ricky Wittman, Lynn Carlin, Rene Auberjonois, Fred Dryer, Janet Maclachan, Rafer Johnson, Patrick Petersen. Dir: Beau Bridges. Screenplay: Judy Farrell. Channel 4, 12 June 1984.

Killdozer (1974). After the killer car with a mind of its own, a murderous bulldozer with a thirst for human blood! This weird thriller, with a touch of science-fiction, stars Clint Walker as a tough building boss on a lonely island with five men... then four... then... Rest of cast: Carl Betz, Neville Brand, James Wainwright, James A. Watson, Robert Uruch. Dir: Jerry London. Screenplay: T. Sturgeon. ITV, 28 May 1984.

Lady With a Badge (1981). Originally made under the title *Incident at Crestridge*, this is the story of a lady who, arriving with her husband in a small Wyoming town finds such corruption and inefficiency in the local arm of the law that she runs for sheriff. But when she wins and sits in the hot seat, she finds life becomes pretty difficult. Cast: Eileen Brennan, Pernell Roberts, Bruce Davison, Cliff Osmond, Maria Richwine, Sandy McPeak. Dir: Jud Taylor. Screenplay: Jim Byrnes. BBC, 30 April 1984.

Legend of the Golden Gun (1979). An American Civil War story concerning the awful outlaw Quantrill and his Raiders gang, pursued here by a vengeful Jeff Osterhage, in yet another TV feature film intended to launch a new series, but which never came about. Rest of cast: Carl Franklin, Hal Holbrook, Keir Dullea, Robert Davi, Michelle Carey, Elisha Leeds, R.G. Armstrong, John McLiam, Richard Slattery, William Bryant, Rex Holman. Dir: Alan J. Levi. Pro: B.W. Sandefur. Screenplay: James D. Parriott. BBC, 28 September 1983.

The Lion, the Witch and the Wardrobe (1978). A simple and amusing feature cartoon film adapted from the C.S. Lewis story, with the voices of Sheila Hancock, Arthur Lowe, Leo McKern, Leslie Phillips, June Whit-

field and other famous names. ITV, 29 December 1983.

The Love Goddesses (1963). A fascinating history of the screen vamp, with some 40 illustrations from before Theda Bara to Brigitte Bardot, etc. Pro and Written by Saul Tarrall and Graeme Feguson. Channel 4, 6 November 1983.

Loving Walter (1982–3). A combination of the two uncomfortably true and revealing one-hour Channel 4 films – *Walter* and *Walter and June* – about 20 years in the life of a mentally handicapped man. Cast: Ian McKellen, Sarah Miles, Barbara Jefford, Arthur Whybrow, Paula Tilbrook, Tony Melody, David Ryall, Linda Polan, Keith Allen, Lesley Claire O'Neill, Marjorie Yates, Jim Broadbent, Kenny Ireland, Donald McKillop, Nabil Shaban, Charles Lewson, Robert Walker, Trevor Laird, Stephen Petcher, Garry Cooper, John Surman, Robin Hooper, Frankie Connolly, John Czeslaw, Bob Flag, Gordon John Sinclair, Tony Doyle, Christine Hargreaves, Catherine Schofield, Debbie Bishop, Rowan Whylie, Tim Potter, Trevor Ray, Jesse Birdsall. Dir: Stephen Frears. Assoc Pro: Patrick Cassavetti. Screenplay: David Cook. ITV, 17 July 1983.

The Man in the Iron Mask (1977). The third screen adaptation – this time specially for television – of the Alexander Dumas classic, with Richard Chamberlain now in the old Fairbanks double role of the French King, Louis XIV, and his twin brother. Rest of cast: Patrick McGoohan, Louis Jourdan, Jenny Agutter, Ian Holm, Ralph Richardson, Vivien Merchant, Dir: Mike Newell. Screenplay: William Bast. ITV, 28 November 1983.

The Man in the Santa Claus Suit (1980). A Christmas fantasy about a trio of Santa-suit-renting characters who all come under the influence of a mysterious figure played by Fred Astaire, who adds his own charm to a comfy sort of movie. Rest of cast: Gary Burghoff, John Byner, Bert Convy, Nanette Fabray, Harold Gould, Danny Wells, David Greenan, Andre Gower. Dir: Corey Allen. Pro: Lee Miller. Screenplay: George Kirgo; based on a story by Leonard Gershe. BBC, 18 December 1983.

The Manions of America (1981). A family saga of love, passion and tears about the marriage of an Irish groom to an English bride, which meets more than its fair share of rocks. Originally a mini-series, the episodes were edited together to create this feature film. Cast: Pierce Brosnan, Kate Mulgrew, Simon MacCorkindale, Linda Purl, David Soul, Anthony Quayle, Peter Gilmore, Steve Forrest, Simon Rouse, Barbara Parkins, T.P. McKenna, Harry Towb. Dir: Joseph Sargent and Charles S. Dubin. Pro: Stanley Kallis. Screenplay: Rosemary Anne Sisson. BBC, 14 September 1983.

Marathon (1980). A film which shows just what jogging can do. In Bob Newhart's case, as a happily married accountant, it leads to passionate love for a female jogger, to Yoga and, finally, to the New York marathon! And it is all very well acted, and directed by Jackie Cooper, the famous child star of the past. Rest of cast: Herb Edelman, Dick Gautier, Anita Gillette, Leigh Taylor-Young, Valerie Landsburg, John Hillerman, Laszlo Tavori. Dir: Jackie Cooper. Screenplay: Ron Freidman. Channel 4, 15 May 1984.

Massarati and the Brain (1983). Massarati, an adventurer with sword for hire, and his clever ten-year-old nephew (the Brain) who lives with him, are employed to rescue a lady in distress – a mission which leads to all sorts of complications and a confrontation with a nasty old Nazi (played by Christopher Lee). Rest of cast: Daniel Pilon, Peter Billingsley, Markie Post, Ann Turkel, Camilla Sparv, Kathy Witt, Christopher Hewett. Dir: Harvey Hart. Screenplay: George Kirgo. ITV, 27 December 1983.

Meantime (1983). A film about present-day family life in London's East End, with all its amusing and less funny moments. Cast: Phil Daniels, Tim Roth, Marion Bailey, Alfred Molina, Jeffrey Robert, Pam Ferris, Eileen Davies, Gary Oldman, Brian Hoskin, Herbert Norville, Tilly Verburgh, Paul Daly, Leila Bertrand, Hepburn Graham, Peter Wright. Dir: Mike Leigh. Pro: Graham Benson. Channel 4, 1 December 1983.

Mission Galactica: The Cylon Attack (1979). Yet another brush between Battlestar Galactica and those nasty robots the Cylons, who for unpleasant reasons are bent on the destruction of the Earth's population. Cast: Richard Hatch, Dirk Benedict, Lorne Greene, Lloyd Bridges, Herbert Jefferson Jr, John Colicos, Maren Jenson, Laurette Spang, Tony Swartz, Anne Lockhart, Terry Carter, George Murdock, Jack Stauffer, William Bryant. Dir: Vince Edwards and Christian Nyby II. Screenplay: Glen A. Larson, Jim Carlson and Terence McDonnell. ITV, 30 December 1983.

More Than Murder (1983). A Mike Hammer feature to lead off a new series of tough private eye episodes from the pen of Mickey Spillane. In this longer adventure, Hammer is determined to prove that his good police captain pal has been framed by the crooks when a cache of cocaine is discovered in his car and he is suspended. Cast: Stacy Keach, Lindsay Bloom, Don Stroud, Kent Williams, Danny Goldman, Tim McIntire, Lynn-Holly Johnson, Sam Groom, Richard Romanus, Denny Miller, Robyn Douglass, Jay Bernstein. Dir: Gary Nelson. Screenplay: Bill Stratton and Stephen Downing. ITV, 7 February 1984.

Moving On: In Tandem (1974). The feature film predecessor of the *Moving On* TV series, with Claude Atkins as a lorry contractor teamed up with law graduate, Frank Converse, to stop the villains preventing the orange grower getting his fruit to market. Rest of cast: Richard Angarola, Sondra Blake, Janis Hansen, Ann Coleman, Michael Chrishel, Chris D'Anthony, Tito Vandis. Dir: Bernard Kowalski. Screenplay: Robert Collins and Herb Meadow. ITV, 14 December 1983.

Murcheson's Creek (1977). A successful young doctor pays a visit to an isolated rural community, built up by his grandfather's efforts, to find his father, the local doctor, has died and the people expecting him to take over the practice. He wants to refuse but is forced to think again. The film is yet another good example of the high standards set by the Australian movie industry. Cast: Mark Edwards, Sandra Lee Paterson, Gordon McDougall, Abigail, Lew Luton. Dir: Terry Bourke. Screenplay: Bob Caswell. ITV, 31 October 1983.

Murder at the Mardi Gras (1978). Against the colourful background of the New Orleans festival, happy tripper Didi Conn sees a very serious killing, and as the only witness is soon being pursued by the killers with very unfestival intent – but British director Ken Annakin never lets it get too far from fun. Rest of cast: David Groh, Gregg Henry, Wolfman Jack. Dir: Ken Annakin. Pro: Richard Nader and Matt Herman. Screenplay: Stanley Ralph Ross. BBC, 21 September 1983.

Murder is Easy – by Agatha Christie (1981). Dear old Miss Fullerton gets it right when, contrary to the village policeman, she guesses the four local deaths have been murders, and she soon has a theory about who committed them; and she is right, as the American visitor helps to prove. Cast: Bill Bixby, Lesley-Ann Down, Olivia de Havilland, Helen Hayes, Patrick Allen, Shane Briant, Freddie Jones, Leigh Lawson, Jonathan Pryce, Trevor T. Smith, Anthony Valentine, Timothy West. Dir: Claude Whatham. Screenplay: Carmen Culver; based on an Agatha Christie story. ITV, 24 December 1983.

Murder Me, Murder You (1983). Mike Hammer – Mickey Spillane's rough, tough detective character, played here by Stacy Keach – in the usual mixture of thick-ear adventures, spiced with sex and excitement, as he delves into the mystery of his beloved's death during a court case in which she is an important witness. Rest of cast: Tanya Roberts, Don Stroud, Delta Burke, Tom Atkins, Jonathan Banks, Kent Williams, Lisa Blount, Michelle Phillips, Randi Brooks, Lee Meredith, Ric Mancini, Madiseon Arnold. Dir: Gary Nelson. Screenplay: Bill Stratton. ITV, 24 January 1984.

Murder Once Removed (1971). Charlie's Angels unseen star, John Forsythe (the voice of Charlie), materializes to good effect in this story about a nasty doctor who is intent on taking, rather than saving, life as he becomes involved with the attractive wife (played by Barbara Bain) of an unhappy marriage. Rest of cast: Richard Kiley, Joe Campanella, Wendell Burton, Reta Shaw, Larry Haddon. Dir: Charles Dubin. Screenplay: Irving Gaynor Neiman. ITV, 17 January 1983.

The New Daughters of Joshua Cabe (1976). The third film in the *Cabe* series and, with the exception of Jack Elam (the original performer in the 'Bitter-root' role in the first movie, *The Daughters of Joshua Cabe*) a brand new cast. These three new 'daughters' decide to break Joshua out of jail when he is put there on a trumped-up murder charge. Rest of cast: John McIntire, Jeanette Nolan, Liberty Williams, Rennie Jarrett, Lezlie Dalton, Geoffrey Lewis, James Lydon, Joel Fabiani, John Dehner, Sean McClory, Ford Rainey, Larry Hovis, Randall Carver. Dir: Bruce Bilson. Screenplay: Paul Savage. ITV, 7 November 1983.

Nice Night for a Hanging (1977). Clu Gulager, as a private eye called Charlie Cobb, finds that delivering a young lady to the rich rancher who thinks she is his long-lost daughter is not as simple as it might appear to be, with a number of shady characters, including villainess Stella Stevens, determined to make his mission impossible. Yet another showcase feature for a series that was never made. Rest of cast: Ralph Bellamy, Blair Brown, Pernell Roberts, Christopher Connelly, Tricia O'Neil. Dir: Richard Michaels. Pro and Screenplay: Peter S. Fischer. BBC, 22 August 1983.

Night Chase (1970). Fugitive David Janssen takes a taxi at Los Angeles Airport at the start of what becomes a pretty exciting and dangerous ride to Mexico. Rest of cast: Yaphet Kotto, Victoria Vetri, Elisha Cook Jr, Joe de Santis, Mel Berger, Karen Carlson, John Carter, Richard Romanos, Laurie Main. Dir: Jack Starrett. Pro: Collier Young. Screenplay: Marvin A. Gluck; based on an original story by the producer. BBC, 5 October 1983.

The Night the City Screamed (1980). Another movie which gets its inspiration from the great New York blackout of the mid 1960s. This time the background is Los Angeles, the cause of the power failure a big storm, and the result – violence and lawlessness in the streets. Cast: Raymond Burr, Clifton Davis, David Cassidy, Robert Culp, Don Meredith, Linda Purl, Vic Tayback, Gary Frank, Shelley Smith, George Stanford Brown, Taurean Blaque. Dir: Harry Falk. Screenplay: Larry Brody. ITV, 15 January 1983.

Not Just Another Affair (1982). A polished comedy-romance about the love-hate affair of a good-looking lawyer and a quite incredibly lovely marine biologist who has taken a vow of celibacy! Cast: Victoria Principal, Gil Gerard, Robert Webber, Barbara Barrie, Richard Kline, Albert Hague, Markie Post, Ed Begley Jr, Judy Strangis, Carmen Zapata, Sharon Stone, William Dozier, Jill Jaconson. Dir: Steven Stern. BBC, 3 June 1984.

Nowhere to Hide (1977). Lee Van Cleef plays a US Marshal assigned to protect gangland informer Tony Musante, whose agreement to testify against his erstwhile underworld boss has brought an expert hit-man on his heels. Rest of cast: Edward Anhalt, Charlie Robinson, Lelia Goldoni, Noel Fournier, Russell Johnson, David Proval, Clay Tanner, John McLaughlin, Robert Hevelone, John Randolph. Dir: Jack Starrett. Screenplay: Edward Anhalt. ITV, 15 August 1983.

Nurse (1980). A young widow returns to her career of nursing in a New York hospital, and the story unfolds of her subsequent public and private life. Cast: Michael Learned, Robert Reed, Tom Aldredge, Hattie Winston, Antonio Fargas, Jon Matthews, Luke Reilly, Leora Dana, Ron McLarty, Cynthia Belgrave. Dir: David Lowell Rich. Screenplay: Sue Grafton; based on Peggy Anderson's best-selling novel. Channel 4, 1 May 1984.

Once They Marched Through a Thousand Towns (1981). Based on fact, the movie, headed by Danny Kaye, traces the events which occurred in a Chicago suburb in 1977 when the mainly Jewish community reacted to the news that their town has been chosen by a Neo-Nazi group as the location for its next big rally. Rest of cast: John Runinstein, Carl Reiner, Kim Hunter, Eli Wallach, Brian Dennehy, George Dzundza, Ed Flanders, Marin Kanter, Charles Levin, Stephan D. Newman, James Sutorious, Lee Strasberg, Robin Bartlett, David Hurst, Joseph Leon, Ruth Nelson, Robin Morse, Michele Shay. Dir: Herbert Wise. Screenplay: Ernest Kinoy. ITV, 30 August 1983.

One Shoe Makes it Murder (1982). Robert Mitchum, in his TV movie debut, plays a kind of Marlowe private eye assigned to solve the mystery of a missing wife. A shoe proves a very important clue, and this leads him on a trail through Nevada to San Francisco and Los Angeles before he cracks the case. Rest of cast: Angie Dickinson, Mel Ferrer, Cathie Sherriff, John Harkins. Dir: William Hale. Pro: Mel Ferrer. Screenplay: Felix Culver. BBC, 30 October 1983.

One Spy too Many (1964). Two TV episodes from the Man from U.N.C.L.E. series have been joined together to make this feature movie. Agents Robert Vaughn and side-kick David McCallum are assigned to track down some lethal gas stolen from the US Army before villain Rip Torn can use it to his evil ends. Rest of cast: Dorothy Provine, Leo G. Carroll, Yvonne Craig, David Opatoshu, David Sheiner, Donna Michelle, Leon Lontoc, Robert Karnes, Clarke Gordon. Dir: E. Darrell Hallenbeck. Screenplay: Dean Hargrove. Pro: David Victor. BBC, 5 August 1983.

The Ordeal of Doctor Mudd (1980). The true story of the unfortunate doctor who unknowingly assisted John Wilkes Booth, the murderer of President Lincoln, and was incarcerated in the notorious jail on Shark's Island. There followed the fight by his wife and lawyer to free him from his terrifying ordeal. Cast: Dennis Weaver, Susan Sullivan, Richard Dysart, Michael McGuire, Nigel Davenport, Arthur Hill, Larry Larson, Clarence Thomas, Bill Gribble. Dir: Paul Wendkos. Pro and Screenplay: Douglas Schwartz and Michael Berk. BBC, 1 August 1983.

A Piano for Mrs Cimino (1982). Bette Davis, in top form in this moving essay on old age, plays a 73-year-old widow who determinedly fights back against medical opinion that she is senile. The film is based on a novel which in turn was based on a true incident. Rest of cast: Penny Fuller, Keenan Wynn, Alexa Kenin, George Hearn, Christopher Guest, Graham Jarvis, Paul Roebling. Dir and Pro: George Schaeffer. Screenplay: John Gay; based on a novel by Robert Oliphant. BBC, 5 September 1983.

Playing for Time (1980). Vanessa Redgrave gives a good performance as a

Jewish cabaret singer (a role which caused a storm of controversy), in the story of the singer's incarceration in Auschwitz where she becomes a member of the Nazi-conscripted prisoner's orchestra, thus saving her life. Rest of cast: Jane Alexander, Marisa Berenson, Viveca Lindfors, Melanie Mayron, Maud Adams, Shirley Knight, Verna Bloom, Anna Kluger Levine, Robin Bartlett, Mady Kaplan. Dir: Daniel Mann. Screenplay: Arthur Miller; based on the memoirs of Fania Fenlon. Channel 4, 22 April, 1984.

Pleasure Cove (1979). Constance Forslund playing the assistant manager at a holiday hotel, tries her best to deal with smugglers, sharks and Tom Jones, the last making his not particularly distinguished straight acting debut in this showcase feature for a projected TV series which never took off. Rest of cast: Joan Hackett, Harry Guardino, James Murtaugh, Melodie Anderson, Ernest Harada, Shelley Fabares, Ron Masak, Tanya Roberts, David Hasselhoff, Jerry Lacy, Barbara Luna, Wes Parker, Sandy Champion. Dir: Bruce Bilson. Pro: Mel Swope. Screenplay: Lou Shaw. BBC, 31 August 1983.

The Possessed (1977). Some nasty things that do more than go bump in the night take up residence in a girls' school, causing terror and death. Can James Farentino, as a cleric expelled from the church, defeat these forces of darkness? And where have we heard that one before? Rest of cast: Joan Hackett, Claudette Nevins, Eugene Roche, Harrison Ford, Ann Dusenberry, Diana Scarwid, Dinah Manoff, Carol Jones. Dir: Jerry Thorpe. Screenplay: John Sacret Young. BBC, 24 March 1984.

The Pot Carriers (1962). The screen adaptation of the 1960 TV play which gave a glimpse into British prison life. Paul Massie plays the inmate most likely to crack (after a year's sentence for his assault on another man) aided by old lags, who soon involve him in their shady life-style. Rest of cast: Ronald Fraser, Carole Lesley, Dennis Price, Paul Rogers, Davy Kaye, Eddie Byrne, Campbell Singer, Alfred Burke, Patrick McAlinney, Neil McCarthy, Vanda Godsell, David Davies, David Ensor. Dir: Peter Graham Scott. Pro: Gordon L.T. Scott. Screenplay: T.J.

Morrison and Mike Watts; based on the teleplay by Watts. BBC, 23 September 1983.

The Power Play (1976). This pilot feature film for an intended TV series has Raymond Burr, playing an investigative journalist. Hired by a newspaper baron and TV executive, he uncovers a nasty web of murder and blackmail organized by a would-be world dictator. Rest of cast: James Canning, Pamela Hensley, Lenka Peterson, Bradford Dillman, Dina Merrill, Biff McGuire, Robert Sampson, Milt Kogan, R.G. Armstrong, Robert Mandan. Dir: Robert Day. Screenplay: Dick Nelson. BBC, 6 March 1984.

The Pride of Jesse Hallam (1981). Johnny Cash plays a Kentucky farmer who finds illiteracy a big handicap when he moves to the Big City – Cincinnati – so that his daughter can be given adequate hospital treatment. Cash and his wife, June Carter Cash, sing the songs he composed for the movie. Rest of cast: Brenda Vaccaro, Eli Wallach, Ben Marley, Crystal Smith. Dir: Gary Nelson. Screenplay: Suzanne Clauser. Channel 4, 2 August 1983.

Puzzle (1978). An Australian-made thriller with plenty of incident, including suicide, murder and blackmail. Cast: James Franciscus, Wendy Hughes, Robert Helpmann, Kerry McGuire, Peter Gwynne, Ivar Kants. Dir: Gordon Hessler. Pro and Screenplay: H.J. Wright. BBC, 25 October 1983.

Red Alert (1977). Power politics and technical arguments are the twin themes in this fast-moving and well directed story of a computer which sounds a warning about an impending disaster in a nuclear power plant, and the resulting disagreements between those who think the computer is right and those who claim it is itself at fault. Cast: William Devane, Michael Brandon, Adrienne Barbeau, Ralph Waite, Lois Fleck, Malcolm Wittman, E. Emett Walsh. Dir: William Hale. Screenplay: Sandor Stern; based on the novel *Paradigm Red* by William Hale. BBC, 9 June 1984.

Reflections of Murder (1974). A reasonably successful American re-

make of the 1955 Henri-Georges Clouzot thriller classic *Les Diaboliques* (*The Fiends*), set against the background of a boys' school. The film revolves around a murder plot and a series of bizarre twists and turns that lead to a really surprising ending. Cast: Tuesday Weld, Sam Walterston, Joan Hackett, Michael Lerner, R.G. Armstrong, Lucille Benson, Ed Bernard, Lance Kerwin, John Levin, William Turner, Jesse Vint. Dir: John Badham. Screenplay: Carol Sobieski; from a novel by Pierre Boileau and Thomas Narcejac. ITV, 10 October 1983.

Relentless (1977). Cops and robbers again, but against a new background this time, the desert and mountains of Arizona, where the cop, a Navajo Indian, his partner and an FBI agent track down and battle with the gang who have robbed a bank and killed a guard in a small wayside town. Cast: Will Sampson, Monte Markham, John Hillerman, Marianna Hill, Larry Wilcox, Anthony Ponzini, John Lawlor, Ted Markland, David Pendleton, Ron Foster, Don Starr, Danny Zapian. Dir: Lee H. Katzin. Screenplay: Sam H. Rolfe; from a novel by Brian Garfield, BBC, 28 January 1984.

Return Engagement (1979). Elizabeth Taylor, movingly impressive as a lonely lady professor at a Californian college, somewhat hesitantly agrees to let one of her rooms to student Joseph Bottoms, and so begins a new chapter in her life. Rest of cast: Allyn Ann McLerie, Peter Donat, James Ray, Susan Buckner, Alston Ahern. Dir: Joseph Hardy. Screenplay: James Prideaux. Channel 4, 10 August 1983.

The Return of the Man from U.N.C.L.E. (1983). Fifteen years after those intrepid agents Napoleon Solo and Illya Kuryakin made their last successful anti-espionage mission, their old enemy THRUSH pops up and they are called back to duty once more – and the interval has not dimmed their amusing style, or brilliance. Cast: Robert Vaughn, David McCallum, Patrick Macnee, Tom Mason, Gayle Hunnicutt, Anthony Zerbe, John Harkins, Geoffrey Lewis, Keenan Wynn, Dick Durock, Simon Williams. Dir: Ray Austin. Screenplay: Michael Sloan. ITV, 21 April 1984.

Revenge of the Stepford Wives (1980). A sequel to the Bryan Forbes shiverer *The Stepford Wives* (1975), with Sharon Glass (of TV's *Cagney and Lacey* series) as the reporter/investigator who arrives in Stepford, in New England, and soon finds a dark side to the apparently peaceful town, especially when her own assistant turns up as another zombie-like woman, similar to all those strangely slave-like wives. Rest of cast: Julie Kavner, Arthur Hill, Audra Lindley, Don Johnson, Mason Adams, Thomas Hill, Howard Witt, Peter Maloney. Dir: Robert Fuest. Pro: Scott Rudin. Screenplay David Wiltse. BBC, 6 November 1983.

The Rise to Power of Louis XIV (1966). Rightly seen as something of a cinematic masterpiece, this French TV film, directed by Italian ace Roberto Rossellini takes a non-professional cast and what must have been a great deal of careful and intelligent research to produce a marvellously visual and detailed examination of French politics in the 17th century. Gourmets will be fascinated by the regal 14-course meal. Cast: Jean-Marie Patte, Raymond Jourdan, Silvagni, Katharina Renn, Dominique Vincent, Pierre Barratt. Dir: Rossellini. Screenplay: Jean Gruault and Jean-Dominique de la Rochefoucauld. BBC, 1 June 1984.

The Roads of Exile (1978). Claude Goretta's 210-minute Franco-Swiss TV feature (shown in two parts) about the life and times of 18th-century philosopher Jean-Jacques Rousseau, whose book *Emile* affronted his native France so much he was banished and thereafter pursued by the Church, Commoners and fellow Thinkers through Europe to a shaky haven in England. The film has all this intelligent movie-maker's visual and intellectual expertise that he displayed in *The Lacemaker*. Cast: François Simon, Dominique Labourier, Martine Chevallier, Corinne Coderey, William Fox, Pierre Loniche, Gabriel Gabin, Didier Haudepin, Maurice Jacquemont, David Markham, John Sharp, Laurence Mercier, Antony Stuart, Vania Vilers. Dir: Claude Goretta. Screenplay: Goretta and George Haldas. BBC, 21 and 22 December 1983.

Saigon – Year of the Cat (1983). Set against the turbulent few months which preceded the fall of Saigon at the end of the Vietnam war, the film tells the story of a romance between a pretty British bank clerk and a CIA agent. Cast: Judi Dench, Chic Murray, Yim Yim Hoontrakul, Pichit Bulkul, Roger Rees, Wallace Shawn, Rong Wongsawan, Manning Redwood, Frederic Forrest, Somsak Seanwilai, Vitoon Win Vitoon, Josef Sommer, Thomasine Heiner, Gerry Bammem. Deborah Eisenberg, Clark Peters, Malinee, Po Pau Pee, Tawes Sub, Bob Sherman, E.G. Marshall, Andrew Winner, Bach Ngoc Tran, Thavisakdi Srimuang, Emily Mann. Dir: Stephen Frears. Pro: Michael Dunlop and Verity Lambert. Screenplay: David Hare. ITV, 29 November 1983.

Salem's Lot (1979). A three-hour, two-part adaptation of Stephen King's eerie best-seller about vampires on the loose in a previously pleasant small town in New England, with lots of famous Hollywood names literally dreadfully involved. Cast: David Soul, James Mason, Lance Kerwin, Bonnie Bedelia, Lew Ayres, Julie Cobb, Elisha Cook, George Dzundza, Ed Flanders, Clarissa Kaye, Geoffrey Lewis, Barney McFadden, Kenneth McMillan, Fred Willard, Marie Windsor, Barbara Babcock, Bonnie Bartlett, Joshua Bryant, Robert Lussier, Brad Savage, Ronnie Scribner, Ned Wilson, Reggie Nalder, James Gallery. Dir: Tobe Hooper. Screenplay: Paul Monash. Pro: Richard Kobritz. BBC, 24 and 26 August 1983.

Savage (1972). Political skullduggery, involving murder, blackmail and revenge, are investigated with (to some) infuriating and certainly dangerous persistency by a television journalist, Martin Landau, in this early Steven Spielberg work. (Was he even then dreaming of *Jaws*?) Rest of cast: Susan Howard, Barbara Bain, Will Geer, Paul Richards, Michele Carey, Barry Sullivan, Dabney Coleman, Louise Latham, Pat Harrington. Dir: Spielberg. Screenplay: Mark Rogers, Richard Levinson and William Link. ITV, 10 January 1984.

The Scarlet Pimpernel (1982). A lavish and well made film of the Baroness Orczy classic tale, with Anthony Andrews doing well as the English titled fop who is also the daring rescuer of French aristocrats from the Terror in France in 1792. Surprisingly, this is only the second filming of this story, the previous version being a British, cinema production in 1935. Rest of cast: Jane Seymour, Ian McKellen, James Villiers, Eleanor David, Malcolm Jamieson, Dennis Lill, Ann Firbank, Richard Morant, Julian Fellowes, Timothy Carlton, David Gant, John Quarmby. Dir: Clive Donner. Screenplay: William Bast. ITV, 27 December 1983.

Scott Free (1976). A confused landowner, Michael Brandon, finds the 25 acres of desert he has won in a poker game a mixed blessing, when a powerful business syndicate and a tribe of Indians both make it plain that they are going to buy the land come hell or high-water. Rest of cast: Susan Saint James, Robert Loggia, Ken Swofford, Michael Lerner, Dehl Berti, Paul Koslo, Tony Giorgio, Allen Rich, Bart Burns, Cal Bellini. Dir: William Wiard. Pro: Alex Beaton. Screenplay: Stephen J. Cannell. BBC, 16 September 1983.

Scream Pretty Peggy (1973). Take a sculptor who likes to sculpt evil things, a pretty young college-girl housekeeper, a recluse mother, a dotty sister *and* Bette Davis, and you have a fairly gripping thriller of the old shivery kind. Rest of cast: Ted Bessell, Sian Barbara Allen, Charles Drake, Allan Arbus, Tovah Feldshuh, Johnie Collins III, Jessica Rains, Christiane Schmidtner. Dir: Gordon Hessler. Screenplay: Jimmy Sangster and Arthur Hoffe. ITV, 28 April 1984.

Sgt Matlovich vs the US Air Force (1977). Brad Dourif plays the title role of a Vietnam veteran who contests his discharge from the USAF when he divulges he is a homosexual. Rest of cast: Mart Singer, Frank Converse, William Daniels, Stephen Elliott, Rue McClanahan, Mitch Ryan, David Spielberg, Barra Grant, Alfred Ryder, David Ogden Steirs. Dir: Paul Leaf. Screenplay: John McGreevey. BBC, 8 June 1984.

Shadow Riders (1982). A Western set at the end of the American Civil War in 1865, it tells the story of two brothers who fought on different sides but who come back and join forces in order to free their family, kidnapped by a gang of outlaws. Cast: Tom Selleck, Sam

Elliott, Katherine Ross, Jeffrey Osterhage, Ben Johnson, Geoffrey Lewis, Gene Evans, Jane Greer, Harry Carey Jr, R.G. Armstrong, Dominique Dunne. Dir: Andrew V. Langlen. Pro: Verne Nobles and Dennis Durney. Screenplay: Jim Byrnes. BBC, 14 October 1983.

A Short Walk to Daylight (1972). A film very similar to *The Poseidon Adventure*, but this time the trapped group of passengers have to find a way out from a New York tube train wrecked by an earthquake instead of a liner at sea. How many of the eight will eventually find their way to the surface and safety? Cast: James Brolin, Don Mitchell, James McEachin, Abbey Lincoln, Brooke Bundy, Lazaro Perez, Suzanne Charney, Laurette Spang, Franklin Cover. Dir: Barry Shear. Pro: Edward J. Montague. Screenplay: Philip H. Reisman Jr, Gerald di Pego and Stevan Bocho. BBC, 15 September 1983.

Sidney Shorr: A Girl's Best Friend (1981). A comedy-drama in which Tony Randall plays a lonely man living in a large New York Apartment he can no longer afford to rent. But he meets a pretty girl who for a while revolutionizes his life until his homosexuality contributes to the unhappy ending of their relationship. Rest of cast: Lorna Patterson, David Huffman, Kaleena Kiff, Ann Weldon, John Lupton, John Villard, Martin Rudy, Tom Fuccello, Berry Carvalho, Daniel Grace. Dir: Russ Mayberry. Screenplay: Oliver Hailey. Channel 4, 23 August 1983.

Slay Ride (1972). A 'whodunit' feature film based on the *Cade's County* TV series in which Glenn Ford, as the local sherrif, solves all the mysteries. In this case an Indian confesses to the murder of a rich rancher and his pretty young lady passenger, but Cade thinks he is lying and so sets out to prove his theory and find the real killer. Rest of cast: Edgar Buchanan, Taylor Lacher, Victor Campos, Betty Ann Carr, Peter Ford, Tony Bill, Gerald O'Loughlin, John Schuck, Dehl Berti, Leslie Parrish, Mark Jenkins. Dir: Robert Day. Screenplay: Anthony Wilson and Rick Husky. ITV, 21 July 1983.

The Solid Gold Kidnapping (1974). 'Six Million Dollar Man', Steve Austin, saves the US President from an international gang of kidnappers in this crime thriller, but then has to face up to the subsequent abduction of the President's chief adviser and a billion-dollar tag for his release. Cast: Lee Majors, Richard Anderson, Alan Oppenheimer, Elizabeth Ashley, Terry Carter, Leif Erickson. Dir: Russ Maybury. Screenplay: Michael Gleason and Larry Alexander. ITV, 31 December 1983.

Someone's Killing the World's Greatest Models (1979). A horror whodunit set against the background of a fashion show which is designed to launch the comeback of a former top couturière. Cast: Eleanor Parker, Jessica Walter, John Rubenstein, Clive Revill, Connie Sellecca, Jim McMullen. Dir: Gus Trikonis. Screenplay: George Lefferts. ITV, 5 September 1983.

Sooner or Later (1979). Teenage 'pashes' against a rock-music background, with Denise Miller as the 13-year-old who tries to look 18 when she falls in love with a guitar and a rock star. Rest of cast: Rex Smith, Barbara Feldon, Judd Hirsch, Lilia Skala, Morey Amsterdam, Vivian Blaine, Lynn Redgrave. Dir: Bruce Hart. Screenplay: Bruce and Carole Hart. BBC 22 June 1984.

Sparkling Cyanide (1983). An adaptation of one of Agatha Christie's 'whodunits': death by cyanide – suicide or murder? Detective Kemp, in spite of all the signs to suggest suicide, doggedly proves it was murder, and sorts out the suspects in routine Christie manner. Cast: Anthony Andrews, Deborah Raffin, Pamela Bellwood, Nancy Marchand, Josef Sommer, David Huffman, Christine Belford, June Chadwick, Barrie Ingham, Harry Morgan. Dir: Robert Lewis. Screenplay: Robert Malcolm Young, Sue Grafton and Steven Humphrey. ITV, 26 April 1984.

The Spy in the Green Hat (1966). Another of the four U.N.C.L.E. features made up of episodes from the TV series. The film includes Jack Palance as the odd character intent on making Greenland a new tropical island. Rest of cast: Robert Vaughn, David McCallum, Janet Leigh, Letitia Roman, Allen Jenkins, Jack La Rue, Leo G. Carroll, Ludwig Donath, John Blondell, Will Kuluva. Dir: Joseph Sargent. Pro: Boris Ingster. Screenplay: Peter Allan Fields. BBC, 26 August 1983.

The Spy with My Face (1966). Yet another of the four U.N.C.L.E. features made up of episodes from the TV series. This time there is lots of skullduggery in Switzerland where Solo finds he has an identical replica. Cast: Robert Vaughn, Senta Berger, David McCallum, Leo G. Carroll, Michael Evans, Sharon Farrell, Fabrizio Mioni, Donald Harron, Bill Gunn, Jennifer Billingsley, Paula Raymond, Donna Michelle, Harold Gould. Dir: John Newland. Pro: Sam Rolfe. Screenplay: Clyde Ware. BBC, 29 July 1983.

Squaring the Circle (1983). Playwright Tom Stoppard's dramatization of the events in Poland in 1980 which led to the formation of Solidarity – with Bernard Hill surprisingly cast as Lech Walesa. Rest of cast: Alec McCowen, Roy Kinnear, John Woodvine, Richard Crenna, Richard Kane, Don Henderson, Frank Middlemass, John Bluthal. Dir: Mike Hodges. Screenplay: Tom Stoppard. Channel 4, 31 May 1984.

The Strange Possession of Mrs Oliver (1977). A neat little occult mystery featuring Karen Black, who turns in an impressive performance as a housewife who gets oppressed by her domestic role and alters appearance, name and character and takes on an entirely new and different personality – that of a girl who has been dead for five years. Rest of cast: George Hamilton, Robert F. Lyons, Lucille Benson, Jean Allison, Gloria Le Roy, Burke Byrnes, Asher Brauner. Dir: Gordon Hessler. Screenplay: Richard Matheson. ITV, 16 February 1984.

Studio Murders (Fantasies in the USA) (1980). A sort of 'who is it whodunit!' film about the cast of a TV soap opera series who are being murdered. Will the killer be caught before the show is ruined? Cast: Suzanne Pleshette, Barry Newman, Robert Vaughn, Ben Marley, Lenora May, Patrick O'Neal, John Gabriel. Dir: William Wiard. Pro and Screenplay: David Levinson. BBC, 18 December 1983.

Summer of my German Soldier (1978). Hailed by the American critics 'The best movie ever made for television' – this is the touching love story of a Nazi POW who escapes from his Southern States prison camp and the young Jewish girl (played beautifully by Kristy McNichol) who offers him refuge and, ultimately, much more. Rest of cast: Bruce Davison, Esther Rolle, Michael Constantine, Barbara Barrie, Margaret Hall, Anne Haney. Dir: Michael Ruchner. Screenplay: Jane-Howard Hammerstein; from the book by Bette Green. BBC, 16 April 1984.

Those Glory, Glory Days (1983). A soccer movie, written by Spurs fan and *Observer* newspaper football correspondent Julie Welch, about the game in the early 1960s. Cast: Zoe Nathenson, Sara Sugarman, Cathy Murphy, Liz Campion, Elizabeth Spriggs, Julia McKenzie, Peter Tilbury, Julia Goodman, Danny Blanchflower, Amelia Dipple, Stephan Chase, Alexei Sayle, Bryan Pringle, John Salthouse, Eva Lohman, Frances Barber, Rachel Meidman, Bob Goody, John Joyce, Lucy Hornak, Chris Jury, Roddy Maude-Roxby, Dudley Sutton, Richard Wilson, Robert Armstrong, Ronald Atkin, Peter Batt, Steve Curry, Bob Houston, David Lacey, Colin Malam, Patrick Bergin, Ron Donachie, Stephen Bent, Glen Murphy, Stuart Organ, John Judd, Jon Iles, Philips Rowlands, David Straun, Dai Bradley. Dir: Philip Saville. Pro: Chris Griffin. Screenplay Editor: Jack Rosenthal. Channel 4, 17 November 1983.

The 3,000 Mile Chase (1977). Cliff de Young plays a courier with the hazardous, often bullet punctuated, assignment of taking scared Glenn Ford 3,000 miles from Los Angeles to New York, where he is due to appear in court as a witness. This film was yet another pilot for a TV series which was never made. Rest of cast: Blair Brown, David Spielberg, Priscilla Pointner. Dir: Rus Mayberry. Pro: Roy Huggins and Jo Swerling Jr. Screenplay: Philip Deguere Jr. BBC, 13 August 1983.

To Trap a Spy (1965). The first of the four U.N.C.L.E. feature films from the American TV series, this one reaching British cinema screens in 1966 before any of the series was shown on our television. Cast: Robert Vaughn, David McCallum, Patricia Crowley, Fritz Weaver, Luciana Paluzzi, William Marshal, Will Kuluva, Eric Berry, Victoria Shaw. Dir: Don Medford. Pro: Norman Felton. Screenplay: Sam Rolfe. BBC, 19 August 1983.

Travis McGee – The Empty Copper Sea (1982). Sam Elliott and partner Gene Evans prove who was and wasn't guilty in a fatal boating accident in this pilot feature for a proposed series, based on the work of crime writer J.D. MacDonald. Rest of cast: Geoffrey Lewis, Katharine Ross, Barry Corbin, Richard Farnsworth, Amy Madigan, Vera Miles, Marshall Teague, Walter Olkewicz. Dir: Andrew V. McLaglen. Screenplay: Stirling Silliphant. ITV, 7 July 1983.

21 Hours at Munich (1976). A stirring, fast-moving drama based on the events of 5 September 1972, when a group of Black September Arab terrorists broke into the Olympic village at Munich and held Israeli competitors hostage, 11 of whom were later killed. Cast: William Holden, Franco Nero, Shirley Knight, Anthony Quayle, Richard Basehart, Gunther Halmer, Paul Smith, Martin Gilat, Noel Willman, James Hurley, Georg Marinschka, Michael Degan, Else Quecke, Dan Van Husen. Dir: William W. Graham. Screenplay: Edward Hume: based on the novel of Serge Groussard. Channel 4, 16 August 1983.

The Underground Man (1974). Peter Graves takes over from Paul Newman in another of Private Eye Lew Archer's cases, this time having to dig into old scandals before he solves the mystery presented to him by a terrified wife who is fleeing from her husband. Rest of cast: Jo Ann Pflug, Jack Klugman, Judith Anderson, Jim Hutton, Celeste Holm, Sharon Farrell, Kay Lenz, Vera Miles, Biff McGuire, Arch Johnson. Dir: Paul Wendkos. Screenplay: Douglas Heyes; based on Ross McDonald's 'whodunit' novel. ITV, 28 June 1983.

Vision of Death (1972). Monte Markham, university lecturer and clairvoyant, makes an unfortunate error of judgement when he reports a vision he has of a future bombing to the police, for he finds himself both suspected of the intended crime by Lieutenant Telly Savalas, and on top of the hit-list of the actual bomber. Rest of cast: Barbara Anderson, Tim O'Connor, Joe Sirola, Lonny Chapman. Dir: Lee Katzin. Screenplay: Paul Playdon. BBC, 7 February 1984.

Young Love, First Love (1979). The story of two teenagers who, although attracted to each other, have to face up to a choice of values as their different backgrounds and upbringing bring them into conflict. Cast: Valerie Bertinelli, Timothy Hutton, Arlen Dean Snyder, Fionnuala Flanagan, Leslie Axkerman, Grant Wilson, James Gallery, David Rupprecht, Cheryl Clark, Charlie Brill. Dir: Steve Stern. Screenplay: Dan Polier Jr. Channel 4, 22 May 1984.

Releases of the Year

In this section you will find details of films released in Great Britain from 1 July 1983 to the end of June 1984 – the period covered by all the reference features in the book. The precise dating of some of these releases is a little tricky in view of the current lack of any rigidity in the release pattern, but dates given refer to the general release and not pre-release.

When it comes to films which are sent out on a 'floating' release I have added, wherever possible, the month of the film's first London showing because usually this is also the first British showing.

The normal abbreviations continue to operate as follows: Dir – for Director; Pro – for Producer; Assoc Pro – for Associate Producer; Ex Pro – for Executive Producer; Pro Ex – for Production Executive; Pro Sup – for Production Supervisor; Pro Con – for Production Controller; Co-Pro – for Co-Producer; Pro Co-Ord – for Production Co-Ordinator; Ph – for Photographer; Ed – for Editor; Art – for Art Director; Pro Des – for Production Designer; M – for Music; and a few others which will be obvious.

Abbreviations for the name of film companies are also pretty obvious when used, such as Fox for 20th Century-Fox, Rank for Rank Film Distributors, and UIP for Universal International Pictures. Where known, the actual production company is given first, the releasing company last.

When it comes to nationality of the film you will find that this is noted wherever possible – those films without any mention of country of origin can be taken as being American – but in these days of increasing international co-productions between two, three and even four countries it is sometimes a little difficult to sort out where the premier credit is due.

Finally, unless otherwise specified (i.e. in black-and-white), it can safely be taken that the film is made in Technicolor or some similar colour process.

Note: The recent change in the former A, AA, U, and X certificates issued by the British Board of Censors has led to some confusion in that some companies still use the old 'X' (for the new '18' certificate). But the new categories are: U (suitable for any age), PG (Parental Guidance – for films which contain scenes some parents would consider unsuitable for their children), 15 (films to which persons under the age of fifteen will not be admitted) and 18 (for audiences of eighteen plus only).

Against All Odds. A rather pale remake of the 1947 gangster piece *Out of the Past*, about the obstinate struggle of a tough, American footballer (Jeff Bridges) to keep playing after he has been humiliatingly sacked. His fight leads to involvement with the underworld characters running the team, and Los Angeles, and an abrasive love affair with a mixed-up heiress who has her own ideas about playing the game. The superb scenic backgrounds include Mexico's island resort, the Mayan-Toltec ruins and other ancient remains in the forests of Yucatan. Rest of Cast: Rachel Ward, James Woods, Alex Karras, Jane Greer, Richard Widmark, Dorian Harewood, Swoosie Kurtz, Saul Rubinek, Pat Corley, Bill McKinney, Sam Scarber, Doug France, Jon St. Elwood, Tamara Stafford, Jonathan Terry, Paul Valentine, Ted White, Stone Bower, Mel Scott-Thomas, Barnetta McArthy, Ginger La Brie, David Dayan, Tom Kelly, August Darnell, Adriana Kaegi, Cheryl Poirer, Taryn Hagey, Gary Davis, Carey Loftin, Carl Ciarfalio, Tundra (the dog). Dir: Taylor Hackford. Pro: Hackford and William Gilmore. Ex Pro: Jerry Bick. Screenplay: Eric Hughes; based on the book by Daniel Mainwaring. Ph: Donald Thorin. Ed: Fredric and William Steinkamp. Art: Richard James Lawrence. Assoc Pro: William Borden. M: Michel Colombier and Larry Carlton. (New Visions/Taylor Hackford–Columbia) Rel: 11 May 1984. 121 mins. Cert 15.

The Alchemist. A minor horror movie about a man in the 1870s who is cursed with everlasting life by a magician because he kills his wife in an effort to free her from the magician's clutches – and the nasty things that happen nearly a century later when they all meet again. Cast: Robert Ginty, Lucinda Dooling, John Sanderford, Viola Kate Stimpson, Robert Glaudini. Dir: Charles Band. Pro: Lawrence Appelbaum. Ex Pro: Billy Fine and Jay Schultz. Assoc Pro: Harvey Genkind. Pro Con: Wanda Cannon. Screenplay: Alan J. Adler. Ph: Andrew W. Friend. Ed: Ted Nicolaou. Assoc Ed: Mark Hebdon. Pro Des: Dale A. Pelton. Art: Pam Warner. M: Richard H. Band. (Video Form Pictures–Ideal Films) Rel: 7 July 1983. 84 mins. Cert X (18).

All Night Long – Toute Une Nuit. This Franco-Belgium co-production set in night-time Brussels consists of a series of assembled shots of men waiting for women, women waiting for men, meetings and partings, mostly without dialogue and none seemingly related to each other. It is the nearest thing to a Marguerite Duras film since she stunned British movie goers with her first movie shown here! Made by Chantal Akerman who directed the hypnotically fascinating *Les Rendez-vous d'Anna* in 1980. The vast list of performers includes: Angelo Abazoglou, Frank Aendenboom, Natalia Akerman, Véronique Alain, Paul Allio and Jacques Bauduin. Dir and Screenplay: Chantal Akerman. Pro: Stéphène Dykman and Séverine Vermersch. Dir of Pro: Nicole Flipo. Ex Pro: Marilyn Watelet. Ph: Caroline Champetier. Ed: Luc Barnier. Pro Des: Michele Blondeel. M: 'Ma Révérence' sung by Véronique Sanson, 'Kindertotenlieder' sung by Lucy Grauman and 'L'Amore Personera' sung by Gino Lorenzi. (Gerick Films/Lyric Films/Partner's Productions, Paris/Centre Bruxellois de l'Audiovisuel, Brussels–Film International, Rotterdam/Cine 380, Quebeck–Paradise Films/Avidia Films Co-Production–The Other Cinema) Rel: floating; first shown London (ICA), March 1984. 90 mins. Cert not fixed.

Almonds & Raisins. This, by turns moving and amusing documentary narrated by Orson Welles, recounts the rise and fall of Yiddish films (about 300 in all) made in the 13 years following the premiere of *The Jazz Singer* in 1927. Illustrated by extracts from some of the best of them, mostly schmaltzy and reflecting the immigrant dream of a United States paradise, but some show the subsequent reality of ghetto poverty. Cast includes: Herschel Bernardi, Joseph Green, Zvee Scooler, Seymour Rechtzeit, Leo Fuchs, Miriam Kressun, David Opatashu. Dir and Co-Pro (latter with David Elstein): Russ Karel. Based on a treatment by Wolf Mankowitz. Ph: Jacee Laskus. Ed: Christopher Barnes. Art: Ralph Steadman. M: John Altman. (Channel 4–Contemporary) Rel: floating; first shown London (Phoenix, East Finchley), Feb 1984. 90 mins. Cert U.

American Boy. A sort of home movies documentary, made on 16mm film by Martin Scorsese in 1978 between his *Taxi Driver* and *New York, New York* movies, profiling Steven Prince. Cast: Prince, Scorsese and friends. Dir: Scorsese. Pro: Bertram Lovitt. Ex Pro: Ken and Jim Wheat. Ph: Michael

Chapman. Ed: Amy Jones and Bertram Lovitt. M: Song 'Time Fades Away' written and sung by Neil Young. (New Empire Films/Scorsese Films–Cinegate) Rel: floating; first shown London (Electric Cinema), July 1983. 55 mins. No cert.

Amityville 3-D. More mysterious happenings in that dark old house where nasty things in the basement go more than bump in the night – and they are now doing it with the added shivers of stereoscopic menace. Claimed by the

Rachel Ward and Jeff Bridges in Taylor Hackford's *Against All Odds*.

producers not to be a sequel to the previous two *Amityville* movies, it is certainly a good lookalike! Cast: Tony Roberts, Tess Harper, Robert Joy, Candy Clark, John Beal, Leona Dana, John Harkins, Lori Loighlin, Meg Ryan. Dir: Richard Fleischer. Pro: Stephen Kesten. Screenplay: William Wales. Ph: Fred Schuler. Ed: Frank J. Urioste. Art: Giorgio Postiglione. M: Howard Blake. (Dino de Laurentis/Orion–Thorn/EMI) Rel: 18 May 1984. 93 mins. Cert 15.

And the Ship Sailed On. Fellini's delightfully idiosyncratic, stylish satire-farce about a group of egocentric operatic passengers on board a luxury liner which has been chartered to carry the ashes of a great opera singer to the small Adriatic island where she was born. The scene is set on the high seas off the Balkans coastline: the time, significantly, July 1914. Typical Fellini jests in-

clude the use of cardboard ships, fabric seas, a seagull apparently anxious to join the mourners in the restaurant and a pet rhino (with a diarrhoea problem) which is taken for a curative 'airing' in a small rowboat. As the dedicated little group interact and periodically break into magnificent song, they refuse to see the ominous portents of the war about to explode. In spite of the serious undertow, it is all good fun and frolics on the surface. Freddie Jones is splendid as the journalist on board who also provides a helpful and larky commentary. Rest of cast: Barbara Jefford, Victor Poletti, Peter Cellier, Norma West, Fiorenza Serra, Pina Bausch, Philip Locke, Pasquale Zito, Elisa Mainardi, Maurice Barrier, Sarah Jane Varley and Janet Suzman. Dir: Federico Fellini. Pro: Franco Cristaldi. Screenplay: Fellini and Tonino Guerra. Ph: Giuseppe Rotunno. Ed: Ruggero Mastroianni. Sets: Dante Ferretti. M: Gianfranco Plenizio. Lyrics: Andrea Zanzotto. (RAI – Vides, Rome/Gaumont, Paris–Gala) Rel: floating; first shown London (Academy), April 1984. 128 mins. Cert PG.

Angel. The third film with this title to arrive within a few months – and that sort of confusion should not be allowed to occur. This one is about a Los Angeles high school kid who doubles as a hooker in her spare time. And in the background there is the usual psycho case with an Oedipus complex whose pleasure it is to murder prostitutes. Cast: Cliff Gorman, Susan Tyrrell, Dick Shawn, Rory Calhoun, John Diehl, Donna Wilkes, Donna McDaniel, Graeme McGavin, Elaine Giftos, Mel Carter, Steven Porter, David Underwood. Dir: Robert Vincent O'Neil. Pro: Roy Watts and Donald P. Borchers. Ex Pro: Mel Pearl and Don Levin. Screenplay: O'Neil and J.M. Cala. Ph: Andy Davis. Ed: Charles Bornstein and Wilt Henderson. Art: Stephen Marsh. M: Craig Saffin. (Adams/Apple–New World–Thorn EMI) Rel: 29 June 1984. 92 mins. Cert 18.

Angelo My Love. Actor Robert Duvall raised a million dollars in order to indulge his desire to make a movie about a gipsy kid (from his own quarter of New York) whose natural talent had so impressed him. Four years in the making, the movie starring the whole Angelo (Evans) family and amateurs (some unable even to read English, hence the obvious stretches of improvised dialogue), this story of a gipsy family, a stolen ring and otherwise paper-thin plot, was slow, indulgent and only periodically fascinating. The precocious kid acted with the confident aplomb of an actor many times his age, but even so, he was hardly endearing. Cast: Angelo, Michael, Ruthie, Tony

Phyllis Logan and Giovanni Mauriello in *Another Time Another Place*.

and Debbie Evans, Steve 'Patalay' and Millie Tsigonoff, Frankie Williams, George Nicholas, Katerina Ribrake, Timothy Phillips, Lachlan Young, Jennifer Youngs, Louis Garcia, Margaret Millan Gonzalez, Kathy Kitchen, Jan Kitchen, Debbie Ristick, William and John Duvall, Nick and Diana Costello, Johnny and Yelka Ristick, John Williams, The Ufie, Ristick and Costello families, The Lucky Brothers. Dir Pro and Screenplay: Robert Duvall. Assoc Pro: Gail Youngs. Ph: Joseph Friedman. Ed: Stephen Mach. M Dir: Michael Kamen. (Miracle) Rel: floating; first shown London (Classic, Tottenham Ct Rd) June 1984. 116 mins. Cert 15.

Another Time, Another Place. Another brilliant and essentially British film which has the hint of a documentary about it as it tells of a group of Italian POWs sent to work on a bleak farm in the far north-east of Scotland, and the tragic love affair that develops between one of them, from Naples, and the farmer's vaguely discontented wife. The contrasts between the two such different ways of life and amusement are beautifully observed. Cast: Phyllis Logan, Gian Luca Favilla, Paul Young, Tom Watson, Denise Coffey, Carol Ann Crawford, Scott Johnston, Giovanni Mauriello, Claudio Rosini, Gregory Fisher, Jennifer Piercey, Yvonne Gilan, Ray Jeffries. Dir: Michael Radford. Pro: Simon Perry. Ex Pro: Timothy Burrill. Assoc Pro: Paul Cowan. Screenplay: Radford; based on the novel by Jessie Kesson.

Ph: Roger Deakins. Ed: Tom Priestley. Art: Hayden Pearce. M: John McLeon: Neopolitan music arr. by Corrado Sfogli and Giovanni Mauriello. Italian Co-ordination by John Francis Lane. (Umbrella Films–Cinegate) Rel: floating; first shown London (Bloomsbury Gate), July 1983. 101 mins. Cert 15.

At First Sight – Coup de Foudre. Diane Kurys's third film, and her best yet, illustrates all the finer qualities of the French movie – a mixture of humour, warmth, reality and wit, with characters drawn in depth, and a fine understanding of human nature, possibly due to the fact that Miss Kurys based some of the characters and experiences on those of her family. The film tells the story of two married couples, the wives meeting in Lyons in 1954 after harrowing war-time adventures and hasty marriages and finding in each other the stimulation their lives lack. This leads to an ever closer relationship and the final break-up of their marriages. Brilliant performances by the quartet: Guy Marchand (particularly), Jean-Pierre Bacri, Miou-Miou and Isabelle Huppert. Rest of cast: Robin Renucci, Patrick Bauchau. Dir: Diane Kurys. Pro: Ariel Zeitoun. Screenplay: Kurys and Alain Le Henry. Ph: Bernard Lutic. Ed: Joële van Effenterre. Art: Jacques Bufnoir. M: Luis Bacalov. (Partner's Productions/Alexandre Films/Hachette Premiere/Films A2/SFPC Productions–Gaumont–Gala Films) Rel: floating: first shown London (Academy), Oct 1983. 110 mins. Cert 15. (Winner of the Critics' Prize at the San Sebastian Film Festival 1983.)

The Balance – La Balance. A brutal and violent – and technically brilliant – French cops and robbers movie which, a little surprisingly, picked up three of France's premier César film awards for Best Film (shared), Best Actor and Best Actress. The film focusses on a loving prostitute and her beloved pimp, and the cops' efforts to force them to become informers. Cast: Nathalie Baye, Philippe Leotard (the award winners), Richard Berry, Christophe Malavoy, Jean-Paul Connart, Bernard Freyd, Albert Dray, Florent Pagny, Jean-Daniel Laval, Luc-Antoine Diquerc, Maurice Ronet, Tcheky Karyo,

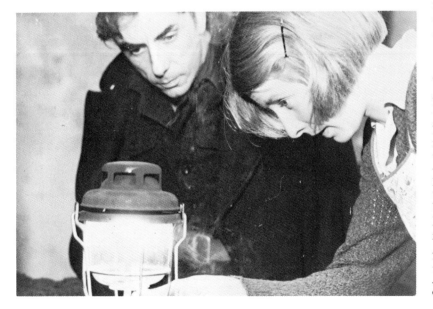

Before the Nickelodeon, a look at the work of film pioneer Edwin S. Porter.

Galia Dujardin, Michel Anphoux, Raouf Ben Yaghlane, Robert Atlan, Guy Dhers, François Berleand, Sam Karmann, Audrey Lazinni, Fiorella de Gennaro, Claude Villers, Mostefa Zerguine, Marc Ballis, Patrick Guillaume, Christian Gaubert, David Overbey, Catherine de Dall, Geffrey Carey, Dir and Screenplay (latter with M. Fabiani): Bob Swaim. Pro Man: Raymond Leplont. Ex Pro: Georges Danvigers and Alexandre Mnouchkine. Ph: Bernard Zitzermann. Ed: Françoise Javet. Art: Eric Moulard. M: Roland Bocquet. (Les Films Ariane/Film A2–Gala) Rel: floating; first shown London (Screen-on-the-Hill, Classic Tott Ct Rd and Odeon, Kensington), March 1984. 102 mins. Cert 18.

The Ballad of Narayama – Narayama-Bushi Ko. Excellently directed and acted, but very, very long (and often slow), this Japanese film, based on the old and now discontinued custom of children taking their aged parents up the mountain to die when they decide their time has come, provides a fascinating glimpse into Japanese village life of the past. Cast: Sumiko Sakamoto, Ken Ogata, Aki Takejo, Mitsuko Baisho, Nijiko Kiyokowa. Dir and Screenplay: Shohei Imamura; based on the book by Shichiro Fukazawa. Pro: Jiro Tomoda. Ph: Masao Toshizawa. Ed: Hajime Okaiasu. M: Shininchiro Ikebe. (Toie–Cannon Film Dist.) Rel: floating; first shown London (Premiere), April 1984. 130 mins. Cert 18.

Basket Case. A gore-and-guts shocker which never manages to get out of one of the lowest of such ruts. Cast: Kevin Van Hentenryck, Terri Susan Smith, Beverly Bonner, Robert Vogel, Diana Browne, Lloyd Pace, Bill Freeman, Joe Clarke, Ruth Neuman, Richard Pierce, Sean McCabe, Dorothy Strongin, Kerry Ruff, Ilza Balodis, Tom Robinson, Chris Babson, Maria T. Newland, Florence Schultz, Mary Ellen Schultz, Constantine Scopas, Charles Stanley, Sydney Best, Johnny Ray Williams, Yousef Abuhamdeh, Lubi Kirsch, Catherine Russell, Mitchell Huval, Noel Hall, Bruce Frankel, Pat Ivers, Emily Armstrong, Russell Fritz. Dir, Ed and Screenplay: Frank Henenlotter. Pro: Edgar Ievins. Ex Pro: Arnie Bruck and Tom Kay. Pro Ex: Ray Sundlin. Ph: Bruce Torbet. Art: Frederick Loren. M: Gus Russo (theme in bar; Davis Maswick). (Basket Case CO./An Ievins–Henenlotter Production/Alpha Films) Rel: 4 July 1983. 90 mins. Cert X.

The Beard. A quite horrific animation short about a beard that won't stop growing and, like the tail that wagged the dog, soon takes over its owner. Dir: Ian Emes. Pro: Chris Brown; based on the illustrations of Peter Till. (Boyd Co/

37

Wife and husband, Patricia Hodge and Ben Kingsley (above), and wife and lover, Jeremy Irons (left), in *Betrayal*.

Nicholas de Rothschild–Mainline Pictures) Rel: 25 Nov 1983. 11 mins. Cert PG.

Before the Nickelodeon. A fascinating documentary, of primary interest to film buffs, telling the story of the movies between 1896 and 1909, and concentrating more particularly on the rise and fall of innovator Edwin S. Porter, whose *The Great Train Robbery* is generally acknowledged to be the first real fictional film feature. Included in the programme are Porter's *The Life of an American Fireman* (1903), and *Rescued from an Eagle's Nest* (1907). With a commentary by Blanche Sweet, the film also gives a marvellous picture of what going to the cinema meant at the turn of the century. Dir and Ed: Charles Musser. Ex Pro: Steve Brier. Assoc Pro: Elizabeth Lennard. Screenplay: Musser and Warren D. Leight. Ph: Rob Issen. With the voices of Milos Forman, Louise Malle, Robert Altman, etc. (BFI) Rel: floating; first shown London (ICA), Nov 1983. 60 mins. No cert (but obviously U). Shown in the same programme were Porter's *The Gay Shoe Clerk* (1903), *The Ex-Convict* (1904), *The White Caps* (1905) and *The Teddy Bears* (1907).

Betrayal. An indelibly stamped Harold Pinter piece adapted from his play, which in a vaguely Noel Coward style tells the story of a ten-year liaison between a publisher's wife and his best friend and literary agent (the best man at his wedding). It is told, somewhat wilfully perhaps, but not inaffectively, in reverse, starting at today and working back to the wedding by one or two year steps. The delightfully typical Pinter dialogue, sprinkled with wit, is finely played by Jeremy Irons as the lover, Patricia Hodge as the wife and mistress, and Ben Kingsley as the betrayed husband. Rest of cast: Avril Elgar, Ray Marioni, Caspar Norman, Chloe Billington, Hannah Davies, Michael Konig, Alexander McIntosh. Dir: David Jones. Pro: Sam Spiegel. Screenplay: Harold Pinter; based on his own play. Ph: Mike Fash. Assoc Pro: Eric Rattray. Ed: John Bloom. Pro Des: Eileen Diss. M: Dominic Muldowney (Horizon Pictures–Virgin Films) Rel: floating; first shown London (Curzon), Oct 1983. 95 mins. Cert 15.

Beyond the Door – Oltre la Porta. A tortuous Italian thriller, with plenty of sexual trimmings and some rather dubious psychological underpinning, about an Italian woman with a 'past' (and in Morocco, too!) who finally leaves her ever-loving American husband in order to go off with her step-father, a sadist played with obvious flamboyant enjoyment by none other than Marcello Mastroianni. Rest of cast: Eleonora Giorgi, Tom Berenger, Michel Piccoli, Paolo Bonetti, Maria Sofia Amendolea, Enrico Bergier, Marcia Briscoe, Cecely Brown, Hadija Lahnida, Leandro Marcoccio, Atik Mohamed, Abdelkader Moutaa, Mahjoub Raji, Fatima Regragui, Giuseppina Romagnoli, Gary Shebex, Hamadi Tounsi, Bill Willis. Dir and Screenplay (latter with Enrico Medioli): Liliana Cavani. Pro: Francesco Giorgi. Ph: Luciano Tovoli. Ed: Ruggero Mastroianni. Art: Dante Ferretti. M: Pino Donaggio. M Dir: Natale Massara. (Futur Film '80 in collaboration with RAI–Radiotelevisione Italiana/Cineriz Distributori Assoc–Premier Releasing) Rel: floating; first shown London (Classics, Tott Ct Rd and Chelsea) March 1983. 116 mins. Cert 18.

Biddy. One of the year's most unusual and in many ways effective examples of British filmcraft, it tells the gentle story of a mid-Victorian nursemaid and her limited world of tidy and moral rectitude, which she colours by quotations from Shakespeare, Byron and other poets as she sits with her charges before the flaming fire, on the guard of which she hangs their sleepwear to warm – a marvellous reconstruction of the Victorian household and its atmosphere.

Cast: Celia Bannerman, Patricia Napier, Sam Ghazoros, Luke Duckett, Miles Parsey, David Napier, Kate Elphick, Sabine Goodwin, Emily Hone, Sally Ashby, John Dalby, Amelda Brown, Frances Lynch, Jason Morell. Dir and Screenplay: Christine Edzard. Pro: Richard Goodwin. Ph: Alec Mills. No art credit. M: Michel Sanvoisin. (Sands Films Ltd) Rel: floating; first shown London (The Minema), Dec 1983. 86 mins. Cert U.

The Big Chill. The story of a small group of 1960s American university graduate pals who are drawn back together in the 1980s by the funeral of one of their number, a drop-out who has committed suicide. In the party afterwards they rediscover each other, old passions are briefly aroused and they gradually reveal the guilt they feel for having sacrificed any teenage dreams and ideals they may have shared for the sake of social and commercial success. A series of vignettes of uneasy and sometimes regretful characters which while not adding up to a strong story do present a subtle and often deep understanding of human nature, resulting in glossy and well acted entertainment. (But it is a pity the string of period-setting musical numbers are belted out with such vigour they sometimes intrude on the dialogue.) Cast: Tom Berenger, Glenn Close, Jeff Goldblum, William Hurt, Kevin Kline, Mary Kay Place, Meg Tilly, Jobeth

The Big Chill – (from l. to r.) Jobeth Williams, Jeff Goldblum, Mary Kay Place, Tom Berenger, William Hurt, Meg Tilly and Kevin Kline and Glenn Close (also below).

Celia Bannerman, the Victorian nursemaid in the marvellously atmospheric *Biddy*.

Williams, Don Galloway, James Gillis, Ken Place, Jon Kasdan, Ira Stiltner, Jacob Kasdan, Muriel Moore, Meg Kasdan, Patricia Gaul. Dir: Lawrence Kasdan. Pro: Michael Shamberg and Kasdan. Ex Pro: Marcia Natasir and Kasdan. Screenplay: Kasdan and Barbara Benedek. Ph: John Bailey. Ed: Carol Littleton. Pro Des: Ida Random. Assoc Pro: Barrie M. Osborne. M Consultant: Meg Kasdan. (Cannon Productions Group–Columbia Delphi Productions–Columbia) Rel: 16 March 1984. 105 mins. Cert 15.

Big Meat Eater. One of, if not actually the craziest movie of the year – a comedy with music which was made entirely on location in the Canadian White-Rock-Vancouver areas for well under a miniscule £100,000. Impossible to describe, the story centres on a butcher's shop where the corpse of the murdered Mayor has been accidentally stowed in the freezer and the murderer frantically tries various ruses to smuggle it out. But other facets of this weirdly insane mix include spaceships that fly on wires, robots that speak good English, a happily singing psychopath, murder most foul and funny, and a butcher whose cheery motto is 'Pleased

Bob Sanderson (right) and Andrew Gillies (left) in Palace's *Big Meat Eater*.

to meet you ... meat to please you'. You'll not find a more bizarre movie in these listings. Cast: George Dawson, Andrew Gillies, Bob Sanderson, Big Miller, Stephen Dimopoulous, Georgine Hegerlos, Ida Carnevali, Howard Taylor, Heather Smith-Harper, Peter Anderson, Gillian Neumann, Sharon Wahl, John Bryden, Shannon Keane, Kim Stebner, Jay Samwald, Neil Macdonald. Dir: Chris Windsor. Pro: Laurence Keane. Ph: Doug Mackay. Screenplay: Phil Savath. M: J. Douglas Dodd. (BCD Entertainment Corration Ltd–Palace Pictures) Rel: floating; first shown London (Screen-on-the-Green) April 1984. 82 mins. Cert 15.

Black Shack Alley – Rue Cases Nègres. Franco/Martinique film which presents a powerful and often moving account of the white man's oppression of his black brothers in the sugar cane fields of the French island in the 1930s. New director Euzhan Palcy (who won a Silver Lion at Venice and a French Cesar for his work) keeps sentimentality at bay as he gets some fine performances from his cast, and injects a strong feeling of sincerity into this adaptation of Joseph Zobel's novel. Cast: Garry Cadenat, Darling Legitimus, Douta Seck, Joby Bernabe, Francisco Charles, Marie-Jo Descas, Marie-Ange Farot, Henri Melon, Eugene Mona, Joel Palcy, Mathieu Crico, Virgine and Celine Delaunay-Belleville, Tania Hamel, Maite Marquet, Laurent Saint-Cyr, Dominique Arfi, Emilie Blameble, Norita Blameble, Leon de la Guigneraye, Andre Lehr, Roger Promard, Joseph Rene-Corail, Lucette Salibur. Dir and Screenplay: Euzhan Palcy; based on the novel *La Rue Cases Nègres* by Joseph Zobel. Ex Pro: Jean-Luc Ormieres. Assoc Pro: Michel Loulegue and Alix Regis. Ph: Dominque Chapuis. Ed: Marie-Joseph Yoyotte. Sets (no Art credit): Hoang Thanh At. (Sumafa Productions/Orca Productions/NEF Diffusion-Artificial Eye) Rel: floating; first shown London (Chelsea Cinema), May 1984. 106 mins. Cert PG.

The Black Stallion Returns. A somewhat sad sequel to the successful 1979 story of a boy and a horse. Now grown into his teens, the lad loses his beloved steed when some Moroccans steal and take him back to their country in order to run him in a big race, which therefore leads to the youngster searching for the animal in the desert wastes. All highly unlikely, to say the least. Cast: Kelly Reno, Vincent Spano, Allen Goorwitz, Woody Strode, Ferdinand Mayne, Jodi Thelen, Teri Garr, Doghmi Larbi, Angelo Infanti, Luigi Mezzanotte, Franco Citti, Robert A. Behling, Joe Murphy, Chris Larrance, Loris Bazzocchi, Angelo Susani, Williw Allen Faiella, Ray Hassett, Gregory Snegoff, Nick Sternberg, Brian Frelino, Adedellal Hadraf, Azis Benzahra, Fouad Hadidi, Bekari Abdurzák, Abgaur Aziz, Zouroule Chaab, Barrio Ben Ahmed, Abdullah El Amrani, Amine Abdenahime, Mustapha M'Hamdi, Hassan Pijani, Tahiri Razim, Abdull Kader, Cass-Ole. Dir: Robert Dalva. Pro: Tom Sternberg, Fred Roos and Doug Claybourne. Ex Pro: Francis Ford Coppola, Screenplay: Richard Kletter and Jerome Kass; based on a novel by Walter Farley. Ph: Carlo di Palma. Ed: Paul Hirsch. Art: Aurelio Crugnola. M: Danda Ortona. (Zoetrope Studios–MGM/UA–UIP) Rel: 20 Oct 1983. 102½ mins. Cert U.

Blind Date. A gimmicky thriller with an interesting if hardly well worked-out basic idea, that of a young man who is blinded in an accident and is given an experimental implant which gives him a radar view of life; and rather uneasily entwined is quite another story about a psycho-case, a failed doctor who goes around with a scalpel and carves up pretty young women. The twain *do* meet up for the climax in which the seeing and – virtually – unseeing battle it out to the death. Cast: Joseph Bottoms, Kirstie Alley, James Daughton, Lana Clarkson, Keir Dullea, Charles Nicklin, Michael Howe, Gerald Kelly, Jerry Sundquist, Marina Sirtis, Kathy Hill, Louis Sheldon, Danos Lygizos, Spyros Papafrantzis, Antigone Amanitis, Ankie Grelson, Noelle Simpson, David Platt, Andrew Johnson. Dir and Pro: Nico Mastorakis (who also wrote the screenplay with Fred C. Perry). Ex Pro: Dimitri T. Skouras. Ph: Andrew Bellis. Ed: George Rosenberg. M: Stanley Myers (songs: John Kongos). (New Line Pictures/Omega in assoc with Wescom Pro–Anglo–American Film Dist) Rel: floating; first shown London (Scene), June 1984. 100 mins. Cert 18.

Kirstie Alley tends to Joseph Bottoms in *Blind Date.*

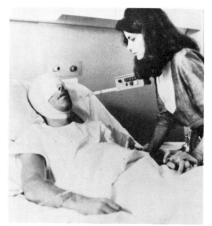

Bloodbath at the House of Death. A farcical send-up of the routine Old Dark House horror movies which veers from the occasionally genuinely comic to bad taste, as it wends its way through the clichés of the genre, finally taking a tilt at the sci-fi movie. The first feature film to star anarchic television favourite Kenny Everett. Rest of cast: Pamela Stephenson, Vincent Price, Sheila Steafel, John Fortune, Gareth Hunt, Don Warrington, John Stephen Hill, Cleo Rocos. Dir: Ray Cameron. Pro: Cameron and John Downes. Ex Pro: Laurence Myers and Stuart D. Donaldson. Screenplay: Cameron and Barry Cryer. Ph: Dusty Miller and Brian West. Ed: Brian Tagg. Art: John Sutherland. M: No credit. (Westwood Productions–Thorn/EMI) Restricted Rel: 30 March 1984. 92 mins. Cert 18.

Bloody Kids. A quite terrifying British film with a social theme, and a final blazing threat to the future. Set in Southend, it tell the story of two 11-year-old kids, who have been nurtured on the violence of the television screen and the more vivid violence in the streets, with the shadowy world of night-time threats, peopled by punks, soccer hooligans, skin-heads and other pathological anti-social youngsters. Their idea of fun is to fake a stabbing but the joke goes sour on them. Made with TV in mind, but so far not seen on the small screen. Cast: Derrick O'Connor, Gary Holton, Richard Thomas, Peter Clarke, Gwynneth Strong, Carline Embling, Jack Douglas, Billy Colvill, P.H. Moriarty, Richard Hope, Niall Padden, John Mulcahy, Terry Paris, Neil Cunningham, George Costigan, Stewart Harwood, Tammy Jacobs, Daniel Peacock, Paul Mari, Mel Smith, C.P. Lee, Jimmy Hibbert, Kim Taylforth, Nula Conwell, Madeline Church, Peter Wilson, Gary Olson, Jesse Birdsall, Roger Lloyd Pack, Brenda Fricker, June Watson, Colin Campbell, Julian Hough, Geraldine James. Dir: Stephen Frears. Pro: Barry Hanson. Assoc Pro: Charles Griffin. Screenplay: Stephen Poliakoff. Ph: Chris Menges. Ed: Peter Coulson. Art: Martin Johnson. M: George Fenton. (Black Lion Films for ITC–Palace Pictures–BFI) Rel: floating; first shown London (ICA), Nov 1983. 91 mins. Cert 15.

Blow to the Heart – Colpire al Cuore. An Italian film about an uneasy father and son relationship (professor and student) seen against a background of terrorism, with the normal situation reversed – it is the father who is involved with 'The Movement' and the son who sternly disapproves. Stimulating performances in their respective roles by Jean-Louis Trintignant and Fausto Rossi. Rest of cast: Laura Morante, Sonia Gessner, Vanni Corbellini, Laura Nucci, Matteo Cerami, Vera Rossi. Dir and Story: Gianni Amelio. Screenplay: Amelio and Vincenzo Cerami. Pro: Enzo Porcelli. Co-Pro: Enea Ferrario. Pro Sup: Riccardo Pintus. Pro Co-Ord: Dino di Dionisio and Conchita Airoldi. Pro Administrator: Roberto Ornaro. Ph: Tonini Nardi. Ed: Anna Napoli. Art: Marco Dentici. M: Franco Piersanti. (RAI Radiotelevisione/Antea Cinematografica–The Other Cinema) Rel: floating; first shown London (ICA), Oct 1983. 105 mins. No Cert.

Blue Thunder. An exciting melodrama based on the dangers to the citizen of a computerized, deadly and constantly snooping Big Brother – in this case a revolutionary new helicopter, 'Blue Thunder', with a watch, seek and destroy potential. Roy Scheider as the expert flying cop is assigned to the new terror and through it becomes aware of a military plot involving federal villains. Determined to make the public aware of this, he is marked down for murder and has to fight a tremendously exciting and brilliantly photographed air war over Los Angeles to survive. Rest of cast: Warren Oates, Candy Clark, Daniel Stern, Paul Roebling, David S. Sheiner, Joe Santos, Malcolm McDowell, Ed Bernard, Jason Bernard, Mario Machado, James Murtaugh, Pat McNamara, Jack Murdock, Clifford Pellow, Paul Lambert, Phil Feldman, John Garber, Anthony James, Robin Braxton, Anna Forrest,

Policeman and pilot Roy Scheider by the revolutionary helicopter in *Blue Thunder*.

Ricky Slyter, Reid Cruickshanks, Billy Ray Sharkey, Fred Slyter, John Gladstein, Ross Reynolds, Karl Wickman, James W. Gavin, Tom Friedkin, James Read, Mickey Gilbert, Bill Lane, Lolly Boroff, Patti Clifton, Ernest Harada, Frances E. Nealy, José Pepe R. Gonzales, Jerry Ziesmer, Tom Lawrence, John Ashby, Tony Brubaker, Norman Alexander Gibbs, Bill Ryusaki, Gary Davis, Tom Rosales, Larry Randles, Kevin P. Donnelly, Peter Miller, Mike McGaughy, Calvin Brown, Lucinda Crosby. Dir: John Badham. Pro: Gordon Carroll. Ex Pro: Phil Feldman and Andrew Fogelson. Assoc Pro: Gregg Champion. Screenplay: Dan O'Bannon and John Jakoby. Ph: John A. Alonzo. Art: Sydney Z. Litwack. Ed: Frank Morriss and Edward Abroms. M: Arthur B. Rubenstein. (Columbia) Rel: 25 August 1983. 110 mins. Cert 15.

Born in Flames. Another of the period's crop of feminist films, this one something of a museum piece in that it took two years to make on a sort of high grade home movies scale. It has ideas bursting out all over, but with amateuristic performances and an unpolished script, it is not always easy to follow as it shows us that in spite of great changes in America ten years on, the position of women in that new society of the future has changed but little from what it is today. And that patently doesn't satisfy writer, director, editor and producer Lizzie Borden! Cast: Honey, Jeanne Satterfield, Adele Bertel, Becky Johnston, Pat Murphy, Kathy Bigelow, Flo Kennedy. Ph: Ed Bowes, Al Sanata and Phil O'Reilly. No art credit listed. M: The Bloods, Ibis and The Red Crayolas. (Lizzie Borden and The Jerome Foundation–Cinema of Women) Rel: floating; first shown London (Screen-on-the-Green), Jan 1984. 90 mins. Cert 15.

Brainstorm. The storyline, characters and nearly everything else are sacrificed to visual gimmickry in this never very clear tale about a scientific 'breakthrough' that creates a machine which can apparently record and play back the human senses, even to the extent of a tape of a dying woman being able to kill anyone who listens to it. It gives the impression that producer-director Douglas Trumball set out to blind us with science! Visually quite remarkable, otherwise notable for the fact that it is Natalie Wood's last performance, for she drowned while the movie was being made. And Louise Fletcher, as the chain-smoking, tough scientist gives a film-stealing performance showing how to triumph over limited material. Rest of cast: Christopher Walken, Cliff Robertson, Jordan Christopher, Donald Hotton, Alan Fudge, Joe Dorsey, Bill Morey, Jason Lively, Darrell Larson, Lou Walker, Stacey Kuhne-Adams, John Hugh, David Wood, Keith Colbert, Jerry Bennett, Mary-Fran Lyman, Jack Harmon, Nina Axelrod, Kelly W. Brown, Desiree Ayres, Debbie Porter, Allen G. Butler, Robert Bloodworth, Georgianne Walken, Jim Boyd, Charlie Briggs, Ann Lincoln, Rev. Robert Terry Young, Jim Burk, Jimmy Casino, Robert Hippard, John Gladstein, Herbert Hirschman, John Vidor, Bill Couch, Robert Gooden, Wallace Merck, Glen Lee, Ernie Robinson, Roger Black, Tommy Huff, May Raymond Ross, Clay Boss, Peter Harrell, Susan Kampe. Dir and Pro: Douglas Trumball. Ex Pro: Joel L. Freedman. Ex in charge of Pro: Jack Grossberg. Screenplay: Robert Stitzel and Philip Frank Messina; from a story by Bruce Joel Rubin. Ph and Assoc Pro: Richard Yuricich. Ed: Edward Warschilka and Freeman Davies. Pro Des: John Vallone. Art: David L. Snyder. M: Harry V. Lojewski. Special Visual Effects: Entertainment Effects Group. (MGM/UA–UIP) Rel: 20 Jan 1984. 106 mins. Cert 15.

Breakdance ... The Movie. The climb to fame, via all the usual, to-be-expected obstacles in their path, of a trio of street dancers, Ozone (Adolfo 'Shabba-Doo' Quinones), Turbo

Natalie Wood, Christopher Walken and Louise Fletcher (centre) in *Brainstorm*.

Turbo (Shrimp) demonstrating what *Breakdance* is all about.

(Michael 'Shrimp' Chambers) and Kelly (Lucinda Dockey), to a background of a score of numbers from 'Tibetan Jam' and 'Boogie Down' to 'Baraque in Blue' and 'Freakshow on the Dance Floor'. And, for the record, 'Beat Box' is performed by 'The Art of Noise'! Rest of cast: Phineas Newborn III, Christopher McDonald, Ben Lokey, Bruno Falcon, Timothy Solomon, Ana Sanchez, Tracey 'Ice T' Marrow, Peter Bromilow, Eleanor Zee, Scott Cooper, Eb Lottimer, T.C. Laughlin, Ric Mancini, Lyla Grahm, Bea Silvern, Gwendolyn Brown, Andre Landzaat, Dalton Cathey, Larry Newberg, Lisa Freeman. Dir: Joel Silberg. Pro: Allen DeBevoise and Gerald Scaife. Ex Pro: Menahem Golan and Yoram Globus. Screenplay: Charles Parker, Allen DeBevoise and Gerald Scaife. Ph: Hanania Baer. Musical numbers staged and choreographed by Jamie Rogers. (Cannon Film Dist) Rel: 1 June 1984. 80 mins. Cert PG.

Breathless. American re-make of the 1959 Jean-Luc Godard film *A Bout de Souffle* (from a Truffaut story), which undoubtedly marked a milestone in motion picture history and was the first triumph of The New Wavers. Updating and transposing the scene from Paris to Los Angeles, the re-make loosely follows the same plot about a devil-may-care crook who suddenly finds life getting serious when he kills a cop and finds love when he comes upon a French girl fascinated by the danger and excitement of his life. Jean-Paul Belmondo managed to elicit some sympathy for the character, but Richard Gere in the role is arrogant, amoral and entirely without any saving graces, in spite of exploiting his torso and on occasion exhibiting himself in full frontal nudity. Rest of cast: Valerie Kaprisky, Art Metrano, John P. Ryan, William Tepper, Robert Dunn, Garry Goodrew, Lisa Persky, James Hong, Waldemar Kalinowski, Jack Leustig, Eugene Lourie, Georg Olden, Miguel Pinero, Henry G. Sanders, Bruce Vilanch, Robert Mark Quesada, Nora Gaye, Andres Aybar, Isabel Cooley, Jerry Greenberg, Javier Grajeda, Robert Snively, Jeni Vici, Carl Munoz, Christopher White, Brien Verady, Keith Addis, Martin Erlichman, Peggy Ann Stevens, Raymond Bear, D. Lee Carson, Tracy and Jesse McBride, Michael B. Aldava, Mickey Alzola,

Valerie Kaprisky, the French girl, and Richard Gere, the crook, in *Breathless*.

Rick Barker, David Burton, Diane Carter, Phil Chong, Bobby Clark, Gilbert G. Combs, Everett Creach, Lauri Ann Creach, Lenny Geer, Marguerite Happy, Jeff Imada, Gene Johnson, William T. Lane, Gary Littlejohn, Vicki Lynn, Steve Maggio. Dir: Jim McBride. Pro: Martin Erlichman. Ex Pro: Keith Addis. Screenplay: L.M. Kit Carson and Jim McBride; based on the French film *A Bout de Souffle* with screenplay by Jean-Luc Godard. Ph: Richard H. Kline. Ed: Robert Estrin. Pro Des: Richard Sylbert. M: Jack Nitzsche. (Erlichman/Miko Productions–Orion–Rank Film Dist) Rel: 13 Oct 1983. 100 mins. Cert 18.

Bronx Warriors – 1990 I Guerrieri del Bronx. A somewhat eccentric action-packed Italian look at New York's Bronx district in the year 1990, by which time it has become an island of lawlessness ruled over by moronic gangs of competing youths. But the reign of terror is brought to an end when the soldiers move in and wipe out the new unified weirdo warriors. Cast: Vic Morrow, Christopher Connolly, Fred Williamson, Mark Gregory, Stefania Girolami, John Sinclair, Enio Girolami, George Eastman, Betty Dessy, Rocco Lerro, Massimo Vanni, Angelo Ragusa, Enzi Girolami. Dir: Enzo G. Castellari. Pro: Fabrizio de Aneglis. Pro Administrator: Otello Tomassini. Screenplay: Castellari, Dardano Sarchetti and Elisa Livia Briganti. Ph: Sergio Salvati. Ed: Gianfranco Amicucci. Pro Des: Massimo Lentini. M: Walter Rizzati. (Deaf Film International–Entertainment) Rel: floating; late June 1982 – early July 1983. 84 mins. Cert 18 (X).

Bullshot. Slaphappy spoof of the old Bulldog Drummond movies which is too broad and pedestrian to be really successful, even though the occasional laugh does crop up as Alan Shearman

Left: Alan Shearman hangs on in aerial pursuit of Count Otto Von Bruno in *Bullshot*. Above: Karen Black and Michael Emil in *Can She Bake a Cherry Pie*.

struts his farcical way through a case of the abduction of a scientist by his old Hunnish adversary – Ron House. Rest of cast: Diz White, Frances Tomelty, Michael Aldridge, Ron Pembev, Christopher Good, Mel Smith, Billy Connolly, Geoffrey Bayldon, Christopher Godwin, Bryan Pringle, Angela Thorne, Peter Bayliss, John Wells, Nicholas Lydhurst, Ray Cooper, Derek Deadman, 'Legs' Larry Smith, John Du Prez, G.B. 'Zoot' Money, Paul Herzberg, Rupert Fraser, Christina Greatrex, Francesa Brill, Lucy Hornak, Ted Moult, Hilary Mason, Ann Way, Ballard Berkeley, Diana Van Proosdy, Albert Evansky, Anthony Milner. Dir: Dick Clement. Pro: Ian La Frenais. Ex Pro: George Harrison and Denis O'Brien. Pro Ex: Ray Cooper. Assoc Pro: David Wimbury. Screenplay: Ron House, Diz White and Alan Shearman. Ph: Alex Thomson. Ed: Alan Jones. Pro Des: Norman Garwood. M: John Du Prez (M Pro: Ray Cooper). (Handmade Films) Rel: 18 Nov 1983. 85 mins. Cert PG.

By Design. A minor Canadian comedy about a lesbian couple who decide they want to consolidate their relationship with parenthood, and the complications that follow their decision as to the male who will do the necessary! Cast: Patty Duke Astin, Saul Rubinek, Sara Botsford, Sonia Zimmer, Alan Duruisseau,

Mina Mina. Dir: Claude Jutra. Pro: Beryl Fox and Werner Allen. Screenplay: Jutra, Joe Weisenfeld and David Eames. Ph: Jean Boffety. Ed: Toni Trow. Art: Reuben Freed. M: Chico Hamilton. (Alpha Films) Rel: floating; first shown London (Gate, Bloomsbury), March 1984. 92 mins. Cert. 18.

Campsite Massacre. Nasty goings-on in California's Redwood National Park, where a crazy creature spoils a trekking trip by four Rangers and their girlfriends, when he unsportingly stabs one of the four to death while he's absorbed in making love. Cast: John Friedrich, Adrian Zmed, Daryl Hannah, Rachel Ward, Ernest Harden Jr, Mark Metcalf, Akosua Busia, Lewis Smith, Cindy Harrell, Joe Pantolinao, Irene Sanders, Richard Jacobs, Donna Pinder, Jim Young, Lori Lee Butler, Tony Maccario. Dir: Andrew Davis. Pro: Joe Roth. Co-Pro: J. Stein Kaplan. Assoc Pro: Gary Shusett and Anthony J. Ridio. Pro Co-Ord: Lenny Fike. Screenplay: Jon George, Neill Hicks and Ronald Scusett; from a story by the first two. Ph: Andreas Davidescu. Ed: Paul Rubell and Erica Flaum. Art: Aleka Corwin. M: Susan Justin. (Watershed Co–ITC) Rel: 14 July 1983. 84 mins. Cert X.

Can She Bake a Cherry Pie? Henry Jaglom follows up his quirky success of *Sitting Ducks* with another oddball,

highly personal movie about a most unusual romance, that between a girl who after her husband walks out on her distractedly walks the New York streets talking to herself, and a balding middle-aged character with a home-spun line in philosophy and an interest in his blood pressure during sexual activity. Karen Black's performance lights up this curiously bitter-sweet comedy. Rest of cast: Michael Emil, Michael Margotta, Frances Fisher, Martin Harvey Friedberg, Anna Raviv, Robert Hallak, Paul Williams, Madeline Silver, Ariela Nicole, Rob Schwimmer, Larry David, Eddie (the pigeon!), The Lost Wandering Blues Band. Dir and Screenplay: Henry Jaglom. Pro: M.H. Simonsons. Ex in charge of Pro: Michael Jaglom. Ph: Bob Fiore. No art credit. M: Karen Black. (International Rainbow Pictures/Jagfilm–Virgin Films) Rel: floating; first shown London (ICA), Jan 1984. 90 mins. Cert 15.

Carmen. Carlos Saura's visually superb follow-up to his previous – and highly successful – ballet film, *Blood Wedding*, with the same outstanding dancing star, Antonio Gades, and using a mixture of Bizet's opera music and flamenco tunes. The high-spot is the marvellously staged 'Tobacco Factory' set-piece. Rest of cast: Laura del Sol, Paco de Lucia, Cristina Hoyos, Juan Antonio Jimenez, Sebastian Moreno, José Yepes, Pepa Flores, José Luna 'Tauro', Enrique Esteve, Antonio Quintana, José Antonio Benitez, Ernesto Lapeña, Carmen Villa, Rocio Navarette, Fernanda Quintana, Ana Yolando Gavino,

José Gaviño, Stella Arauzo. Singers: Gomez de Jerez and Manolo Sevilla. Guitarists: Antonio Solera, Manuel Rodriguez and Lorenzo Virseda. Plus many guest artistes. Dir and Screenplay (latter with Antonio Gades): Carlos Saura. Pro: Emiliano Piedra. Pro Sup: Gustavo Quintana. Ph: Teo Escamilla. Ed: Perdo del Rey. Art: Felix Murcia. M: Paco de Lucia (and Bizet). Choreography: Saura and Gades. (Emiliano Piedra Productions in assoc with Television Espanola–Curzon Film Dist) Rel: floating; first shown London (Curzon), March 1984. 98 mins. Cert 15.

Carry Greenham Home. A documentary about the Greenham Common women protesters (made by students, Beeban Kidron and Amanda Richardson, from the National Film & Television School of Beaconsfield) which may prove not to be quite the good propaganda for the camp it was apparently meant to be. But it is a fascinating glimpse of this long-running effort to

John Hurt as Bob Champion and 'Aldaniti' in the winner's enclosure in *Champions*.

show opposition to the placing of American missiles in the Berkshire countryside. (Contemporary) Rel: floating; first shown London (Everyman, Hampstead), Oct 1983. 66 mins.

Champions. A brilliant, if somewhat overlong, large-scale, essentially British movie telling the true story of jockey Bob Champion, who heroically overcame cancer and returned to racing to win the 1981 Grand National. An outstanding story of a man and a horse (Aldaniti), and the will to win. John Hurt, gaunt and lugubrious, is perfectly cast in the title role. Rest of cast: Edward Woodward, Ben Johnson, Jan Francis, Peter Barkworth, Ann Bell, Judy Parfitt, Alison Steadman, Kirstie Alley, Michael Byrne, Carolyn Pickles, Fiona Victory, Mark Burns, Richard Leech, Frank Mills, Jonathan Newth, Hubert Rees, John Woodnutt, Noel Dyson, Julia Adams, Guy Keith-Miller, Glynn Edwards, Francesca Brill, Ceri Jackson, Trevor Clarke, Andrew Fell, Andrew Wilde. Dir: John Irvin. Pro: Peter Shaw. Assoc Pro: Eva Monley. Screenplay: Evan Jones; based on the book *Champion's Story* by Bob Champion and Jonathan Powell. Ph: Ronnie Taylor. Ed: Peter Honess. Art:

Left to right, the destructive Charno, Ostrander and Danare in *Christine*.

Roy Stannard. M: Carl Davis. (Embassy Pictures in assoc with Ladbroke Entertainments–United British Artists–Fox) Rel: 30 March 1984. 114 mins. Cert PG.

Christine. A John Carpenter thriller following pretty closely in the footsteps of previous devil-car movies like *Duel* and *The Car*. In this case an easily dislikable college lad becomes pos-

Andrew McCarthy bedding best friend's mother, Jacqueline Bisset, in *Class*.

sessed by the (very) second-hand 1958 Plymouth 'Fury' model automobile which has a nasty reputation after one of its assembly team is asphyxiated in it and its various owners suffer disaster and death. After he has lovingly restored the beast to pristine beauty it begins to show its maniacal as well as mechanical paces. All very short on credibility, but long on macabre atmosphere. Cast: Keith Gordon, John Stockwell, Alexandra Paul, Robert Prosky, Harry Dean Stanton, Christine Belford, Roberts Blossom, William Ostrander, David Spielberg, Malcolm Danare, Steven Tash, Stuart Charno, Kelly Preston, Marc Poppel, Robert Darnell, Richard Collier, Bruce French, Douglas Warhit, Keri Montgomery, Jan Burrell. Dir: John Carpenter. Pro: Richard Kobritz. Ex Pro: Kirby McCauley and Mark Tarlov. Co-Pro: Larry Franco. Screenplay: Bill Phillips; based on the book by Stephen King. Ph: Donald M. Morgan. Ed: Marion Rothman. Pro Des: Daniel Lomino. M: John Carpenter, in assoc. with Alan Howarth. Assoc Pro: Barry Bernardi. Pro Co-Ord: Bridget Murphy. (Columbia Delphi–Columbia) Rel: 2 March 1984. 110 mins. Cert 18.

City of Lost Souls. West German film about an oddball parade of assorted figures—black, gay, erotic acrobats, trans-sexuals and the like, all doing their thing—who move in and out of Angie Stardust's 'Fast Food Joint & Pension' in Berlin; a 'cabaret' movie whose nearest relative is *The Rocky Horror Picture Show*. With songs by Angie Stardust, Alexander Kraut, Holger Munzer and Jayne County. Director Rosa von Praunheim is male and gay. Others in the cast: Judith Flex, Tara O'Hara, Tron von Hollywood, Lorraine Muthke, Wolfgang Schumacher, Helga Goetze, Gary Miller, Joaquin La Hanban, Sally Karter, Manfred Finger, Gerjard Helle, Rolf Holzhutter, Bert Henkels, Rainer Gotz Otto, Burkhard Mauer, Lotti Huber, Katja Kunik. Dir, Pro, Ed and Screenplay: Rosa von Praunheim. Ex Pro: Dietmar Schings. Pro Sup: Renée Gundelach, Pro Controller: Traute Göres. Ph: Stephan Koster. (Praunheim in assoc with Hessische Runfunk Sender Fries, Berlin–The Other Cinema) Rel: floating; first shown London (ICA), April 1984. 89 mins. No Cert at present.

Class. Another survey of American college youth, which this time tries to cover rather too much ground and venture in too many directions in a story about an innocent, but very aware, young student who has a love affair with his best friend's mother, with rather obvious unpleasant results. Cast: Jacqueline Bisset, Rob Lowe, Andrew McCarthy, Cliff Robertson, Stuart Margolin, John Cusack, Alan Ruck, Rodney Pearson, Remak Ramsey, Virginia Madsen, Deborah Thalberg, Fern Persons, Casey Siemaszko, Aaron Douglas, Anna Maria Horsford, Hal Frank, Dick Cusak, William Visteen, James O'Reilly, Caithlin Hart, Virginia Morris, Stewart Figa, Paula Clarendon, Gita Tanner, John Cusack, John Kapelos, George Womack, Christopher Brake, Dan Moriarty, Maria Ricossa, Candice Collins, Marty Britton, Bruce Norris, Kevin Swerdlow, Wayne Kneeland, J. Todd Shaughnessy, Carole Arterbery, Nancy Serlin, Bruno Aclin, Molly Landgraf, Mike Bacarella, Edna Garza, Albert Stevens, Lance Kinsey, Gary Houston, Lolita Davidovich, Sue Snyder, Meg Thalken, Lance Kinsey, Dean Hill. Dir: Lewis John Carlino. Pro: Martin Ransohoff. Ex Pro: Cathleen Summers. Assoc Pro: Jim Kouf, David Greenwalt and Jill Chadwick. Pro Co-Ord: Linnea Ebba Wicklund. Screenplay: Jim Kouf and David Greenwalt. Screenplay Sup: Luca Kouimelis. Ph: Ric Waite. Ed: Stuart Pappe and Dennis Dolan. Art: Jack Poplin. M: Elmer Bernstein; with add M by (and perf by) Tom Scott. (Martin Ransohoff/Orion Rank Film Dist) Rel: 11 Nov 1983. 98 mins. Cert 15.

The Colour of Pomegranates – Sayat Nova. Sergo Paradjanov's 1969 film, of which a blown-up 16mm smuggled print was shown at the ICA in August 1982, is now revealed in all its colourful glory for the first time on 35mm film by Artificial Eye. For full details of the film, cast, etc, see the entry in the 1983–84 *Film Review* (Poseidon Films). Rel: floating; first shown London (Camden Plaza), Oct 1983.

Come Back to the Five and Dime, Jimmy Dean, Jimmy Dean. Robert Altman's adaptation of a play based on the classic and oft-used theme of a group of people (in this case assistants in a small-town Woolworth's store who formed a James Dean fan club) who after a 20-year interval meet again for a reunion in the store which, after a little loosening liquor, produces a number of surprises as the truth comes out to shame the lies they have lived till then: and the biggest surprise comes when it is revealed that one of the girls has fathered (yes, that's correct!) another's child. Always stagey, but well directed, and by far Altman's best work in years. Cast: Sandy Dennis, Cher, Karen Black, Susie Bond, Kathy Bates, Marta Heflin, Mark Patton, Caroline Aaron, Ruth Miller, Gena Ramsel, Ann Risley, Dianne Turley Travis. Dir: Robert Altman. Pro: Scott Bushnell. Ex Pro: Giraud Chester. Screenplay: Ed Graczyk; based on his stage play. Pro Ex: Peter Newman. Ph: Pierre Mignot. Ed: Jason Rosenfield. Pro Des: David Gropman. M: Various popular songs of the late 1950s (Mark Goodson Presentation in assoc with Viacom–Sandcastle 5 Productions–Alpha Films) Rel: floating; first shown London (Lumiere Cinema), Sept 1983. 109 mins. Cert 18.

The Concrete Jungle. A somewhat lame women's prison movie with soft-pedalled sex and sadistic trimmings. Cast: Jill St. John, Tracy Bregman, Barbara Luna, June Barrett, Aimee

Left to right, Sandy Dennis, Cher and Karen Black in *Come Back to the Five and Dime, Jimmy Dean, Jimmy Dean.*

Eccles, Sondra Currie, Peter Brown, Susan Mechsner, Robert Miano, Niki Dantine, Nita Talbot, Marcia Karr, Sally Julian, Justine Lemore, Kendal Kaldwell, Carol Ita White, Maria Caso, Cynthia Grant, Karole Le Man, Camille Keaton, Mae E. Campbell, Brianna Clark, Kimberly Binion, Millie Baron, Chris de Rose, Greg Finley, Robert De Simone, Patrice Bousson, Betty Bridges, Linda Alznsuer, Angeline Butler, Joel Redlin, Ron Shotola, Debra Louise Morris, Mary Cowan, Tiana Pierce, Greta Blackburn, Shanit Keter, Karen Shepard, Linda Arocha, Carol Connors, Dir: Tom de Simone. Ex Pro: Jay Schultz and Richard D. Reinberg. Pro: Billy Fine. Screenplay: Alan J. Adler; add dialogue by Jack Cummins. Ph: Andrew W. Friend. Ed: Nino de Marco. M and M Dir: Andrew W. Friend: song 'I'm on my Own' by J. Conlan and T. Bregman, perf by Deborah Davis. (Ideal Films–Video Form Pictures) Rel: 1 July 1983. 101 mins. Cert X.

The Country Girls. A charming, pictorially beautiful Irish story of two girls, from their schooldays in a severe convent school through adolescence and life in the big city to their final decision to emigrate, all seen with sympathy and a lovely sense of quiet humour. And there are some excellent performances to match. Cast: Sam Neill, Maeve Germaine, Jill Doyle, John Kavanagh, Niall Toibin. Dir: Desmond Davis. Pro: Aida Young. Ex Pro: Mark Shelmerdine and David Conroy. Screenplay: Edna O'Brien; from her own novel. Ph: Denis Lewiston. Ed: Timothy Gee. Art: Arden Gantly. (London Films–Enterprise

Boatman Rip Thorn and authoress Mary Steenburgen in *Cross Creek*.

Pictures) Rel: floating; first shown London (Minima), April 1984. 107 mins. Cert PG.

Cross Creek. A small treasure which leisurely relates the apparently true story of the life of American writer Marjorie Kinnan Rawlings, whose great achievement was in writing the classic best-seller *The Yearling*. Kinnan gave up New York and her journalist husband for the backwoods pleasures of an isolated orange grove in Florida, where the richly human life of her few neighbours gave her the material for her first published success after years of frustrating failure. Overlong, but beautifully directed and superbly played, especially by Mary Steenburgen as the authoress. Rest of cast: Rip Torn, Peter Coyote, Dana Hill, Alfred Woodard, Joanna Miles, Ike Eisenman, Cary Guffey, Toni Hudson, Bo Rucker, Jay O. Sanders, John Hammond, Tommy Alford, Norton Baskin, Terrence Gehr, Keith Michel, Nora Rogers, Kenneth V. Vickery, C.T. Wakefield, Malcolm McDowell. Dir: Martin Ritt. Pro: Robert B. Radnitz. Co-Pro: Terry Nelson. Screenplay: Dalene Young. Ph: John A. Alonzo. Ed (and 2nd Unit Dir): Sidney Levin. Pro Des: Walter Scott Herndon. M: Leonard Rosenman. (Thorn–EMI) Rel: floating; first shown London (ABC Haymarket and several Classics), May 1984. 120 mins. Cert U.

Besieged Dee Wallace and Danny Pintauro in the bloody and brutal *Cujo*.

Cujo. A well made thriller about a woman in a car with her small son besieged by a rabid dog. But the film never quite achieves its object of sending a violent shudder down the watcher's spine – perhaps it was a basic mistake to make the monster that most gentle and agreeable of dogs, a St Bernard. Cast: Dee Wallace, Danny Pintauro, Daniel Hugh-Kelly, Christopher Stone, Ed Lauter, Kaiulanilee, Billy Jacoby, Mills Watson, Sandy Ward, Jerry Hardin, Merritt Olsen, Arthur Rosenberg, Harry Donovan-Smith, Robert Elross, Robert Behling, Claire Nono, Daniel H. Blatt. Dir: Lewis Teague. Pro: Daniel H. Blatt and Robert Singer. Assoc Pro: Neil A. Machlis. Pro Sup: Elliott Friedgen. Ex Pro Man: George Goodman. Screenplay: Don Carlos Dunaway and Lauren Currier; based on a novel by Stephen King. Ph: Jan de Bont. Ed: Neil Travis. Pro Des: Guy Comtois. M: Charles Bernstein. (Taft Entertainment Co–ITC) Rel: 18 Nov 1983. 91mins. Cert 18.

The Curse of the Pink Panther. Blake Edwards gets away with almost murder as he manages successfully to pull off this first of the 'PP' series not to star the late Peter Sellers. The film introduces a likeable Harold Lloyd-look-alike hero in Ted Waas, who plays a similarly accident-prone character in New York detective Clifton Sleigh, assigned to solve the mystery of Inspector Clousseau's disappearance. And Edwards climaxes the nicely paced series of classic and corn-fed gags with the appearance of Roger Moore (uncredited) as the face-lifted, unrecognizable Inspector! It's all good, if daring, fun stuff. Rest of cast: David Niven (one of his last performances), Robert Wagner, Herbert Lom, Joanna Lumley, Capucine, Robert Loggia, Harvey Korman, Burt Kwouk, Leslie Ash, Andre Maranne, Graham Stark, Peter Arne, Patricia Davis, Michael Elphick, Steve Franken, Ed Parker, Denise Crosby, Emma Walton, Sidi Bin Tanney, Pat Corley, William Hootkins, Donald Sumpter, Harold Kasket, Mollie Maureen, Liz Smith, Danny Schiller, Lawrence Davidson, Joseph Morton, Bill Nighy, Arthur Howard, William Abney, Hugh Fraser, 'Special Guest Star' Turk Thrust II! Dir, Pro (with Tony Adams)

and Screenplay (with Geoffrey Edwards): Blake Edwards. Ex Pro: Jonathan D. Krane. Assoc Pro: Gerald T. Nutting. Ph: Dick Bush. Ed: Ralph E. Winters. Pro Des: Peter Mullins. Sup Art Dir: Tim Hutchinson. Art: Alan Tomkins and John Siddal. M: Henry Mancini. Title animation based on David H. de Patie and Friz Freleng characters written and directed by Arthur Leonardi. Stunts, etc: Rocky Taylor, Roy Alon, Mark McBride, Romo Gorrara, Dinny Powell, Gerry Crampton, Malcolm Weaver, Graeme Crowther, Wendy Leech, Jack Cooper, Andy Cowley, Brian Gaskin and John Harbutt. (Blake Edwards Entertainment–Jewel Productions–MGM/UA-UIP) Rel: 17 Feb 1984. 110 mins. Cert PG.

Daniel. E.L. Doctorow's own screen adaptation of his 1971 book *The Book of Daniel* which was obviously based around the story of Julius and Ethel Rosenberg, who in 1953 were arrested, tried and sentenced to death on the charge of passing atomic secrets to the Soviets. Sidney Lumet's movie, assem-

Ted Waas (right) startled by Clousseau's effigy in *The Curse of the Pink Panther*.

bled in a complex now-and-then pattern, appears reasonably balanced and never tries to answer the still unanswered question as to *how* guilty the pair were, but it does emerge, more by omission than anything else, as being sentimentally on their side. Lumet, however, seems even more concerned with the effect the execution had on their children (played by Timothy Hutton and Lindsay Crouse), but somehow he does not bring out any sympathy for them. Cast: Mandy Patinkin, Edward Asner, Ellen Barkin, Julie Bovasso, Tovah Feldshuh, Joseph Leon, Carmen Matthews, Norman Parker, Amanda Plummer, Lee Richardson, John Rubinstein, Colin Stinton, Maria Tucci, Rita Zohar, Ilan M. Mitchell-Smith, Jena Greco, Dael Cohen, Peter Friedman, Will Lee, David Margulies, George Axler. Dir: Sidney Lumet. Pro: Burtt Harris. Ex Pro: E.L. Doctorow and Lumet. Screenplay: Doctorow; based on his own novel *The Book of Daniel*. Assoc Pro: John Van Eyssen. Ph: Andrzej Bartowiak. Ed: Peter C. Frank. Pro Des: Philip Rosenberg. M: No credit, but songs sung by Paul Robeson. (World Film Services–Fox) Rel: floating; first shown London (Gate cinemas), Jan 1984. 129 mins. Cert 15.

Daniel Takes a Train – Szerencsés Dániel. Boldly, for an East European country, this Hungarian film takes a look at its recent history, and in particular the 1956 uprising, seeing it in a balanced, non-partisan way. It tells the story of two young men trying to reach the freedom of the Austrian border, one a young Jew, seeking his sweetheart, and the other searching for his father. And behind these two, is the whole story of the flight of the refugees. Swift-paced, and with a warm understanding of human nature under stress. Cast: Péter Rudolf, Sándor Zsótér, Kati Szerb, Mari Törócsik, Dezsó Garas, Gyula Bodrogi, András Kern, Ági Margittai. Dir: Pál Sándor. Screenplay: Zsuzsa Tóth and Zsuzsa Biró; based on a short story by András Mezei. Ph. Elemér Ragályi. M: György Selmeczi. No Pro, Art or Ed credits. (Mafilm/Hunnia Studio, Budapest–Cinegate) Rel: floating; first shown London (Gate, Notting Hill), April 1984. 92 mins. Cert 15.

Mandy Patinkin and Lindsay Crouse at the trial in *Daniel*.

Danton. Polish Andrzej Wajda's French film looks at some of the events of the 'Terror' that led to the ending of the French Revolution, and in particular the duel between Robespierre, the aesthetic lawyer, bloodily ruthless and utterly incorruptible, and another lawyer, the self-indulgent Danton, a magnificent orator. With the duel won by Robespierre, Danton and his friends are sent to the guillotine, where, ironically, Robespierre meets his own end a few months later. Some have seen in this contest a parallel to the present Polish political situation, with Walenska as Danton, something denied by Wajda, but not entirely convincingly. Wordy, well acted and absorbing, Gérard Départdieu gives his usual apparently careless, untidy but withal impressive performance in the title role, although he is almost outclassed by Polish actor Wojcieh Pszoniak's steely portrait of his opponent, a performance to be long remembered. Rest of cast: Patrice Chereau, Angela Winkler, Boguslaw Linda, Roland Blanche, Anne Alvora, Roger Planchon, Serge Merlin, Lucien Melki, Andrzej Seweryn, Franciszek Starowieyski, Emmanuelle Debeverm, Jerzy Trella, Tadeusz Huk, Jacques Villeret. Dir: Andrzej Wajda. Pro: Margaret Menegoz. Screenplay: Jean Claude-Carriere; based on the play *The Danton Affair* by Stanislawa Przybyszewska. Script collaborators: Wajda, Agnieszka Holland, Boleslaw Michalek and Jacek

Gasiorowski. Ph: Igor Luther. Ed: Halina Prugar-Ketling. Art: Allan Starski and Gilles Vaster. M: Jean Prodromides. (Les Films du Losange/Margaret Menegoz/Gaumont/TFI Films/SFPC/TM Co-productions, with the participation of the French Ministry of Culture and Films Polski, and the collaboration of the X Production Group of Warsaw/Barbara Pec–Slesinka–Artificial Eye) Rel: floating; first shown London (Chelsea Cinema), Sept 1983. 136 mins. Cert PG.

Dark Circle. One of two documentary features (the other: *In the King of Prussia*) shot in the United States, Nagasaki and Hiroshima, which sets out through personal stories the cost, danger and terror of nuclear weapons. Dir/Pro: Chris Beaver, Judy Irving and Ruth Landy. Ph/Ed: Beaver and Irving. Assoc Pro: Judith Lit. Narrator: Judy Irving. M: Gary Remal and Bernard Kraus. (The Other Cinema/Concord Films) Rel: floating; first shown London (Electric, Rio and Ritzy), July 1983. 81 mins. Cert PG.

The Dead Zone. A David Cronenberg thriller which rather oddly mixes second-sight thrills with political chicanery, and somehow jells them into a pretty good package of entertainment. Christopher Walken, the victim of a car crash which loses him five years of his life, lies in coma, but he is able to look into the future; and when he sees what this has in store for U.S. Presidential candidate Martin Sheen, he decides to

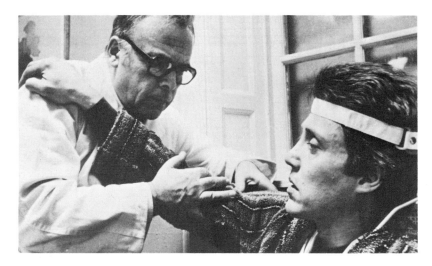

Doctor Herbert Lom (left) and comatose Christopher Walken, in *The Dead Zone*.

act selflessly to manipulate history. Rest of cast: Brooke Adams, Tom Skerritt, Herbert Lom, Anthony Zerbe, Colleen Dewhurst, Nicholas Campbell, Sean Sullivan, Jackie Burroughs, Geza Kovacs, Roberta Weiss, Simon Craig, Peter Dvorsky, Julie-Ann Heathwood, Barry Flatman. Dir: David Cronenberg. Pro: Debra Hill, Assoc Pro: Jeffrey Chernov. Screenplay: Jeffrey Boam; based on the novel by Stephen King. Ph: Mark Irwin. Ed: Ronald Sanders. Pro Des: Carol Spier. Art: Barbara Dunphy. M: Michael Kamen. (Dino de Laurentis–Lorimar–Thorn EMI) Rel: 11 May 1984. 103 mins. Cert 18.

The Death of Mario Ricci. A French/ Swiss film about a crippled TV reporter assigned to interview a famous scientist who, driven to the edge of mental breakdown by the refusal of the richer nations to do anything about the problems of the poorer, has retired to a small Swiss village where he lives with his pretty young American assistant. During his short stay the reporter becomes involved in a fatal accident that stirs up local animosity and finds angry undercurrents to the quiet flow of village life. Superb atmosphere, fine performances (Gian-Maria Volonte as the TV reporter won the Cannes Festival 'Best Actor of the Year' Award for 1983) and assured direction add up to an unobtrusively brilliant movie. Rest of cast: Jean-Michel Dupuis, Heinz Bennent, Magali Noel, Mimsy Farmer. Dir: Claude Goretta. Pro: Yves Peyrot and Norbert Saada. Assoc Pro: Yves

Gasser. Screenplay: Goretta and Georges Haldas. Ph: Hans Liechti. Ed: Joële van Effenterre. Art: Yanko Hodjis. M: Arie Dzierlatka and Orchestre Osmose. (Gala) Rel: floating; first shown London (Academy), Dec 1983. 100 mins. Cert PG.

Dial M for Murder. The famous Hitchcock film, originally released on 23 August 1953, in its 'flat' form, has now been brought back in 3-D – as originally made but never seen as such in Britain. It tells the story about a clever but warped character who bribes his old schoolfriend to murder the former's wife. Cast: Ray Milland, Grace Kelly, Robert Cummings, John Williams, Anthony Dawson, Patrick Allen, George Leigh, George Alderson, Robin Hughes. Dir and Pro: Alfred Hitchcock. Screenplay: Frederick Knott; based on his stage play. Ph: Robert Burks. Ed: Rudi Fehr. Art: Edward Carrere. M: Dimitri Tiomkin. (Warner) Rel: floating; first shown London (ICA), August 1983. 105 mins. Cert PG.

The Divine Emma – Božská Ema. This Czech film, made in 1979 but only now reaching British screens, relates the story of famous Czech soprano Emma Destimm whose World War I adventures included being held as a suspected spy, a period of house arrest, and giving concerts for the locals, at which, defying the authorities, she included the National Anthem as one of the items. But even her international status did not save her from a lonely, penniless death, having earlier seen all her goods sold up. All somewhat confusingly episodic, but musically inter-

esting, with Božidara Turzonovová (actress) and Gabriela Beňačová (singer) combining to present a warm and charming portrait of the diva. Rest of cast: Juraj Kukura, Miloš Kopecký, Jiří Adamíra, Josef Somr, Cestmír Randa, Josef Kemr, Václav Neužil, Václav Lohnisky, Karel Augusta,Vlastimil Bedrna, Jana Smrčková, František Rehák, Zdeněk Dítě, Milena Svobodová, Stanislav Zindulka, Milan Karpíšek, František Husák, Karel Urbánek, Augustine Kubáň, Otto Sevčik, Bořik Procházka. Dir: Jiří Krejčik. Pro/Man: Jan Syrový. Opera Dir: Ladislav Stros. Screenplay: Krejčik and Zdeněk Mahler. Ph: Miroslav Ondricek. Ed: Miroslav Hajek. Art: Jindřich Goetz. M: Zdeněk Liška and Svatopluk Havelka: and extracts from *Carmen, Don Giovanni, Aida, Salome, La Gioconda, I Pagliacci, Russalka, The Bartered Bride, The Kiss, Dalibor, Tannhäuser, The Flying Dutchman, Tosca, La Bohème, Madame Butterfly.* (Filmove Studio Barrandov-Ambassador Films) Rel: floating; first shown London (Classic, Chelsea), Nov 1983. 105 mins. Cert PG.

Dream Flights – Polioty Vo Sne I Naiavou. An odd little Soviet film about an irresponsible character who behaves outrageously to wife, family, lovers, friends and fellow workers; and whose reaction to reaching his 40th birthday is to play a joke on them at the party they throw for him, which finally alienates all of them and leaves him isolated. Beneath the more superficial lesson, that to take all and not give in return leads to moral disaster, some see a hidden message about the Soviet worker's dream of rebellion against the political system. Whether you see this or not, the film provides an interesting glimpse of contemporary Soviet life and character. Cast: Oleg Tankovsky, Ludmilla Gurchenko, Nikita Mikalkov, Oleg Tabakov, Liudmila Zorina, Elena Kostina, Liudmila Ivanova, Oleg Menshikov, Liubov Rudneva, Alexander Adabashian, Nikita Mikhalkov, Elena Chernvak, Alyona Odinokova. Dir: Roman Balayan. Pro: No credit. Screenplay: Victor Merezhko. Ph: Vilen Kalyuta. Art: Vitaly Volynsky. M: Vadim Khrapachev. (The Aleksandr Dovzhenko Kiev Film Studios-Thorn EMI) Rel: floating; first shown London (Gate), Jan 1984. 90 mins. Cert PG.

Albert Finney (left), about to play King Lear, with Tom Courtenay in *The Dresser*.

The Dresser. Two outstanding, Oscar-nominated performances, among the many fine supporting ones, by Finney and Courtenay, some marvellously amusing situations, and lines that are often laced with wit lift this basically stagey tragi-comedy into the realms of unforgettable cinema. Primarily a portrait of a dictatorial, flamboyant British actor-manager who is beginning to show signs of mental stress as he tries to keep the Shakespearean show on the road in spite of the bombs and other wartime hazards, it is at the same time a wonderfully observed picture of a touring company of players seen from the other side of the proscenium arch. It may just be pertinent that the original stage play's author, Ronald Harwood, served and toured with Sir Donald Wolfit's wartime company – if so it may be thought a mite unfairly cruel! Cast: Albert Finney, Tom Courtenay, Edward Fox, Zena Walker, Eileen Atkins, Michael Gough, Cathryn Harrison, Betty Marsden, Sheila Reid, Lockwood West, Donald Eccles, Llewellyn Rees, Guy Manning, Anne Mannion, Kevin Stoney, Ann Way, John Sharp, Kathy Staff, Roger Avon, Christopher Irvin, Stuart Richman, Sandra Gough, Joe Belcher, Johnny Maxfield, Paul Luty, Lori Wells, Alan Starkey. Dir and Pro: Peter Yates. Screenplay: Ronald Harwood; based on his own stage play. Assoc Pro: Nigel Wooll. Ph: Kelvin Pike. Ed: Ray Lovejoy. Pro Des: Stephen Grimes. Art: Colin Grimes. M: Comp and Con by James Horner. (Goldcrest Films/World's Film Services–Columbia) Rel: 11 May 1984. 118 mins. Cert PG.

Due to an Act of God – Im Zeichen des Kreuzes. A West German frightener about a town (in 1990) stricken by a plutonium leak after a lorry smash, and the ruthless way the authorities deal with the panic that follows – largely by a massacre of the fleeing inhabitants! Slow, implausible and a long way from real life. Cast: Renate Schroeter, Wigand Witting, Joanna Rudolph, Mathias Nitschke, Antje Hagen, Karl-Heinz von Hassel, Werner Schwuchow, Rainer Christian Mehring, Hermann Lause, Gunnar Möller, Edith Neitzel-Görler, Werner Eichhorn, Jo Bolling, Günter Bothur, Ulrich von Bock, Peter Faerber, Christian Fuchs, Werner Haindl, Thomas Kollhoff, Alexander May, Lore Moor, Hans Günther Reibold, Robert Tillian, Rita Ziegler, plus the citizens of Duttenstedt. Dir: Rainer Bolt. Pro: Hermann Wolf. Ex Pro: Helmut Wietz. Screenplay: Hans Rüdiger Minow. Ph: Karl Kases. Ed: Elke Boisch. Art: Winfried Hennig. M: Jens-Peter Ostendorf. (Common Film Produktion in assoc with Cikon Film Produktion/Co-Pro with WDR & SFB–Blue Dolphin Films) Rel: floating; first shown London (Everyman, Hampstead), April 1984. 106 mins. Cert 15. (Apparently the film was made for TV but shelved by the channel which funded it.)

Emmanuelle 4 in 3D. Sylvia Kristel bows out of the series in a story which has her undergoing major cosmetic surgery in order to escape the attentions of an old lover. She emerges from the surgeon's couch as a new woman, in fact lovely new star Mia Nygen, who carries on with various sexual adventures in the good old Kristel manner. And with Miss Nygen's body and looks nobody is surely likely to complain about Sylvia's departure. Rest of cast: Patrick Bauchau, Deborah Power, Sophie Berger, Sonia Martin, Dominique Troyes, Gerard Dimiglio, Christian Marquand. Dir and Screenplay: Francis Leroy and Iris Letand; from a story by Emmanuelle Arsan. Pro: Alain Siritzky. Ph: Jean-François Gondre. Ed: Hélène Plemiannikov. Art: Jean-Baptiste Poirot. M: Michel Magne. (French AAA/Sedpa-Sara Films/ASP Productions) Rel: 8 June 1984. 90 mins. Cert 18.

The Evil That Men Do. Iron Man (Charles) Bronson literally gets away with multi-murder as a retired hit-man lured from his idyllic island home to rub out some nasties on learning that an ex-pal and journalist has been tortured to death for writing the truth about a South American state. All luridly unlikely and, somehow surprisingly, directed by our own J. Lee Thompson. Rest of cast: Theresa Saldana, Joseph Maher, Jose Ferrer, Rene Enriquez, John Glover, Raymond St. Jacques, Antoinette Bower, Enrique Lucero, Jorge Luke, Mischa Hausserman, Roger Cudney, Constanza Hool, Joe Seneca, Jorge Zepeda, Alan Conrad, Ernesto Gomez Cruz, Angelica Aragon, Rodrigo Puebla, Nicole Thomas, Anais de Mello, Eduardo Lopez Rojas, Carlos Romano, Miguel Angel Fuentes, Richard Brodie, Alfredo Gutierrez, Jorge Humberto Robles, Fernando Saenz, Ernie Orsatti, Ken Fritz. Dir: J. Lee Thompson. Pro: Pancho Kohner. Ex Pro: Lance Hool. Assoc Pro: David Pringle and Jill Ireland. Screenplay: David Lee Henry and John Crowther; based on the novel by R. Lance Hill. Ph: Javier Ruvalcaba Cruz. Ed: Peter Lee-Thompson. 2nd Unit Dir: Ernie Orsatti. Pro Sup: Marco Aurelio Ortiz. Ex in charge of Pro: Howard P. Alston. M: Ken Thorne. (Kohner/Hool–ITC Entertainment) Rel: 8 June 1984. 89 mins. Cert 18.

Exposed. Not highly credible but an interesting terrorist thriller set against the world of fashion and models. Nastassja Kinski, as a waitress, becomes

Rudolf Nureyev plays a passionate sonata on Nastassja Kinsky's neck in *Exposed*.

one of New York's most photographed women, and through a relationship with a man she meets and falls in love with becomes his undercover agent as he seeks a way to get even with the international Paris-based gang whose bombings killed her mother. The melodrama rears its roaring head in the final bullet-spitting confrontation. Rudolf Nureyev plays the star violinist and anti-terrorist. Rest of cast: Harvey Keitel, Ian McShane, Bibi Andersson, Ron Randell, Pierre Clementi, Dov Gottesfeld, James Russo, Marion Varella, Murray Moston, Stephanie Farrow, Carmen, Carl Lee, Mariana Magnasco, Miguel Pinero, Jeff Silverman, Ray Sawhill, Michel Delahaye, Brian Hamill, Tony Sirico Jr, Geoffrey Carey, Dennis McGovern, Patrick Baker, Emil Tchakarov, Madeleine De Blonay, Jacques Preyer, Vincent Lascoumes, Eleonore Klarwein, Mostefa Stiti, Djeoul Beghoura, David Jalil, Aina Walle, Sylvie George, Maryline Abecassis, Anne Aor, Rosine Young. Dir, Pro and Screenplay: James Toback. Ex Pro: Serge Silberman. Ph: Henri Decae. Ed: Robert Lawrence. Pro Des: Brian Eatwell. Assoc Pro: Brian Hamill. M: George Delerue. Pro Sup: (France) Ulrich Pickardt; (USA) Ralph S. Singleton. Pro Assoc: Ibrahim Moussa. (Toback–MGM/UA–UIP) Rel: floating, first shown London (Cinecenta), Nov. 1983. 99½ mins. Cert 15.

Fade to Black. A thriller about a movie buff, driven mad by some pretty hard blows from fate, who sets out to commit a series of killings in the same way as he has seen them carried out in various famous movies. But he is finally trapped by his passion for a Marilyn Monroe look-alike who has stood him up on their first date. Cast: Dennis Christopher, Linda Kerridge, Tim Thomserson, Morgan Paull, Hennen Chambers, Marya Small, Eva Brent Ashe, Norman Burton, Gwynne Gilford, James Luisi. Dir and Screenplay: Vernon Zimmerman. Pro: George Braunstein and Ron Hamady. Ex Pro: Irwin Yablans and Sylvia Tabet. Ph: Alex Phillips Jr. Ed: Howard Kumin. No Art or M credits listed. (GTO Films) Rel: 2 August 1983. 101 mins. Cert X.

Family Business. American feature documentary about the struggle of a pizza parlour owner to hold on to his franchise and at the same time keep his family and self-respect intact. An amusing and often moving slice-of-life examination of the tensions and the traumas of family and business life in America. Dir: Tom Cohen. (BFI) Rel: floating: first shown London (ICA), Dec 1983. 87 mins. No cert.

Finally, Sunday! – Vivement Dimanche! Masterly, beguiling François Truffaut comedy-thriller which while paying tribute to his favourite director, Alfred Hitchcock, makes references to many of Truffaut's former movies; and, in black-and-white, it also pays tribute to some of the most famous of the American movies of the Bogartian era. Delectable Fanny Ardant as the estate agent's secretary turns amateur sleuth when her boss is accused of triple murder and solves the case for the cops. A delightful lesson on the making of top-class cinematic entertainment. Rest of cast: Jean-Louis Trintignant, Philippe Laudenbach, Caroline Sihol, Phillippe Morier-Genoud, Xavier Saint Macary, Jean-Pierre Kalfon, Anik Belaubre, J-L. Richard, Yann Dedet, Nicole Felix, Georges Koulouris, Roland Thenot, Pierre Gare, Jean-Pierre Kohut-Svelko, Pascale Pellegrin. Dir: François Truffaut. Pro Dir: Armand Barbault. Pro Administrator: J-F. Lentretien. Screenplay: Truffaut, Suzanne Schiffman and Jean Aurel; adapted from the novel *The Long Satur-*

day Night by Charles Williams. Ph: Nestor Almendros, Florent Bazin and Tessa Racine. Ed: Martine Barraque and Marie-Aimee Debril. Set Design: Hilton McConnico. M: Georges Delarue. (Les Films du Carosse/Films A2/ Soprofilms, Co-Production /Artificial Eye) Rel: floating; first shown London (Chelsea Cinema), Nov 1983. 111 mins. Cert PG.

First Name Carmen – Prénom Carmen. The usual Jean-Luc Godard mixture: a disjointed story, sex and self-indulgence, with quite a bit of violence, the occasional touch of humour, and not a little crudity. It is the tale of a girl crook (luscious newcomer Maruschka Detmers) and a young cop (Jacques Bonnaffe) tempted into assisting her escape after a bank robbery and who then comes under her spell until the climax, when she goes off with someone else, is cornered, shot and dies in her new lover's arms while he is copped. Some fine photography of rolling breakers, and Godard playing himself, as a vague and pre-occupied film director. All a very odd mix indeed. Rest of cast: Myriem Roussel, Christophe Odent, Hyppolite Girardot, Bertrand Liebert, Alain Bastien-Thiry. Dir and Ed: Jean-Luc Godard. Screenplay/Adaptation: Anne-Marie Mieville. Ph: Raoul Coutard. M: Beethoven Quartets 9, 10, 14, 15 and 16 played by the Quatuor Prat; song 'Ruby's Arms' written and sung by Tom Watts. (Sara Films, France/Jean-Luc Godard Films, Switzerland/Films A2, France–Artificial Eye) Rel: floating; first shown London (Lumiere), Jan 1984. 85 mins. Cert 18.

The First Turn-On! Entombed by a cave fall-in caused by a feminine shriek of fear, engendered by a tarantula, five Big-Tee-Pee campers are freed by a further fall caused by their orgasmic shouts of pleasure! In between which they tell imaginative (and false) stories of their sexual experiences. And that should explain all. Cast: Georgia Harrell, Michael Sanville, Googy Gress, Heidi Miller, John Flood, Al Pia, Betty Pia, Gilda Gumbo, Lara Grills, Kristina Marie Wetzel, Frank Trent Saladino, David Berardi, Ted Henning, Donna Winter, Sheila Kennedy, Mark Torgi, Donna Barnes, Siobhan Fergus, Steve Hollander, Vincent D'Onofrio, Russell Matthews, Mitchell

Whitfield, Nick Pannone, Michel Schoffel, Randy Matthews, Gretchen Weiner, Ebb Miller, William Kirksey, Steve Chambers, Dennis Berrigan, Thur Adams, Katya Goldman, Deborah Whitley, Vicki Juditz, Rubin Ruzan, Arleen O'Brien, William Cheverino, Julie Anne Parker, Andrea Suter, Catherine Hayes, Barbara Gurskey, Michael Corcoran, Kevin Rice, Alex Ross Harper, Rondell Sheridan, John and Bob Stoltzfus, Carla Bragoli, Ron Conroy, Al Spellman, Don Costello, Konni Novinger, Rachel Allisyn, Joanne Jarvis, Joe and Sam Simpson, Dana Rossi, June De Young, Amy Montinari, Gary Pratt, Cris Costello, Sloane Herz, Ellen Christiansen, Scherzo Harrell. Dir: Michael Herz and Samuel Weil. Pro: Lloyd Kaufman and Michael Herz. Ex Pro: William E. Kirksey and Spencer A. Tandy. Assoc Pro: Stuart Strutin. Pro Sup: Nelson Vaughn. Screenplay: Stuart Strutin. Ph: Lloyd Kaufman. Ed: Adam Fredericks and Richard King. Art: Ellen Christiansen. (Manley Productions for Grand Co, Troma–Premier Releasing) Rel: 25 Nov 1983. 87 mins. Cert 18.

Jennifer Beals with boyfriend Michael Nouri, and (below) dancing her way to fame in *Flashdance*.

Flashdance. A virtually plotless piece about a pretty young girl welder in Pittsburg who dreams of a ballet career, and by luck, and a nudge in the right direction by her boyfriend boss, eventually achieves her dream. All highly incredible, but on the credit side is the charming performance of Jennifer Beals (though rumour has it that her highly acrobatic dancing was done by an un-named double) and the several flashy modern dance numbers. Rest of cast: Michael Nouri, Belinda Bauer, Lilia Skala, Phil Bruns, Malcolm Danare, Lucy Lee Flippin, Kyle T. Heffner, Sunny Johnson, Ron Karabat-

sos, Durga McBroom, Nicole Mercurio, Cynthia Rhodes, Lee Ving, Richard Colon, Wayne Frost, Kenneth Gabbert, Marc Lemberger, Norman Scott, Bettina Birnbaum, Don Brockett, Deirdre L. Cowden, Hank Crowell, Marjean Dennis, Tony de Santis, Helen Dexter, David di Manna, Michael Epps, Debra Gordon, Colin Hamilton, Bob Harks, Roy L. Jones, Matt Landers, Erika Leslie, Jim McCardle, Larry John Meyers, Mark Anthony Moschello, Ann Muffly, Frank Pesce, Stacey Pickren. Dir: Adrian Lyne. Pro: Don Simpson and Jerry Bruckheimer. Ex Pro: Jon Peters and Peter Guber. Screenplay: Tom Hedley and Joe Eszterhas; from a story by Hedley. Ph: Don Peterman. Ed: Bud Smith and Walt Mulconery. Pro Des: Charles Rosen. M: Giorgio Moroder arr and con by Sylvestor Levay. M Sup: Phil Ramone. Choreography: Jeffrey Hornaday. Assoc Pro: Tom Jacobson and Lynda Rosen Obst. (Paramount–UIP) Rel: 1 July 1983. 95 mins. Cert 15.

Flight to Berlin. A perfect 'festival' film, made in West Germany, with lots of style, fine photography, a set of odd characters (well played), modern editing, and then very little, and ambivalent content. The story follows a mysterious woman who flies to Berlin seemingly on impulse, meets her sister there and is only gradually revealed to be trying to get away from an immediate past that includes involvement with a possible murder – an off-beat, trickily set out mystery melodrama. Cast: Tusse Silberg, Paul Freeman, Lisa Kreuzer, Jean-François Stevenin, Ewan Stewart, Eddie Constantine, Ellen Umlauf, Larry Lamb, Tatjana Blacher, Sema Poyraz, Jonathan Kinsler, Udo Helland, Gisela Gluck, Sonja Warnke, Claud D. Strauber. Dir: Christopher Petit. Ex Pro: Chris Sievernich. Assoc Pro: Walter Donahue, Peter Sainsbury and Lynda Myles. Screenplay: Petit and Hugo Williams; based on the novel by Jennifer Potter. Ph: Martin Schafer. Ed: Peter Przygodda. Art: Rainer Schaper. M: Irmin Schmidt. (Geba Filmproduktion GmbH Gerhard and Barbara von Halem/Road Movies Filmproduktion GmbH Berlin in assoc with the BFI) Rel: floating; first shown London (Lumiere), March 1984. 90 mins. Cert 15.

Footloose. A young persons' musical which pays tribute to films like *Flashdance* and *Saturday Night Fever* (and others going back as far as *Rebel Without a Cause*) in its story of a youth (played by Kevin Bacon) from Chicago who runs up against older generation prejudice in the small Mid-Western town to which his mother has moved after her husband deserted her. But he eventually persuades the local anti-rock preacher that he's not so moronic after all... Luckily Kevin Bacon has some talent and so, too, have some of the supporting players. Rest of cast: Lori Singer, John Lithgo, Dianne Wiest, Christopher Penn, Sarah Jessica Parker, John Laughlin, Elizabeth Gorcey, Frances Lee McCain, Jim Youngs, Douglas Dirkson, Lynne Marta, Arthur Rosenberg, Timothy Scott, Alan Haufrect, Linda MacEwan, Kim Jensen, Michael Telmont, Leo Geter, Ken Kemp, Russ McGinn, Sam Dalton, H.E.D. Redford, Jay Bernard, David Valenza, Meghan Broadhead, Mimi Broadhead, Gene Pack, Marcia Yvette Reider, John Perryman, Mary Ethel Gregory, Oscar Rowland, J. Paul Broadhead, John Bishop, Carmen Trevino, Melissa Renee Graehl, Monica M. Da Silva, Terri Gay Ulmer. Dir: Herbert Ross. Pro: Lewis J. Rachmil and Craig Zadan. Ex Pro: Daniel Melnick. Screenplay: Dean Pitchford. Ph: Ric Waite. Ed: Paul Hirsch. Pro Des: Ron Hobbs. M: Miles Goodman and Becky Shargo. (Paramount–UIP). Rel: 13 April 1984. 107 mins. Cert 15.

Forbidden Relations – Visszaesok. Thoughtful, visually beguiling, and in somewhat Jancso style, this Hungarian film takes a cool and unbiased look at incest, director-writer Zsolt Kézdi-Kovács basing his story on a recent case. A twice divorced and not too honest man (prone to a bit of embezzling) meets a woman whose husband has committed suicide (for reasons never known), goes to bed with her and then finds she is his half-sister. By this time their physical passion for each other is such that in spite of punishments they cannot part and so have to face up to further prison sentences for co-habiting; nor is the outlook for the two children resulting from the liaison a very happy one. An extremely well presented film which gives a picture of sympathetic and helpful authorities.

Cast: Lili Monori, Miklos B. Szekely, Mari Torocsik, Jozsef Horvath, Jozsef Toth, Tibor Molnar, Gyorgy Banffy, Laszlo Horvath. Dir and Screenplay: Zsolt Kézdi-Kovács. Pro Sup: Jozsef Mark. Ph: Janos Kende. Ed: Eva Karmento. Art: Tamas Banozich. (Mafilm–Objectiv Studio Budapest–Cinegate) Rel: floating; first shown London (Gate, Bloomsbury), Sept 1983. 90 mins. Cert 18.

Fords on Water. A minor British film with strong political allusions in a not always clear story about a white and a black youth adventuring North at a time when political unrest over a 'no strikes' Parliamentary bill has led to massive police and army intervention. Cast: Elvis Payne, Mark Wingett, Kathryn Apanowicz, Jason Rose, Allister Bain, David Ryall, Michele Winstanley, Kate Rabett, Mona Hammond, Paola Dionisotti, Mike Horsburgh, Christine Kimberley, Howard Lew Lewis, Peter Postlethwaite, Sheila Grant, Johnny Mulcahy, Shay Gorman, Alex Blythe, Jules Mannheim, Roger Monk, Jerry Judge, Lydia Burke, Stephen Calcutt, Sam Cox, Chris Flynn, David Grahame, Sidney Johnson, Judith Nelmes, Barrie Houghton, John Bardon, Dick McCullough, Steve Michaels, David Napthine, Holly Searle, Ralph Hawkes, Jim McCabe, Rick Shifter, Peggy Gosschalk, Dick Irwin, Andrew Byatt, Stephen Brigden, Norman Cooley, Raymond S. Gardener, Jeremy Swift, Andrew Bicknell, Mike Hurd, Geoffrey Swann. Dir and Screenplay: Barry Bliss. Pro: Nita Amy and Jill Pack. Ex Pro: Peter Sainsbury. Screenplay: Bliss and Billy Colvill. Ph: Russell Murray. Ed: Neil Thomson. Art: Ian Watson and Caroline Amies. M: Keith Donald. (BFI in assoc with Cannel 4–BFI) Rel: floating; first shown London (Ritzy), May 1984. 83 mins. Cert 15.

For Love or Money. An Australian compilation film about Women, Work and Money, made up of news snippings, clippings from feature films and still photographs, all adding up to history re-examined from the female point of view. Dir: Megan McMurchy and Jeni Thornley, with the duo plus Margot Oliver also credited with Research, Screenplay and Production. Ed: Margot Nash. Ph: Erika Addis. M:

Elizabeth Drake. Narration: Noni Hazlehurst. Cast: Narrative Voices – Jane Clifton, Diane Craig, Nick Enright, Vivienne Garrett, Richard Meikle, Margot Nash, Robyn Nevin, Emu Nugent, Justine Saunders, Kay Self, Carole Skinner, Maureen Watson. (Flashback Films in assoc with Creative Development and Project Development branches of the Australian Film Commission and Women's Film Fund-Contemporary). Rel: floating; first shown London (Phoenix, E. Finchley) June 1984. 109 mins. Cert 15.

Friday the 13th Part IV: The Final Chapter. Some more butcherings in this popular gore-and-guts series (No. 1 took $17 million, No. 2 $9½ and No. 3 $15 million) with about a dozen characters getting the chop from knives, axes, harpoons and the like, in that deceptively pleasant forest campsite by the lake. Cast: Crispin Glover, Kimberly Beck, Barbara Howard, E. Erich Anderson, Corey Feldman, Alan Hayes, Judie Aronson, Ted White, Lawrence Monson, Joan Freeman, Peter Barton, Camilla More, Carey More, Lisa Freeman, Bruce Mahler. Dir: Joseph Zito. Pro: Frank Mancuso Jr. Co-Pro: Tony Bishop. Screenplay: Barney Cohen. Ph: Joao Fernandes. Ed: Joel Goodman. Pro Des: Shelton H. Bishop III, Art: Joe Hoffman. M: Harry Manfredini. (Paramount–UIP Friday Four). Rel: 15 June 1984. 91 mins. Cert 18.

Friends and Husbands. A somewhat heavily Germanic, feminine-weighted Margarethe Von Trotta film concerning the friendship between a shy professor's wife, with a penchant for painting, and a strong-willed lecturer in German literature – a friendship eventually spoiled by the professor's jealousy. Cast: Hanna Schygulla, Angela Winkler, Peter Striebeck, Franz Buchrieser, Jochen Striebeck, Christine Fersen, Felix Moeller, Wladimir Yordanoff, Thérèse Affolter, Agnes Fink, Helga Ballhaus. Dir and Screenplay: Margarethe Von Trotta. Pro: Eberhard Junkersdorf. Ph: Michael Ballhaus. Ed: Dagmar Hirtz. Art: Jürgen Henze. M: Nicolas Economou. (Bioskop Film, Munich/Les Films du Losange, Paris/WDR, Cologne–Miracle Films) Rel: floating; first shown London (Academy), June 1983. 105 mins. Cert 15.

Funny Money. A wild, British crime thriller based on the serious topical problem of credit card fraud, which after a good start slides away into more and more uproarious melodrama. Elizabeth Daily plays a young American girl crook who comes to London to exploit her bag-full of stolen cards and tries with increasing desperation to persuade night-club pianist Gregg Henry to join her in the big swindle. Rest of cast: Gareth Hunt, Derren Nesbitt, Annie Ross, Stephen Yardley, Al Matthews, Rosa Alba, Mildred Shay, Nigel Lambert, Robert Henderson, Joe Praml, Bill McAllister, Charles Keating, Carol Cleveland, Lyndham Gregory. Dir and Screenplay: James Kenelm Clarke. Pro: Greg Smith. Ph: John Wyatt. Ed: Bill Lenny. Pro Des: Harry Pottle. Assoc Pro: Selwyn Roberts. (Norfolk International Picture/Greg Smith Productions–Cannon Film Dist.) Rel: floating; first shown London (Classic Haymarket), June 1983. 92 mins. Cert 18.

Ghost Dance. A visually impressive and complex examination of ideas and ghosts, memory, and the past, seen through the adventures of two women, one in London, the other in Paris; with quite a bit of anarchic humour. Cast: Leonie Mellinger, Pascale Ogier, Robbie Coltrane, Dominque Pinon, Stuart Brisley, Jacques Derrida. Dir, Pro and Screenplay: Ken McMullen. Ph: Peter Harvey. M: David Cunningham, Michael Giles and Jamie Muir. (The Other Cinema) Rel: floating; first shown London (ICA), Jan 1984. 96 mins. No cert.

The Girl from Trieste – La Ragazza Di Trieste. Ben Gazzara, as an American cartoonist, tries to gain inspiration by getting away from it all in a small seaside town near Trieste, where he becomes involved with a nubile young girl (Ornella Muti), who turns out to be a voluntary patient at a nearby psychiatric clinic. The passionate affair ends when the girl decides, in a moment of sane assessment, to release him by walking into the sea. An Italian film which never quite achieves the poetic ambiance it seems was intended. Rest of cast: Jean-Claude Brialy, Mimsy Farmer, Andrea Ferreol, William Berger, Consuelo Ferrara, Romano Puppo, Diego Pesaola. Dir: Pasquale Festa Campanile. Pro: Angelo Zemella.

Elizabeth Daily (right) makes full use of a bag full of stolen credit cards in *Funny Money*.

Screenplay: Ottavio Jemma; based on the director's novel of the same title. Ph. Alfio Contini. Ed: Amedeo Salfa. Art: Ezio Altieri. M: Riz Ortolani. (Faso Films–Golden Era) Rel: 25 Nov 1983. 103 mins. Cert 18.

The Gold Diggers. A curious, made-by-women film with an *avante garde* (and whatever) surface covering lots of symbolism and the like, which all adds up to an involved and not easy to follow picture. Take for example: one gold digger, a black women called Celeste, a city bank computer operator, who investigates the complex world of high finance and rides into a dancehall on a horse to rescue beautiful blonde Ruby from the men dancers! Cast includes: Julie Christie, Colette Laffont, Hilary Westlake, David Gale, Tom Osborn, Jacky Lansley, George Yiasoumi. Dir and Ed: Sally Potter. Pro Sup: Nita Amy and Donna Grey. Pro Co-Ord: Kristin Olafsdottir. Screenplay: Potter, Rose English and Lindsay Cooper. Ph: Babette Mangolte. Art: Rose English. M: Lindsay Cooper. (BFI in assoc with Channel 4–BFI) Rel: floating; first shown London (NFT), May 1984. 89 mins. Cert U.

The Golden Seal. A real Disneyish charmer for all the family which is nearer in spirit, story and beauty to the classic *Storm Boy* than any movie made since. It tells the simple, heart-tugging, often exciting story of a boy, living with his mother and salmon-fishing father on a remote but gloriously scenic island in the Aleutians, who finds a golden seal

Friends at play – Torquil Campbell stars as Eric in The Golden Seal.

which give birth to a pup which becomes his trusted friend. As there is a fortune waiting for the golden hide, the boy has to defend his playmate from father, the hunting Aleuts and a villainous visitor. Marvellous photography, wonderful storm scenes, breath-taking backgrounds all add to perhaps a minor and certainly a cinematic gem. Cast: Steve Railsback, Michael Beck, Penelope Milord, Torquil Campbell, Seth Sakai, Richard Narita, Sandra Seacat, Peter Anderson, Terence Kelly, Tom Heaton, Jacob Rupp, Tony Morelli, Suzanne Brown, John Thomas, Bary Beales. Dir: Frank Zuniga. Pro: Samuel Goldwyn Jr. Assoc Pro: Russell Thacher. 2nd Unit Dir: Joe Canutt. Screenplay: John Groves; based on the novel *The River Ran Out of Eden* by James Vance Marshall. Ph: Eric Sarrinen. Ed: Robert Q. Lovett. Pro Des: Douglas Higgins. M. Scored by Dana Kaproff; main theme comp by John Barry. (Samuel Goldwyn Co–New Realm) Rel: 13 April 1983. 94 mins. Cert PG.

Goodie-Two-Shoes. An amusing half-hour British comedy about the dancing lessons a comprehensive school headmistress introduces to his class and the Terpsichorean and romantic rivalry that develops between the little thug and the nice lad over the punk-style lass, and the nice girl who eventually wins the day, not to say the end of term competition. Cast: Michael Waterman, Ann-Marie Gwatkin, Stephen Sweeney, Suzanna Hamilton, Francis Victory, Holli Hoffman, Cary Carp, Beverley Martin, Lila Kaye, Allan Mitchell, Jim Barclay, Christine Edmonds, Christopher Coll, Clark Flanagan, Martin Murphy, Elaine Lordan, Sally Watkins, Kathy Burke, Paul Sims. Dir, Pro and Screenplay: Ian Emes. Assoc Pro: Heather Anderson. Pro Co-Ord: Tricia de Lacy. Ph: Ray Orton. Ed: David Spiers. Art: Deborah Youens. M: Rod Thompson. (Timeless

Students Ann-Marie Gwatkin and Michael Waterman in Goodie-Two-Shoes.

Films/Paramount–UIP) Rel: 22 Sept 1983. 30 mins. Cert U.

Gorky Park. A classically constructed 'whodunit' thriller with a story about illegal trade in Russian sables, interfactional squabbling and crooked dealings in high Moscow places. Chief militia investigator William Hurt grimly, in spite of the obstacles placed in his way, tries to solve the mystery of the three faceless and fingertipless bodies buried in the snow of Moscow's Gorky Park. Often convoluted and not so easy to follow, it nicely succeeds in sending chills down watchers' spines, with its callous action, snowy backgrounds and bitterly chilling atmosphere. Rest of cast: Lee Marvin, Brian Dennehy, Ian Bannen, Joanna Pacula, Michael Elphick, Richard Griffiths, Rikki Fulton, Alexander Knox, Alexei Sayle, Ian McDiarmid, Niall O'Brien, Henry Woolf, Tusse Silberg, Patrick Field, Jukka Hirvikangas, Marjatta Nissinen, Hekki Leppanen, Lauri Torhonen, Elsa Salamaa, Anatoly Davydov, Lasse Lindberg, Jussi Parvianen, Black Pearls (Russian Tea Band), Bad Signs (Rock & Roll band). Dir: Michael Apted. Pro: Gene Kirkwood and Howard W. Koch Jr. Ex Pro: Bob Larson. Assoc Pro: Efrem and Uri Harkham. Screenplay: Dennis Potter; based on the novel by Martin Cruz Smith. Ph: Ralph D. Bode. Ed: Dennis

Virkler. Pro Des: Paul Sylbert. M: James Horner. Cadavers by Carl Fullerton Co! (Eagle Associates–Koch/Kirkwood–Orion–Rank Dist) Rel: 3 Feb 1984. 128 mins. Cert 15.

Gregorio Cortez. Stylish and in part memorable western set along the Texas-Mexican border at the turn of the century, when the authorities were trying to impose some sort of law and order in the territory. Outlaw Gregorio Cortez is hunted down like an animal and so responds like one – a fine performance by Edward James Olmos. Rest of cast: James Gammon, Tom Bower, Bruce McGill, Brion James, Alan Vint, Timothy Scott, Pepe Serna, Michael McGuire, William Sanderson, Barry Corbin, Jack Kehoe, Rosana DeSoto, Victoria Plata, Nico Olmos, Lawrence De Yapp Jr., Cleo Ann De Yapp, Amos De Yapp, Buddy Vigil, Zach Porter, Lilli Young, Cletus Tafoya, Waymond Vessels, Weldon Minzenmayer, James Pamplin, Curtis Akin, Fred Collins, Rod Hudson, Dan Delk, Mark Burner, Ben Zeller, Joshua Tree, Laurence Steib, Doug Kaess, Jack Caffrey, William Paxton, Odile Kelly, Raina Barrett, Vance Sorrells, Eloy Hernandez, Judge E.W. Patteson, Jose Gomez, Margo Chavez Charles, Harry Fish, Fredrick Lopez, Getulio Rivera, Ruben Romero, Carlos Villegas, Ned Beatty. Dir and Screenplay (latter based on the book *With a Pistol in his Hand* by Americo Paredes): Robert M. Young. Pro: Moctesuma Esparza and Michael Hausman. Ex Pro: David Ochoa and H. Frank Dominguez. Assoc Pro and Sup Ed: Richard Soto. Ed: Arthur Coburn and John Bertucci. Pro Des: Stuart Wurtzel. M: W. Michael Lewis and Edward James Olmos. Assoc Pro: Soto, Olmos and David Wisnievitz. (Mainline Pictures) Rel: floating; first shown London (Electric Screen), May 1984. 105 mins. Cert 15.

Greystoke: The Legend of Tarzan, Lord of the Apes. Forget all the previous Tarzan movies, this one is for real, a serious, spectacular and warmly human adaptation from the famous Edgar Rice Burroughs novels. A young man who has been brought up by apes has to come to terms with civilization when he is brought out of the jungle and has to face up to the fact that he is a wealthy Lord and owner of one of England's stately homes. Director Hugh Hudson (of *Chariots of Fire* fame) brings out the basic tragedy of a man who cannot fit into either of the two worlds; and in the end he leaves pretty, civilized, Jane to return to the African Jungle knowing he will never again be

Below: William Hurt (foreground right) and Brian Dennehy (left), in *Gorky Park*, which also features Joanna Pacula (right).

The young Tarzan and the man, Christopher Lambert (above left), with Ian Holm and Sir Ralph Richardson in *Greystoke*.

able to recapture his former innocent happiness there. Cast: Christopher Lambert, Andie MacDowell, Ralph Richardson, Ian Holm, Emile Abossolo, Bridget Biargi, Philemon Blake Andhoua, Paul Brooke, Cheryl Campbell, Colin Charles, Ian Charleson, Elaine Collins, Nigel Davenport, David Endene, Nicholas Farrell, James Fox, Paul Geoffrey, Richard Griffiths, Tristam Jellineck, Eric Langlois, Sheila Latimer, Alison Macrae, Roddy Maude-Roxby, Tali McGregor, Hilton McRae, Messanga Messanga, Atangana Messi, Andrea Miller, Jean Mingele, Ali Mvondo, Emanuelle Obeya, Daniel Potts, Ravinder, Anne Scott-Jones, David Suchet, Harriet Thorpe, John Wells, Jacobin Yarro. Dir and Pro (latter with Stanley S. Canter): Hugh Hudson. Assoc Pro: Garth Thomas. Screenplay: P.H. Vazak and Michael Austin; based on the story *Tarzan and the Apes* by Edgar Rice Burroughs. Ph: John Alcott. Ed: Anne V. Coates. Pro Des: Stuart Craig. M: John Scott (add M by Elgar, D'Albert and Boccherini). M Dir: John Warrack; con Norman del Mar. Sup Art: Simon Holland. Filmed on location at Floors Castle, Blenheim Palace, Hatfield House, The Natural History Museum and in the Cameroons. (Warner) Rel: 13 April 1984. 127 mins. Cert PG.

The Heartbreakers – Die Heartbreakers. A West German film about a youthful quartet, plus manager, who in the early 1960s set out to form a 'Beat Band'. And they come up against all the snags before they – so nearly – make it. Woven into this simple tale is a love theme and a hard look at the whole business of forming and holding together a group. Cast: Sascha Disselkamp, Mary Ketikidou, Uwe Enkelmann, Michael Klein, Mark Eichenseher, Harmut Isselhorst, Esther Christinat, Rolf Zacher, Werner Eichhorn, Werner Schwuchow, Rudolf Voss, Dieter Prochnow, Klaus Lochthove, Rainer Chrostian Mehring, Gerd Weidenhofen, Nils Hansen, Christiane Lentz, Frank Holtmann, Werner Hansch, Udo Kerber, Jens Ingo Muller, Dirk Raschke. The Bands: Pille Palle und die Otterpotter, The X-Rays, Treff, etc. Dir: Peter F. Bringmann. Pro: Herbert Rombach. Pro Sup: Erich Raschke. Pro Co-Ord: Michael Wiedmann. Screenplay: Mathias Seelig. Ph: Helge Weindler. Ed: Annette Dorn. Art: Toni Ludi. M. Sup: Lothar Meid. (Tura–Film/Project Filmproduktion/WDR–Contemporary) Rel: floating; first shown London (ICA), April 1984. 113 mins. Cert 15.

Heartland Reggae. A feature film about reggae music, largely made up of footage from several concerts given in Jamaica during 1977–78. Commentary by Ras Lee Morris. Dir: Jim Lewis. Pro: John W. Mitchell. Assoc Pro: Cheryl M. Taub and Randal J. Torno. Ph: John Swaby, Lewis and Tony Marsh. Add Ph: Haines Cameron and Dennis Miller. Ed: Lewis, Torno and John Mayes. M. Co-Ord: Pamela Hulme. (Canada Offshore Cinema in assoc with Tuff Gong Productions International and Media Aides Ltd–Blue Dolphin Films) Rel: floating; first shown London (Screen-on-the-Green), August 1983. 87 mins. Cert 15.

Heart Like a Wheel. And it beats in a lady, too! The well told story of America's first lady of the Hot Rod, the woman who created a stir by going in for the business and then, after becoming local champion, went on to win the National Hot Rod Assoc. World Championship on no less than three occasions. Both feminists and rodracers should approve of the fun, sentiment and thrills on offer, all ably melded together. Cast: Bonnie Bedelia, Beau Bridges, Leo Rossi, Hoyt Axton, Bill McKinney, Anthony Edwards, Dean Paul Martin, Paul Bartel, Dick Miller, Missy Basile, Michael Cavanaugh, Ellen Geer, Nora Heflin, Byron Thames, Tiny Wells, Brandon Brent Williams, Jesse Aragon, Bruce Barlow, Michel Barrere, Creed Bratton, Tiffany Brissette, Paul Bryar, James Burton, Jill Carroll, Martin

Casella, Sandy Chanley, Mark Dawson, Diane Delano, Tom Duffield, Steve Evans, Dennis Fetchet, Chris Fontana, Marvin Graham, Mitzi Hoag, Marvin 'Swede' Johnson, Tim Kimber, Terence Knox, Sam Laws, Paul Linke, Dave McClellan, Mike Milgrom, Bob Minor, Harry Northup, Catherine Polone, Sam Posey, Bob Ridgely, Jennifer Roven, Michael Talbott, Leonard Termo. Dir: Jonathan Kaplan. Pro: Charles Roven. Ex Pro: Rich Irvine and James L. Stewart. Screenplay: Ken Friedman. Ph: Tak Fujimoto. Ed: O. Nicholas Brown. Pro Des: J. W. Newport. M: Laurence Rosenthal. Assoc Pro: Arne Schmidt. 2nd Unit Dir: Conrad Palmisano. (Aurora in assoc with Michael Nolin-Fox-Mainline) Rel: floating; first shown several London cinemas, June 1984. 112 mins. Cert PG.

Heaven's Gate. The first public showing in Britain of the controversial $18-million Michael Cimino disaster in the form and length the director originally presented it to the producers, running for 207 instead of the 148 minutes it was cut to for its 1981 release. It looks much better now than then! Full details of the film will be found in the 1982–83 *Film Review*. (UIP) Rel: floating; first shown (in new form) London (National Film Theatre), August 1983.

Hellcat Mud Wrestlers. A British documentary about an evening's mud wrestling between women at a club 'somewhere near London', with interviews of some of the stars and plenty of views of their naked bodies. Including: Queen Kong, Shelley Selina Savage, Sadistic Sadie, Vickie Scott, Helen Hammer, Rosie Rock, Sandra Wolshin, Miss Death Wish, Big Harry, Hal 'Animal' Stone, Jock McPhearson. Dir: David Sullivan and John M. East, with the latter doing the interviews. Ph: Alan Hall. Ed: Jim Connock. M: De Wolfe. (Roldvale–ITC) Rel: floating. 48 mins. Cert X.

High Road to China. Action, action all the way in this extremely entertaining film. Set in the 1930s, a handsome, macho hero and a gutsy, filthy-rich girl fall in love and then face danger and adventure together in their efforts to find her father. After flying in two old biplanes across Afghanistan to Wariris-

tan and Nepal, and across the Himalayas to Sinkiang Province in China, they eventually discover him happily leading the locals in the defence of their hilltop town from the attacks of a nasty local War Lord. Good leading performances by Tom Selleck (the air-ace hero), Bess Armstrong (the headstrong lass), Jack Weston (the fat but not always jolly mechanic) and Wilford Brimley (an eccentric father and inventor who does wonders with gumption and gunpowder). Rest of cast: Robert Morley, Brian Blessed, Cassandra Gava, Michael Sheard, Lynda Marchal, Timothy Carlton, Shayur Mehta, Terry Richards, Jeremy Child, Peter Williams, Dino Shafeek, Robert Lee, Peggy Sirr, Anthony Chinn, Chua Kah Joo, Ric Young, Simon Prebble, Daniel Clucas, John Higginson, Timothy Bateson, Wolf Kahler, Marc Boyle, Zdenka Hersak, Domagoj Mukusic, Sime Jagarinac, Hai Ching Lim, Kim Fook Teoh. Dir: Brian G. Hutton. Pro: Fred Weintraub. Screenplay: Sandra Weistraub Poland and S. Lee Pogostin; based on the book by Jon Cleary. Ex Pro: Raymond Chow. Assoc Pro: Frederick Muller. Ph: Ronnie Taylor (aerial ph by Peter Allwork). Ed: John Jympson. Pro Des: Robert Laing. M: John Barry. (Golden Harvest/Jadran Films–City Films–Videoform Pictures in assoc with Miracle) Rel: 27 April 1984. 104 mins. Cert PG.

The Honorary Consul. Michael Caine, in the lesser of the main roles in this adaptation of the Graham Greene novel, acts his co-stars into deep shade with his brilliant performance as a drunken yet likeable British Consul in a small Argentinian town where his power is small but his spirit is big. Richard Gere, as the half-English doctor refugee from Paraguay, becomes unwillingly involved in a political plot which goes badly wrong, leading to his and the conspirators deaths. Impressive support from Bob Hoskins and a pretty

Bess Armstrong (below) and Tom Selleck (above) in *High Road to China*.

debut performance by Mexican beauty Elpidia Carrilo. Rest of cast: Joaqim de Almeda, A. Martinez, Stephanie Cotsirilos, Domingo Ambriz, Eric Valdez, Nicholas Jasso, Geoffrey Palmer, Leonard Maguire, Jorge Russek, Erika Carlsen, Josefina Echanove, Ramon Alvarez, George Belanger, Juan Antonio Llanez, Aline Davidoff, Zohra Segal, Anais de Melo, Arturo Rodriguez Doring, Alejandro Compean, Mario Valdez. Dir: John Mackenzie. Pro: Norma Heyman. Assoc Pro: Richard F. Dalton. Screenplay: Christopher Hampton; based on the novel by Graham Greene. Ph: Phil Meheux. Ed: Stuart Baird. Pro Des: Alan Cameron. M: Stanley Myers (Theme Music comp and played by Paul McCartney). (World Film Services Ltd in assoc with Parsons and Whittemore Lyddon Ltd–Fox) Rel: 13 Jan 1984. 103 mins. Cert 18.

Hot Dog . . . The Movie. Sex-obsessed youngsters at Squaw Valley ski resort in Lake Tahoe country, apart from chasing possible sleeping partners, indulge in a form of ski-ing called 'hot dogging' which seems to mix acrobatics with Terpsichorean efforts. But the hackles are raised when a rivalry develops between 'our lads' and a lot of nasty Austrians, including their world champ. Cast: David Naughton, Patrick Houser, Tracy N. Smith, John Patrick Reger, Frank Koppola, James Saito, Shannon Tweed, George Theobald, Marc Vance, Erik Watson, Lynn Wieland, Sandy Hackett, Crystal Smith, Peter Vogt, Robert Fuhrmann, Mark Costello, Deborah Dutton, Anders Stenstedt, Daniel K. Moore, Michael Moore,

Patrick Houser and David Naughton bearing Tracy N. Smith on their shoulders star in *Hot Dog . . . The Movie.*

Unfaithful wife Elpidia Carrilo eyes Richard Gere as husband Michael Caine opens the bubbly in *The Honorary Consul.*

Linda Briggs McCulloch, Ami Julius, M. Lisa Cooper, Lauri Price, Robin Rael, Victoria Rae Walker, Gregory Beck, Mike Marvin, Jim Clark, Ronald Hurley, Robin Haynes. Stunt Skiers: Frank Beddor 3, Jeffrey J. Chumas, Dan Herby, Robert Huntoon, Lane Parrish, Paul Rosenberg, Todd Smith, Scott Sproule, Robert Vogel, Kevin Wightman. Dir: Peter Markle. Pro: Edward S. Feldman. Ex Pro: Christopher W. Knight. Screenplay and Co-Pro: Mike Marvin. Assoc Pro: Tim Tennant. Ph: Paul G. Ryan. Ed: Stephen Rivkin. Art: Don DeFina. M: Peter Bernstein. Ski sequences dir by Mike Marvin. (Edward S. Feldman Productions/The Hog Dog Partnership–Entertainment Film Dist) Rel: 8 June 1984. 98 mins. Cert 18.

House of Evil (American title: The House on Sorority Row). An efficient thriller, with occasional gore-and-guts effects, about a psycho case who having seen his mother accidentally killed sets out to have his own back on those responsible. Cast: Kathryn McNeil, Eileen Davidson, Lois Kelso Hunt, Christopher Lawrence, Janis Zido, Robin Meloy, Harley Kozak, Jodi Draigie, Ellen Dorsher, Michael Kuhn, Michael Sergio, Ruth Walsh, Ed Heath, Jean Schertler, Larry Singer, Charles Serio, Peter McClung, Brian T. Small, Alan Treadwell, Ken Myers, Ruth Moss, Hilary Crowson, Nanna Ingvarsson, Arthur Crockett, Tom

Bothwell, Van Santvoord, Kathryn Davidov, Celeste Poirier, Patti Chambers, Eric Smith, Karl B. Bromwell. Dir and Screenplay: Mark Rosman. Pro: Rosman and John G. Clark. Ex Pro: John Pinchock and .W. Thomas McMahon. Co-Pro: Ed Beyer. Assoc Pro: Alec Rabonowitz. Pro Assoc: Rene Eram. Add dialogue: Bobby Fine. Ph: Timothy Suhrstedt. 2nd Unit Ph: Tom Loizeaux. Ed: Jean-Marc Vasseur. Co-Ed: Paul Trejo. Art: Vincent Peranio. M: Richard H. Band. (VAE Productions–Miracle) Rel: floating; first shown London (Classic, Oxford and ABC Edgware Rd.) Dec 1983. 116 mins. Cert 18.

Humongous. A minor horror movie about six youngsters wrecked on a small island where a recluse's house harbours something very nasty and homicidal in the cellar. And the six little teenagers then go very much the way of Agatha Christie's *Ten Little Niggers.* Cast: Janet Julian, David Wallace, John Wildman, Janet Baldwin, Joy Boushel, Layne Coleman, Shay Garner, Page Fletcher, John McFadyen, Garry Robbins, Mary Sullivan. Dir: Paul Lynch. Pro: Anthony Kramreither. Ex Pro: Michael M. Stevenson. Pro Co-Ord: Angela Gruenthal. Screenplay: William Gray. Ph: Brian R.R. Hebb. Ed: Nick Rotundo. Sup. Art: Carol Spier. Art: Barbara Dunphy. M: John Mills Cockell (song 'Magic to Me' by Cockell and Lisa J. Sweeting, sung by Sawn Aitken). (Humongous Productions in assoc with Manesco Films–Entertainment) Rel: 1 July 1983. 85 mins. Cert 18.

Hysterical. A comedy spoof of *The Exorcist* and other similar chillers, which is obviously tailored to present the talents of the former American TV act the Three Hudson Brothers (William, Mark and Brett). But the trio are never likely to upstage the Marxes. Rest of cast: Cindy Pickett, Richard Kiel, Julie Newmar, Bud Cort, Robert Donner, Murray Hamilton, Clint Walker, Franklin Ajaye, Charlie Callas, Keenan Wynn, Gary Owens. Dir: Chris Bearde. Pro: Gene Levy. Ex Pro: William Immerman. Ph: Donald Morgan. Ed: Stanley Frazen. (Cinema Works/H & W–Entertainment Films) Rel: floating; first shown London (Classic, Tott Ct Rd and Electric, Chelsea), Oct 1983. 86 mins. Cert 15.

In the King of Prussia. A reconstruction of the court trial in the US of 'The Plowshares Eight' – the Jesuit-trained pacifist and his friends who broke into a GEC factory in King of Prussia, Pennsylvania, in 1980, as an anti-nuclear protest. One of two films (the other *Dark Circle*), the distribution of which has been financially assisted by the GLC. Cast: Martin Sheen; and the 'Eight' played by themselves – Daniel Berrigan SJ, Philip Berrigan, John Schuvhardt, Dean Hammer, Father Karl Kabat, Sister Anne Montgomery, Elmer Maas and Molly Rush. Dir, Screenplay and Ed: Emile de Antonio. Ph: Judy Irola and Julian Abio. M: Joe Walsh and Craig Doerge. (Turin Films, USA–Concord Films Council). Rel: floating; first shown London (Electric, Rio and Ritzy), July 1983. 92 mins. Cert U.

In the White City – Dans la Ville Blanche. A leisurely paced, meandering and somewhat ambiguous but always fascinating Alain Tanner Swiss–Portuguese production about a Swiss marine engineer who jumps ship at Lisbon and drifts aimlessly as he toys with the idea of a new life. He enjoys an affair with the hotel's barmaid, and makes interminable home movies, sending them back to his wife with letters which indicate his indecision about his future. But his plight is made more problematical when he is robbed of all his money and stabbed by the thief when he challenges him. A remarkable performance by Gruno Ganz, who, hardly ever off screen, is ably supported by talented Teresa Madruga,

as the girl. Also look for the wonderful atmospheric backgrounds of old Lisbon. Rest of cast: Julia Vonderlinn, José Carvalho, Francisco Baiao, José Wallenstein, Lidia Franco, Pedro Efe, Cecilia Grimaraes, Joana Vicente. Dir and Screenplay: Alain Tanner. Pro: Tanner, Paulo Branco and Antonio Vaz da Silva. Ex Pro: Branco and Tanner. Ph: Acacio de Almeida. Ed: Laurent Uhler. Art: Maria Jose Branco. M: Jean-Luc Barbier. (Metro Filme, Lisbon/Filmograph, Geneva–Contemporary Films) Rel: floating; first shown London (Phoenix, East Finchley) Oct 1983. 105 mins. Cert 15.

Italianamerican. A home-movie documentary by Martin Scorsese about his immigrant parents, which he made originally as a contribution to the American TV series called 'Storm of Strangers'. Hard times in Hester Street. Dir: Martin Scorsese. Pro: Saul Rubin and Elaine Ettias. Assoc Pro: B. Lovitt. Ph: Alan Hirshfeld. Ed: Bertram Lovitt. Cast: Catherine, Charles and Martin Scorsese. (The National Endowment for Humanities/The National Communications Foundation–Cinegate) Rel: floating; first shown London (Electric Cinema), July 1983. 49 mins. No cert.

Dennis Quaid and Bess Armstrong school a pet whale in *Jaws 3-D*.

Jaws 3-D. For once, a 3-D film which uses the usual gimmicks with some discretion, but unfortunately this third in the *Jaws* movies has a somewhat threadbare story. A giant killer fish gets into the Florida 'Sea World' entertainment complex and proceeds to chew up some of the workers preparing to launch a new 'Undersea Kingdom' section. Surely it is time to lay old *Jaws* to rest even if the – sometimes gory – exciting high-spots of the movie attract curious movie-goers *en masse*. Cast: Dennis Quaid, Bess Armstrong, Simon MacCorkindale, Louis Gossett Jr, John Putch, Lea Thompson, P.H. Moriarty, Dan Blasko, Liz Morris, Lisa Maurer, Harry Grant, Andy Hansen, P.T. Horn, John Edson Jr, Kaye Stevens, Archie Valliere, Alonzo Ward, Cathy Cervenka, Jane Horner, Kathy Jenkins, Steve Mellor, Ray Meunnich, Les Alford, Gary Anstaett, Muffet Baker, William Bramley, Scott Christoffel, Debbie Connoyer, Mary Davis Duncan, Barbara Eden, John Floren, John Gaffey, Joe Gilbert, Will Knickerbocker, Jackie Kuntarich. Dir: Joe Alves. Pro: Rupert Hitzig. Ex Pro: Alan Landsburg and Howard Lipstone. Screenplay: Richard Matheson and Carl Gottlieb; from a story by Guerdon Trueblood, suggested by Peter Benchley's novel *Jaws*. Ph: James A. Contner. Ed: Randy Roberts. Assoc Pro: David Kappes. Pro Des: Woods Mack-

Claudia Udy, the nubile star of *Joy*.

intosh. M: Alan Parker (Shark theme by John Williams). (Alan Landsburg Productions/Universal–UIP) Rel: 16 Dec 1983. 98½ mins. Cert PG.

Joy. A French-Canadian soft-core adaptation of Joy Laurey's erotic best-selling book about a photographic model with a father complex ('My heart belongs to daddy!') and a hang-up which sends her away from him when she sees him making love to her mother in front of the fire. Later she gets involved with a lover who takes her around the kinkier parts of Paris – the opportunity to get down to the sexual knitty-gritty. Introducing a nubile beauty, Claudia Udy. Rest of cast: Gerard Antoine Huart, Agnes Torrent, Elisabeth Mortensen, Manuel Gelin, Kenneth Le Gallois. Dir: Serge Bergon. Pro: Benjamin Simon. Screen-play: Marie-Françoise Hans, Christian Charriere and Serge Bergon. (Dia-logues by Charriere and Bergon). Ph: Rene Verzier (and Richard Ciupke). Ed: Michael Lewin. Art: Eric Moulard.

M: Alain Wisniak (title song by Fran-çoise Valery sung by Debbie Davis). (ATC 3000/RSL Films–Avatar Com-munications) Rel: floating; first shown London (Prince Charles), Feb 1984. 90 mins. Cert 18.

Killpoint. A semi-documentary-style cops and robbers piece about a Chinese-American martial arts expert Los An-geles cop, teamed with a government agent. Together they are assigned to track down and remove, one way or another, the menace of a gang who, having stolen a number of guns from an armoury, are selling them to the local crooks. Cast: Leo Fong, Richard Round-tree, Cameron Mitchell, Stack Pierce, Hope Holiday, Diana Leigh. Dir Co-Pro (with Diane Stevenett) Ed Screenplay and Ph: Frank Harris. Ex Pro: Roger Jacobson and Dana Welch. M: Herman Jeffreys and Daryl Stevenett. (Lorimar/ Universal–Miracle/ Videoform) Rel: floating; 113 mins. Cert 18.

King Blank. Controversial Michael Ob-lowitz movie about King and Queenie Blank and their vituperistic and scatalogical abuse of each other, which ends with the wife shooting the hus-band dead during a struggle for the gun – and finding it hysterically amusing. All very, very odd and for highly specialized tastes. Cast: Rosemary Hochschild, Ron Vawter, Will Patton, Fred Neuman, Nancy Reilly, Peyton Smith, Cookie Mueller, Marina Meline, Larry Watson, Ray McReady, Mark Heidrich, Eric Himes, Peter Richardson, Susan Mitchell, Francine Berman, Pearllinda Hill, Marilyn Darden, Tony Piazza, Joaqim de Alme-da, Libby Howes, David Damrosch, Fiona Templeton, Jane Weinstock. Dir Pro and Ph: Michael Oblowitz. Ex Pro: David T. Goldberg. Assoc Pro: Rose-mary Hochschild, Dunja Sagov and Henry S. McNeil Jr. Screenplay: Ob-lowitz and Hochschild. Ed: Susanne Rostock. M: Anton Fig. (King Blank Productions–BFI) Rel: floating; first shown London (ICA), Dec 1983. Black-and-white. 90 mins. No Cert.

The King of Comedy. Jerry Lewis is surprisingly impressive in his first straight acting role; suggesting that he is a better straight man than comic. He plays the star of a late-night TV chat show who is pestered by a more than brash character – Robert de Niro – who is convinced he has a great comic gift, and when turned down by Lewis ab-ducts him and holds him to ransom, threatening to kill him unless the pro-ducer allows him to appear on the show

Jerry Lewis (centre) about to evict Robert de Niro and Diahanne Abbott from his house, in *The King of Comedy*.

that night. The outcome is as ironically amusing as it is unexpected. Rest of cast: Diahanne Abbott, Sandra Bernhard, Ed Herlihy, Lou Brown, Doc Lawless, Marta Heflin, Richard Baratz, Catherine Scorsese, Cathy Scorsese, Chuck L. Low, Liza Minnelli, Leslie Levinson, Margo Winkler, Tony Boschetti, Shelley Hack, Matt Russo, Dr. Joyce Brothers, George Kapp, Victor Borge, Ralph Monaco, Ron Jamere-Wess, Kim Chan, Audrey Dummett, June Prud'homme, Fred de Cordova, Edgar J. Scherick, Thomas M. Tolan, Ray Dittrich, Richard Dioguardi, Jay Julien, Harry Ufland, Scotty Bloch, Jim Lyness, Bill Minkin, Diane Rachell, Jimmy Raitt, Martin Scorsese, Tony Randall, Charles Scorsese, Merdik Martin, William Jorgensen, Marvin Scott, Chuck Stevens, William Littauer, Jeff David, Mick Jones, Joe Strummer, Paul Simmion, Kosmo Vynil, Ellen Foley, Pearl Harbour, Gaby Salter, Jerry Baxter-Worman, Dom Letts. Dir: Martin Scorsese. Pro: Arnon Milchan. Ex Pro: Robert Greenhut. Screenplay: Paul D. Zimmerman. Ph Dir: Fred Schuler. Pro Sup and Ed: Thelma Schoonmaker. Pro Des: Boris Leven. Assoc Pro: Robert F. Colesberry. Art: Edward Pisoni and Lawrence Miller. M Pro: Rabbie Robertson. (Embassy International Pictures NV–Fox) Rel: floating; first shown London (Gate and Screen-on-the-Hill), July 1983. 108 mins. Cert PG.

Koyaanisqatsi. A quite extraordinary and in many ways outstanding film by Godfrey Reggio, who uses in turn speeded-up, normal and slow-motion photography, a brilliant specially-composed sound track (by Philip Glass) – but not a word of commentary or dialogue, or even a single sound-effect – to produce what in so many ways is a moving picture poem, keyed to the title, which in Hopi Indian language means 'Life Out of Balance'. Marvellous land- and city-scapes, with colour, light and shadow, and incredible patterns and effects, produce sequences which alternate between great beauty and a subtle threat of horror. Forget any underlying significance about the threat of an automated world or other implications and enjoy some of the most breathtakingly impressive film sequences ever to reach the screen. Dir and Pro: Godfrey Reggio. Assoc Pro:

Koyaanisqati – brilliant camera work uses the dramatic possibilities of light and shadow to the full to present a pageant of natural and man-made beauty.

Lawrence S. Taub, T. Michael Powers, Anton Walpole, Roger McNew and Mel Lawrence. Screenplay: Ron Fricke, Godfrey Reggio, Michael Hoenig and Anton Walpole. Ph: Ron Fricke. Assoc Ph: Christine Gibson. Additional Ph: Hilary Harris and Louis Schwartzberg. M: Philip Glass. M Dir (and add M): Michael Hoenig. Dramaturge: Walter Bachauer. (Institute for Regional Education, Santa Fé–Francis Ford Coppola–Blue Dolphin) Rel: floating; first shown London (Lumiere), Sept 1983. 86 mins. Cert U.

Krull. An openly derivative, likeable, amusing science-fiction film which sets a *Star Wars* world against a background of ancient, fairy-tale castles and the like. Part of the fun is in trying to put one's finger on the various sources. The film tells the story of a young hero king on a besieged planet fighting not only the alien invaders but the Beast who holds his beloved in its clutches. Cast: Ken Marshall, Lysette Anthony, Freddie Jones, Francesca Annis, John Welsh, David Battley, Bernard Bresslaw, Graham McGrath, Tony Church, Bernard Archard, Liam Neeson, Todd Carty, Robbie Coltrane, Dicken Ashworth, Bill Weston, Andy Bradford, Bronco McLoughlin, Gerard Naprous, Belinda Mayne, Clare McIntyre. Dir:

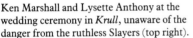

Ken Marshall and Lysette Anthony at the wedding ceremony in *Krull*, unaware of the danger from the ruthless Slayers (top right).

Peter Yates. Pro: Ron Silverman. Ex Pro: Ted Mann. Assoc Pro: Geoffrey Helman. 2nd Unit Dir: Derek Cracknell. Screenplay: Stanford Sherman. Ph: Peter Suscitzky. 2nd Unit Ph: Chic Anstiss. Ed: Ray Lovejoy. Animation: Steven Archer. Pro Des: Stephen Grimes. Art: Colin Grimes, Tony Reading, Norman Dorme, Tony Curtis and Francesco Chianese. M: James Horner. (Columbia) Rel: 27 Dec 1983. 120 mins. Cert PG.

L'Argent – Money. Based on a short story by Tolstoy, Robert Bresson's typically spare and lean film tells how a Paris schoolboy by passing off a dud note to a photographic shop sets off a chain of events which leads to several murders. Winner of the Grand Prix for Creative Cinema at the 1983 Cannes Festival, and a fine example of Bresson's unique and fascinating style, hinting both of his early philosophic successes and his training as an artist. Cast: Christian Patey, Sylvie van den Elsen, Michael Briguet, Caroline Lang, Vincent Risterucci, Beatrice Tabourin, Didier Baussy, Marc Ernest Fourneau, Bruno Lapeyre, Dir and Screenplay: Robert Bresson; based on the Tolstoy story *The False Note*. Pro: Jean-Marc Henchoz. Ph: Emmanuel Machuel and Pasqualino de Santis. Ed: Jean-François Ughetto. Ex Pro: Antoine Gannage. Assoc Pro: Jean-Pierre Baste.

No Art credit. M: by Bach. (Eros Films, Switzerland/Marion Films, & FR3, France–Artificial Eye) Rel: floating; first shown London (Camden Plaza), July 1983. 85 mins. Cert PG.

The Last Winter. An Israeli story about the aftermath of the war against Egypt, when two women both identify a POW shown on a Dutch TV newsreel as their missing husband and become close friends as they set out to find which of them is right. And then, at last, the POWs return.... Cast: Yona Elian, Kathleen Quinlan, Stephen Macht, Zipora Peled, Michael Schnider, Avi Uria, Brian Aaron, Michael Shilo, Yossi Werzanski, Yehuda Fux, Naomi Sharon, Zafrir Kochonovsky, Mel Penson, Biatris Shimshoni, Dana Ben-Yehuda, Avishai Milshtein, Sybil Lampkin, Dafna Karte, Daniel Schwartzman, Aba Zuriel, Norman Ravis, Shlomo Somech, Lennie Ravitz, Herzel Yaakobi, Saray Zuriel, Kavin Shepherd, Jerry Hyman, Yonni Lucas, Larry Price, Ruth Reachel Parciaspe, Jill Goldwasser, Zohar Laskov, Motti Cohen. Dir: Riki Shelach Missimoff. Pro: Jacob Kotzky. Ex Pro: Avi Lerner and Mota Gorfund. Script: Riki Shelach, Yona Elian, Nava Semel and Dror Schwartz: based on an idea by Dan Wolman and short script by Ruth Epstein. Screenplay: John Herzfeld. Ph: Amnon Salomon. Art: Ofer Lalush. M: Nahun Heyman. (Lerko Productions–Tri-Star Pictures) Rel: 15 June 1984. 89 mins. Cert 15.

La Traviata. Franco Zeffirelli's marvellous screen adaptation of the Verdi opera – the best operatic film ever made. Wonderful artistry, outstanding camerawork, perfect arrangement and superb operatic performances bring the old, trite story to life and make it tremendously exciting and moving. Zeffirelli starts with the opera's final scene – all sad blues and shadows – then switches suddenly to the spectacle, colour and movement of the opera's normal beginning, reverting finally to the same blue-and-shadow for Violetta's death scene. Two dominating performances by Teresa Stratas (Violetta) and Placido Domingo (Alfredo) set the standard for a cast that can both sing and act. Rest of cast: Cornell Macneil, Allan Monk, Axell Gall, Pina Cei, Maurizio Barbacini, Robert Sommer, Ricardo Oneto, Luciano Brizi, Tony Ammirati, Russell Christopher, Charles Antony, Geraldine Decker, Michael Best, Ferruccio Furlanetto, Ariel Bybee, Richard Vernon, Ekaterina Maksimova and Vladimir Vassiljev of the Bolshoi State Academic Theatre (the two main dancers). Dir, Screenplay and Design: Franco Zeffirelli. Pro: Tarak Ben Ammar. Metropolitan Opera Assoc Orch and Chorus con James Levine (M Dir). Assoc Pro: Carlo Lastricati. Ph: Ennio Guarnieri. Ed: Peter Taylor and Franca Sylvi. Art: Gianni Quaranta. Set Dir: Bruno Carlino. Choreographer: Alberto Testa. (Accent Films/FAI–ITC) Rel: floating; first shown London (Odeon, Haymarket), Oct 1983. 105 mins. Cert U.

L'Etoile du Nord. Masterly performances by Philippe Noiret and Simone Signoret lift this otherwise not wholly satisfactory adaptation of a Georges Simenon story into a moving and compelling movie. Noiret plays a likeable character who, when his employer dies in Alexandria, finds the gift she has left him as a nest egg is worthless. In desperation and sudden fury, he commits a murder, about which he can subsequently remember nothing, until revelation and retribution. A very attractive performance too, by Fanny Cottencon in her first major film role. Rest of cast: Julie Jezequel, Jean Rogerie, Jean-Pierre Klein, Jean-Yves Chatelais, Michel Koniecny, Jean Dautremay, Patricia Malvoisin, Gamil Ratib, Liliana Gerace, Pierre Forget, Julien Bukowsky, Abdallah Chahed, Serge Coursan, Michele Couty, Malek Eddine Kateb, Slim Mahfoudh, Mohsen Zaaza, Dominique Zardi, Jean-Pierre Dauzun, Dany Jacquet. Dir: Pierre Granier-Deferre. Pro: Alain Sarde. Pro Sup: Gerard Gaultier. Screenplay: Jean Aurenche, Michel Grisolia and Pierre Granier-Deferre; based (somewhat loosely) on the Georges Simenon novel *Le Locataire*. Ph: Pierre-William Glenn. Ed: Jean Ravel. Art: Dominique Andre. M: Phillipe Sarde. (Sara Films/Antenne 2–Gala) Rel: floating; first shown London (Odeon, Kensington), July 1983. 120 mins. Cert PG.

Lianna. Writer-director-editor John Sayles has given this bitter-sweet story of a woman and mother in her thirties, who finds she prefers women to men for lovemaking, something of a documen-

Linda Griffiths as Lianna (left) and Jane Hallaren as Ruth, in *Lianna*.

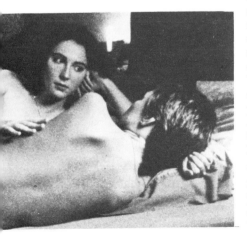

tary style, making his rough corners and loose construction all work towards a sense of moving reality. Having divorced, gone through the trauma of trying to explain things to her two children, loved and lost her first feminine passion, Lianna begins to come to terms with life and herself. Cast: Linda Griffiths, Jane Hallaren, Jon DeVries, Jo Henderson, Jessica Wight MacDonald, Jesse Solomon, John Sayles, Stephen Mendillo, Betsy Julia Robinson, Nancy Mette, Maggie Renzi, Madelyn Coleman, Robyn Reeves, Christopher Elliott, Marta Renzi, D. David Porter, Rochelle Oliver, Nancy-Elizabeth Kammer, Jean Passanante, Maggie Task, Marisa Smith, Amanda Carlin, Madeline Lee, Deborah Taylor. Dir, Screenplay and Ed: John Sayles. Pro: Jeffrey Nelson and Maggie Renzi. Ph: Austin de Besche. Art: Jeanne McDonnell. M: Mason Daring. (Winwood Co./United Artists Classics–Mainline Pictures) Rel: floating; first shown London (opening of the Screen cinema in Baker St.), Feb 1984. 112 mins. Cert 18.

Life is a Bed of Roses – La Vie est un Roman. That master of cinematic ambiguity and creator of fascinating film puzzles, Alain (*Hiroshima Mon Amour*, *Last Year in Marienbad* etc.) Resnais, goes well over the top in this dense, confused and far too contrived, many-layered story set in three different periods of time. Centred on a sugar-plum-style chateau in the Ardennes, the action wanders through time from the chateau's wealthy but eccentric builder's abortive plan to create an Ideal City around him, to the equally eccentric progressive school now occupying the premises. The third tale is a fairy-story dreamed up by a trio of small pupils. And just to add to the confusion, at any moment, and intercutting all three, any of them may take off into grand opera. A visually fascinating exercise but way below the best Resnais. On the asset side however, are some nice performances, particularly from Sabine Azema, Fanny Ardant, Martine Kelly and Vittorio Gassman. Rest of cast: Ruggero Raimondi, Andree Dussollier, Pierre Arditi, Samson Fainsilber, Robert Manuel, Veronique Silver. Dir: Alain Resnais. Pro: Philippe Dussart. Screenplay: Jean Gruault. Ph: Bruno Nuytten. Ed: Albert Jurgenson. Art: Jacques

Saulnier and Enki Bilal. M: Philippe-Gerard. (Soprofilms/Films A2/Fideline Films/Les Films Ariane/Filmedis–Artificial Eye) Rel: floating; first shown London (Chelsea Cinema), April 1984. 110 mins. Cert PG.

The Lift. Dutch (dubbed into English) chiller-thriller which, in telling the story of a wayward, lethal lift (arbitrarily killing a number of characters in horrible ways before a service engineer solves the problem and reveals the villain) never really explains clearly the motivation of the villainy. But director-writer Dick Maas comes up with some highly effective, horrifying scenes. Cast: Huub Stapel, Willeke van Ammelrooy, Josine van Dalsum, Piet Römer, Hans Veerman, Ab Abspoel, Onno Molenkamp, Manfred de Graaf, Serge Henri Valcke, Siem Vroom, Aat Ceelen, Gerard Thoolen, Kees Prins, Michiel Kerbosch, Luk van Mello, Hans Dagelet, Dick Scheffer, Cor Witscge, Paul Gieske, Carola Gijsbers van Wijk, Arnica Elsendoorn, Guus Hoes, Peer Mascini, Jan-Anne Drenth, Liz Snoijink, Wiske Sterringa, Huib Broos, Pieter Lutz. Dir and Screenplay: Dick Maas. Pro: Matthijs van Heijningen. Ph: Marc Felperlaan, Ed: Hans van Dongen. Art: Harry Ammerlaan. No M credit. (Warner) Rel: floating; first shown London (Warner), Dec 1983. 99 mins. Cert 15.

Liquid Sky. An ambiguous mixture of sex and science-fiction concocted by a group of German expatriates living in New York. An alien arrives in a minute flying saucer and – though never seen – gets his 'kicks' (i.e. dope – Liquid Sky

Ann Carlisle in one of the year's less attractive cinematic curiosities – *Liquid Sky*.

is apparently a slang word for heroin) from a substance released in the human brain at the moment of orgasm, after which it neatly disposes of the males by a crystal shard prior to dematerialization! No doubt many of the actors involved may now wish they had stayed that way. Cast: Anne Carlisle, Paula E. Sheppard, Bob Brady, Susan Doukas, Elaine C. Grove, Stanley Knap, Jack Adalist, Otto von Wernherr, Lloyd Ziff, Harry Lum, Roy McArthur, Sara Carlisle, Nina K. Kerova, Alan Preston, Christine Hatfull, Perry Iannaconi, Roger Martencen, Calvin Haugen, Marcel Fieve, Deborah Jacobs, Inamsi, Tom Cote, Michael Dreschler, Jose Preval, etc. Dir and Pro: Slava Tsukerman. Screenplay: Tsukerman, Anne Carlisle and Nina V. Kerova. Ex Pro: Robert Field. Pro Ex: Mark Slater. Ph: Yuri Neyman. Ed: Tsukerman and Sharyn Leslie Ross. M: Tsukerman and Brenda I. Hutchinson. (Z Films–Virgin Films in assoc with VTC) Rel: floating; first shown London (ICA and Chelsea Classic), Dec 1983. 112 mins. Cert 18.

Little Ida (Growing Up) – Liten Ida. Highly effective Norwegian film set in a small coastal town during the German Occupation. It relates the story of Ida (a brilliant, winning performance by little Sunniva Lindekleiv) who is ostracized by the other children because her mother not only works for the Germans but takes one of them into her bed. The

Pia Zadora caught in a watery clinch in *The Lonely Lady*.

film's greatest achievement is the way in which, with cool balanced perception, it presents a human problem not uncommon in many countries during the war. Rest of cast: Howard Halvorsen, Lise Fjeldstad, Arne Lindtner Naess, Ellen Westerfjel, Roennaug Alten, Gunnar Olram, Anne Toft Olsen, Bernt Lindekleiv, Anne Lise Tangstad, Odd Remen, Erik Hivju, Randi Koch, Jan Erik Aune. Dir: Laila Mikkelsen. Ex Pro: Harald Ohrvik and Svein Johansen. Screenplay: Marit Paulsen and Laila Mikkelsen; based on the former's novel. Ph: Hans Welin and Kjell Vassdal. Ed: Peter Falck. Art: Anders Barreus. M: Eyvind Solas. (Liten Ida Norsk Film A/S, Oslo-Svenska Filminstitutet Stockholm-Minema Releasing) Rel: floating; first shown London (Minema), Oct 1983. 88 mins. Cert PG.

The Lonely Lady. Having launched his wife Pia Zadora as a potential new cinematic sensational sexpot in *Butterfly* in 1982, her gallant millionaire spouse tries again in this adaptation of a typical Harold Robbins novel in which Miss Z plays a writer in Hollywood who finds that beds are the surest way to producers' hearts! Rest of cast: Lloyd Bochner, Bibi Besch, Joseph Cali, Anthony Holland, Jared Martin, Ray Liotta, Carla Romanelli, Olivier Pierre, Kendal Kaldwell, Lou Hirsch, Kerry Shale, Sandra Dickinson, Shane Rimmer, Nancy Wood, Ed Bishop. Dir: Peter Sasdy, Pro: Robert R. Weston. Assoc Pro: Tino Barzie. Screenplay: John Kershaw and Shawn Randall;

based on the Harold Robbins novel, adapted by Ellen Shepard. Ph: Brian West. Ed: Keith Palmer. Pro Des: Enzo Bulgarelli. M: Charles Calello. (Universal–Thorn EMI) Rel: 18 Nov 1983. 92 mins. Cert PG.

Lone Wolf McQuade. Modern Western in the Sergio Leone spaghetti Westerns tradition of the sixties, with plenty of action, double-dyed villainy, self-sacrifical love and bullet-splattered death: all of which would be repellently brutal if taken seriously instead of as the often amusing business it is. Chuck Norris is excellent as the super-tough lone-wolf Texas Ranger who finally comes to respect his young Mexican partner (Robert Beltran) as the battle against arms-smuggling villain David Carradine gets more deadly. Rest of cast: Barbara Carrera, Leon Isaac Kennedy, L.Q. Jones, Dana Kimmell, R.G. Armstrong, Jorge Cervera Jr., Sharon Farrell, Daniel Frishman, William Sanderson, John Anderson, Robert Arenas, Tommy Ballard, Jeff Bannister, Anthony E. Caglia, Eli Cummins, Jesus 'Chuy' de Layo, Oscar Hidalgo, Robert Jordan, Joe Kaufenberg, Susan Kaufenberg, Velma Nieto, Aaron Norris, Don Pike, Gary Pike, Gil Reyes, Martha Saldana, Hector Serrano, Deborah Shore, Richard Terschel, Franco Toth, William J. Wagner, Stunt persons: J. Barrett, D.L. Benjamin, S. Boisseree, C. Boss, J. de Pland, R. Dodson, A. Gibbs, D. Hansen, D. Heide, K. Hodder, S. Hulin, J. Jensen, M. Johnson, A. Jones, A. Marcus, R. McCallum, R. Mendez, L. Morarles, B. Orrison, C. Skeen. Dir: Steve Carver, Pro: Carver and Yoram Ben-Ami, Screenplay: B.J. Nelson; from the story by H. Kaye Dyal and B.J. Nelson. Ph: Robert Shearman (Texas), Jerry Callaway and Michael Sibley. Ed: Anthony Redman. Pro Des: Norm Baron. M: Francesco de Maso: (Harmonica Player: Franco de Gemini) Assoc Pro: Kathryn Petty and Aaron Norris. Pro Con: Nava Levin. (Orion Pictures–Rank Dist) Rel: 25 Nov 1983. 107 mins. Cert 18.

Loose Connections. A minor British romantic comedy about an eventful car journey from London to Munich undertaken by a feminist girl and her (advertised-for) co-pilot, a chauvinis-

Chuck Norris (above and left) gives a convincing macho performance as the Texas Ranger in *Lone Wolf McQuade*.

The Lords of Discipline. Brutalizing and – hopefully – quite incredible goings-on at a Carolina Military Institute which makes the similarly tough institution pictured in *An Officer and a Gentleman* look like a kids' nursery school. At the CMI you are likely to be castrated, tortured, and otherwise violently abused if your face doesn't fit in with the officially tolerated secret society. David Keith plays the final year cadet who rebels against the system when a negro inductee is nearly maimed for life. A fast moving, tightly directed, most ably acted, but nevertheless repelling picture of one facet of America's military life. Rest of cast: Robert Prosky, G.D. Spradlin, Barbara Babcock, Michael Biehn, Rick Rossovich, John Lavachielli, Mitchell Lichtenstein, Mark Breland, Malcolm Danare, Judge Reinhold, Greg Webb, 'Wild' Bill Paxton, Dean Miller, Ed Bishop, Stuart Milligan, Katharine Levy, Jason Connery, Rolf Saxon, Michael Horton, Ian Tyler, Norman Chancer, Ronald Fernee, Michael Fitzpatrick, Richard Oldfield, Matt Frewer, William Hope, Peter Hutchinson, Peter Merrill, Sheridan Earl Russel, Simon Shepherd, Aaron Schwartz, Graham Cull, Mark Eadie, Tom Fry, Lee Galpin, Dean Lawrence, Martin Phillips, Joe Searby, Christopher Warrick, Sarah Brackett, Mart Ellen Ray, Helena Stevens, Valerie Colgan, Nichola King, Sallyanne Law, Elizabeth Morton, Kim Thomson, Sophie Ward. Dir: Franc Roddam. Pro: Herb Jaffe and Gabriel Katzka.

tic, almost moronic Liverpudlian. With a ticket – which he has won – but without funds, he seizes the chance of a free ride to Munich to see his team play an international match. Cast: Lindsay Duncan, Stephen Rea, Carole Harrison, Frances Low, Andrew de la Tour, David Purcell, Keith Allen, Robbie Coltrane, Ruth Bruck, Gary Olsen, Ingrid Domann, Jan Niklas, Henny Reinheimer, Anneliese Dobbertin, Eberhard Melzer, Ken Jones, Nevzat Yuceyildiz, Uwe-Karsten Koch, Joachim Regelien, Otto Bleidner, Benjamin Kramer. Dir: Richard Eyre. Pro: Simon Perry. Assoc Pro: Paul Cowan. Screenplay: Maggie Brooks. Ph: Clive Tickner. No Ed credit. M: Dominic Muldowney ('Loose Connections'), 'Living Apart Together', 'You Can Kick Me Out of the Country', M. and lyrics by Andy Roberts, sung by him and Melanie Harrold). Filmed on location in Britain, Belgium and West Germany. (National Film Finance Corp/Virgin Films–Fox) Rel: 18 May 1984. 95 mins. Cert PG.

Stephen Rea and Lindsay Duncan as the 'odd couple' in *Loose Connections*.

Officer Robert Prosky details David Keith to protect negro cadet Mark Breland (above) in *The Lords of Discipline*.

Assoc Pro: Basil Rayburn. Screenplay: Thomas Pope and Lloyd Fonvielle; based on the novel by Pat Conroy. Ph: Brian Tufano. Ed: Michael Ellis. Pro Des: John Graysmark. Art: Alan Cassie. M: Howard Blake. Pro Con: John Sargent. (Paramount–UIP) Rel: 1 Sept 1983. 102½ mins. Cert 15.

Losin' It. More American schoolboys seeking sex, this time a trio of teenagers hoping to exchange cash for carnal experience in Tijuana. During their journey South the lads (three rather nice performances, lifting the all too familiar theme a notch or two above the groove) meet various characters and adventures, all finally climaxed by the routine comedy car chase. Cast: Tom Cruise, Jackie Earle Haley, John Stockwell, Shelley Long, John P. Navin Jr., Henry Darrow, Hector Elias, Daniel Faraldo. Dir: Curtis Hanson. Pro: Bryan Gindoff and Hannah Hampstead. Ex Pro: Joel B. Michaels and Garth H. Drabinsky. Screenplay: B.W.L. Norton. Ph: Gil Taylor. Ed: Richard Halsey. Pro Des: Robb Wilson King. Art: Vance Lorenzini. M: Ken Wannberg. (Embassy Pictures–Alpha/Intervision) Rel: 6 April 1984. 105 mins. Cert 18.

Love Streams. The 1984 Golden Bear winner at the Berlin Film Festival. Although most certainly some of director/writer John Cassavetes's best work yet – and likely to prove to be among his three most successful B.O. movies – it still probably appeals to festival and like audiences rather than the general cinemagoer. It is far too long for its own good, with plenty of prunable repetition, but with a lot of good stuff in it. A complex story about a writer using his home for research into the subject of his next book – on love for sale – and his sister, who is on the losing side of a custody battle, both trying and finally failing to come to terms with life and ending up with only each other. Cast: John Cassavetes, Gena Rowlands, Diahnne Abbott, Seymour Cassel, Margaret Abbott, Jakob Shaw, Risa Blewitt, John Roselius, Michelle Conaway, Eddy Donno. Dir: John Cassavetes. Pro: Menahem Golan and Yoram Globus. Ex Pro: Al Ruban. Screenplay: Cassavetes and Ted Allan; based on the latter's play. Ph: Al Ruban. Ed: George Villasenor. Pro Des: Phedon Papamichael. M: Bo Harwood. (Cannon Group) Rel: floating; first shown London (Classic, Shaftesbury Ave), March 1984. 138 mins. Cert 15.

The Man from Snowy River. An Australian film previously shown in this country at a few spots but only now getting a proper release. The story, set in the Mountains of the Great Divide in the late 1800s, about a young man who finds it far from easy to prove himself a real mountain man, but eventually succeeds in doing so by bringing in the prize horse he has himself gentled, after it has been let loose by a couple of villainous characters – at the same time winning the rancher's pretty daughter. A sort of 'down-under' Western with something of a *Wilderness Family*-cum-Disney atmosphere. Cast: Kirk Douglas, Jack Thompson, Tom Burlinson, Sigrid Thornton, Lorraine Bayly, Terence Donovan, June Jago, Gus Mercurio, David Bradshaw, Tony Bonner, Chris Haywood, Tommy Dysart, Bruce Kerr, Kristopher Steele, Howard Eynon, John Nash, Jack Lovick, Charlie Lovick, John Lovick, Frank Hearn, Jack Purcell, Gerald Egan, Bill Stacey, Ken Connley, Brandan Purcell, Greg Purcell, Mick Hulse, Max Scalon, Paul Purcell, Peter McElroy, Rob Purcell, Dick Forrest, Ron Purcell, Chester Wallis, Noel Egan, Brian Wallis, Basil Egan, Peter Wallis, Ricky Spottiswood, Bernie Wallis, Bruce McCornack, Terry Walsh, John Coombes, Geoff Burrowes, Adrian Daniels, Graeme Stoney, Gerard Comerford, Lloyd Parkes, Bill Wil-

loughby, Rocky Black, Tom Purcell, Heath Harris, Kevin Stewart, Jim James, Louis Trifunovic, Joe Jury, Bob Vienna, Peter Maher, Jim Walsh, Stan McKay. Dir: George Miller. Pro: Geoff Burrowes. Pro Sup: Michael Lake. Ex Pro: Michael Edgley and Simon Wincer. Pro Co-Ord: Trish Foley. Screenplay: John Dixon; from an original script by Fred Cul Cullen; based in turn on a poem by A. B. Paterson. Ph: Keith Wagstaff. Ed: Adrian Carr. Art: Leslie Binns. M: Bruce Rowland. (Michael Edgley/International/Cambridge Films-Fox) Rel: floating; 104 mins. Cert PG.

Man of Flowers. A remarkable Australian film from Paul Cox which is highly individual, superbly artistic, consistently fascinating, and contains one of the finest performances of the year from any source. Norman Kaye as the Oedipus-scarred middle-aged recluse writes to his dead mother every day, collects works of art, loves and smothers his home in flowers, plays his own works on the nearby church organ, and every week pays a pretty girl to come and strip to the buff for his visual pleasure, to background music by Donizetti. When the girl's crude charlatan painter boyfriend attempts to blackmail him, he deals with him in his own bizarre, cold but highly effective way. It is a marvellously controlled performance by the actor-musician in a film of endless sexual and artistic subtleties. Rest of cast: Alyson Best, Chris

Haywood, Sarah Walker, Julia Blake, Bob Ellis, Barry Dickins, Patrick Cook, Victoria Eagger, Werner Herzog, Hilary Kelly, James Stratford, Eileen Joyce, Marianne Baillieu, Lirit Bilu, Juliet Bacskai, Dawn Klingberg, Tony Llewellyn-Jones. Dir Screenplay and Co Pro: (with Jane Balantye) Paul Cox. Assoc Pro: Tony Llewellyn-Jones. Ph: Yuri Sokol. Ed: Tim Lewis. Dialogue: Bob Ellis. Art: Asher Bilu. M: excerpts from Donizetti's *Lucia di Lammermoor* sung by Montserrat Caballé and José Carreras, with New Philharmonia Orch con Jesus Lopez Cobos. (Palace Pictures) Rel: floating; first shown London (Screen-on-the-Hill), June 1984. 91 mins. Cert 18.

The Man Who Loved Women. A minor Reynolds . . . Burt as the wealthy Los Angeles sculptor whose passion for women gets a jolt when sudden inner confusion is allied to impotence. So lovely and sympathetic lady psychiatrist Julie Andrews has to help him back to male confidence . . . ! Rest of cast: Kim Basinger, Marilu Henner, Cynthia Sikes, Jennifer Edwards, Sela Ward, Ellen Bauer, Denise Crosby, Tracy Vaccaro, Barry Corbin, Ben Powers, Shelly Manne, Don Menza,

Burt Reynolds turns his attentions to Marilu Henner in *The Man Who Loved Women.*

James G. Rowles, Andrew Simpkins, Jill Carroll, Schweitzer Tanney, Regis Philbin, Joseph Bernard, John J. Flynn Jr., Jim Knaub, Jim Lewis, Roger Rose, Jennifer Ashley, Tony Brown, Philip Alexander, Jonathan Rogal, Margie Denecke, Jerry Martin, Sharon Hughes, Nanci Rogers, Kai J. Wong, Walter Soo Hoo, Marilyn Child, Cindi Dietrich, Arnie Moore, Lisa Blake Richards, Noni White, Lynn Webb, Jason Ross, Alisa Lee, Cis Rundle, Marcheline Bertrand, Cathy St. George, Ola Marie Ray, Sheila Ryan, Susan Mechsner, Jeri Gale, Chanelle Lea, Maureen O'Connor, Sondra Theodore, Judy Balduzzi, Suzanne Kent, Mary Lynne Gehr, Cindy Landis, Lori Scott, Mayra Fornos, Mary Steele, Paula Jones, Ellyn Stern, Tamara Barkley, Bruiser Reynolds (the dog). The ballet *Swan Lake*, performed by the Los Angeles Ballet Co. Dir: Blake Edwards. Pro: Edwards and Tony Adams. Ex Pro: J.D. Krane. Assoc Pro: Gerald T. Nutting. Screenplay: Edwards, Milton Wexler and Geoffrey Edwards. Ph: Haskell Wexler. Ed: Ralph E. Winters. Pro Des: Roger Maus. Art: Jack Senter. M: Henry Mancini (theme song 'Little Boys' by Mancini, lyrics by Alan and Marilyn Bergman perf by Helen Reddy). (Columbia/Delphi–Columbia) Rel: 15 June 1984. 110 mins. Cert 15.

Martin Sheen with his son from a casual Paris liaison (Sebastian Dugan), and his wife, Blythe Danner (far right), in *Man, Woman and Child*.

Man, Woman & Child. Charming domestic comedy, marred only by the most unlikely and illogical ending, about an American professor who suddenly discovers that a 10-year-old orphan is his own – French – son and whose decision to bring him to America for a holiday leads to family upheavals between him, his wife and his two young daughters. Convincing, intelligent, thoughtful (apart from the ending) and beautifully acted, with little Sebastian Dungan giving a most impressive performance as the very self-contained little boy. Rest of cast: Martin Sheen, Blythe Danner, Craig T. Nelson, David Hemmings, Nathalie Nell, Maureen Anderman, Arlene McIntyre, Missy Francis, Billy Jacoby, Ruth Silveira, Jacques François, Randy Dreyfus, Lisa Figieroa, Frank Koppola, David O. Thomas, Jan Stratton, John Wyler, Gwil Richards, Lila Waters, James Beach, Richard McGonagle, Grace Woodward, Louis Plante, Dennis Redfield, Frederick Contron, Anne Bruner, Eve Douglas,

Lorraine Williams, Mark E. Boucher, David E. Boucher, Homey Taylor. Dir: Dick Richards. Pro: Elmo Williams and Elliott Kastner. Ex Pro: Stanley Beck. Ex in charge of Pro: David Selven. Assoc Pro: Stacy Williams. Screenplay: Erich Segal and David Z. Goodman; based on the novel by Segal. Ph: Richard H. Kline. Ed: David Bretherton. Pro Des: Dean Edward Mitzner. M: Georges Delerue (Song 'Never Gone' by Delerue, with lyrics by David Pomeranz and Buddy Kaye, sung by Edie Lehmann). (Gaylord Productions/Elliott Kastner Presentations–Columbia) Rel: 15 Sept 1983. 100 mins. Cert PG.

Merry Christmas Mr. Lawrence. That extreme rarity, a British-Japanese co-production. A quite remarkable achievement by Nagisa Oshima in bringing to the screen the Laurens Van Der Post novel *The Seed and the Sower*, which examines in some depth the clash of Western and Eastern social and moral codes and philosophies and comes up with the conclusion that both races are prisoners of their respective upbringing and outlook. The package in which this message is carried is an

absorbing story of brutal life in a Japanese POW Camp in Java in 1942, where the constant beatings and degradation of the British and Allied prisoners is occasionally lightened by a curious affinity between captured and captors. A high level of direction only very slightly flawed by the flashbacks to a strangely unreal Britain. A superb performance by Tom Conti as the Japanese-speaking Lieut-Col. Lawrence, a fine one by Takeshi and effective ones by David Bowie, Jack Thompson and Ryuichi Sakamoto, a Japanese Pop Star who also wrote the fascinating musical soundtrack. Rest of cast: Johnny Okura, Alastair Browning, James Malcolm, Chris Broun, Yuya Uchida, Ryunosuke Kaneda, Takashi Naito, Tamio Ishikura, Rokko Toura, Hiroshi Mikami, Yuji Honma, Daisuke Itjima, Hideo Murota, Barry Dorking, Geoff Clendon, Grant Bridger, Richard Adams, Geoff Allan, Michael Baxter-Lax, Marc Berg, Marcus Campbell. Dir: Nagisa Oshima. Pro: Jeremy Thomas. Ex Pro: Masato Hara, Eiko Oshima, Geoffrey Nethercott and Terry Glinwood. Assoc Pro: John Herlihy and Larry Parr. Screenplay: Oshima and Paul Mayersberg, based on the novel by Laurens Van Der Post. Ph: Toichiro Narushima. Ed: Tomoyo Oshima. Pro Des: Shigemasa Toda. Art: Andrew Sanders. M: Ryuichi Sakamoto. (Palace Pictures) Rel: 10 Nov 1983. 120 mins. Cert 15.

Metalstorm – The Destruction of Jared-Syn. Stereovision 3-D minor *Star Wars* spin-off, in which interstellar lawman Jeffrey Byron confronts villain Mike Preston on some far-off arid planet. Space 'Western' presumably aimed at young audiences. Rest of cast: Tim Thomerson, Kelly Preston, Richard Moll, David Smith, Mickey Fox. Dir and Co-Pro (with Alan J. Adler): Charles Band. Ex Pro: Albert Band and Arthur H. Maslansky. Screenplay: Alan J. Adler. Ph: Mac Ahlberg. Ed: Brad Arensman. Art: Pamela B. Warner. M: Richard Band (Charles Band–Universal–Arista Films–Entertainment Film Dist) Rel: 25 Feb 1984. 83 mins. Cert PG.

Mickey's Christmas Carol. After an interval of almost thirty years Walt Disney's most famous creation makes a highly entertaining comeback in a half-hour cartoon based on the Dickens classic seasonal story. And Mickey is surrounded by a very famous supporting cast, which includes Donald Duck, Goofy and Jiminy Cricket among others. (Walt Disney Productions–U.K. Film Dist) Rel: 16 Dec 1983. 26 mins. Cert U.

Mighty Mouse in the Great Space Chase. Animated feature which combines some sixteen episodes from an American TV series starring Paul Terry's 1940s cartoon creations such as Harry the Heartless, the feline villain, and Mighty Mouse the hero, with Pearl Pureheart, another pussycat, as heroine. Dir: Ed Friedman, Lou Kachivas, Marsh Lamore, Gwen Wetzier, Kay Wright and Lou Zukor. Pro: Lou Scheimer, Norm Prescott and Don Christensen. Pro Con: Bob Wilson. Ph: R.W. Pope. Ed: James Blodgett, Ann Hagerman and Earl Biddle. M: Yvette Blais and Jeff Michael. With the voices of Allen Oppenheimer and Diane Pershing. (Filmation Assoc/Viacom International–Miracle) Rel: floating. 87 mins. Cert U.

The Mission. Extremely topical (when premiered) anti-Khomeini Iranian-American film about a young hit man

Mickey Mouse takes the role of Bob Cratchit in *Mickey's Christmas Carol.*

sent from Iran to murder a dissident refugee living in New York, who quite by accident becomes friendly with the man he has been ordered to kill. Through this association with the refugee and his free-thinking daughter, the assassin gradually recognizes the true nature of the casual brutality and corruption of the 'New' regime. Refusing to kill without proof of the victim's guilt, he decides to go home with his assignment unfinished but is himself murdered by His Eminence on the way to the airport – just as another young Iranian replacement hit man arrives with a murder assignment. A carefully balanced, intelligent and thought-provoking movie, well acted and

Bowie with small brother James Malcolm and below right Commandant Ryuichi Sakamoto, in *Merry Christmas Mr. Lawrence.*

polished in every technical department. Cast: Houshang Touzie, Parviz Sayyad, Mary Apick, Mohammed B. Gaffari, Hedyeh Anvar, Hatam Anvar, Kamran Nozad. Dir, Pro and Written by Parviz Sayyad: based on an idea by Sayyad and Hesam Kowsar. Ph: Reza Aria. (New Film Group, USA/Aria–Film, FGR–Palace Pictures) Rel: floating; first shown London (Academy), May 1984. 104 mins. Cert PG.

Monkey Grip. Another superior Australian contribution; exploring the depressing sexual life-style of the Melbourne arty set (actors, writers, pop people and the like) in general, and a year in the life of one member in particular. A thirty-ish divorcee becomes hopelessly embroiled with a drug-addict, a totally unreliable and self-obsessed actor who treats her like an object, but whom she continually takes back into her bed. An outstanding (and Australian Awards winning) performance by Noni Hazelhurst as the unhappy lady. Rest of cast: Colin Friels, Alice Garner, Harold Hopkins, Candy Raymond, Michael Caton, Tim Burns, Christina Amphlett, Don Miller-Robinson, Lisa Peers, Cathy Downes. Dir: Ken Cameron. Pro: Patricia Lovell. Ex Pro: Danny Collins. Screenplay: Ken Cameron in assoc with Helen Garner. Ph: David Gribble. Ed: David Huggett. Pro Des: Clark Munro. Assoc Pro: Treisha Ghent. M: Bruce Smeaton: special rock music composed by Mark McEntee and Christina Amphlett, perf by Divinyls. (Pavilion Films–Mainline Pictures) Rel: floating;

Noni Hazel (below and right), a delightfully natural actress, in *Monkey Grip*.

John Cleese offering gargantuan diner Terry Jones the last fateful mouthful in *Monty Python's The Meaning of Life*.

first shown London (Cinecenta, ABC Fulham Rd and Screen-on-the-Hill), Nov 1983. 102 mins. Cert 18.

Monty Python's The Meaning of Life. If the rumour is true that this is the last cinema movie the Python people will make as a team, it seems a very wise decision, for this one shows the original impact lessened, the wit and the craziness running out, and the efforts to

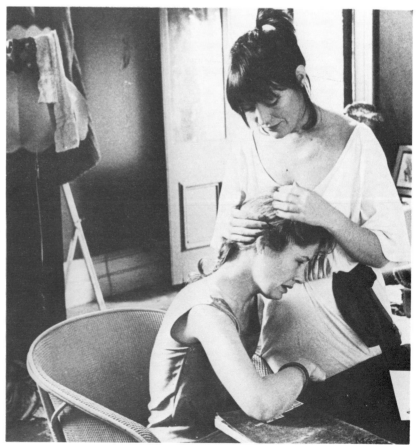

provoke becoming more and more desperate as the humour becomes sicker – literally in one episode where a gourmand, after spraying the restaurant and diners with his vomit, explodes; and most certainly in the Live Transplant episode in which the kidneys are torn from a live, protesting donor. But every so often the old wit and superb comic invention shines through the muck, to some extent balancing the balance sheet. Of the team, Eric Idle scores most heavily, not only appearing in many of the 'chapters' but writing lyrics and music for some excellent numbers. Rest of cast: Graham Chapman, John Cleese, Terry Gilliam, Terry Jones and Michael Palin (all of whom are also credited with the writing), Carol Cleveland, Judy Loe, Simon Jones, Andrew Maclachlan, Valerie Whittington, Patricia Quinn, Mark Holmes, Jennifer Franks, Imogen Bickford-Smith, George Silver, Angela Mann, Chris Grant, Peter Lovstrom. Dir: Terry Jones. Pro: John Goldstone. Dir of Animation and Special Sequences: Terry Gilliam. Ph: Peter Hannan. Ed: Julian Doyle. Pro Des: Harry Lange. Art: Richard Dawking. M: 'The Meaning of Life', 'Galaxy Song' and 'Accountancy Shanty'; lyrics and/or music by Eric Idle and John du Prez: 'Oh Lord Please Don't Burn Us', lyrics by John Cleese and Graham Chapman, music by Idle and du Prez: 'Every Sperm is Sacred', lyrics by Michael Palin and Terry Jones, music by Andre Jacquemin and Dave Howman; 'Penis Song', lyrics and music by Idle; 'Christmas in Heaven', lyrics by Terry Jones, music by Idle. (Universal–UIP) Rel: 25 Aug 1983. 106½ mins. Cert 18.

The Moon in the Gutter – La Lune dans le Carniveau. Jean-Jacques Beineix's Franco-Italian screen adaptation of the David Goodis whodunit. A wilfully, and often rather woefully, stylish, periodically pictorially stunningly effective, over-arty yet overall consistently fascinating story of love, desire, violent death and revenge, set fairly and squarely in 1938 *Quai des Brumes* territory. Gérard Dépardieu as the stolid stevedore searching for the man who raped his sister and sent her to a suicide's death, Nastassja Kinski as the lovely, slumming little rich girl who is attracted by the muscles. An overlong mixture of the bad, the (often very)

Michael Keaton, the husband who changes roles with his wife, in *Mr. Mum.*

good and the indifferent, all adding up to a real collector's piece. Rest of cast: Victoria Abril, Vittorio Mezzogiorno, Dominique Pinon, Bertrice Reading, Gabriel Monnet, Milena Vukotic, Bernard Farcy, Ann-Marie Coffinet, Katia Berger, Jacques Herlin, Rudo Alberti, Ross Fumeto, Grasiano Giusti, Fred Ulysse, Victor Cavallo, Jean-Roger Milo, Jean-Pierre Laurent, Claudia Pola. Dir and Screenplay (latter with Olivier Mergault): Jean-Jacques Beineix: based on the book of the same title by David Goodis. Pro: Lise Fayolle. Pro Sup: Hubert Niogret. Ph: Philippe Rousselot. Ed: Monique Prim and Yves Deschamps. Art: Hilton McConnico. Set Designs: Sandro Dell'Orco and Angelo Santucci. M: Gabriel Yared. (Gaumont & TFI Productions–Palace Pictures) Rel: floating; first shown London (Lumiere), Jan 1984. 130 mins. Cert 18.

Mr. Mum. A big box-office success in America, this quite charming and sometimes chuckly comedy is about the sacked hubbie who looks after the home and kids while Mom takes off her apron and goes back to work, and is soon the brightest light in her approving – and soon lecherous – boss's formerly not very successful advertising agency. Nice performances from Michael Keaton as the male mum and Teri Garr as the efficient worklady. Rest of cast: Frederick Koehler, Taliesin Jaffe, Courtney and Brittany White, Martin Mull, Ann Jillian, Jeffrey Tambor, Christopher Lloyd, Tom Leopold, Graham Jarvis, Carolyn Seymour, Michael Alaimo, Valri Bromfield, Charles Woolf, Miriam Flynn, Derek McGrath, Michael Ensign, Ken Olfson, Frank Birney, Hilary Beane, Edie McClurg, Patti Deutsch, Estelle Omens, Patty Dworkin, Bernadette Birkett, James Gallery, Tom Rayhall, Danny Mora, Maurice Sneed, Phil Simms, Bruce French, Henry Flores, Roger Menache, Dennis Landry, Lisa Freeman, Marley Simms, Kay Dingle, Robert Lussier, Jacque Lynn Colton, Mandy Ingber, Ken Hixon, Jane Atkins, Gerry Black, Lisa Balke Richards, Larry Flash Gordon, Leigh Walsh, John O'Leary, Valerie O'Donnell, Jacklyn McQuery, Bruce Barrington, Ted Grossman, Phil Adams, Victor Paul, Joe Dunne, Joanne Anderson, Michael Cassidy. Dir: Stan Dragoti, Pro: Lynn Loring and Lauren Shuler. Co-Pro: Harry Colomby. Ex Pro: Aaron Spelling. Screenplay: John Hughes. Ph: Victor J. Kempber. Ed: Patrick Kennedy. Pro Des: Alfred Sweeney. M: Lee Holdridge. (Thorn EMI) Rel: 25 May 1984. 91 mins. Cert PG.

My Nights With Messalina – Bacanales Romanas. Shoestring-budget Spanish soft-porn-and-corn chapter of ancient Roman orgies and the like, and unlike. A few good laughs sprinkled along the Appian Way but, one suspects, not always intentional! Cast: Raquel Evans, King Gomes, Carla

Day, 'Pipper', Tony Marono, Mirna Vec, Red Mills, Ajita Wilson, Julia Caballero, Concha Valero, Eva Wagner, Olga Rodriguez, Carlos Perez, Anjo Solon. Dir and Screenplay: Jacob Most. Pro: J. Olives and P. Balcazar. Ph: Carlos Gusi. Ed: Tony Puig. Art: Marta Cabezas. M: Jaime A. Puig. (Este Films/Balcazar/Cine d'or–Cannon Film Dist) Rel: floating; first shown London (Eros), Jan 1984. 81 mins. Cert 18.

My Tutor. The lady is given the job of teaching teenager Bobby French, but introduces an extra subject when she decides to go to bed with him. A teenage sex romp with the lads after the girls and the girls generally not objecting to the chasing. Cast: Caren Kaye, Matt Lattanzi, Kevin McCarthy, Clark Brandon, Bruce Bauer, Arlene Golonka, Crispin Glover, Amber Denyse Austin, John Vargas, Maria Melendez, Graem McGavin, Rex Ryon, Kathleen Shea, Brioni Farrel, Shelley Taylor Morgan, Kitten Natividad, Jewel Shepard, Michael Yarma, Robin Honeywell, Mora Gray, Derek Partridge, Gene Patton, Eric Lantis, Lyle Kanouse, Marilyn Tokuda, Jacqueline Jacobs, Jim Kester. Dir: George Bowers. Pro: Marilyn J. Tenser. Ex Pro: Mark Tenser. Co-Pro: Michael D. Castle. Pro Assoc: Stephen Lillis. Screenplay: Joy Roberts; from a story by Mark Tenser. Ph: Mac Ahlberg. Ed: Sidney Wolinsky. Add Ed: George Berndt. Art: Linda Pearl (Add Art: Robert Lowy). M: Webster Lewis. (Marimark–Anglo American Dist) Rel: floating; first shown London (Classic, Haymarket), Oct 1983. 97 mins. Cert 18.

Caren Kaye giving Matt Lattanzi more than French lessons in *My Tutor*.

Anne Archer is gunned down while Roger Moore, aided by Art Carney (inset), is on the murderer's trail in *The Naked Face*.

The Naked Face. James Bond Two – Roger Moore – takes times off from Bonding to play a Chicago psychiatrist in a smooth and polished Brian Forbes film, in which he is suspected of having murdered one of his patients. He has a 'hard day's night' in finding the real killer, helped by the private eye he hires – another scene (and almost film) stealing performance by Art Carney. One of the neatest – and less violent – whodunit thrillers of the year. Rest of cast: Rod Steiger, Elliott Gould, Anne Archer, David Hedison, Deanna Dunagan, Ron Parady, Dock Sollenberger, James Spinks, John Kapelos, Cynthia Baker Schuyler, Virginia Smith, Joe E. Lauck, Jimmie F. Skaggs. Mary Demas, Frankie Hill, Nancy Serlin, Sarah Partridge, Richard Burton Brown, Sheila Keenan, Roslyn Alexander, Ron Beattie, Cyndi Maxey, Rosemary Schoeninger, Jerry Tullos, Edward L. Burba, Will Zahrn, Paul Ilmer, Michael E. Meyers, Ann Bernadette Coyle, Rob Maxey, Les Podewell, John T. Stibich, Caemelo Melendez, Richard Henzel, Mark Houston, Jeffrey Feathergill, Jeff Jenkins, Corney Morgan, Martin Grace, Hank Baumert, Ed Fernandez, John Maldonado. Dir and Screenplay: Bryan Forbes (based on the book by Sidney Sheldon). Pro: Menahem Golan and Yoran Globus. Assoc Pro: Rony Yacov. Ph: David Gurfinkel. Sup Ed: Philip Shaw. Pro Des: William Fosser. M: Michael J. Lewis. (Cannon Films) Rel: 15 June 1984. 105 mins. Cert 18.

National Lampoon's Vacation. Generally mildly amusing comedy with some very funny moments, notably in two black comedy sequences. Chevy Chase takes his family by car from Chicago to Florida's 'Walley World' Entertainment Centre (which looks remarkably like Disneyland) and becomes involved in a series of comic disasters *en route*, climaxed by the final disaster of finding the place closed for renovations. There is, though, what might be termed a Happy Ending to all this, and Chase, at possibly his screen best yet, is well supported by a nice case of farceurs. Rest of cast: Beverly D'Angelo, Imogene Coca, Randy Quaid, Anthony Michael Hall, Dana Barron, Eddie Bracken, Brian Doyle-Murray, Miriam Flynn, James Keach, Eugene Levy, Frank McRae, John Candy, Christie Brinkley, Jane Krakowski, John Navin,

Nathan Cook, Christopher Jackson, Mickey Jones, John Diehl, Jeannie Dimter Barton, Randolph Dreyfuss, Virgil Wyaco II, Gerry Black, James Staley, Adelaide Wilder, Tessa Richarde, Fritz Ford, Eric Stacey Jr., Scott Perry, Dennis Freeman, Michael Talbot, John Craigmile, Dick Ziker, Pam Bebermeyer, Jophery Brown, Chere Bryson, Bill Burton, Jim Connors, Mike Deluna, David Ellis, Tony Epper, Hugh Hooker, Don Pulford, J.N. Roberts, Kenny Studer, Glenn R. Wilder, John Woodward, Julian Richard Sylvester. Dir: Harold Ramis. Pro: Matty Simmons. Assoc Pro: Robert Grand. Pro Assoc: Trevor Albert. Screenplay: John Hughes. Ph: Victor J. Kemper. Ed: Pam Herring. Pro Des: Jack Collis. M: Ralph Burns (Add M: Chris Boardman). (Warner) Rel: 20 Oct 1983. 88 mins. Cert 15.

Never Cry Wolf. Based – so 'tis claimed – on fact, this Disney movie is about a young scientist-innocent pitchforked into the Arctic with an assignment to study the wolves and their effect on the Caribou herds. The animals, the frozen wild, and a couple of delightful Eskimo characters bring the young man to a new understanding of nature, himself and the conviction that the wolves benefit rather than reduce the numbers of healthy deer. And all this never less than amusing. Cast: Charles Martin Smith, Brian Dennehy, Zachary Ittimangnaq, Samson Jorah,

The wolf, watched by Smith, Ittimangaq and Jorah, in *Never Cry Wolf.*

Chevy Chase gave one of his best screen performances in *National Lampoon's Vacation.*

Hugh Webster, Martha Ittimangnaq, Tom Dahlgren, Walker Stuart. Dir: Carroll Ballard. Pro: Lewis Allen, Jack Couffer and Joseph Strick. Ex Pro: Ron Miller. Screenplay: Curtis Hanson, Sam Hamm and Richard Kletter; based on the book by Farley Mowat. Narration written by C.M. Smith, Eugene Corr and Christina Luescher. Assoc Pro: Walker Stuart. Ph: Hiro Narita. Ed: Peter Parasheles and Michael Chandler. Art: Graeme Murray. M: Mark Isham. (Disney) Rel: 20 April 1984. 105 mins. Cert PG.

Never Say Never Again. It has taken twelve years to persuade Sean Connery to reverse his decision and once more don his old 007 role in what proves to be a sort of updated, refurbished *Thunderball.* A lively, likeable James Bond tale, decorated with plenty of humourous touches, excitement, and less – but good – gimmicks. First-rate if familiar entertainment. Good performances,

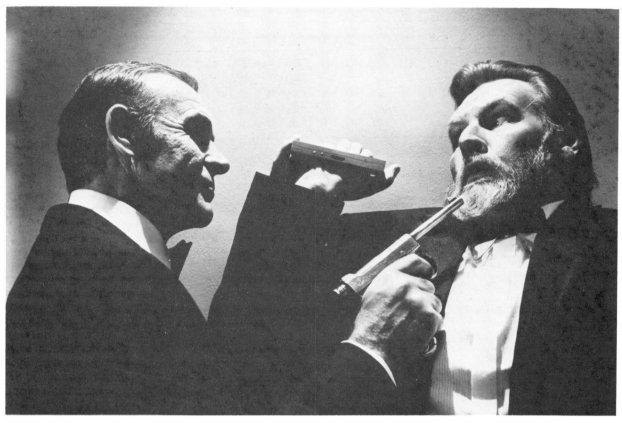

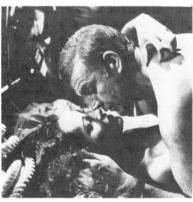

Sean Connery, *the* James Bond, at work in *Never Say Never Again*.

too, more especially by Connery, Klaus Maria Brandauer as the debonair Spectre playboy villain and Barbara Carrera as the lethal lady. Rest of cast: Max Von Sydow, Kim Basinger, Bernie Casey, Alec McCowen, Edward Fox, Pamela Salem, Rowan Atkinson, Valerie Leon, Milow Kirek, Pat Roach, Anthony Sharp, Prunella Gee, Gavan O'Herlihy, Ronald Pickup, Robert Rietty, Guido Adorni, Vincent Marzello, Christopher Reich, Billy J. Mitchell, Manning Redwood, Anthony Van Laast, Saskia Cohen Tanugi, Sylvia Marriott, Dan Meaden, Michael Medwin, Lucy Hornak, Derek Deadman, Joanna Dickens, Tony Alleff, Paul

Tucker, Brenda Kempner, Jill Meager, John Stephen Hill, Wendy Leech, Roy Bowe. Dir: Irvin Kershner. Pro: Jack Schwartzman. Ex Pro: Kevin McClory. Assoc Pro: Michael Dryhurst. Screenplay: Lorenzo Semple Jr.; based on an original story by Kevin McClory, Jack Whittingham and Ian Fleming. Ph: Douglas Slocombe. Sup Ed: Robert Lawrence. Ed: Ian Crafford. Pro Des: Philip Harrison and Stephen Grimes. Art: Michael White and Roy Stannard. Sup Art Dir: Leslie Dilley. M: Michel Legrand. Pro Sup: Alex de Grunwald. (Taliafilm in assoc with Producers Sales Org–Warner Bros) Rel: 16 Dec 1983. 134 mins. Cert PG.

New York Nights. A sort of pornographic spin-off from *La Ronde*. The sexual merry-go-round starts with the abduction and seduction of a pop star by a beautiful, drug-addicted debutante (who has him tossed out of the car when she has obtained her satisfaction); and ends with the same girl seducing her business magnate stepfather—with a lot of nude squirming, gasping and such-

like in between. Cast: Corrine Alphen, Nicholas Cortland, George Ayer, Marcia McBroom, Bobbi Burns, Cynthia Lee, Peter Matthey, William Dysart, Missy O'Shea. Dir and Screenplay: Romano Vanderbes. Production-Dir: Simon Nuchtern. Ph: Alan Dobeman. Ed: Victor Zimet. M: Linda Schreyer. (International Talent Marketing–Brent Walker) Rel: floating; first shown London (Prince Charles), Nov 1983. 109 mins. Cert 18.

Corrine Alphen in *New York Nights*.

Octopussy – brilliantly polished hokum with Roger Moore in the mantle of Bond.

Nostalgia-Nostalghia. Winning the 'Grand Prize for Creative Cinema' as well as the Critics' Prize at the 1983 Cannes Film Festival, this Andrei Tarkovsky, Russian, film, made mostly in Italy, seems destined to become a great highbrow classic, flawed though it is by a complete lack of pace, far too dark and shadowed photography and, at times, seemingly wilful lack of clarity in its storytelling. But it is poetic, personal and full of stunning images as well as being philosophical and full of allusions, both religious and political. It tells of a Russian poet researching an 18th-century musician, a fellow countryman, who lived in Italy; both find separation from, and nostalgia for, Mother Russia difficult to bear. The remarkably effective scenes include the attempt to cross a pond with a lighted candle and a madman's protest in Rome, climaxed by setting himself alight. Cast: Oleg Yankovsky, Domiziana Giordano, Erland Josephson, Patrizia Terreno, Laura de Marchi, Delia Boccardo, Milena Vukotic, Alberto Canepa. Dir: Andrei Tarkovsky. Ex Pro: Manolo Bolognini. Screenplay:

Tarkovsky and Tonino Guerra. Ph: Giuseppe Lanci. Ed: Amedeo Salfa and Erminia Marani. Art: Andrea Grisanti. M Consultant: Gino Perguri. (Rai Rete 2/Opera Film–Artificial Eye) Rel: floating; first shown London (Lumiere Cinema), Nov 1983. 125 mins. Cert 15.

Octopussy. The 007 mixture much as before; a lush and lavish fun film which mixes thrills with laughs and lots of utter incredibility, and jells them into top-class light-hearted entertainment. With Roger Moore as the imperturbable, if sometimes careless, British agent, Maud Adams, the delectable lady with doubtful morals of the title, and Louis Jourdan as the villain – all of them involved in a wildly improbable plot by a power-crazy Soviet General to double-cross his Kremlin mates and start up a nuclear war with the Americans. Rest of cast: Kristina Wayborn, Kabir Bedi, Steven Berkoff, David Meyer, Vijay Amritraj, Desmond Llewelyn, Robert Brown, Walter Gotell, Geoffrey Keen, Suzanne Jerome, Cherry Gillespie, Albert Moses, Douglas Wilmer, Andy Bradford, Lois Maxwell, Michaela Clavell, Philip Voss, Bruce Boa, Richard Parmentier, Paul Hard-

wick, Dermot Crowley, Peter Porteous, Eva Rueber-Staier, Jeremy Bullock, Tina Hudson, William Derrick, Stuart Saunders, Patrick Barr, Gabor Vernon, Hugo Bower, Ken Norris, Tony Arjuna, Gertan Klauber, Brenda Cowling, David Grahame, Brian Coburn, Michael Halphie. Stunters: Dorothy Ford, Clive Curtis, Del Baker, Pat Banta, Bill Weston, Rocky Taylor, Jim Dowdall, Wayne Michaels, Nick Hobbs, Jazzer Jeyes, Christopher Webb, Malcolm Weaver; Stunt Supervisors: Martin Grace, Paul Weston and Bill Burton. The Girls: Mary Stavin, Carolyn Seaward, Carole Ashby, Cheryl Anne, Jani-Z, Julie Martin, Joni Flynn, Julie Barth, Kathy Davies, Helene Hunt, Gillian de Terville, Safira Afzal, Louise King, Tina Robinson, Alison Worth, Janine Andrews, Lynda Knight. Dir: John Glen. Pro: Albert R. Broccoli. Ex Pro: Michael G. Wilson. Assoc Pro: Thomas Pevsner. Story and Screenplay: George Macdonald Fraser, Richard Maibaum and Michael G. Wilson. Ph: Alan Hume. Pro Des: Peter Lamont. M: John Barry. Lyrics: Tim Rice (title song sung by Rita Coolidge). Sup Ed: John Grover. Special Effects Sup: John Richardson. 2nd Unit Dir and Ph: Arthur Wooster. Pro

George C. Scott (far left), Tim Curry, Cherie Lunghi and Richard Charles (also above) in *Oliver Twist*.

Sup: Hugh Harlow. Art: John Fenner. (Broccoli–MGM/UA–UIP) Rel: 4 August 1983. 130 mins. Cert PG.

Oliver Twist. Somewhat surprisingly, this appears to be only the third time that the Dickens classic has been adapted to the screen; once in 1948, again twenty years later (the film of the stage musical *Oliver*) and now – made primarily for television. Unfortunately the verve and pace of the musical makes this straightforward version seem a little mundane; yet obviously this particular *Oliver* is nearer to the original. Richard Charles presents the workhouse boy as a wan little waif and it is left to George C. Scott as Fagin to get what acting honours there are going. Rest of cast: Tim Curry, Michael Hordern, Timothy West, Eileen Atkins, Cherie Lunghi, Oliver Cotton, Martin Tempest, Matthew Duke, Eleanor David, Philip Locke, Spencer Rheult, Ann Tirard, Ann Beach, Brenda Cowling, John Barrard, Bill Dean, Declan Mulholland, Dax Jackson, Dominic Martinelli, Paul Davies Prowles, Robert Russell, Roy Evans, Astra Sheridan, Lysette Anthony, Artro Morris, Philip Davis, Michael Logan, Debbie Arnold, Nicholas Davies, John Savident. Dir: Clive Donner. Pro: Ted Childs and Norton Romsey. Ex Pro: William F. Storke. Screenplay: James Goldman; based on the Charles Dickens novel. Pro Sup: Ron Fry. Ph: Norman Langley. Ed: Peter Tanner. Pro Des: Tony

Curtis. M: Nick Bicat. (Claridge Group/ Grafton Productions–Trident Television–Enterprise Pictures) Rel: 3 Nov 1983. 103 mins. Cert. PG.

One from the Heart. The musical with which Francis Ford Coppola launched his ambitious Zoetrope filming method

in his own special studios. An expensive enterprise costing, according to report, some $25 million, and in America (up to mid-1983) only bringing back $1 million in revenue, which sad fact forced Coppola into putting the studios up for sale. The story concerns a vulgar slob whose pretty wife, after an adventure with a handsome waiter-dancer-singer, finds she can't leave the by now

Raul Julia and Teri Garr (also inset) dance the night away in *One from the Heart*.

weeping lover. All somewhat incredible but technically fascinating and innovative, with some exciting sequences, colourful Vegas backgrounds and charming performances by Teri Garr – as the silly girl – Natassja Kinski and Raul Julia. Rest of cast: Frederick Forrest, Lainie Kazan, Harry Dean Stanton, Allen Goodwitz, Jeff Hamlin, Italia Coppola, Carmine Coppola. Dir: Francis Ford Coppola. Pro: Gray Frederickson and Fred Roos. Ex Pro: Bernard Gerstein. Co-Pro: Armyan Bernstein. Screenplay: Bernstein and Coppola: from the former's story. Dir of Ph: Ronald V. Garcia. Ph: Vittorio Storado. Ed: Anne Goursaud, with Rudi Fehr and Randy Roberts. Pro Des: Dean Tavoularis. Special Visual Effects: Robert Swarthe. M: Tom Waits (songs by him, sung by Crystal Gayle and Tom Waits). (Zoetrope Studios–Artificial Eye) Rel: floating; first shown London (Lumiere), July 1983. 107 mins. Cert 15.

Order of Death. Italian film (made in New York) about a cop killer which packs so much in that, bad as it often is, it remains consistently fascinating with it's killings, torture, psychological trimmings and weird excursions into Hitchcockian territory. A remarkable performance by Harvey Keitel as a guilt-ridden cop and a debut for John Lydon, who is better known as former punk pop performer Johnny Rotten. Rest of cast: Nicole Garcia, Leonard Mann, Sylvia Sidney, Carla Romanelli, Bob Kelly, Tony Mayer, Harriet Kurland, Paul Ragonese, Al Sheppard, Mike Tremont. Dir: Robert Faenza. Pro: Elda Ferri. Assoc Pro: Roberto Cicutto. Pro. Co-Ord: Bob Colesberry and Gianmaria Vismara. Screenplay: Faenza, Hugh Fleetwood and Ennio de Concini; based on Fleetwood's novel of the same title. Ph: Giuseppe Pinori. Ed: Nino Baragli. Art: Giantito Burchiellaro. M: Ennio Morricone. (Jean Vigo Srl in assoc with RAI Radiotelevisione Italiana–Virgin Films) Rel: floating; first shown London (Classic, Oxford St), Oct 1983. 105 mins. Cert 18.

The Osterman Weekend. Making his come-back after five years, Sam Peckinpah has made a pretty good job of this adaptation of Robert Ludlum's book, although he can't make the story any more credible or easy to follow than the

John Hurt as the ruthless CIA agent in *The Osterman Weekend.*

original. It is all about the CIA and its villainy, with ambitious politician Burt Lancaster assigning John Hurt the job of convincing unfortunate TV journalist Rutger Hauer that his best friends are Soviet agents, brutally manipulating everyone to achieve his ends. Rest of cast: Dennis Hopper, Chris Sarandon, Meg Foster, Helen Shaver, Cassie Yates, Sandy McPeak, Christopher Starr. Dir: Sam Peckinpah. Pro: Peter S. Davis and William N. Panzer. Ex Pro: Timothy Murphy, Larry Jones and Marc W. Zavat. Assoc Pro: Don Guest and E.C. Monell. 2nd Unit Dir: Rod Amateau. Screenplay: Alan Sharp, from an adaptation by Ian Masters; based on the thriller by Robert Ludlum. Ph: John Coquillon. Ed: Edward Abroms and David Rawlins. Art: Robb

C. Thomas Howell (right) and friend Ralph Macchio on the run in *The Outsiders.*

Wilson King. M: Lalo Schifrin. (Fox) Rel: 29 June 1983. 102 mins. Cert 18.

The Outsiders. Francis Ford Coppola's screen version of 17-year-old Susie Hinton's first (of, now, four) novels about teenage life in her home town of Tulsa, Oklahoma. A not particularly edifying mix of violence and sentimentality, relating the adventures of three youngsters mixed up in moronic gang warfare which ends in tragedy after one has knifed one of the opposition to death. The unpleasantness of the film coughs up the old, old excuse for such anti-social behaviour by suggesting that it is all a matter of environment; and the equally familiar suggestion that beneath the dross is gold—the latter revealed in this case when the trio put their lives on the line to rescue some small children trapped in a fire. But in fact, the film's gold, if any, is to be found in the several good performances. Cast: Matt Dillon, Ralph Macchio, C. Thomas Howell, Patrick Swayze, Rob Lowe, Emilio Estevez, Tom Cruise, Glenn Withrow, Diane Lane, Leif Garrett, Darren Dalton, Michelle Meyrink, Gailard Sartain, Tom Waits, William Smith. Dir: Francis Ford Coppola. Pro: Fred Roos and Gray Frederickson. Screenplay: Kathleen Knutsen Rowell; based on the novel of the same title by S.E. 'Susie' Hinton. Assoc Pro: Gian-Carlo Coppola. Ph: Stephen H. Burum. Ed: Anne Goursaud. Pro Des: Dean Tavoularis. M: Carmine Coppola (song

'So Gold' sung by Stevie Wonder: 'Loveless Motel' perf by R.C. Bannon; 'Jack Daniels If You Please' perf by David Allen Coe, and 'Gloria' composed and performed by Van Morison). (Zoetrope–Warner) Rel: 18 Aug 1983. 91 mins. Cert PG.

Over the Brooklyn Bridge. Warmly affectionate tribute to New York and its ethnic population, seen as a background to the story of a Brooklyn café-owning Jew who dreams of moving on and up to a top-flight restaurant in Manhattan, and has to choose between the opportunity to achieve his dream (courtesy of his uncle, who offers him financial backing) and his gentile beloved (vetoed by uncle, who wants to see his nephew marry a good Jewish girl). An amusing and often moving film which has all the appearances of a 1960s movie; very nicely performed. Cast: Elliott Gould, Sid Caesar, Margaux Hemingway, Burt Young, Shelley Winters, Carol Kane, Robert Gosset, Karen Shallo, Jerry Lazarus, Francine Beers, Leo Postrel, Rose Arrick, Matt Fischel, Lynnie Greene, Amy S. Ryder, Sal Richards, Leib Lensky, Lou David, Tom McDermott, Zvee Schooler, Mort Freeman, Marh Gutzi. Dir: Menahem Golan. Pro: Golan and Yoram Globus. Screenplay: Arnold Somkin. Ph: Adam Greenberg. Ed: Mark Goldblatt. Art: John Lawless. M: Pino Donaggio. Assoc Pro: Christopher Pearce. Fashion Show sequence by Tracy Mills. (Golan–Globus/City Films–Entertainment/Cannon Group) Rel: floating; first shown London (Classic, Haymarket), Mar 1984. 107 mins. Cert 15.

Parade. Jacques Tati's last film, made for video in 1974, transferred to film and shown at the London Film Festival the following year, but never, until now, released. A Franco-Swedish production in which Tati is the MC at a small-time circus performance, during which he performs some of his most famous mimes – for instance, the tennis player – seen in his previous features. Obviously made on a shoe-string, it is something of a fascinating rag-bag, with moments of illuminating vintage Tati comedy, but somehow looking more like a series of notes for what might have been another of the master's feature comedies. A real collector's item. Rest of cast: Karl Kossmayer and

his Mule, Les Williams, Les Veterans, Les Siholo, Pierre Bramma, Michel Brabo, Pia Colombo, Hall, Norman and Ladd, Les Argentinos, Johnny Lonn, Bertilo, Jan Swahn, Bertil Berglund, Moniqa Sunnerberg. Dir and Screenplay: Jacques Tati. Pro: Karl Haskel. Assoc Pro: Michael Chauvin. Ph: Jean Badal and Gunnar Fischer. Ed: Sophie Tatischeff, Aline Asseo, Per Carlesson, Siv Lundgren and Jonny Mair. Art: Ulla Malmer-Lagerkvist. Artistic Dir: François Bronett. M: Charles Dumont. (Gray Film, Paris/Sveriges Radio TV2, Stockholm–Premier Releasing) Rel: floating; first shown London (Barbican), 1 Dec 1983. 85 mins. Cert U.

Patu! (Maori for Kill, Strike Out or Chastise). New Zealand-made documentary about the 1981 South African Rugby tour of New Zealand and the controversy, confrontation and violence that accompanied it. Dir and Pro: Merata Mita. Ph: Barry Harbert. Ed: Annie Collins. M: Diatribe. (Vocals by Tia Kingi). (Contemporary) Rel: floating; first shown London (Phoenix, Finchley), June 1984. 110 mins. Cert PG.

Pauline at the Beach – Pauline à la Plage. The third in Eric Rohmer's 'Comedies & Proverbs' series of movies, winner of the first prize at the 1983 Berlin Film Festival and very much the conversational, discussion (on love) piece so typical of this most literary of French directors. A leisurely, refined and stylish variation on the old mistaken identity farce, with five characters dancing around the flames of love, seduction and jealousy against a

Kevin Kline (left), Angela Lansbury and Rex Smith in *The Pirates of Penzance*.

background of a sun-drenched Normandy coastal resort at the end of the season. Cast: Arielle Dombasle, Amanda Langlet, Pascal Greggory, Feodor Atkine, Simon de la Brosse, Rosette. Dir and Screenplay: Eric Rohmer. Pro: Margaret Mengoz. Ph: Nestor Almendros. Ed: Caroline Thivel. M: Jean-Louis Valero. (Les Films du Losange/Les Films Ariane–Gala) Rel: floating; first shown London (Academy), June 1983. 95 mins. Cert 15 (AA).

The Pied Piper of Hamelin. Animation – model – film of the fairy story by Cosgrove Hall Productions (Mark Hall, Brian Cosgrove and John Hambley) which won the 1982 *Prix Jeunesse*, and BAFTA's Best Children's Programme Award in the same year. Parcelled at the ICA Children's Cinema with another of the studio's half-hour productions, *Captain Noah and the Floating Zoo*, along with two shorts – *Cockleshell Bay* (model animation, 11 mins) and *Dangermouse* (cartoon animation, 5 mins). Founded in 1976, the company has made 3,000 minutes of animated film (equal to about 30 feature films) and employs 70 people. (Cosgrove Hall Productions–ICA) Rel: floating; first shown London (ICA), Nov 1983. Cert U.

The Pirates of Penzance. Straightforward (made in Britain) film of the big American stage success which considerably peps up the original Gilbert and Sullivan operetta, presenting it as a lively, lilting and thoroughly entertaining show with some nice touches of wit along the way. A remarkably athletic (shades of Douglas Fairbanks Snr!) performance as the Pirate King by Kevin Kline, and a pleasant one by pop music recruit Rex Smith as the hero with the high morals. Sterling support comes from a well-voiced Angela Lansbury, Clara-Bowish Linda Ronstadt, nimble dancer Tony Azito and richly comic George Rose, as the Major-General. And as incidental information, this film made history by being premiered simultaneously in the cinema and by Cable TV. Rest of cast: (Pirates) David Hatton, Anthony Arundell, Tim Bentinck, Ross Davidson, Mike Grady, Simon Howe, Tony Millan, Zoot Money, Andrew Paul, Ken Rogers-Johnson, Mike Walling; (Daughters) Teresa Codling, Louise Gold, Leni

Harper, Clare McIntryre, Louise Papillon, Tilly Vosburgh, Nancy Wood. And; Frankie Cull, David Hampshire, Phillip Harrison, Jerry Manley, Rhys Nelson, Kenny Warwick, Peppi Borza, Nicolas Chagrin, Maurice Lane, Neil McCaul, Garry Noakes, Chris Power, Mohamed Aazzi, Mohamed Serhani, Ali Tahari, Larbi Ben Mansour, Mohamed Larbi Hammani. Dir and Screenplay: Wilford Leach. Pro: Joseph Papp. Ex Pro: Edward R. Pressman. Assoc. Pro: Stephen Katz and Andrew Tribe. Pro Sup: Alexander de Grunwald. Ph: Douglas Slocombe. Ed: Anne Coates. Pro. Des: Elliot Scott. Art: Ernest Archer and Alan Cassie. Choreographer: Graciela Daniele. M Adaptation: William Elliott. M Pro: Peter Asher. M Ed: John Strauss. Based on the Broadway production of the Gilbert and Sullivan operetta. (Universal–UIP) Rel: floating; first shown London (Classic, Shaftesbury Ave), Sept 1983. 112 mins. Cert U.

Police Academy. Comedy built around a group of cop cadets in an American Police Academy, which has been aston-

Anthony Perkins as the menacing killer, and Meg Tilly in a re-run of the shower scene (inset), in *Psycho II*.

ishingly successful in the States. Cast: Steve Guttenberg, G.W. Bailey, George Gaynes, Michael Winslow, Kim Cattrall, Bubba Smith, Andrew Rubin, Donovan Scott, Leslie Easterbrook, David Graff, Marion Ramsey, Scott Thomson, Brant Van Hoffman, Georgina Spelvin. Dir: Hugh Wilson. Pro: Paul Maslansky. Screenplay: Neal Israel, Pat Proft and Hugh Wilson; from a story by Israel and Proft. Ph: Michael D. Margulies. Ed: Robert Brown and Zach Staenberg. Pro Des: Trevor Williams. M: Robert Folk. (Ladd Co–Warner Bros) Rel: 29 June 1984. 95 mins. Cert 18.

Porky's II – The Next Day. *Porky's I* continued, with the same sort of rude fun and tasteless frolics that made the original movie such a money-spinner – at least in home-town America. Bill Wiley as the Reverend gent who wants to kill the school's Shakespeare Festival because of the sexiness of the bard's works, supported by the gym mistress and the local Ku Klux Klan. Jokes include sending a snake up into the lady's toilet and running the shaven-headed, nude KKKs through the streets. Rest of cast: Dan Monahan, Wyatt Knight, Mark Herrier, Roger Wilson, Cyril O'Reilly, Tony Ganios,

Kaki Hunter, Scott Colomby, Nancy Parsons, Joseph Running Fox, Eric Christmas, Edward Winter, Cisse Cameron, Else Earl. Dir: Bob Clark. Pro: Don Carmody and Clark. Ex Pro: Melvin Simon, Harold Greenberg and Alan Landsburgh. Assoc Pro: Gary Goch and Ken Heeley-Ray. Screenplay: Clark, Roger E. Swaybill and Alan Ormsby. Ph: Reginald H. Morris. Ed: Stan Cole. Art: Fred Price. M: Carl Zittrer. (Simon/Reeves/Landsburg Productions–Astral Bellevue Pathe-Fox) Rel: 8 Sept 1983. 95 mins. Cert 18.

The Prize of Peril – Le Prix du Danger. Highly incredible, if cinematically highly efficient, Franco-Yugoslavian fantasy thriller from Yves Boisset which presents a future in which those daft panel games on TV have reached the stage when contestants stake their life against an enormous prize – but as the result is always rigged they inevitably fail *and die!* Each eager entrant after those millions of dollars is given four hours to reach a predetermined spot in the town, with the blood-thirsty mob in pursuit, primed to kill the prey before the goal is reached. Cast: Gérard Lanvin, Michel Piccoli, Marie-France Pisier, Bruno Cremer, Andréa Ferreol, Jean Rougerie, Jean-Claude Dreyfus, Jean-Pierre Bagot, Henri-Jacques Huet, Dragan Stupljanin, Steve Kalfa, Zlata Numanacic, Julien Bukowski, Gabrielle Lazure, Catherine Lachens, Jacques Chailleux. Dir: Yves Boisset. Pro: Norbert Saada. Screenplay: Boisset and Jean Curtelin; based on a short story by Robert Sheckley. Ph: Pierre-William Glenn. Ed: Michelle David, Elizabeth Guido, Nicole Gauduchon, Claire Pinheiro and Françoise Lefèvre. Pro Des: Serge Douy. Art: Aleksandar Milovic. M: Vladimir Cosma. (Swanie Productions/TFI Films/UGC Top 1, Paris–Avala Films, Belgrade–Brent Walker) Rel: floating; first shown London (ABC Edgware Rd & Classics at Chelsea and Tott Ct Rd), Feb 1984. 98 mins. Cert 18.

Psycho II. One of the rare reasonably successful efforts at following up a former feature success. The 1960 Hitchcock classic chiller to which this sequel continually makes pictorial reference, even using the famous murder-in-the-shower sequence as a prelude

81

and, later on, artfully offering something of a parallel. Anthony Perkins gives a performance several times larger than life as the released psycho case who goes back to the scenes of his old crime some 22 years later, only to be almost immediately involved in strange goings-on, murders most foul and the final repeat killing of his 'mother', the crime which originally sent him to the asylum. Plenty of tension, initial restraint (lessening towards the end), nice touches of humour and a number of authentic Hitchcock touches. Rest of cast: Vera Miles, Meg Tilly, Robert Loggia, Dennis Franz, Hugh Gillin, Claudia Bryar, Robert Alan Browne, Ben Hartigan, Lee Garlington, Tim Maier, Jill Carroll, Chris Hendri, Tom Holland, Michael Lomazow, Robert Destri, Osgood Perkins, Ben Frommer, Gene Whittington, Robert Traynor, George Dickerson, Thaddeus Smith, Sheila K. Adams, Victoria Brown, Bob Yerkes. Dir: Richard Franklin. Pro: Hilton A. Green. Ex Pro: Bernard Schwartz. Screenplay: Tom Holland. Ph: Dean Cundey. Ed: Andrew London. Pro Des: John W. Corso. Special Visual Effects: Albert Whitlock. M: Jerry Goldsmith. (Universal Oak–UIP) Rel: 15 Sept 1983. 113 mins. Cert 15.

Querelle. Rainer Werner Fassbinder's final movie (completed in June 1983, only a short time before his death) which, based on the famed French homosexual writer Jean Genet's 1947 novel *Querelle de Brest*, was the most overtly homosexual of all his 42 feature films. A stylized story – in a deliberately artificial setting – of male love, lust, corruption and violence seen against the sordid background of the docks, brothels and back alleys of Brest. Quotations from Genet's high-flown poetry are introduced, possibly to alleviate the wholly nasty taste in the mouth it all leaves. Quite a number of unpleasantly explicit scenes of homosexual couplings are shown as the film follows the self-discovery of the sailor of the title, whom it would seem, all men desire! Cast: Brad Davis, Franco Nero, Jeanne Moreau, Laurent Malet, Hanno Poschl, Gunther Kaufmann, Berkhard Driest, Dieter Schidor, Roger Feitz, Michael McLernon, Neil Bell, Harry Baer, Nadja Brunkhorst. Dir and Screenplay: Rainer Werner Fassbinder. Pro: Dieter Schidor. Ph: Xavier

Schwarzenberger. Ed: Juliane Lorenz. Sets: Rolf Zehetbauer. Artistic Collaboration (no Art credit as such): Harry Baer. M. (and songs): Peer Raben. (Palace Pictures) Rel: floating; first shown London (Screen-on-the-Hill), August 1983. 105 mins. Cert 18.

Real Life. Showing obvious signs of his TV background, writer-director Francis Megahy makes an impressive debut on the large screen with this leisurely but charming comedy about a young man who, to liven up his rather depressing existence, dreams up a story about a Rembrandt theft and manages to convince a couple of Fleet Street scribes that it is geniune. But, suddenly, daydream merges into reality... with a real thief and a real theft. A splendid lead performance by Rupert Everett. Rest of cast: Christina Raines, Catherine Rabett, James Faulkner, Isla Blair, Norman Beaton, Warren Clarke, Lyndsey Baxter, Annabel Leventon, Sharon Haywoode, Brian Bovell, Nick Rodding. Michael Cochrane. Dir: Francis Megahy. Pro: Mike Dineen. Screenplay: Megahy and Bernie Cooper. Ph: Peter Jessop. Ed: Peter Delfgou. M: David Mindel. (Bedford Productions–Entertainment Century Film Dist) Rel: floating: first shown London (Studio &

Rupert Everett as the Walter Mitty character in *Real Life*.

Gabriel Byrne returns to Dublin at the end of an eventful but unproductive summer, in *Reflections*.

Kensington Odeon) June 1984. 93 mins. Cert PG.

Reflections. Slow, dreamy – and at times dangerously near dreary – Irish film about a self-centred Dublin writer who rents a country cottage in order to complete his book on Isaac Newton. However, in true Irish style he becomes involved instead with the family at the big old house (who are his landlords), casually entering into an affair with the niece, a drinking friendship with the husband, and a fleeting desire for the wife, ending up with the realization that he has got all their characters wrong, and returning to Dublin at the end of the summer with no book but a better understanding of people. A film of long silences, egotistical characters, halting conversations, sombre undercurrents and considerable visual beauty. Cast: Gabriel Byrne, Donal McCann, Harriet Walter, Fionnula Flanagan, Gerard Cummins, Niall Tobin, Paedar Lamb, Des Nealon, Margaret Wade, Larry O'Driscoll, Noel O'Flaherty. Dir: Kevin Billington. Pro: Billington and David Deutsch. Screenplay: John Banville: based on the novella *The Newton Letter*. Ph: Mike Molloy. Ed: Chris Ridsdale. Art: Martin Johnson. M: Rachel Portman. (Court House Films–Artificial Eye) Rel: floating; first shown London (Chelsea Cinema), March 1984. 103 mins. Cert 15.

Return Engagement. A curious but consistently provoking and amusing documentary about two of America's least-loved men, former opponents and completely contrasting characters—who now earn what is obviously a very good living by taking their lecture-debate around the country, staging it in real showbiz style. Former lawyer, DA and mastermind of the bungled burglary which helped drive President Nixon out of the White House, G. Gordon Liddy and the former hippy, advocate of drugs, Harvard Professor (and banned from Britain character) Dr Timothy Leary—With this 'debate' – which ranges across pally meals, inebriated candidness, lectures to junior classes, and other revealing moments – the two men are fully revealed. Outstanding in its way, and quite unique. Debate Moderator: Carole Hemmingway. Dir: Alan Rudolph. Pro: Carolyn Pfeiffer. Ex in charge of Pro: David Blocker. Assoc Pro: Barbara Leary. Ph: Jan Keisser. Ed: Tom Walls. M: Adrian Belew. (Island Alive Enterprises–Mainline) Rel: floating; first shown London (Screen on the Green), Sept 1983. 89 mins. Cert 15.

The Return of Martin Guerre. A French triple award winner by Daniel Vigne, based on an old classic story, which was in turn an adaptation of a court case recorded by a Toulouse magistrate in the 16th century. A fascinating tale of a man who claimed to be another, was quick-witted enough to carry on the masquerade throughout legal examinations, and was just about to win his case when the real Martin turns up in court. . . and so to a hanging rather than happy ending. Marvellously atmospheric, outstandingly photographed (one can almost smell the dung-and-dirt atmosphere of the period) and equally finely acted: but with a leisurely, measured pace. Cast: Gérard Dépardieu, Nathalie Baye, Roger Planchon, Maurice Jacquemont, Isabelle Sadoyan, Rose Thiery, Maurice Barrier, Stephane Pean, Sylvie Meda, Chantal Deruaz, Valerie Chassigneux, Tcheky Karyo, Dominique Pinon, Adrien Duquesne, Andre Chaumeau, Philippe Babin, Axel Bogousslavsky, Neige Dolsky. Dir: Daniel Vigne. Pro: Marcel Dassault. Screenplay: Vigne and Jean-Claude Carriere. Ph: Andre Neau. Ed: Denise de Casabianca. Art: Alain Nègre. M:

Familiar faces, and machines, in the third Star Wars film *Return of the Jedi.*

Michel Portal. (Société Française de Production Cinematographique/Société de Production de Films-Palace Pictures) Rel: floating; first shown London (Curzon) June 1984. 111 mins. Cert 15.

Return of the Jedi. With this third *Star Wars* film George Lucas winds up the first – actually central in time scale – of his planned three trilogies about life long ago and far away in space. In this episode, Luke Skywalker (Mark Hamill) learns that the villainous Emperor's henchman (Darth Vader) is actually his dad and decides to confront him; he learns, too, that pretty Princess Leia (Carrie Fisher) is really his sister. And this time around there's something like a happy ending. Probably the most imaginative, and least human of the three movies, full of weird and wonderful creations, imaginative sequences and some remarkable movie magic. A vast and spectacular creation for children which will appeal to millions of their young-in-heart elders. Rest of cast: Harrison Ford, Billy Dee Williams, Anthony Daniels, Peter Mayhew, Sebastian Shaw, Ian McDiarmid, Frank Oz, David Prowse, James Earl Jones, Alec Guinness, Kenny Baker, Michael Pennington, Keneth Colley, Michael Carter, Denis Lawson, Tim Rose, Dermot Crowley, Caroline Blakiston, Warwick Davis, Jeremy Bulloch,

Revolt of the astronauts, (from left to right) Paulin, Quaid, Frank, Henriksen and Harris (also below), in *The Right Stuff*.

Femi Taylor, Annie Arbogast, Claire Davenport, Jack Purvis, Mike Edmonds, Jane Busby, Malcolm Dixon, Mike Cottrell, Nicki Reade, Adam Bareham, Jonathan Oliver, Pip Miller, Tom Mannion, Toby Philpott, Mike Edmonds, David Barclay, Michael McCormick, Deep Roy, Simon Williamson, Hugh Spirit, Swim Lee, Michael Quinn, Richard Robinson. Dir: Richard Marquand. Pro: Howard Kazanjian. Screenplay (with Lawrence Kasdan), story and Ex Pro: George Lucas. Co-Pro: Robert Watts and Jim Bloom. Ph: Alan Hume. Pro Des: Norman Reynolds. Ed: Sean Barton, Marcia Lucas and Duwane Dunham. Visual Effects: Richard Edlund, Dennis Muren and Ken Ralston. M: John Williams. Art: Fred Hole and James Schoppe (Lucasfilm Ltd–Fox) Rel: 14 July 1983. 133 mins. Cert PG.

Revenge of the Ninja. A follow-up to the same company's (Cannon) first martial arts epic *Enter the Ninja*, which was originally released earlier but revived now to make a *Ninja* double feature programme! Starting in Japan, the scene moves to America, where the unfortunate Sho Kosugi, minus most of his family – wiped out by the Ninjas – sets up as a doll importer but innocently becomes involved with dope smugglers, gangsters and more Ninjas. Lots of action, some awful acting, martial arts, delicious choreography and so – if you like this sort of thing – quite of lot of fun. Rest of cast: Keith Vitali, Virgil Frye, Arthur Roberts, Mario Gallo, Grace Oshita, Ashley Ferrare, Kane Kosugi, John La Motta, Melvin C. Hampton, Oscar Rowland, Professor Toru Tanaka, Dan Shanks. Dir: Sam Firstenberg. Pro: Menahem Golan and Yoran Globus. Assoc Pro: David Womark. Screenplay: James R. Silke. Ph: David Gurfinkel. Sup Ed: Michael J. Duthie. Ed: Mark Helfrich. Art: Paul Staheli. M: Rob Walsh (add M: W. Michael Lewis and Laurin Rinder). (MGM–UA–Cannon) Rel: 2 Dec 1983. 88 mins. Cert 18.

The Right Stuff. After so much variable sci-fi fiction, at last some fine sci-fact! The very long (3-hour plus), sprawling, highly competent, glossy story of America's conquest of space, from – rocketry – failure to success with the triumphal orbiting of John Glenn. In a deft mix of semi-documentary seriousness and light-hearted human comedy-satire, the film follows the training of the first seven US astronauts to the point (and beyond) when they rebelled at being treated as robots and demanded some control of the experiments. It includes the equally fascinating side-by-side story of the initial breaking of the sound barrier and the dangers faced by dedicated test pilots. All-in-all a fine example of the big American film at its best; even if in this instance there is but little feminine appeal. Cast: Sam Shepard, Scott Glenn, Ed Harris, Dennis Quaid, Fred Ward, Barbara Hershey, Kim Stanley, Veronica Cartwright, Pamela Reed, Scott Paulin, Charles Frank, Lance Henriksen, Donald Moffat, Levon Helm, Mary Jo Deschanel, Scott Wilson, Kathy Baker, Mickey Crocker, Susan Kase, Mittie Smith, Royal Dano, David Clennon, Jim Haynie, Jeff Goldblum, Harry Shearer, Scott Beach, Jane Dornacker, Anthony Munoz, John P. Ryan, Darryl Henriques, Eric Severeid, William Russ. Dir and Screenplay: Philip Kaufman; based on the book by Tom Wolfe. Pro: Robert Chartoff and Irwin Winkler. Ex Pro: James D. Brubaker. Ph: Caleb Deschanel. Ed: Glenn Farr, Lisa Fruchtman, Stephen A. Rotter, Tom Rof and Douglas Stewart. pro Des: Geoffrey Kirkland. Art: Richard J. Lawrence, W. Stewart Campbell and Peter Romero. M: Bill Conti, add M by Garth Hudson and Todd Boekelheide. (Ladd Company–Warner Bros) Rel: floating; first shown London (Warner), March 1984. 193 mins. Cert 15.

Risky Business. Fresh and often funny comedy which suffers a bit from curiously mixed ethical underpinning and, apart from the likeable young hero, the usual squad of foul-mouthed, sex-obessed schoolboys. It's all about a nice young lad coerced by circumstances into converting his holidaying parents' mansion into a one-night super-brothel and trying to come to terms with the fact that he has lost both his innocence and his heart to a very pretty if businesslike young hooker! Cast: Tom Cruise, Rebecca de Mornay, Curtis Armstrong, Bronson Pinchot, Raphael Sbarge, Joe Pantoliano, Nicholas Pryor, Janet Carroll, Shera Danese, Richard Masur, Bruce A. Young, Kevin C. Anderson, Sarah Partridge, Nathan Davis, Scott Harlan, Sheila Keenan, Lucy Harrington, Jerry Tullos, Jerome Landfield, Ron Dean, Bruno Aclin, Robert Kurcz, Jonathan Chapin, Jimmy Baron, Harry Teinowitz, Francine Locke, Ann Cole, Candace Collins, Elizabeth Curran, Jill DeVries, Debra Dulman, Joyce Hazard, Kerry Hill, Megan Mullally, Lora Staley, Vivian Victor, Fern Persons, Cynthia Baker,

Wayne C. Kneeland, Jade Gold, Dana Balkin, Karen Grossman, Brett Baer, Vinny Argiro, Eric Minsk, Michael Genovese, Steven Charous, Reid Rondell, Steven M. Davison, Rick LeFevour, Joe Shapiro. Dir and Screenplay: Paul Brickman. Pro: Jon Avnet and Steve Tisch. Assoc Pro: James O'Fallon. Ph: Reynaldo Villalobos and Bruce Surtees. Ed: Richard Chew. Pro Des: William J. Cassidy. M: comp and played by Tangerine Dream. (Geffen Co–Warner) Rel: 9 March 1984. 99 mins. Cert 18.

Rumblefish. Another Francis Ford Coppola movie about American teenagers – actually made back-to-back with his *The Outsiders* (released in 1983), to which it bears more than a passing resemblance. In black-and-white, it relates the story of two problem lads, brothers alienated from Society, of which the elder – the more unpleasant 'Motorcycle Boy' – is killed by a cop and the younger, inheriting his brother's bike, symbolically sets off (and there's lots of symbolism around here) toward the Californian coast and . . .? Well made, if on the dullish side, with main appeal obviously for the younger generation. Cast: Matt Dillon, Mickey Rourke, Diane Lane, Dennis

Hopper, Diana Scarwid, Vincent Spano, Nicolas Cage, Christopher Penn, Larry Fishburne, William Smith, Michael Higgins, Glenn Withrow, Tom Waits, Herb Rice, Maybelle Wallace, Nona Manning, Domino, Gio, S.E. Hinton, Emmett Brown, Tracey Walter, Lance Guecia, Bob Maras, J.T. Turner, Keeva Clayton, Kirsten Hayden, Karen Parker, Sussannah Darcy, Kristi Somers. Dir and Ex Pro: Francis Ford Coppola. Pro: Fred Roos and Doug Claybourne. Screenplay: Coppola and S.E. Hinton; based on the latter's novel. Ph: S.H. Burum. Ed: Barry Malkin. Pro Des: Dean Tavourlaris. M: Stewart Copeland. (Hot Weather Films–Universal Pictures–UIP) Rel: floating; first shown London (Lumiere), Feb 1984. 94 mins. Cert 18.

Runners. British film about an apparently quite happy and contented 14-year-old schoolgirl whose smashed bicycle is found one morning on her route to school. The girl has seemingly vanished without trace, and the story follows the two-year-long persistent search carried on by her loving dad, who puts both his marriage and his job on the line as he follows every possible clue to her whereabouts, doggedly certain she is alive, and well, and somewhere . . . And what happens when he does eventually run her to earth in London? A topical, newspaper headline theme, but often just that bit too far-

Tom Cruise takes the profits of vice from Shera Danese, while Rebecca de Mornay looks on, in *Risky Business*.

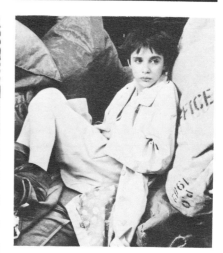

Jane Asher and James Fox (left) hunt down obdurate daughter Kate Hardie (above) in *Runners*.

fetched for belief, particularly in the later stages of the story. James Fox as the worried dad, Eileen O'Brien as the wife who gives up hope, Jane Asher as another runaway-child parent who not only shares the man's refusal to believe the worst, but also shares, for one night, his bed; and Kate Hardie, as the petulant cause of all the bother. Rest of cast: Robert Lang, Ruti Simon, Paul Angelis, Bernard Hill, Bridget Turner, Bridget Mead, Holly Hoffman, John Homes. Dir: Charles Sturridge. Pro: Barry Hanson. Screenplay: Stephen Poliakoff. Ph: Howard Atherton. Pro Des: Arnold Chapkis. Art: Mark Nerini. Ed: Peter Coulson. M: George Fenton. (Hanstoll Productions/Goldcrest Films–Cinegate) Made on location in Nottingham and London. Rel: floating; first shown London (Gate, Notting Hill), Aug 1983. 106 mins. Cert 15.

Running Brave. Another addition to the present spate of sporting epics, this one (a minor one) from Canada. The running brave of the title is a Sioux Indian from South Dakota who showed his running prowess at university, but was only able to prove it after joining the US Marines and, gaining confidence and polish from them, went to the Tokyo Olympics to carry off the long-distance running prize to the apparent astonishment of everyone concerned. The film was financed by an

oil-rich group of Cree Indians. Cast: Bobby Benson, Pat Hingle, Claudia Cron, Jeff McCraken, August Schellenberg, Denis Lacroix, Graham Greene, Margo Kane. Dir: 'D.S. Everett' (apparently the original director, Donald Shebib did not want any credit!). Pro: Ira Englander. Assoc Pro: Maurice Wolf. Screenplay: Henry Bean and Shirl Hendryx. Ph: François Protat. Ed: Tony Lower and Earl Herdan. Art: Barbra Dunphy. M: Mike Post. (Englander Productions–in assoc with the Ermineskin Band–ITC) Rel: 29 June 1983. 105 mins. Cert PG.

Sahara. Wild and woolly story about a lovely lady (Brooke Shields) who promises her dying daddy that she will drive his specially designed car in the world's toughest, cross-Sahara race, in which to

take part she must necessarily disguise herself as a man! Rest of cast: Lambert Wilson, Horst Buchholz, John-Rhys Davies, Ronald Lacey, John Mills, Steve Forrest, Perry Lang, Cliff Potts, Terence Hardiman. Dir: Andrew V. McLaglen. Pro: Menahem Golan and Yoram Globus. Ex Pro: Teri Shields. Screenplay: James R. Silke and Leslie Stevens. Ph: David Gurfinkel. Pro Des: Luciano Spadoni. M: Ennio Morricone. (Cannon Group–Columbia) Rel: Jan 20 1984. 104 mins. Cert PG.

Sans Soleil – Sunless. French film 'tone' poem by Chris Marker about memories of moviemaking in Japan, Africa and other places which won him the BFI award for the most imaginative and original film to be shown in their theatre during 1983. English narrator: Alexandra Stewart. Pro: Anatole Dauman. M: Sibelius, Krasna and Mussorgsky. (The Other Cinema) Rel:

Brooke Shields, as a man, and being protected by Lambert Wilson, in *Sahara*.

floating; first shown London (ICA) June 1984. 100 mins. No cert.

Scandalous. A lively, never boring, but somewhat uneasy mixture of light comedy, romance, farce and whodunit which tries very hard but never quite succeeds in recreating the atmosphere and charm of similar (successful) movies of the '40s. This one is about a TV reporter (Robert Hays) who falls in love with the female half (Pamela Stephenson – deluscious) of a high-powered 'con' team (other half: John Gielgud) and becomes involved with the murder of his rich wife. And there's a completely daft, over-the-top portrait of a CID Inspector provided by Jim Dale. Rest of cast: M. Emmet Walsh, Nancy Wood, Conover Kennard, Ron Trains, Ed Dolan, Paul Reeve, Slita Kennedy, Kevin Elyot, Duncan Preston, Maureen Bennett, Peter Dennis, Preston Lockwood and Bow-Wow-Wow. Dir: Rob Cohen. Pro: Arlene Sellers and Alex Winitsky. Ex Pro: Carter De Haven. Co-Pro: Martin C. Schute. Screenplay: Rob Cohen and John Byrum. Ph: Jack Cardiff. Ed: Michael Bradsell. Pro Des: Peter Mullins. M: Dave Grusin. (Lantana/Sellers: Winitsky/De Haven Production–Hemdale) Rel: 1 June 1984. 94 mins. Cert 15.

Scarface. Basically an up-dated and otherwise modified re-make of the 1932 movie made from the Armitage Trail novel about the bullet-punctuated rise and drug-soaked, machine-gun-perforated end of a gangster. This time around it is 1980, and an ignorant, brutal, amoral young thug from Cuba arrives in the United States as a refugee. But thanks to his Bolivian drug connections, he is soon climbing the ladder to cash unlimited. A technically polished, finely produced, well enough acted, bloodily violent, broad modern morality play which appears generally more concerned with the violence than the moral. Ruthlessly tailored for B.O. success, it would have been a better movie if the script had been pre-washed in carbolic soap, some of the players had taken a few elocution lessons, and the editors had used their shears more cuttingly. Cast: Al Pacino, Steven Bauer, Michelle Pfeiffer, Mary Elizabeth Mastrantonio, Robert Loggia, Miriam Colon, F. Murray Abraham, Paul Shenar, Harris Yulin, Angel

Wounded mobster Al Pacino surveys the carnage of the shoot-up in *Scarface*.

Salazar, Arnaldo Santana, Pepe Serna, Michael P. Moran, Al Israel, Dennis Holahan, Mark Margolis, Michael Alldredge, Ted Beniades, Richard Belzer, Paul Espel, John Brandon, Tony Perez, Garnett Smith, Loren Almaguer, Gil Barreto, Heather Benna, Dawnell Bowers, Tina Leigh Cameron, Victor Campos, Robert Hammer Cannerday, Rene Carrasco, Albert Carrier, John Carter, Richard Caselnova, Gary Cervantes, Carlos Cestero, John Contardo, Robert Contreras, Caesar Cordova, Gregory N. Cruz, Dante D'Andre, Richard Delmonte, Wayne Doba, Michel François, Ben Frommer, Edward R. Frommer, John Gamble, Troy Isaacs, Ronald Joseph, Mario Machado. Dir: Brian DePalma. Pro: Martin Bregman. Ex Pro: Louis A. Stroller. Screenplay: Oliver Stone. Ph: John A. Alonzo. Ed: Jerry Greenberg and David Ray. Art: Ed Richardson. Visual Consultant: Ferdinando Scarfiotti. Co-Pro: Peter Saphier. M: Giorgio Moroder: 'Scarface' perf by Paul Engemann; 'Rush, Rush' by Deborah Harry; 'Turn Out the Light' by Amy Holland; 'Vamos a Baillar' by Maria Conchita; 'Tony's Theme' by Giorgio Moroder; 'She's On Fire' by Amy Holland; 'Shake It Up' by Elizabeth Daily; 'Dance Dance Dance' by Beth Andersen; 'I'm Hot Tonight' by Elizabeth Daily; 'Gina's & Elvira's

Theme' by Giorgio Moroder. (Universal–UIP) Rel: 10 Feb 1984. 170 mins. Cert X.

Screwballs. This more than aptly named epic concerns five young morons in an American High School whose object in life is to revenge themselves on the Institution's only virgin by baring her breasts in public – her crime, it seems, was doing her level best to get them detention. Which just about says it all. Cast: Peter Keleghan, Kent Deuters, Lynda Speciale, Alan Deveau, Linda Shayne, Jason Warren, Jim Coburn, Terrea Foster, Donnie Bowes, Raven de la Croix, Kim Cayer, Astrid Hildebrandt, Angela Jensen, Allison Smith, Shannon McMahon, Stephanie Murgaski, Kimberly Brooks, Nicky Fylan, Paula Farmer, Joe Crozier, Heather Smith, Nola Wale, Nancy Chambers, John Fox, Jan Taylor, Caroline Tweedle, John Glossop, Tim Dunphy, Mitch Sherman, Leslie Lahoda, Howard Nemetz, Simon Rakoff, Rosalia Martino. Dir: Rafal Zielinski. Pro: Maurice Smith. Assoc Pro: Peter McQuillan and Nicky Fylan. Pro Co-Ord: Debbie Cooke. Screenplay: Linda Shayne and Jim Wynorski. Ph: Miklos Lente. Ed: Brian Ravok. Art: Sandra Kybartas. M: Tim McCauley. (Crazy Times Film Corp, with participation of the Canadian Film Development Corp/Famous Players Ltd–Avatar Communications) Rel: 9 Dec 1983. 79 mins. Cert 18.

The Second Awakening of Christa Klages. Yet another in the more than usually heavy crop of feminist films that reached the screen during the 1983/4 period. This one from Germany's Margarethe von Trotta tell the story of the tragic events that follow a bank hold-up by a group of women trying to get enough money to support the day-centre built by one of them, which is threatened with closure. Cast: Tina Engel, Silvia Reize, Katharina Thalbach, Marius Müller-Westernhagen, Peter Schneider. Dir and Pro: Margarethe von Trotta. Screenplay: von Trotta and Luisa Francia. Ex Pro: Eberhard Junkersdorf. Ph: Franz Rath. Ed: Anette Dorn. No art credit. M: Klaus Doldinger. (Bioskop–Film, Munich, In assoc with WDR, West German Television, Cologne–First City Films/Cinema of Women–Contemporary) Rel: floating; first shown London (Everyman, Hampstead), Jan 1984. 88 mins. Cert 15.

Siege. The 1981 Halifax, Nova Scotia, Police strike provides a convenient peg on which to hang this bloody Canadian thriller about an underworld gang's efforts to wipe out the witness of a mass killing of innocent people, who has taken refuge in a house in a deserted area of the town. Several characters on both sides meet varyingly violent and mostly bloodsoaked ends in this tense and shocking drama. Despite the well manufactured thrills, it is all rather nasty, and very good if unintentional propaganda for ensuring that *our* cops stay on the job! Cast: Tom Nardini, Brenda Bazinet, Doug Lennox, Darel Haeny, Terry Despres, Jeff Pustil, Jack Blum, Keith Knight, Fred Wadden,

Tom Nardini in *Siege*.

Lax safety procedures, plutonium contamination and a cover up – the nub of *Silkwood* starring Meryl Streep.

Gary Dempster, Dennis O'Connor, Rick Collins, Dug Rotstein, Ted Germaine, Barbara Jones, Patricia Vroom, Alan MacGillivray, Kevin Jollimore, John D'Arte, Glen Radman, Carolyn Van Gurp, Blaine Henshaw. Dir: Paul Donovan and Maura O'Connell. Pro: Donovan, O'Connell and John Walsh. Ex Pro: P.M. Robinson. Assoc Pro: Iris Essex. Screenplay: Donovan; based on an idea by Marc Vautour. Ph: Les Krizsan. Ed: Ian McBride. Pro Des: Malachi Salter. M: Peter Jermyn and Drew King. (Salter Street Films, Canada–New Realm) Rel: 8 Oct 1983. 83 mins. Cert 18.

Silkwood. A leisurely and generally low-toned movie about a factory worker in a nuclear 'parts' firm who becomes contaminated and drifts leftwards into Union affairs. Later, contaminated again and determined to reveal the dangers of the plant's work to a New York reporter, she somewhat conveniently dies in her car on the way home. Based on true facts, but always carefully – and obviously unavoidably – ambiguous in its allusions to management villainy. Meryl Streep offers a determined, not very sympathetic portrait of a working-class lass with a not very delicate air. Rest of cast: Kurt Russell, Cher, Craig T. Nelson, Diana Scarwid, Fred Ward, Ron Silver, Charles Hallahan, Josef Sommer, Susie Bond, Henderson Forsythe, E. Katherine Kerr, Bruce McGill, David Strathairn, J.C Quinn, Kent Broadhurst, Richard Hamilton, Les Lannom, M. Emmet Walsh, Graham Jarvis, James Rebhorn, Ray Baker, Michael Bond, Bill Cobbs, Norm Colvin, Haskell Craver, Kathie Dean, Gary Grubbs, Susan McDaniel, Tana Hensley, Anthony Fernandez, Betty Harper, Tess Harper, Anthony Heald, Nancy Hopton, Betty King, Dan Lindsey, John Martin, Will Patton, Vern Porter, Christopher Saylors, Don Slaton, Tom Stovall. Dir and Pro (latter with Michael Hausman): Mike Nichols. Ex Pro: Buzz Hirsch and Larry Cano. Assoc Pro: Joel Tuber and Tom Stovall. Screenplay: Nora Ephron & Alice Arlen. Ph: Miroslav Ondricek. Ed: Sam O'Steen. Pro Des: Patrizia von Brandenstein. Art: Richard James. M: Georges Delerue. Ex in charge of Pro: Herb Jellinek. (ABC Motion Pictures–Rank Film Dist) Rel: 11 May 1984. 131 mins. Cert 15.

Sisters: or the Balance of Happiness – Die Balance des Glücks. Leisurely told, but very serious and essentially Germanic film from Margarethe von Trotta which, (rather confusingly) predates by two years her more recently shown and – in Germany – far more commercially successful film *The German Sisters*. The increasing alienation of two formerly inseparable sisters the elder of whom becomes a successful, highly efficient secretary, whilst the younger finds both her studies and her life without purpose. Ultimately, the younger girl commits suicide, not so much from despair as a desire to punish her sister. But there's a lot more to it then appears on the surface, adding up to a sombre but fascinating work. Cast: Jutta Lampe, Gudrun Gabriel, Jessica Fruh, Rainer Delventhal, Konstantin Wecker, Heinz Bennent, Agnes Fink, Fritz Lichenhahn, Günther Schütz, Ilse Bahrs, Barbara Sauerbaum, Maria-Helena Diekmann, Lieselotte Arnold, Editha Horn, Heinrich Marmann, Edith Garden, Ellen Esser, Kathie Thomsen, Volker Schwab, Dionysos Kawathas. Dir and Screenplay: Margarethe von Trotta. Ex Pro: Eberhard Junkersdorf. Ph: Franz Rath. Ed: Annette Dorn. Art: Winnifried Hennig. M: Konstantin Wecker. (Bioskop Film, Munich-First City Films-Blue Dolphin Films) Rel: floating; first shown London (ICA & Phoenix, E. Finchley) July 1983. 95 mins. Cert AA.

Slayground. Ex-cameraman Terry Bedford concentrates on arty visuals in his directing debut with this minor British crime thriller about the pursuit of a hold-up gang who run down and kill a rich man's daughter during their getaway. The outraged father hires a gunman to hunt down and kill the killers and the scene moves from New York (the crime) to Britain (retribution) and the final encounter between pursued and pursuer in Southport. There is quite a bit of fun to be had from it all, albeit not always intentional. Cast: Peter Coyote, Mel Smith, Billie Whitelaw, Philip Sayer, Bill Luhrs, Marie Masters, Clarence Felder, Ned Eisenberg, David Hayward, Michael Ryan, Barret Mulligan, Kelli Maroney, Margareta Arvidssen, Rosemary Martin, Malcolm Terris, John Morrison, Cassie Stuart, Debby Bishop, Stephen Yardley, P.H. Moriarty, Ziggy Byfield, Erick Ray Evans, Bill Dean, Ozzie Yue. Dir: Terry Bedford. Pro: John Dark and Gower Frost. Ex Pro: Bob Mercer. Pro Ex: Paul Esposito. Pro Sup: Ron Fry. Screenplay: Trevor Preston: based on the book by Richard Stark. Ph: Stephen Smith (USA) and Herb Wagreich (GB). Ed: Nicholas Gaster. Pro Des: Keith Wilson. Art: Denjis Bosher (GB) Edward Pisoni (USA). M: Colin Towns. (EMI in assoc with Jennie & Co Film Production–Thorn EMI) Rel: 6 April 1984. 89 mins. Cert 18.

The Slumber Party Massacre. Minor spin-off – originally titled *Sleepless Nights* in America – from the psychopathic-killer-on-the-loose cycle. In this one, the killer despatches several youngsters with the power drill and other equipment he has obtained from his first victim, a telephone maintenance engineer. But he finally gets his come-uppance when three of his female prey turn on him to extract a grisly revenge. Cast: Michele Michaels, Robin Stille, Michael Villeia, Debra De Liso, Andree Honore, Gina Mari, Jennifer Meyers, Joe Johnson, David Milbern, Jim Boyce, Pamela Roylance, Brinke Stevens, Ryan Kennedy, Jean Vargas, Anna Patton, Howard Purgason, Pam Canzano, Aaron Lipstadt, Francis Menendez, Joe Dante. Dir and Pro: Amy Jones. Co-Pro: Aaron Lipstadt. Assoc Pro: Mark Allan. Screenplay: Rita Mae Brown. Ph: Steve Posey. Ed: Sean Foley. Art: Francesca Bartoccini. M: Ralph Jones. (Santa Fe Productions–Enterprise Films) Rel: 3 Nov 1983. 84 mins. Cert 18.

Smash Palace. An outstanding film from New Zealand, only slightly marred by a sudden dip into incredibility and melodrama at the end of what has until then been an entirely convincing and absorbing movie. It features a *Grand Prix* driver, married to a pretty young French girl, who returns to New Zealand to take up his inheritance, a vast wrecked-car dump known as 'Smash Palace', which had been collected over 50 years by his dad for spare parts sales. His refusal to move, his offhand and often brutal treatment of his wife, leads to her leaving him with his beloved small daughter, and this in turn leads to his increasing battles with the law. And just to add spice to the mix – though quite acceptably within context – there's male full-frontal nudity, beatings up, explicit sex scenes and some remarkable *Grand Prix* racing sequences. A splendidly convincing performance by ex-pop and jazz star Bruno Lawrence as the 'thick' hubbie,

Bruno Lawrence with pretty hostage and in the climactic siege at the end of *Smash Palace*.

Jonathan Pryce leads the carnival parade in *Something Wicked This Way Comes.*

a nice one by Anna Jemison as the finally rebelling wife, and a quite remarkable and outstanding one by Greer Robson as the small daughter. Also good performances from Keith Aberdein and Des Kelly. Rest of cast: Lynne Robson, Margaret Umbers, Sean Duffy, Bryan Johnson, Terence Donovan, Dick Rollo, Ian Barber, Mike Beytagh, Brian Chase, Ross Davies, Colin Fredricksen, Thomas King, Chris Pasco, Evan Sommerville, Frank Taylor, Mike Wiggins, Ray Littlewood, Doug McKenzie, Don Lee, Jazz. Dir Pro and Story: Roger Donaldson. Assoc Pro: Larry Parr. Screenplay: Donaldson, with Peter Hansard and Bruno Lawrence. Ph: Graeme Cowley. Ed: Mike Horton. Art: Reston Griffiths. M: Sharon O'Neill. (Aardvark Films in assoc with the New Zealand Film Commission–Mainline Pictures) Rel: floating; first shown London (Screen on the Green & Cinecenta), July 1983. 108 mins. Cert 18.

Something Wicked This Way Comes. The 'Wicked' being a travelling show run by a sombre and creepy magician (Jonathan Pryce in top form) who uses the powers of darkness to try and trap two small boys so that he can carry them off as two more 'freaks' for his show, to join the many he has already entrapped by simply offering them fulfilment of their 'deepest, darkest desires'. All this is set against some superbly caught and photographed small-town settings in full autumnal glory, yet the thriller is never quite as creepy as it might have been. Jason Robards is excellent as the ailing local librarian who is forced to fight the devil in order to save his small son. The superbly stormy finale is most impressive with its thunder, lightning and various other devilish manifestations. (And best-seller author Ray Bradbury actually has gone on record as saying it's the most satisfying filming of his work for thirty years!). Rest of cast: Diane Ladd, Pam Grier, Royal Dano, Vidal Peterson, Shawn Carson, Angelo Rossitto, Peter D. Risch, Tim T. Clark, Jill Carroll, Tony Christopher, Sharan Lea, Scott De Roy, Sharon Ashe, Arthur Hill, Mary Grace Canfield, Richard Davalos, Jake Dengel, Jack Dodson, Bruce M. Fisher, Ellen Geer, Brendan Klinger, James Stacy. Stunt Players: Gary Combs, Bobby Porter, George Robotham, Patrick Romano, Charles Tamburro, Jeff Viola. (And the many – and real – tarantulas supplied by 'The Animal Actors of Hollywood'). Dir: Jack Clayton. Pro: Peter Vincent Douglas. Screenplay: Ray Bradbury; based on his own novel. Ph: Stephen H. Burum. Ed: Argyle Nelson and Barry Mark Gordon. Pro Des: Richard Macdonald. Special Visual Effects: Lee Dyer. M: James Horner. (UK Film Dist) Rel: 20 Oct 1983. 95 mins. Cert PG.

The South – El Sur. Marvellously atmospheric, leisurely, gently low-key Spanish movie about a little girl in Northern Spain who adores her father but finds it difficult to communicate with him, more so when he takes to drink and despair before finally committing suicide – leaving his now teenager offspring to achieve her ambition of 'going South'. Which she does, armed with a telephone number found on a piece of paper from her father's desk, determined to delve into her parent's past and find the reason for his downhill slide. Cast: Omero Antonutti, Lola Cardona, Sonsoles Aranguren, Iciar Bollan, Rafaela Aparicio, Germaine Montero, Aurore Clement, Maria Caro. Dir: Victor Erice. Ex Pro: Jean Pierre Fougez. Screenplay: Jose Luis Lopez Linares; based on a story by Adelaida Garcia Morales. Ph: Jose Luis Alcaine. Ed: Pablo G. del Amo. (Elias Querejeta, Spain/Chloe Productions, France—Connoisseur/Contemporary) Rel: floating; first shown London (Academy), March 1984. 94 mins. Cert U.

Spacehunter – Adventures in the Forbidden Zone. Good spatial fun in this 3-D science-fiction film, which is remarkably restrained in the usual stereoscopic gimmick department. It tells the tale of salvage pilot Peter Strauss and his pals, and their efforts to rescue three young damsels marooned on a plague-infested planet in the 22nd century. All of them *parfait*, if not exactly gentle, knights. Rest of cast: Molly Ringwald, Ernie Hudson, Andrea Marcovicci, Michael Ironside, Beeson Carroll, Hrant Alianak, Deborah Pratt, Aleisa Shirley, Cali Timmins, Paul Boretski, Patrick Rowe, Reggie Bennett. Dir: Lamont Johnson. Pro: Don Carmody, John Dunning and Andre Link. Ex Pro: Ivan Reitman. Assoc Pro: Stewart Harding. Screenplay: Edith Rey, David Preston, Dan Goldberg and Len Blum; from a story

They look scarier and lovelier in 3-D in *Spacehunter.*

by Stewart Harding and Jean Lafleur. Ph: Frank Tidy. Ed: Scott Conrad. Pro Des: Jackson DeGovia. M: Elmer Bernstein. Stunt Co-Ord: Walter Scott. (Columbia) Rel: 20 Oct 1983. 89 mins. Cert PG.

Space Riders. The action focuses on the 1983 500cc Motor Cycling World Championship, with lots of footage from the actual races and stars like Barry Sheene playing themselves. Rest of cast: Gavan O'Herlihy, Toshiya Ito, Stephanie McLean, Sayo Inaba, Caroline Evans, Hiroshi Kato, Jeff Harding, Marina Sirtis, Akira Kobayashi, Isamu Mochisuki, Tago Sakamoto, Maria Kamon, Yuriko Takagi, Geraldine Marsh, Maureen Moody, Teresa Powell, Steve Parrish, Steve Rogers, Ken Fletcher, Andrew Marriott, Roald Knutsen, Stu Avant, Wayne Gardner, Chris Guy, Ron Haslam, Steve Henshaw, Keith Huewen, Paul Lewis, Rob McElnea, Roger Marshall, Steve Parrish, Mark Salle, Terry Haslam. Dir: Joe Massot. Pro: Felicity Hibberdine. Assoc Pro: Julian Seddon and Chris Courtney. Pro Sup: David Ball. Screenplay: Felicity Hibberdine, from a story by Herv and Massot. Ph: Alec Mills. Ed: John Foster. Art: Brian Savager. Theme M: Alan Darby. (Condor Films) Rel: floating; first shown London (several cinemas) June 1984. 99 mins. Cert PG.

Spetters. A value-for-money Dutch film, aimed at the teenager, about a fish'n'chips stall serving siren (a very promising, nubile young actress, Renee Soutendijk), and the three motorcycle-mad pals who are attracted to her.

Along the incident-packed way are explicit sex (including triple male rape), motocross races, horrific accident and suicide scenes, religious fervour and parental sadism, with a few laughs thrown in for good measure. All of which helps to illustrate the movie's sub-title: *Living life like there's no tomorrow.* Rest of cast: Toon Agterberg, Maarten Spanjer, Hans Von Tongeren, Marianne Boyer, Jeroen Krabbe, Rutger Hauer. Dir: Paul Verhoeven. Pro: Joop Van Den Ende. Screenplay: Gerard Soeteman. Ph: Jost Vacano. Ed: Ine Schenkkan. Art: Dick Schillemans. M: Kayak. Pro Co-Ord: Marianne Van Wijnkoop. (VSE–Embassy Home Entertainment) Rel: floating; first shown London (several Classic cinemas), 27 Oct 1983. 109 mins. Cert 18.

Spring Break. Something of an American equivalent to Britain's *Crossroads* TV series, with everything happening at a motel (situated in this case at Fort Lauderdale, Texas) during the Easter vacation. A careful mixture of romance, villainy and curvacious, sun-tanned female pulchritude. Cast: David Knell, Perry Lang, Paul Land, Steve Bassett, Jayne Modean, Corinne Alphen, Donald Symington, Mimi Cozzens, Jessica James, Richard B. Shull, Daniel Faraldo, John Archie, Robert Small, Fred Buch, Mark Pellicori, Bobbi Fritz, Rhonda Flynn, Bert Sheldon, Alex Panas, Barry Hober, Ronn Carroll, Roger Minami, Paul Lorenzo, John Terry, Marilyn Max, Lois Chamberlain, Laura J. Galgozy, Johanna Mileschikowsky, Elenore Raabe, Sheila Kennedy, Kathy Ryan, Maria Sedano, Christine Georgopulo. Dir and Pro: Sean S. Cunningham. Ex Pro: Mitch Leigh and Milton Herson. Assoc Pro: Barbara de Fina. Screenplay: David Smilow. Ph: Stephen Poster. Ed: Susan Cunningham. (Add Ed. Angie Ross). Pro Des: Virginia Field. Art: Nicholas Romanac. M: Harry Manfredini. M Ed: Vern Carlson. (Sean S. Cunningham Films–Columbia/EMI/Warner) Rel: 7 July 1983. 101 mins. Cert AA.

The Star Chamber. Thoughtful and interesting drama based on the all too frequent gap between justice and the law, seen particularly from the American angle, where it appears unscrupulous lawyers exploit technical legal loopholes by which confessed killers and other criminals walk out of the

The Star Chamber, with the leading role played by Michael Douglas (top of table, left).

courts free and legally untouchable. On a more personal level, it is the story of a confused and angry young judge who becomes a member of a secret judicial court whereby such escapees are retried in absentia, convicted and summarily executed. The plot is not always clear in legal and other motivation but it always holds, even at the sudden, melodramatically thrilling, physical climax. A nice cinematic debut by TV actress Sharon Glass of TV's *Cagney & Lacey* fame. Rest of cast: Michael Douglas, Hal Holbrook, Yaphet Kotto, James B. Sikking, Joe Regalbuto, Don Calfa, John Disanti, DeWayne Jessie, Jack Kehoe, Larry Hankin, Dick Anthony Williams, Margie Impert, Dana Gladstone, David Proval, Robin Gammell, Matthew Faison, Fred McCarren, Michael Ensign, Jason Bernard, Jerry Taft, Mike Austin, Sheldon Feldner, James Margolin, Hexin E. McPhee, Diana Douglas, Keith Buckley, Dom-

ingo Ambriz, Frances Bergen, Charlie Stavola, Robert Costanzo, Paul Brennan, Kate Zentall, George Cooper, Gary Rebstock, David Faustino, Jason Tomarken, George Dickerson, Eddy C. Dyer, John Garrett, Danna Hyams, Alan Oliney, Don Pulford, Ron Cummins, Jack Slate. Dir: Peter Hyams. Pro: Frank Yablans. Assoc Pro: Kurt Neumann and J.A. Zimbert. Screenplay: Roderick Taylor and Peter Hyams; based on the former's story. Ph: Richard Hannah. Ed: Jim Mitchell. Pro Des: Bill Malley. M: Michael Small. (Fox) Rel: 3 Nov 1983. 109 mins. Cert 15.

Star 80. The sad story of pretty (Canadian) Playboy Pet and movie starlet Dorothy Stratton who – according to the movie – was wooed and won by a sleek and nasty self-worshipping spiv who helped her to gain Playboy King Hugh Hefner's attention by sending him nude pictures of his wife. A not too easy to follow plot as it proceeds with

leaps and editing bounds, moving pretty superficially over the surface of a tragedy which ends in the murder of the girl by the estranged husband. Cast: Mariel Hemingway, Eric Roberts, Cliff Robertson, Carroll Baker, Roger Rees, David Clennon, Josh Mostel, Lisa Gordon, Sidney Miller, Keith Hefner, Tina Willson, Shelly Ingram, Sheila Anderson, Cis Rundle, Kathryn Witt, Jordan Christopher, James Luisi, Neva Patterson, Robert Fields, Keenen Ivory Wayans, Sandy Wolshin, Robert Perault, James Blendick, Jacqueline Coleman, Don Granbery, Stuart Damon, Ernest Thompson, Budd Friedman, Doborah Geffner, Norman Browning, Hagen Beggs, Bobby Bass, Gilbert S. Combs, Terence Kelly, Tabitha Herrington, Dean Hajum, Dan Zaleski, Paul Ryan, Michael Joel Shapiro, Fred Pierce, John Horn, David W. Rose, Stanley Kamel, Liz Sheridan, Liis Kailey, Robert Picardo, Erica Yohn, Marilyn Madderom. (Playboy Mansion Guests; Lonny Chin, Tracy Vaccaro, Kim St. Leon, Cathy

St. George, Carol Hills, Catherine Gilmore, Venus Pinkston, Michele Hill, Sulinda Watson, Katrina von Splawn, Kristine Garbo, Charlene Howell: Paul's Party Guests; David O. Cameron, Michael Levittan, Bonnie Kanner, Stacey M. Toten, Lorraine Michaels, Toni Petrie: Getaway/Prom Band; Don Jones, George McKensie, Jim Cross, Rick Webb, Martin Eade, Don Kitchen, Peter Ohrnberger). Dir and Screenplay: Bob Fosse. Pro: Wolfgang Glattes and Kenneth Utt. Story: Fosse; partly based on Teresa Carpenter's Pulitzer Prize-winning feature in *Village Voice – Death of a Playmate*. Ph: Sven Nykvist. Ed: Alan Heim. Art: Jack G. Taylor Jr. and Michael Bolton. M: Ralph Burns. Assoc Pro: Grace Blake. (Ladd Co–Warner Bros) Rel: floating; first shown London (Warner) Feb 1984. 103 mins. Cert 18.

A Star is Born. A re-issue of the 1954 classic, co-starring Judy Garland and James Mason, with an extra 26 minutes running time – including two Garland musical numbers – which were edited out of the original release. And that additional footage does no harm at all to this great movie. Rel: floating; first shown – in the new edition – London (Gate, Notting Hill), December 1983. (Warner) 180 mins.

Star Struck. A rather untidy, unconventional pop-musical about an ambitious barmaid of 18 summers (Jo Kennedy) who is launched towards stardom by an impresario of just 14 summers! An obviously youth-orientated Australian epic directed – somehow surprisingly in view of style and content – by Gillian Armstrong of *My Brilliant Career* fame. Rest of cast: Ross O'Donovan, Margo Lee, Max Cullen, Pat Evison, John O'May, Dennis Miller, Norman Erskine, Melissa Jaffer, Philip Judd, Dwayne Hillman, Ian Gilroy, Ned Lander, Ian Spence, Kerry McKay, Mark Little, Peter Davies, Carol Burns, Frances Spackman, Max Simms, Pat Rooney, Vola Vandere, Giselle Morgan, Ken Lambeth, Jamie Campbell, Warren Lewis, Lucky Grills, Bernard Curran, Frankie James, Syd Heylen, Doug Scroope, Judith Woodroffe, John Sheerin, Peter Boswell, Brett Nevill, Michael Moody, Ben Franklin, Lyn Lovett, Painee Skinner, John Garfield, Brian Blain, Geoffrey Rush, Janice Finn, Katherine

Mariel Hemingway, the model, and Eric Roberts the spiv husband, in *Star 80*.

Romaine, Kay Eklund, Geoffrey Rhoe, Doug Hull, Donnie Sutherland, Camille Linden, Elyse Clare, Rona Coleman, Stuart Campbell, Kaarin Fairfax, Sam (the dog). Dir: Gillian Armstrong. Pro: David Elfick and Richard Brennan. Screenplay and Assoc Pro: Stephen MacLean, Ph: Russell Boyd. Ed: Nicholas Beauman. Pro Des: Brian Thomson. Art: Kim Hilder. M Dir: Mark Moffatt. Choreographer: David Atkins. M Co-Ord: Jenny Keath. (Palm Beach Pictures–Entertainment Film Distributors) Rel: floating; first

Ambitious Jo Kennedy (centre) singing her way to success in *Star Struck*.

shown London (Gate, Bloomsbury), Feb 1984. 95 mins. Cert PG.

Staying Alive. The six-years-after sequel to *Saturday Night Fever*, with John Travolta now in New York waiting for his big chance, which comes when the male lead dancer is sacked from a new musical. Naturally, Travolta steps into the breach on the eve of the Broadway first night, having incidentally been loved and left by the beautiful star of the show along the way. Several Bee Gees songs, lots of jerky dance numbers to – literally – hellish backgrounds, and an athletic, beefcake performance by Travolta who to please his fans strips down to a loincloth for one of his numbers. And top marks to Finola Hughes, as the man-eating star,

Above: Travolta and Finola Hughes in *Staying Alive*. Right: Paul LeMat and Lulu Sylbert against the aliens (unmasked below) in *Strange Invaders*.

for best elocution – the only member of the cast who makes sure we can hear every word she says! Rest of cast: Cynthia Rhodes, Steve Inwood, Julie Bovasso, Charles Ward, Steve Bickford, Patrick Brady, Norma Donaldson, Jesse Doran, Joyce Hyser, Deborah Jenssen, Robert Martini, Sarah Miles, Tony Munafo, Susan Olar, Cindy Perlman, Ross St. Phillip, Kurtwood Smith, Frank Stallone. Dir: Sylvester Stallone. Pro: Stallone and Robert Stigwood. Screenplay: Stallone and Norman Wexler; based on the characters created by Nik Cohn. Ex Pro: Bill Oakes. Ph: Nick McLean. Ed: Don Zimmerman and Mark Warner. Pro Des: Robert F. Boyle. Art: Norman Newberry. M: Songs written and sung by The Bee Gees with add music by Johnny Mandel. M Co-Ord: Robin Garb. Choreography: Dennon Rawles and Sayhber Rawles. (Paramount–UIP) Rel: 22 Sept 1983. 96 mins. Cert PG.

Strange Invaders. A good straightforward sci-fi movie which very successfully manages to blend humour, horror and fantasy (the 'Blue Ball' ending is sheer kids' fairy-tale stuff). There is skulduggery in high places when some Aliens from another planet in the 1950s fix up a secret contract with the US Government to stay for 25 years (in plastic-covered humanoid disguise) whilst observing life on the – American – Earth. The 'cover-up' is revealed in the '80s, when in preparation for their return, the Aliens abduct the wife (who's one of them), daughter and dog of Paul LeMat, who then sets out with delightful young journalist Nancy Allen to get his family back. Some neat satire as well as some startling effects when the visitors, getting literally too hot under the collar, tear off their human disguise to reveal the ET-like creatures beneath. Rest of cast: Diana Scarwid, Michael Lerner, Louise Fletcher, Wallace Shawn, Fiona Lewis, Kenneth Tobey, June Lockhart, Charles Lane, Lulu Sylbert, Joel Cohen. Dir: Michael Laughlin. Pro: Walter Coblenz. Screenplay: William Condon and Laughlin. Ph: Louis Horvath. Ed: John W. Wheeler. Pro Des: Susanna Moore. M: John Addison. Assoc Pro: Richard Moore and Joel Cohen. (Orion–Thorn EMI) Rel: floating; first shown London (Studio), Feb 1984. 92 mins. Cert PG.

Kelly Nichols and Jerry Butler, the 'hungry' couple in *Strangers in Love*.

Strangers in Love. Boy meets Girl; Boy and Girl hungrily copulate; Boy loses Girl – he seeks her here, and there, and everywhere, in vain. Years later Boy meets Girl again, and they hungrily copulate again – and, presumably, live happily ever after! A trite romance decorated with plenty of sexual incident – but presented tastefully enough to lift this minor sex film well above the pornographic mark. Cast: Kelly Nichols, Jerry Butler, Michael Knight, Tish Ambrose, Veronica Hart, Samantha Fox, Michael Bruce, Susan Nero, Beth Alison Broderick, Rachel Orion, Dan Stephens, Jack Wrangler, Joanna Storm. Dir and Pro: Chuck Vincent. Assoc Pro: Bob Meyer. Screenplay: Rick Marx and Chuck Vincent; from a story by Henri Pachard. Ph: Larry Revene. Ed: James Macreading. Pro Des: Larry Revene. M: Ian Shaw. (Theme Song, *That First Love* sung by Kate Robbins). (Black Cat Films) Rel: floating; first shown London (Studio, Oxford Circus), March 1984. 72 mins. Cert 18.

Strangers Kiss. A refreshingly original movie about moviemaking in Hollywood, circa the mid 1950s, with a fanatical director who, for the sake of realism, encourages his leading man and woman to fall in love, even though he is aware that the girl is being kept by a gangster whose money is backing the production. Technically clever in the way the real and film romance run in tandem, side by side, but separated by the colour tones. There is quite a lot of wit around, too. Cast: Peter Coyote (splendid as the director), Victoria Tennant, Blaine Novak, Dan Shor, Richard Romanus, Linda Kerridge, Carlos Palomino, Vincent Palmieri, Jay Rasumny, Jon Sloan, Arthur Adams, Joseph Nipote, Jeanette Joseph, Cecil Hill, Frank Moon, Larry Dilge. Dir: Matthew Chapman. Pro: Douglas Dilge. Ex Pro: Michael White. Co-Pro: Hercules Bellville. Assoc Pro: Sean Ferrer. Screenplay: Blaine Novak and Matthew Chapman; from a story by Novak. Ph: Mikhail Suslov. No Ed credit. (but Ed Consultant: William Carruth and Visual Con: J. Michael Riva). Art: Ginny Randolph. M: Gato Barbieri. (Enterprise Pictures) Rel:

Victoria Tennant and Blaine Novak share a romantic scene on screen in *Strangers Kiss*.

floating; first shown London (Gate, Notting Hill), June 1984. 100 mins. Cert 15.

Streamers. Robert Altman's film of a play by David Rabe about a quartet of US Army draftees; two white (an upper-class homosexual and a nice ex-college lad) and two black (one easy-going, the other dangerously touchy on some subjects). All four are waiting at home base to be called – this is 1965 – to the Vietnam front and filling in the boring interval by whoring, boozing and getting dangerously on each other's nerves. Cast: Matthew Modine, Michael Wright, Mitchell Lichtenstein, David Allen Grier, Albert Macklin, Guy Bond, George Dzundza. Dir and Pro. (latter with Nick J. Mileti): Robert Altman. Ph: Pierre Mignot. Ed: Norman Smith. Pro Des: Wolf Kroeger. Art: Steve Altman. M: Stephen Foster's *Beautiful Dreamer* with new words added. (United Artists Classics–Rank Film Dist) Rel: floating; first shown London (Classic Haymarket and Odeon Swiss Cottage), March 1984. 118 mins. Cert 18.

Street Fleet. Rough and raucous story of the metamorphosis of a run-down Washington taxi firm with the advent and good influence of a bright young lad from the South. Lots of action and some very loud musical numbers. Cast: Adam Baldwin, Charlie Barnett, Irene

Paul Rodriguez, one of the drivers of the D.C. Cab Co., in *Street Fleet*.

Cara, Anne de Salvo, Max Gail, Gloria Gifford, De Wayne Jessie, Bill Maher, Whitman Mayo, Mr. T, Jose Perez, Paul Rodriguez, David Barbarian, Peter Barbarian, Marsha Warfield, Gary Busey, Bob Zmuda, Jim Moody, Denise Gordy, Alfredine P. Brown, Scott Nemes, Senta Moses, Jill Schoelen, Diana Bellamy, John Diehl, Bonnie Keith, J.W. Smith, Moriah Shannon, Newton D. Arnold, Michael Elliott Hill, Dennis Stewart, Paula Earlette Davis, Jacki Clark, Don Jacob, Ann Guildford-Grey. Dir and Screenplay: Joel Schumacher; from a story by Topper Carew and Schumacher. Pro: Topper Carew. Ex Pro: Peter Guber and John Peters. Assoc Pro: Peter V. Herald. Co-Pro: Cassius Vernon Weathersby. Ph: Dean Cundey and Ron Van Nostrand. Pro Des: John Lloyd. Art: Bernie Cutler. Ed: David Blewitt. M: Giorgio Moroder. (RKO/Universal–UIP) Rel: 2 March 1984. 99 mins. Cert 15.

Stryker. Another filmic – this time Phillipino – glimpse into a pretty unpleasant, post-atomic war world where water is the main commodity in short supply and much fought over. When a warring group of females find the only pure water spring left on earth, sexual struggle intervenes before bringing eventual peace between the warring factions and the dawn of a new era! Cast: Steve Sandor, Andria Savio, William Ostrander, Michael Lane, Julie Gray, Monique St. Pierre, Ken Metcalfe, Jon Harris III, Joe Zucchero. Dir

and Pro: Cirio H. Santiago. Screenplay: Howard R. Cohen; from a story by Leonard Hermes. Assoc Pro: Jose Buenaventura and Vincent Dayrit. Ph: Dick Remias. Ed: Bas Santos. M: Ed Gatchlian (Add M: Susan Justin: M Ed: Jim Matheny). (H.C.I. Trading Co–New World Pictures–EMI) Rel: 23 Dec 1983. 86 mins. Cert 18.

The Subjective Factor – Der subjektiv Faktor. Feminist-slanted West German film which sets a fictional story against the factual background of the 1960–70s and the beginnings of the German women's movement. Cast: Angelika Rommel, Tobias Delius, Nils Delius, Kai Opitz, Nikolaus Dutsch, Lutz Weidlich, Dominik Bender, Johanna Sophia, Tillmann Braun, Klaus Trebes, Karin Mumm, Charlotte Matthiesen,

The Amazonian gang take stock of their male opponents in *Stryker*.

Bill Foster, Felix Backe, Hans-Jörg Frey, Hannes Hellmann, Ulrich Huber, Hans-Dieter Wohlmann, Jockel Baumann, Klaus Mehner, Roswitha Soukup, Paul Adler, Peter Scharf, Barbara von Baur, Monika Albrecht, Elmar Altvater, Detel Aurand, Beate Banck, Jan Berg, Rainer Berson, Eberhard Delius, Dagmar Franz, Christiane Grass, The Hirt Family, Jürgen Hoffmann, Inga Humpe, Ivuschka, Nils Kadritzke, Silvo Lahtela, Michael Marondel, Verena Meinhardt, Jürgen Rieger, Gabriele Ruthmann, Helma Sanders-Brahms, Wolf-Dietrich Schilhab, Claudia Schilinski, Peter Schmidt, Ingrid Schmidt-Harzbach, David Schröder, Traute Siebert, Petra du Sold, Gesine Strempel, Martina Wehner, Hildegard Westbeld, Eva Wexler, Helga Wullweber. Dir and Screenplay: Helke Sander. Pro: Marianne Gassner. Ph: Martin Schäfer. Ed: Ursula Höf and Dörte Völz. Art: Jürgen Rieger. M: Heiner Goebbels. (Helke Sander Filmproduktion in assoc with ZDF–Resistance Films) Rel: floating; first shown London (ICA), 5 Oct 1983. 144 mins. No cert.

Subway Riders. Vaguely 'undergroundish' Warhol-reminiscent movie about a saxophone player who commits a series of random murders, serenading his victims beforehand! But this aspect of the plot seems almost incidental to the director's purpose of examining the individual's isolation in a big city. More of a curiosity than a movie. Cast: Robbie Coltrane, Charlene Kaleina, Cookie Mueller, John Lurie, Amos Poe, Susan Tyrrel, Bill Rice, Leigh Tyler, Babs Egan, M. de Muro, S. Moss, C.

Clint Eastwood in *Sudden Impact*, again playing 'Dirty Harry', the detective who meets violence with violence.

Yee, F. Kutlik, S. Vermont, A. Mashkov, J. Zaloga, Paul Ricci, Emilo Cubero, Lance Loud, Tony Schfrazi, Henry Benenutti, Nina Gaidarova, Lindzee Smith, Ed Buck, Emily Poe, Glenn O'Brien, Chris Kosburg, Jane, Tom Wright. Dir and Screenplay: Amos Poe. Pro: Poe and Johanna Heer. Ph: Johanna Heer. (Hep Pictures–Mainline) Rel: floating; late June and July, 1983. 118 mins. No cert.

Sudden Impact. Fourth in the 'Dirty Harry' detective series and the first to be directed by the films' star Clint Eastwood. Here – in what is almost certainly the most rough and violent of the quartet – our anti-hero is sent out of town (San Francisco) by his superiors in order to let the municipal heat created by his strong-arm methods to cool. Needless to state, on arriving in the small Californian resort, he soon finds even more work for his ever-ready gun

and ruthless determination to bring the bad men to brutal book. There are some pretty controversial ethics involved, too, when he saves a multi-murderess from justice. Rest of cast: Sondra Locke, Pat Hingle, Bradford Dillman, Paul Drake, Audrie J. Neenan, Jack Thibeau, Michael Currie, Albert Popwell, Mark Keyloun, Kevyn Major Howard, Bette Ford, Nancy Parsons, Joe Bellan, Wendell Wellman, Mara Corday, Russ McCubbin, Robert Sutton, Nancy Fish, Carmen Argenziano, Lisa Britt, Bill Reddick, Lois de Banzie, Matthew Child, Michael Johnson, Nick Dimitri, Michael Maurer, Pat DuVal, Christian Phillips, Steven Kravitz, Dennis Royston, Melvin Thompson, Jophery Brown, Bill Upton, Lloyd Nelson, Christopher Pray, James McEachin, Maria Lynch, Ken Lee, Morgan Upton, John X. Heart, David Gonzales, Albert Martinez, David Rivers, Robert Rivers, Harry DeMopoulos, Lisa London, Tom Spratley, Eileen Wiggins, John Nowack. Stunts by Carey Loftin, Fritz Manes, Debby Porter, Christine Baur, Jade

David, Scott Dockstader, Jerry Gatlin, Larry Holt, Kristy Horak, Jack Lilley, Paula Moody, George Orrison, Chuck Waters, Al Silvani. Dir and Pro: Clint Eastwood. Ex Pro: Fritz Manes. Assoc Pro: Steve Perry. Screenplay: Joseph E. Stinson; story by Earl E. Smith and Charles B. Pierce, based on characters created by Harry Julian Fink and R.M. Fink. Ph: Bruce Surtees. Ed: Joel Cox. Pro Des: Edward Carfagno. M: Lalo Schifrin. (Warner Bros) Rel: 27 Jan 1984. 117 mins. Cert 18.

Superman III. Inevitably, with the initial novelty impact long since gone, this third movie about the incredible flying knight hero seems – despite immense effort, some good ideas and novel sequences – somewhat less amusing than its predecessors. Quirky director Richard Lester replaces the firm morals of the earlier epics with lots of slapstick – notably most successfully (in spite of some loss of good taste in getting laughs from an unfortunate blind man whose guide dog has run off) in the opening credits sequence. But

Superman III, and again Christopher Reeve is in action as the flying hero, with Richard Pryor, while (left), as Clarke Kent, he dallies with Annette O'Toole.

apart from these personal reservations, undoubtedly a film with immense general appeal. Cast: Christopher Reeve, Richard Pryor, Jackie Cooper, Marc McClure, Annette O'Toole, Annie Ross, Pamela Stephenson, Robert Vaughn, Margot Kidder, Gavan O'Herlihy, Nancy Roberts, Graham Stark, Henry Woolf, Gordon Rollings, Peter Wear, Justin Case, Bob Todd, Terry Camilleri, Stefan Kalipha, Helen Horton, Lou Hirsch, Bill Reimbold, Shane Rimmer, Al Matthews, Barry Dennen, Enid Saunders, Kevin Harrison Cork, Robert Henderson, Paul Kaethler, R.J. Bell, Pamela Mandell, Peter Whitman, Ronnie Brody, Sandra Dickinson, Philip Gilbert, Pat Starr, Gordon Signer, John Bluthal, George Chisholm, David Fielder, Robert Beatty, Chris Malcolm, Larry Lamb. Stunt Cast: Richard Hammatt, Mark Stewart, Greg Elam, Roy Alon, Dicky Beer, Marc Boyle, Ken Baker, Sue Crosland, Clive Curtis, Tracy Eddon, Reg Harding, Billy Horrigan,

Wendy Leech, Wayne Michaels, Colin Skeaping, Eddie Stacey, Terry Walsh. Dir: Richard Lester. Pro: Pierre Spengler. Ex Pro: Ilya Salkind. Assoc Pro: Robert Simmonds. Pro Ex: Pauline Coutelenq. Screenplay: David and Leslie Newman. Ph: Robert Paynter. Ed: John Victor Smith. Assoc Ed: Peter Hollyman. Pro Des: Peter Murton. Art: Terry and Brian Ackland-Snow, and Bert Davey. M: Ken Thorne; with original songs composed by Giorgio Moroder. Flying and 2nd Unit Dir: David Lane. Special Effects Dir: Colin Chilvers. (Dovemead Ltd–For Canthavus Productions/Alexander and Ilya Salkind–Warner Bros) Rel: 21 July 1983. 120 mins. Cert PG.

Swann in Love – Un Amour de Swann. The French-West German co-production of a small but significant fillet from the first part of Marcel Proust's enormous literary work: 24 hours in the life of the rich and sophisticated Jew Charles Swann (Jeremy Irons) and the lovely, former lady of the town Odette de Crecy (Ornella Muti). A tale of obsessive passion, violent jealousy and superficiality seen against the background of Paris society of the period. And tacked on is a kind of epilogue set fifteen years later, with Swann doomed to an early death and Odette enjoying the prestige of being married. Even though Proust remains basically unworkable in visual terms, the film does capture a great deal of the atmosphere of the period and ambiance of the characters, and though leisurely and undramatic is consistently fascinating to watch, thanks a great deal to the decor, the photography and the performances, including a – surprisingly – marvellously apt one by Alain Delon as the homosexual poet and wit, the Baron de Charlus. Rest of cast: Fanny Ardant, Marie-Christine Barrault, Anne Bennent, Nathalie Juvet, Charlotte Kerr, Catherine Lachens, Philippine Pascale, Charlotte de Turckheim, Nicolas Baby, Jean-François Balmer, Jacques Boudet, Jean-Louis Richard. Bruno Thost, Geoffroy Tory, Roland Topor, Jean-Pierre Coffe, Vincent Martin, Marc Arian. Dir: Volker Schlöndorff. Pro: Margaret Menegoz, Nicole Stephane and Eberhard Junkersdorf. Screenplay: Peter Brook, Jean-Claude Carrière and Marie-Hélène Estienne; based on *Du Côte de Chez Swann*, the first part of Marcel Proust's *A la Recherche du Temps Perdu*, adapted by Schlöndorff. Ph: Sven Nykvist. Ed: Françoise Bonnot. Costumes (no Art credits): Yvonne Sassinot de Nesle. M: Hans Werner Henze. (Gaumont/Bioskop Films/FR3/SFPC–Artificial Eye) Rel: floating; first shown London (Lumiere), April 1984. 110 mins. Cert 18.

Sweet Body of Bianca. Minor Greek sex film, with the usual sequence of couplings to moaning accompaniment. Cast: Grazia de Giorgi, Marina Frajese, Mario Cutini, Panos Fitos, Sabrina Mastrolorenzi, Bruno Alias, Vanessa Dariou, Mara Johnson, Antonis Leonardo, Nicolas Georgiou, Aleca Venardou, Rosella Oramis. Dir: Ilia Milonako. Pro and Screenplay: Vagelis Fournistakis. Pro Direction: Vorgo Statiras. Ph: Vasilis Christomoglou. Ed: Daniele Alabiso. No art credit. M: Giovanni Ullu. (Andromeda International–Golden Era) Rel: 21 July 1983. 73 mins. Cert X.

Failed singer Robert Duvall and religious young widow Tess Harper in *Tender Mercies*.

Tender Mercies. A simple and entirely delightful story which, however basically unlikely, is treated with such delicacy by Australian director Bruce Beresford (though it is an American film) that it is entirely acceptable. It tells of the marriage of a down-and-out country-and-western singer with a former drink problem to the deeply religious and attractive young widow who runs a small motel in remote Texas. The marriage works so well, that it not only survives the little bumps given it by the singer's ex-wife, but also the tragic death of his daughter. Old-fashioned in the best cinematic sense of the word. Cast: Robert Duvall, Tess Harper, Allan Hubbard, Betty Buckley, Ellen Barkin, Wilford Brimley. Michael Crabtree, Lenny von Dohlen, Stephen Funchess, James Aaron, Rick Murray, Roy R. Russell, Paul Gleason, Dir: Bruce Beresford. Pro: Philip S. Hobel. Assoc. Pro: Mary Ann Hobel. Screenplay: Horton Foote. Ph: Russell Stewart Boyd. Ed: William Anderson. Pro Des: Jeannine Oppewall. M: George Dreyfus. (Antron Media Inc–EMI) Rel: floating; first shown London (ABC, Shaftesbury Ave), June 1983. 91 mins. Cert PG.

Shirley Maclaine (right, above) with Debra Winger, and (left) with Jack Nicholson, in *Terms of Endearment*.

Terms of Endearment. The story of a close if sometimes uneasy mother-daughter relationship which veers erratically between lively comedy and soap-opera drama as it tries (but fails) to cram into its 132 episodic minutes enough plot for a whole TV series. Shirley MacLaine (mother) and Jack Nicholson (ex-astronaut, hard-drinking lover) do marvels with their roles (both of them winning Oscars) but cannot make their parts any more likeable or morally acceptable than most of the other characters in the piece. And some of the players would certainly have benefited from elocution lessons. Rest of cast: Debra Winger, Danny De Vito, Jeff Daniels, John Lithgow, Lisa Hart Carroll, Betty R. King, Huckleberry Fox, Troy Bishop, Shane Serwin, Megan Morris, Tara Yeakey, Norman Bennett, Jennifer Josey, Kaye Charleson, Tom Wees, Paul Manzel, F. William Parker, Amanda Watkins, Buddy Gilbert, David Wohl, Shelley K. Nielsen, Bette Croissant, Charles Beall, Leslie Folse, Sharisse Parker,

Judith A. Dickerson, Devon O'Brien, Dana Vance, Alexandra O'Karma, Nancy E. Mette, Holly Beth Holmberg, Lear Levin, A. Brooks, Lanier Whilden, Helen Stauffer, Barbara Balik, Michelle Watkins, John C. Conger, Sandra Newkirk, Elaine McGown, Jeannie Epper, Alan R. Gibbs, Mary Kay Place. Dir Pro and Screenplay: James L. Brooks; based on the novel by Larry McMurtry. Co-Pro: Penney Finkelman and Martin Jurow, Ph: Andrzej Bartkowiak. Ed: Richard Marks. Pro Des: Polly Platt. M: Michael Gore. (Paramount–UIP) Rel: 30 March 1984. 132 mins. Cert 15.

The Terry Fox Story. It took well over a year for this excellent Canadian film to cross the Atlantic, the more suprising in that it is considerably better than many others that did the trip in far less time. It is a warm, and even inspiring, real-life tale about a young man who, after losing a leg from cancer, set out to run more than 5000 miles across Canada in aid of cancer research and successfully raised more than ten million pounds by doing it. Not an easy character – egocentric and liable to outbursts of temper – but an amazingly strong one. Against medical advice but with the cancer fund's support, and despite initial parental opposition and little public interest, he doggedly ran on beyond exhaustion, to his goal. A fine performance in the title role by newcomer Eric Fryer, himself an amputee. Rest of cast: Robert Duvall, Eric Fryer, Michael Zelniker, Chris Make-

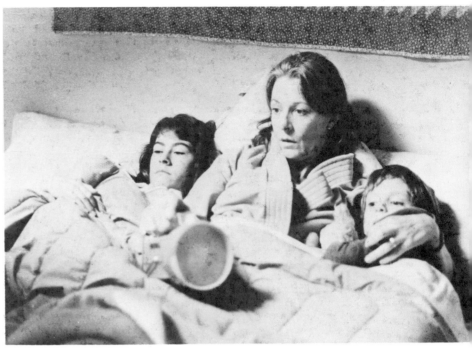

Mother Jane Alexander and children Roxana Sal and Lukas Haas in *Testament*.

peace, Rosalind Chao, Elva Mai Hoover, Frank Adams, Marie McCann, R.H. Thomson, Saul Rubine, Gary Darycot, Matt Craven, Chuck Shamata, Patrick Watson. Dir: Ralph L. Thomas. Pro: Robert Cooper. Ex Pro: Gursten Rosenfeld and Michael Levine. Assoc Pro: John Eckert. Screenplay: Edward Hume; based on a story by John and Rose Kastner. Ph: Richard Ciupka. Ed: Ron Wisman. Art: Gavin Mitchell. M: Bill Conti. (Astral Films in co-op with CTV & Bank of Montreal–ITC) Rel: 15 June 1984. 97 mins. Cert PG.

Testament. Another 'After The Bomb' movie; this one a very restrained, and deliberately ambiguous (no hints of international tension; is the explosion an accident?) but credible one as it follows the gradual debilitation of a typical middle-class American family's slide down the slope to radiation death against a background of almost normal conditions (they were too far away to feel the blast). Sober, depressing and, within the context, extremely well done. Cast: Jane Alexander, William Devane, Ross Harris, Roxana Zal, Lukas Haas, Philips Anglim, Lilia Skala, Leon Ames, Lurene Tuttle, Rebecca de Mornay, Kevin Costner, Mako, Mico Olmos, Gerry Murillo, J. Brennan Smith, Lesley Woods, Wayne Heffley, William Schilling, David Nichols, Gary Bayer, Martin Rudy, Jamie Abbott, Rocky Krakoff, Rachel Gudmunson, Keri Houlihan, Pauline Lomas, Jesse Wayne, Clete Roberts. Dir: Lynne Littman. Pro: Littman and Jonathan Bernstein. Assoc Pro: Andrea Asumow. Screenplay: John Sacret Young; based on the story of the same title by Carol Amen. Ph: Steven Poster. Ed: Suzanne Pettit. Pro Des: David Nichols. M: James Horner. Filmed entirely on location in Sierra Madre, California. (Entertainments Events in assoc with American Playhouse–Paramount–UIP) Rel: floating; first shown London (Plaza), March 1984. 90 mins. Cert PG.

Triumph in sport, *The Terry Fox Story*, with Eric Fryer (left) the young athlete.

Mel Brooks and Anne Bancroft, with Charles Durning (inset), in *To Be or Not To Be*.

To Begin Again – Volver a Empezar. Somewhat surprisingly an Oscar winner as 'Best Foreign Film of 1983, this low-toned, leisurely and often highly sentimental story from Spain is about a Nobel Prize Winner for Literature (working at the University of California) with an incurable disease, who returns to his Gijon birthplace (left for the New World in 1938) to recapture some of his early joys and meet old friends and mistresses before making a final return to America to live out the short span left to him. Cast: Antonio Ferrándis (the Professor), Encarna Paso, José Bódalo, Agustin González, Pablo Hoyos, Marta Fernandez Muro, Pablo del Hoyo. Dir Pro and Screenplay (last with Angel Llorente): José Luis Garcia. Ex Pro: Estaban Alenda and Angel Llorente. Ph: Manuel Rojas. Pro Des: Gil Parrondo. M: Johann Pachelbel (and Cole Porter). (Nickel Odeon-Premier Releasing). Rel: floating; first shown London (Minema) June 1984. 93 mins. Cert PG.

To Be or Not To Be. Updated and otherwise retailored re-make of the 1942 Ernst Lubitsch comedy adapted to fit the considerable talents of Mel Brooks. He plays the star and producer of the Warsaw Bronski Theatrical Company, caught up in the Nazi occupation of Poland, who increasingly and gallantly supports the agent sent from England to prevent the list of Warsaw Underground members falling into the hands of the Gestapo. Slow in starting but soon warming up and finishing on a high note of farcical comedy. Rest of cast: Anne Bancroft (Mrs Brooks of course), Tim Matheson, Charles Durning, Jose Ferrer, Christopher Lloyd, James Haake and 'Scamp', George Gaynes, George Wyner, Jack Riley, Lewis J. Stadlen, Ronny Graham, Estelle Reiner, Zale Kessler, Earl Boen, Ivor Barry, William Glover, John Francis, Raymond Skipp, Marley Sims, Larry Rosenberg, Max Brooks, Henry Kaiser, Milt Jamin, George Caldwell, Wolf Muser, Henry Brandon, Lee E. Stevens, Frank Lester, Roy Goldman, Robert Goldberg, John McKinney, Eda Reiss Merin, Manny Kleinmuntz, Phil Adams, Curt Lowens, Dieter Curt, Howard Goodwin, Robin Haynes, Ron Kuhlman, John Otrin, Blane Savage, Joey Sheck, Gillian Eaton, Paddi Edwards, Terence Marsh, Winnie McCarthy, Paul Ratliff, Scott Beach, Sandra Gray, Lainie Manning, Antonette Yuskis, Clare Culhane, Leeyan Granger, Stephanie Wingate, Ian Bruce, John Frayer, Edward J. Heim, Spencer Henderson, George Jayne, Bill K. Richards, Neil J. Schwartz, Tucker

Smith, Ted Sprague. Dir: Alan Johnson. Pro: Mel Brooks. Ex Pro: Howard Jeffrey. Assoc Pro: Irene Walzer. Screenplay: Thomas Meehan and Ronny Graham. Ph: Gerald Hirschfeld. Ed: Alan Balsam. Pro Des: Terence Marsh. M: John Morris. (Songs; 'Ladies' and 'A Little Peace', lyrics & music by Mel Brooks and Ronny Graham). Pro Sup: Jack Frost Sanders. Based on the film of same title by Ernst Lubitsch; screenplay by Edwin Justus Mayer and story by Melchior Lengyel. (Brooksfilms Productions–Fox) Production suggested by William Allyn and David Lunney. Rel: Mar. 16 1984. 108 mins. Cert PG.

Tokyo Story – Tokyo Monogatari. Yasujiro Ozu's gentle, rather melancholy but leisurely 1953 family piece, made in black-and-white. An elderly couple, invited by their children to spend a holiday with them in Tokyo, find the trip somewhat less satisfactory than they had hoped, as they realise that the family tie has been loosened by distance and time. On returning to their far-away village, the mother dies, and we then see the various reactions of family and in-laws at and after the funeral. Lovely, graceful performances. Cast: Chishu Ryu, Chiyeko Higashiyama, Setsuko Hara, Haruko Sugimura, So Yamamura, Kuniko Miyake, Kyoko Kagawa, Nobuo Nakamura, Eijiro Tohno, Hisao Toake, Shizuka Murase, Michihiro Mohri. Dir and Screenplay (latter with Kogo Noda): Yasujiro Ozu. Pro: Takeshi Yamamoto. Ph: Yushun Atsuta. Ed: Yoshiyasu Hamamura. Art: Tatsuo Hamada. M: Takanori Saito. (Shochiku Pro. Co–Cinegate) Rel: floating; first shown London (Gate, Notting Hill), Oct 1983. 135 mins. Black-and-White. Cert U.

To our Loves – A Nos Amours. A leisurely, meandering film about a young girl who finds it impossible either to love or hate with any depth. She indulges in numerous, unsatisfying, love affairs, has frighteningly violent rows with her mother and brother (head of the family after father – with whom alone she has some affinity) – walks out on it all and, eventually marrying, almost immediately goes off to America with another man ... still searching for something she will doubtless never find. A wonderful performance by young newcomer Sandrine Bonnaire and excellent ones from the mixed professional and amateur cast, including director Maurice Pialat (father), Evelyne Ker (mother) and Dominique Besnehard (brother). Rest of cast: Anne-Sophie Maille, Christophe Odent, Cyr Boitard, Maite Maille, Pierre-Loup Rajot, Cyril Collard, Nathalie Gureghian, Guenole Pascal, Caroline Cibot, Jacques Fieschi, Valerie Schlumberger, Tom Stevens, Tsilka Theodorou, Vanghel Theodorou, Isabelle Prades, Herve Austen, Alexandre de Dardel, Alexis Quentin, Pierre Novion, Eric Viellard. Dir and Co-Screenplay (with Arlette Langmann): Maurice Pialat. Ex Pro: Micheline Pialat. Assoc Pro: Emmanuel Schlumberger. Ph: Jacques Loiseleux. Ed: Yann Dedet. Sets (no art credit): Jean-Paul Camail and Arlette Langmann. (Les Films du Livradois/Gaumont/FR3–Artificial Eye) Rel: floating; first shown London (Camden Plaza) June 1984. 102 min. Cert 15 (Awarded Prix Louis Delluc 1983, and Best Film César 1984).

The Toy. An ungainly farce about a business magnate who, to satisfy his small son's whim, 'buys' one of his accident-prone employees – Richard Pryor no less! – on a week's lease as a present. But this is almost certainly the most awkward, strained and unfunny performance that Pryor has given so far, perhaps, one speculates, because he has not been allowed that profusion of four-letter words with which his dialogue is usually splattered. Rest of cast: Jackie Gleason, Ned Beatty, Scott Schwartz, Teresa Ganzel, Wilfrid Hyde-White, Annazette Chase, Tony King, Don Hood, Karen Leslie-Little, Virginia Capers, B.J. Hopper, Linda McCann, Ray Spruell, Stocker Fontelieu, Stuart Baker-Bergen, Robert Adams, Mark Bennett, John R. Wilson, Robert Costley, Robert Earle, Pauline Barcelona, Juan Coleman, Valerian Smith, Elbert Andre Patrick, Orwin Harvey, Jim Clancy, Davis Hotard, Debra Cole, Marilyn Gleason, Charles Detraz, Steven Kahan, Paul Tuerpe, Jim Beyer, Tot Beyer, Robert M. Stevens, Sally Birdsong, Louis Weinberg, Annie McGuire, Beverley Tagg, George Howard, Helen Howard, Alex Hyde-White, Bill Holliday, J.D. Martin, James Roddy, Lucy Campbell Rowland, Robert Cherry, Delana Renay Cole, Lewis Baker, La Monica Matthews, Bruce Langley, Dawnis Kaye Smith, Santos Swing, Willie Swing. Dir: Richard Donner. Pro: Phil Feldman. Assoc Pro; Margaret Booth. Screenplay: Carol Sobieski; based on a previous film by Francis Veber. Ph: Laszlo Kovacs. Ed: Richard Harris and Michael A. Stevenson. Pro Des: Charles Rosen. M: Patrick Williams: song 'I Want to be Your Friend' by Trevor Lawrence and Frank Jusker, perf by Jeffrey Osborne. (Columbia) Rel: 3 Nov 1983. 102 mins. Cert PG.

The Toy proved that even Richard Prior (centre) can do little with poor material.

Left to right: Don Ameche, Eddie Murphy and Ralph Bellamy in *Trading Places*.

Trading Places. A splendid farce-comedy built on old-fashioned, vintage foundations—a ludicrously impossible story, lots of fun, and a number of superb performances, including those of veterans Ralph Bellamy and Don Ameche, ably supported by younger farceurs like Dan Aykroyd, Jamie Lee Curtis and Eddie Murphy, with a solid contribution from Denholm Elliott. All about a bet by a couple of cute and crooked old brokers which involves the disgrace of their financial wizard tipster and his replacement by a young negro whose only previous business experience has been as a blind (!) beggar. All so silly – but, oh, *so* effectively amusing. Rest of cast: Kristin Holby, Robert Curtis-Brown, Nicholas Guest, John Bedford-Lloyd, Tony Sherer, Tom Mardirosian, Charles Brown, Avon Long, Paul Gleason, P. Jay Sidney, Clint Smith, Ron Taylor, James D. Turner, Gwyllum Evans, Frank Oz, Bill Cobbs, Kelly Curtis, Tracy K. Shaffer, Susan Fallender, Bo Diddley, Al Franken, Tom Davis, Don McLeod. Dir: John Landis. Pro: Aaron Russo. Ex Pro: George Folsey Jr. Screenplay: Timothy Harris and Herschel Weingrod. Assoc Pro: Sam Williams and Irwin Russo. Ph: Robert Paynter. Pro Des: Gene Rudolf. Ed: Malcolm Campbell. M: Elmer Bernstein. (Paramount–UIP) Rel: 13 Jan 1984. 116 mins. Cert 15.

The Tragedy of Carmen. A brilliant 'chamber-music' Peter Brook production of the Bizet opera, which to judge by its concentration on close-shot and close-up, has been designed more for the television than the cinema screen. But a delight in any case, with fine acting performances allied to outstanding singing. No opera-lover should let this little gem slip by unvisited. Cast: Hélène Delavault, Howard Hensel, Agnes Host, Jake Gardner, Jean-Paul Denizon, Alain Maratrat. Dir: Peter Brook. Pro: Micheline Rozan. Ex Pro: Pierre Jourdan. Based on the work of Georges Bizet (music), Prosper Mérimée (original story) and Meilhac and Halvey (libretto) adapted by Marius Constant, Jean-Claude Carrière and Peter Brook. Ph: Sven Nykvist. M (dir and con): Marius Constant. Set Designer: Georges Wakhevitch. Filmed at Théâtre des Bouffes du Nord from the perf by Théâtre National de l'Opéra de Paris and Centre International à Créations Théâtrales. (Antenne 2/Channel Four/Bavaria Atelier, Munich/Alby Films–BFI) Rel: floating; first shown London (Barbican), May 1984. 85 mins. Cert PG.

Tribute – The Overlord Embroidery. The story of a modern Bayeux Tapestry, designed by Miss Sandra Lawrence (with advice from the three Services) which took twenty ladies of the Royal School of Needlework almost seven years to complete. Depicting the events of D-Day – 6 June 1944 – the tapestry is not only a unique work of art, it is also the largest embroidery of its kind in the world, measuring more than 90 yards in length. (Overlord Embroidery Educational & Promotional Services Ltd) floating; first shown London (Minema), Nov 1983. 22 mins. Cert U.

Triumphs of a Man Called Horse. Third in the 'Horse' Western series, with most of the action handed over this time to White Man (Richard Harris), Sioux Chief Yellow Hand's son Koda, a law student when his dad is ambushed and mortally wounded. And despite endless provocation the youngster finally defeats the ruthless seekers after gold in his tribe's territory, and sees them run out by a none too enthusiastic US Calvalry. Good old-fashioned cowboys-and-'injuns' stuff. Rest of cast: Michael Beck, Ana de Sade, Vaughn Armstrong, Buck Taylor, Sebastian Ligarde, Ann Seymour, Miguel Angel Fuentes, Regino Herrera, Lauturo Murua, Roger Cudney, Simon Andreu, John Chandler, Walter Wyatt, Gerry Gatlin. Dir: John Hough. Pro: Derek Gibson. Ex

Ana de Sade draws a bow on a surprised gunman in *Triumphs of a Man called Horse*.

Pro: Sandy Howard. Screenplay: Ken Blackwell. Assoc Pro: Don Borchers. Action Dir: Terry Leonard. Ph: John Alcott. Pro Des: Alan Roderick-Jones. Ed: Roy Watts. No M credit. (VTC Films) Rel: floating; first shown London (Classic Tottenham Ct Rd), Nov 1983. 85 mins. Cert 15.

The 12 Chairs. Re-issue of the 1970 movie based on the 1920s novel by Ilya Ilf and Eugene Petrov about the frantic search for the chair, one of a set of twelve now distributed, in which a fortune in jewels has been hidden. The search is given a fine degree of lunacy by Ron Moody, Frank Langella and Dom Deluise. This was the second film in which Mel Brooks doubled as writer-director, as well as playing an important role. Rest of cast: Bridget Brice, Robert Bernal, David Lander, Diane Copeland, Nicholas Smith, Elaine Gar-

reau, Will Stampe, Andreas Voutsinas, Branka Veselinovic, Paul Wheeler Jr., Vlada Petric, Aca Stojkovic, Mavid Popovic, Peter Banicevic, Vojislav Micovic, Radomir Popovic, Dusah Vujisic, Luca Alavija, Petar Slovenski, Jovan Vukovic, Stanimir Avranovic, Menad Jeftanovic, Relja Basic, Ljuba Cipranic, Dejan Cavic, Mladja Veselinovic, Tamanija Dzuricko, Mel Brooks. Dir and Screenplay: Mel Brooks; based on the novel of the same title by Ilya Ilf and Eugene Petrov. Pro: Michael Hertzberg. Ex Pro: Sidney Glazier. Ex in charge of Pro: William A. Berns. Ph: Djordje Nikolic. Ed: Alan Heim. Art: Mile Nikolic. (Columbia) Rel: floating: first shown London (Warner), July 1983. 93 mins. Cert U.

The Twilight Zone – The Movie. A four-part feature based on the long-running American TV series which ended a five-year, regular run in 1964. Although the introduction and first of the four episodes are original, the remaining three filmlets are all actually versions of some of the old TV segments. After a neat serio-comic Introduction, the first story is about a man in a bar who loudly blames Blacks, Jews and other Foreigners for his present bad fortune. Thrown out of the bar he finds himself somewhat inexplicably in a Paris street during the Occupation, and is soon fleeing from the Nazis ... escaping only to become a victim of the Ku Klux Klan, then a fugitive in Vietnam and, finally, is forced aboard a

Four clips from the four segments of *Twilight Zone – The Movie*, which was based on a '60s American TV series.

train of Jews bound for the gas chambers. In the second story a coloured philosopher brings enlightenment and a new understanding of life to the occupants of an Old People's Home. The third episode is about a small boy with mysterious and ugly powers who is taken in hand by a pretty schoolteacher. Each episode caps the one before, and in the final, and best, episode, a terrified passenger of an airliner (which is battling through the inevitable storm) is the only one to see a little green man on the wing tearing and smashing one of the engines. In toto, a pretty good cinematic package, ranging from the gently amusing to the flesh-creeping scary, persuasively suggestive of a Twilight Zone somewhere outside our ken, which sometimes asserts and insinuates itself within it. Cast: Prologue: Dan Aykroyd and Albert Brooks. Segment 1: Vic Morrow, Doug Mc-Grath, Charles Hallahan, Remus Peets, Kai Wulf, Sue Dugan, Debby Porter, Steven Williams, Annette Claudier, Joseph Hieu, Albert Leong, Stephen Bishop, Thomas Byrd, Vincent J. Isaac, William B. Taylor, Domingo Ambriz, Eddie Donno, Michael Milgram, John Larroquette, Norbert Weisser. Segment 2: Scatman Crothers, Bill Quinn, Martin Garner, Selma Diamond, Helen Shaw, Murray Matheson, Peter Brocco, Priscilla Pointer, Scott Nemes, Tanya Fenmore, Evan Richards, Laura Mooney, Christopher Eisenmann, Richard Swingler, Alan Haufrect, Cheryl Socher, Elsa Raven. Segment 3: Kathleen Quinlan, Jeremy Light, Keven McCarthy, Patricia Barry, William Schallert, Nancy Cartwright, Dick Miller, Cherie Currie, Bill Mumy, Jeffrey Bannister. Segment 4: John Lithgow, Abbe Lane, Donna Dixon, John Dennis Johnston, Larry Cedar, Charles Knapp, Christina Nigra, Lonna Schwab, Margaret Wheeler, Eduard Franz, Margaret Fitzgerald, Jeffrey Weissman, Jeffrey Lambert, Frank Tooth. Dir Intro and Seg 1: John Landis. Seg 2: Steven Spielberg. Seg 3: Joe Dante. Seg 4: George Miller. Pro: Steven Spielberg and John Landis. Ex Pro: Frank Marshall. Screenplays: Intro and 1: John Landis. 2: George Clayton Johnson, Richard Matheson and Josh Rogan; based on a story by Johnson. 3 & 4: Richard Matheson; based on stories by Jerome Bixby (3) and Matheson (4). Assoc Pro: George Folsey Jr. (Intro & 1), Kathleen Kennedy (2), Michael Finnell (3) and John Davison (4). Ph: Stevan Larner (Intro & 1), Allen Daviau (2 & 4) and John Hora (3). Ed: Malcolm Campbell (Intro & 1), Michael Kahn (2), Tina Hirsch (3) and Howard Smith (4). Pro Des: James D. Bissell. M: Jerry Goldsmith ('Nights Are Forever' comp Goldsmith and John Bettis, sung by Jennifer Warnes; 'Anas-

thesia' comp Joseph Williams and Paul Gordon, perf. by '213'). (Footnote: this was the film during the production of which a fatal helicopter crash led to a headline court case) (Warner) Rel: 8 Sept 1983. 101 mins. Cert 15.

Two of a Kind. John Travolta and Olivia Newton-John re-teamed for the first time since *Grease* in a wacky sort of comedy sprinkled with a few musical numbers but otherwise sadly lacking in merit. The tale hinges on God being persuaded by his angels to change his mind about ending the corrupt Earth, giving the mortals one more chance to show they have some good left in them. But, alas, there doesn't appear to be a great deal of charm in either Heaven or on Earth – and that goes for the two stars, too. Rest of cast: Charles Durning, Oliver Reed, Beatrice Straight, Scatman Crothers, Richard Bright, Vincent Bufano, Toni Kalem, James Stevens, Ernie Hudson, Jack Kehoe, Bobby Constanzo, Castulo Guerra, Warren Robertson, Deborah Dalton, Tony Crupi, Kurek Ashley, Jill Andre, Ann Travolta, John Hudkins, Sheila Frazier, Michael Melon, Ellen Whyte, Kitty Muldoon, Michael Aronin, Tony Munafo, Kathy Bates, Tammy Brewer, Deborra Hampton, Roxanne Byrd, Steven Hirsch, Pam Bowman, Jacque Foti, Ted Grossman, Rochelle Kravit, Dee Griffin, Robin Adler, Phil Romano, Richard Adams, Donna Porter, Jeff Lawrence, Gary Woodward, Joe Cirillo, Christopher Loomis, Dennis McKenzie, Michael Prince, Ric Diangelo, Jerome Michaels, John Dresden, Charles Picerni, Walt Robles. Dir and Screenplay: John Herzfeld. Pro:

Alas, no bells at the box office for Olivia and John in *Two of a Kind*.

Roger M. Rothstein. Assoc Pro: Michele Panelli, Joan and Kate Edwards. Pro Co-Ord: Claire MacTague. Ph: Fred Koenekamp and Warren Rothenberger. 2nd Unit Ph: John Moio. Ed: Jack Hofstra (add Ed: Lynzee Klingman). Pro Des: Albert Brenner. Art: Spencer Deverell. M Adapt: Patrick Williams. Ed: Ken Wannberg. (Fox) Rel: 24 Feb 1984. 87 mins. Cert PG.

Uncommon Valour. Grieving dad Gene Hackman, with the backing of another, richer sorrowing father (Robert Stack), leads his hand-picked mini-Army back to Vietnam to try and find their 'missing-in-action' soldier sons. A sort of *Missing* combined with *The Dirty Dozen* but, alas, not as good as either of those movies. Rest of cast: Fred Ward, Reb Brown, Randall 'Tex' Cobb, Patrick Swayze, Harold Sylvester, Tim Thomserson, Lau Nga Lai, Kwan Hi Lim. Dir and Ex Pro: Ted Kotcheff. Pro: John Milius and Buzz Feitshans. Screenplay: Joe Gayton. Ph: Stephen H. Burum. Ed: Mark Melnick. Pro Des: James L. Schoppe. Art: Jack G. Taylor Jr. Asoc Pro: Burton Elias and Wings Hauser. (Paramount–UIP) Rel: 23 March 1984. 105 mins. Cert 18.

Undercover. Video with the Rolling Stones group which, after being banned by BBC and ITV, was released (with the feature *Videodrome*) by Palace Pictures in the cinemas on 25 Nov 1983.

Under Fire. A generally thoughtful thriller about an American war photographer in Nicaragua in the late 1960s. His attempts to remain neutral in his reportage of the Civil War there, are overtaken by events. He is inevitably led to take sides with the rebels when he fakes a 'live' photograph of their dead leader and so unwittingly brings about the death of his best friend, a Foreign Correspondent whose girlfriend he has stolen. Beneath all the brilliantly staged action are comments on loyalty, integrity and moral values, as well as a certain criticism of American-South American politics, although the film is careful never to step out to any great degree from its general and deliberate ambivalence. Cast: Nick Nolte, Ed Harris, Gene Hackman, Joanna Cassidy, Alma Martinez, Holly Palance, Ella Laboriel, Samuel Zar-

Confrontation and revolutionary confusion provide the nub of *Under Fire*.

zosa, Jonathan Zarzosa, Raul Picasso, Oswaldo Doria, Fernando Elizondo, Hamilton Camp, Jean-Louis Trintignant, Richard Masur, Jorge Santoyo, Lucina Rojas, Raul Garcia, Victor Alcocer, Eric Valdez, Andaluz Russel, E. Villavicencio, Enrique Kucero, Enrique Beraza, Jenny Gago, Elpidia Carrillo, Martin Palmares, Gerardo Moreno, Eloy Phil Casados, Carlos Romano, Rene Enriquez, Jose Campos Jr., Halim Camp, Antonio Mata Jr., Julio Cesar Vazquez, Martin Lasalle, Filipe Ytuarte, Jorge Zepeda, Anfredo Gutierrez, Jose Marin, J.A. Ferral, E. Baramona, Octavio Cruz, Leonor Llausas, Juan Carlos Meizveiro, Humberto Vilches, Roberto Dumant, Ahui Camacho, Arturo R. Doring, Bruno Bichir, Richardo Ramirez, Jose Carlos Rodriguez, Enrique Hernandez, Monica Miguel, Luisa Sanchez, Carlos Lenin Vazuez, 'Los Folkloristas', Clay Wright, Michael Crowley, Eugene Vagnone: Stunt People: Gilbert Combs, Gene Walker, Benny Moore, Harold Jones, Tanya Russell, Mike Vendrell, Kerrie Cullen, George Fisher, Bruce Barbour, David Zeletti, Lamont Cox, Eddie Smith, Tony Brubaker, Alex Brown, John Ashby. Dir: Roger Spottiswoode. Pro: Jonathan Taplin. Ex Pro: Edward Teets. Screenplay: Ron Shelton and Clayton Frohman; from the latter's story. Ph: John Alcott. Ed: Mark Conte. Sup Ed: John Bloom. Assoc Pro: Anna Roth. Art: Augustin Ytuarte and Toby Rafelson. M: Jerry Goldsmith: 'Dear John' and '1979'

comp and perf by Pat Metheny; 'Our Love May Never See Tomorrow' by Peggy Turner. (Lion's Gate–Orion–Rank Film Dist) Rel: 24 Feb 1984. 128 mins. Cert 15.

Variety. A modestly made avant-garde movie about a woman who, unable to find employment elsewhere, takes a job at a sex cinema – 'Variety Photoplays' – drifts into a fantasy world and, it is suggested, possibly also into the criminal underworld. A most disjointed and odd piece which is open to all sorts of critical interpretation. Cast: Sandy McLeod, Luis Guzman, Will Patton, Nan Goldin, Richard Davidson, Lee Tucker, Peter Rizzo, Mark Boone Jr., April Andres, Suzanne Fletcher, Peyton Green, Cookie Mueller, Norma Rodriguez, Sally Rodwell, Scotty Snider, Spalding Gray, Dr. Usharbudh Arya. Dir: Bette Gordon. Pro: Renee Shafransky. Screenplay: Gordon with Kathy Acker. Ph: Tom Dicillo and John Foster. Ed: Ila von Hasperg. M: John Lurie. (Variety Motion Pictures in assoc with ZDF Television & Channel 4–BFI) Rel: floating; first shown London (Screen-on-the-Green), May 1984. 100 mins. Cert 18.

Vassa. A marvellously well played Russian adaptation of the 1910 Maxim Gorky stage play (which he revised in 1933) about a remarkable woman who is forced by circumstances into taking over the large and flourishing shipping business from her drunken and criminally lecherous husband. She rules it, as she does her family, with a will of iron. When she suddenly dies, every-

thing disintegrates and is taken over by her equally unfeminine but greedy and uncaring secretary. Against the *art nouveau* background is seen the emergence of the bourgeoisie who did so much for the Russian economy before they were killed or ruined by the revolution. The film's politics are subtle and shaded out by the magnificent performances, the superb photography and impressive, if sometimes awfully slow, direction. Cast: Inna Churikova, Vadim Medvedev, Nikolai Skorobogatov, Olga Mashnaya, Yana Poplavskaya, Valentina Yakunina, Vanya Panfilov, Valentina Telichkina, Vyacheslav Bogachov, Tatiana Kravchenko, Albert Filosov. Dir and Screenplay: Gleb Panfilov; based on the Maxim Gorky play. Ph: Leonid Kalashnikov. Sets (no art credit as such): Nikolai Dvigubsky. M: Vadim Bibergan. (Mosfilm–Contemporary) Rel: floating; first shown London (Academy), Jan 1984. 136 mins. Cert PG. (Winner of the 1983 Moscow Festival Grand Prix).

Videodrome. David (*Scanners*) Cronenberg's macabre thriller which, in dealing with (and supposedly exposing) the business of distributing and making video 'nasties', is itself about as vilely nasty as any movie could be. A mixture of sadism, masochism and horrific hallucination in an off-putting and eye-averting whole. The story, set in the 'near future' concerns the experimentation by a ruthless organization with mind-bending hypnosis through the medium of the TV video, which leads to appalling violence and death. The

James Wood, the video dealer, and Deborah Harry in *Videodrome*.

film's (somewhat dubious) message appears to be: 'You are what you watch'. Cast: James Woods, Sonja Smits, Deborah ('Blondie') Harry, Peter Dvorsky, Les Carlson, Jack Creley, Lynne Gorman, Julie Khaner, Reiner Schwarz, David Bolt, Lally Cadeau, Henry Gomez, Harvey Chao, David Tsubouchi, Kay Hawtrey, Sam Malkin, Bob Church, Jayne Eastwood, Franciszka Hedland. Dir and Screenplay: David Cronenberg. Pro: Claude Heroux. Ex Pro: Victor Solnicki and Pierre David. Ph: Mark Irwin. Assoc Pro: Lawrence Nesis. Pro Co-Ord: Roger Heroux. Ed: Donald Sanders. Art: Carol Spier. M: Howard Shore (Filmplan International, for Guardian Trust Co with Canadian Film Development Corp/Famous Players–Palace Pictures) Rel: 25 Nov 1983. 89 mins. Cert 18.

War Games. A movie with a message! And the message, the somewhat naive one that the only way to win a nuclear war is not to start it. In this case American missiles come within a few seconds from launching thanks to a young lad who is something of a computer nut. He accidentally breaks into the American nuclear programme and sets off a 'game' which soon becomes terrifyingly real – and with the computer's automatic finger on the buzzer it all seems (at least to a non-computerized member of society) all too horrifyingly possible. Initially, it is somewhat difficult for a non-com to

fathom but later it switches into a really classic, 'edge-of-seat' thriller. Cast: Matthew Broderick, Dabney Coleman, John Wood, Ally Sheedy, Barry Corbin, Juanin Clay, Kent Williams, Dennis Lipscomb, Joe Dorsey, Irving Metzman, Michael Ensign, William Bogert, Susan Davis, James Tolkan, David Clover, Drew Snyder, John Garber, Duncan Wilmore, Billy Ray Sharkey, John Spencer, Michael Madsen, Erik Stern, Gary Bisig, Gary Sexton, Jason Bernard, Frankie Hill, Jesse Goins. Dir: John Badham. Pro: Harold Schneider, Ex Pro: Leonard Goldberg. Screenplay: Lawrence Lasker and Walter R. Parkes. Ph: William A. Fraker. Ed: Tom Rolf. Pro Des:

Matthew Broderick shows his computer skills to Ally Sheedy in *War Games*.

Angelo P. Graham. Art: James J. Murakami. M: Arthur B. Rubenstein. (MGM/UA–UIP) Rel: 29 Sept 1983. 113 mins. Cert PG.

We of the Never Never. Another superior Australian film set in the outback at the turn of the century, this time the story of a young woman who marries a loving and devoted husband who takes her with him when he sets off into the interior to take up his job of manager of a cattle station. There she has to conquer the distrust of both the tough white stockmen and the ill-treated aborigines, and finally, having achieved both, face up to life without her man when he dies of fever. A little long, but superbly photographed, beautifully acted and consistently credible; another plum in Down-Under's rich celluloid pudding. Cast: Angela Punch McGregor, Arthur Dignam, Tony Barry, Tommy Lewis, Lewis Fitz-Gerald, Martin Vaughan, John Jarratt, Tex Morton, Donald Blitner, Kim Chiu Kok, Mawuyul Yanthalawuy, Cecil Parkee, Brian Granrott, Danny Adcock, John Cameron, Sibina Willy, Jessie Roberts, Christine Conway, Ray Pattison, George Jadarku, Sally McKenzie, Sarah Craig, Fincina Hopgood, Lisa Rodgers, Dayle Alison, Jenni Cunningham; and the People of Bamyili, Djembere, Beswick, Roper Valley and Ngukkur. Dir: Igor Auzins. Pro: Greg Tepper. Ex Pro: Phillip Adams. Co-Pro: John B. Murray. Assoc Pro: Brian Rosen. Screenplay: Peter Schreck. Ph: Gary Hansen. Ed: Clifford Hayes. M: Peter

Best. Pro Des: Josephine Ford. (Adams Packer Film Productions Pty Ltd/Film Corp of Western Australia Pty Ltd/ General Television Corp–Mainline Films). Made on location at Elsey Station and Mataranka with asst of the Northern Territory Govt and developed with the assist of the Victoria Film Corp. Rel: floating; first shown London (Screen-on-the-Hill, and Kensington Odeon), Sept 1983. 134 mins. Cert U.

When the Mountains Tremble. Feature documentary about the struggle going on in Guatemala (and the wider South American conflicts) seen through the eyes of one of its Indian sufferers, whose experiences turned her from simple peasant to exiled voice of protest. Dir: Pamela Yates and Thomas Sigel. Pro and Ed: Peter Kinoy. Ph: Thomas Sigel. M: Ruben Blades. The Storyteller: Rigoberta Menchu (the woman). (Skylight Pictures/Cori & Orient). Rel. floating; first shown London (Rio Cinema), Jan 1984. 83 mins.

Angela Punch McGregor in the Outback (top) after the death of husband Arthur Dignam (above) in *We of the Never Never*.

Where the Buffalo Roam. Possibly the most unfunny comedian in the unfunniest comedy of the year. The plot hovers vaguely around a writer and an attorney, but is all such an eccentric mixture that it is quite impossible to categorize. Cast: Peter Boyle, Bill Murray, Bruno Kirby, Rene Auberjonois, R.G. Armstrong, Danny Goldman, Rafael Campos, Leonard Frey,

Leonard Gaines, De Wayne Jessie, Mark Metcalf, John Matthews, Joseph Ragno, Quinn Redeker, Lisa Taylor. Dir and Pro: Art Linson. Screenplay: John Kaye; based on the book *The Twisted Legend of Dr. Hunter S. Thompson*. Ph: Tak Fujimoto. Ed: Christopher Greenbury. Pro Des: Richard Sawyer. M: Neil Young. Ex Consultant: Dr. Hunter S. Thompson. Assoc Pro: Mack Bing. (Universal/MCA–Blue Dolphin) Rel: floating; first shown London (ICA and Chelsea Classic), May 1984. 91 mins. Cert PG.

White Dog. Los Angeles provides the background in this story of a movie actress who, accidentally running down a white alsatian dog, takes it into her home, only to discover that it is a very colour-conscious canine, apparently programmed to attack blacks! Of course, there is plenty of symbolism around, but not too many moviegoers are going to worry unduly on that score, being quite satisfied by the surface entertainment offered by what was originally a Romain Gary tale. Cast: Kristy McNichol, Paul Winfield, Burl Ives, Jameson Parker, Lynne Moody, Marshall Thompson, Bob Minor, Vernon Weddle, Christa Lang, Tony Brubaker, Samuel Fuller, Paul Bartel, Martine Dawson, Alex A. Brown, Parley Baer, Karl Lewis Miller, Karrie Emerson, Helen J. Siff, Glen D. Garner, Terrence Beasor, Richard Monahan, Neyle Morrow, George Fisher, Hubert Wells, Dick Miller, Robert Ritchie, Cliff Pellow, Sam Laws, Samantha Fuller, Jamie Crowe, Joseph R. Hornok. Dir: Samuel Fuller. Pro: Jon Davison. Ex Pro: Edgar J. Scherick and Nick Vanoff. Assoc Pro: Richard Hashimoto. Screenplay: Fuller and Curtis Hanson; based on the novel by Romain Gary. Ph: Bruce Surtees. Ed: Bernard Gribble. No art dir credit. M: Ennio Morricone. (Paramount–UIP) Rel: floating; first shown London (Cinecenta and Electric), April 1984. 90 mins. Cert 18.

Who's Singing Over There – Ko To Tamo Peva. A delightful little Yugoslavian comedy (made in 1980) about a group of assorted characters on board an old bus heading for Belgrade in the Spring of 1941, on the eve of the German invasion of the country. The arguments and eventual violence that centre on the dillapidated old vehicle

South Bronx NY, graffiti, loud music, disco dancing – *Wild Style*.

can be seen as a slyly comic comment on the end of an era; with the physical violence starting at the moment the bombs begin to fall. Cast: Pavle Vuisic, Dragan Nikoloc, Danilo Stojkovic, Aleksandar Bercek, Neda Arneric, Milivoje Tomic, Tasko Nacic, Borislav Stjepanovic, Slavko Stimac, Miodrag I. Nenas Kostic. Dir: Slobodan Sijan. Pro: Milan Zmukic. Screenplay: Veljko Desrotovic; from a story by Dusan Kovacevic. Ph: Nikola Popovic. Ed: Lana Vukobratovic. (Cannon Film Dist) Rel: floating; first shown London (Premiere, Shaftesbury Ave), March 1984. 86 mins. Cert 15.

Kate Nelligan interviewed about her son's disappearance in *Without a Trace*.

Wild Style. An essentially American romantic musical, set against the poverty of the largely black New York South Bronx, where graffiti artists ply their trade and the youngsters get their (literal) kicks from their noisy music and dancing at the disco. Cast: 'Lee' George Quinones, Sandra 'Pink' Fabara, Frederick Braithwaite, Patti Astor, Zephyr, Busy Bee, Carlos Morales, Alfredo Valez, Niva Kislac, Glenn O'Brien, Bill Rice, Johnny 'Crash' Matos, Chris 'Daze' Ellis, Fred 'Caz' Glover, Edwin 'Obe' Ortez, Lisa Lee, Henrietta Henry, Pamela Smith, Diane Parker, Lillian 'Cookie' Brown, Lil Marcky 'C', Lil Sput, Michael Martin, Nathan Ingram, Joe Lewis, Vernon 'Pookie' Daniels, Kenndy Lee Howard, Perry 'B'. Dir Pro and Screenplay: Charlie Ahearn. Assoc Pro: Frederick Braithwaite and Jane Dickson. Ph: Clive Davidson and John Foster. Ed: Steve Brown. Assoc Ed: Nathalie Le Guay. M: Fab 5 Freddy and Chris Stein. No Art credit. Songs: 'Pretty Baby' and 'Rapture' by Chris Stein and Deborah Harry perf by Blondie: 'Good Times' by Bernard Edwards and Nile Rogers perf by Chic. (Wild Style Productions–ICA Projects) Rel: floating; first shown London (ICA), Sept 1983. 82 mins. No cert.

Without a Trace. The story of the trauma that ensues when a six-year-old boy goes missing. The police are constantly baffled as they come up against one dead-end after another every time they find something that makes them

think they are solving the case. The ending is contrived and – to say the least – unlikely, revealing the weakness of the movie beneath the considerable polish. Cast: Kate Nelligan, Judd Hirsog, David Dukes, Stockard Channing, Jacqueline Brookes, Keith McDermott, Kathleen Widdoes, Daniel Bryan Corkill, Cheryl Giannini, David Simon, William Duell, Joan McMonagle, Louise Stubbs, Deborah Carlson, Charles Brown, Sheila M. Coonan, Peter Brash, L. Scott Caldwell, Ellen Barber, Theodore Sorel, Sam J. Coppola, Elaine Bromka, Roger Karol, Caroline Aaron, Lee Sandman, Fred Coffin, Marissa Ryan, Dan Lauria, Donny Burke, Stephanie Ann Levy, Peggy Woody, Kathrin King Segal, Marcella Lowery, Jane Cecil, Todd Winters, Timothy Minor, Lynn Cohen, Kymbra Callaghan, Ronald Barber, Carlotta A. De Vaughn, Luke Sickle, Robert Ott Boyle, Joseph M. Costa, Richmond Hoxie, Elizabeth Lathram, Terrance, K. O'Quinn, Angela Pietropinto, Tory Wood, Don Amendolia, Tony Devon, Thomas Kopache, Lou Leccese, Mark McGovern, Steve Mendillo, Bob Scarantino, Martin Shakar, Bill Smitrovich, Ashby Adams, Hy R. Angens, MacKenzie Allen, Peter Burnell, Bruce Carr, Maria Cellario, Gregory Chase, Paul Collins, Ken Cory, Freda Foh Shen, William Fowler, Edmund Genest, Roxanne Gregory, Gracie Harrison, W.H. Macy, James Storm, Brenda Thomas, Allan Weeks, Hattie Winston, Tom Dunn, Sara Lee Kessler, Phyllis Haynes, Mary Ellen McPhillips, Edward O. Downes, Hugo Weisgall, Joe Mandelbaum, Dir and Pro: Stanley R. Jaffe. Assoc Pro: Alice Shure. Pro Co-Ord: Mary Jane Nolan Kelly. Screenplay: Beth Gutcheon; based on her novel. Ph: John Bailey. Ed: Cynthia Scheider. Pro Des: Paul Sylbert. Art: Gregory Bolton. M: Jack Nitzsche. M Ed: Curt Sobel. (Fox) Rel: 22 Sept 1983. 117 mins. Cert 15.

The Year of Living Dangerously. One of Australia's finest directors, Peter Weir, triumphantly makes the transition to American production with this story about an ambitious Australian journalist. Set against the background of the upheaval and dangerous days of Indonesia in 1965, our hero spends his time chasing sensational scoops in an

Mel Gibson and Linda Hunt in *The Year of Living Dangerously*.

effort to establish himself, and also becomes passionately involved with a British girl attaché during her last weeks at the Embassy. A highly individual effort, visually superb, with remarkable atmosphere, and most notable for a most extraordinary performance as a local dwarf *male* photographer by New York actress Linda Hunt! Altogether a notable movie. Rest of cast: Mel Gibson, Sigourney Weaver, Bill Kerr, Michael Murphy, Noel Ferrier, Bembol Roco, Domingo Landicho, Hermino de Guzman, Paul Sonkkila, Ali Nur, Dominador Robridillo, Joel Agona, Mike Emperio, Bernardo Nacilla, Coco Marantha, Kuh Ledesma, Norma Uatuhan, Lito Tolentino, Cecily Polson, David Oyang, Mark Egerton, Joonee Gamboa, Pudji Waseso, Joel Lamangan, Mario Layco, Jabo Djohansjan, Agus Widjaja, Chris, Quivak. Dir: Peter Weir. Pro: James McElroy. Screenplay: David Williamson, Peter Weir and C.J. Koch; based on the novel by the latter. Ph: Russell Boyd. Ed: Bill Anderson. Des Co-Ord: Wendy Weir. Art: Herbert Pinter. M: Maurice Jarre. (McElroy & McElroy Productions/Peter Weir–MGM/UA–UIP) Rel: 7 July 1984. 114½ mins. Cert PG.

Yellowbeard. Slaphappy, loosely constructed comedy about pirates and the like, with lots of good stars but, alas, considerably less laughs. Cast: Graham Chapman, Peter Boyle, Richard 'Cheech' Marin, Tommy Chong, Peter Cook, Marty Feldman (Marty's final film, he was found dead the morning after completing his role), Martin Hewitt, Michael Hordern, Eric Idle, Madeline Kahn, James Mason, John Cleese, Kenneth Mars, Spike Milligan, Stacy Nelkin, Nigel Planer, Susannah York, Beryl Reid, Ferdinand Mayne, John Francis, Peter Bull, Bernard Fox, Ronald Lacey, Greta Blackburn, Nigel Stock, Kenneth Danziger, Monte Landis, Gillian Eaton, Bernard McKenna, John Diar, Carlos Romano, Alvaro Carcano, Leopoldo Frances, Ava Harela, Garry O'Neill, Buddy Van Horn, Mike Cassidy, Terry Walsh, George Wilbur, Walt Robles, Loren Janes, Chuck Waters. Dir: Mel Damski. Pro: Carter de Haven. Ex Pro: John Daly. Screenplay: Graham Chapman, Peter Cook and Bernard McKenna. Ph: Gerry Fisher. Ed: William Reynolds. Pro Des: Joseph R. Jennings. M: John Morris. Filmed on location in England & Mexico. (Hemdale–Orion–Rank) Rel: 22 Sept 1983. 96 mins. Cert PG.

Yentl. Barbra Streisand boldly continues her one-woman-band movie career by starring, directing, producing and co-writing this story about a young woman culture-vulture in the chauvinistic world of Russia (or rather 'Fiddler on the Roof' country) at the turn of the century. She has to disguise herself as a boy in order to achieve the passionately desired education; a masquerade which leads to obvious complications, including falling in love with a fellow student whose fiancé falls in love with her! This somewhat slender story is punctuated by plenty of Barbra's breaks into song. Rest of cast: Mandy Patinkin, Amy Irving, Nehemiah Persoff, Steven Hill, Allan Corduner, Ruth Goring, David Keyser, Bernard Spear, Doreen Mantle, Lynda Barron, Jack Lynn, Anna Tzelniker, Miriam Margolyes, Mary Henry, Robbie Barnett, Ian Sears, Frank Baker, Anthony Rubes, Renata Buser, Kerry Shale, Gary Brown, Peter Whitman, Danny Brainin, Jonathan Tafler, Teddy Kempner. Dir Pro and co-writer (the last with Jack Rosenthal): Barbra Streisand; based on the book by Isaac Bashevis Singer, *Yentl, The Yeshiva Boy*. Co-Pro: Rusty Lemorande. Ex Pro: Larry Dewaay. Ph: David Watkin. Ed: Terry Rawlings. Pro Des: Roy Walker. M: Michel Legrand (Lyrics by Alan and Marilyn Bergman). (Ladbroke/Barwood–MGM/UA–UIP) Rel: 18 May 1984. 133 mins. Cert PG.

Young Giants. Charmingly, warmingly simple story about a happy orphanage saved from 'redevelopment' extinction by the efforts of the dying old priest who has run it for many years. He is aided by the, initially, less-than-enthusiastic young priest sent to help him

Walter Huston, Pelé and the football team he coaches in *Young Giants*.

Barbra Streisand (left) in boyish disguise in *Yentl*.

out and football wizard Pelé, one of the home's more distinguished old boys who, answering an appeal, returns to train the boys' soccer team, leading them to victory over very formidable opposition. In the course of all this activity enough public interest, and cash, is raised to defeat the planners and ensure the home's continued existence. Pelé shows that when it comes to acting he really has quite a flair; John Huston makes the old priest a very real character; and Peter Fox as the young priest completes a nice trio of performances. Rest of cast: Lisa Wills, David Ruprecht, F. William Parker, Mark Schenider, Pamela McKee, René Portugal, Aldo Tassara, Donté I. Henry, Varney Fahnbulleh, Brian Jay Frederick, David Ruprecht, Severn Darden, Richard Grant, Christopher Bringard, Erik Briggard, Michael Kafka, German Laverde, Kenneth McMurphy, Brian J. Stankiewicz, Jay Louden, E. Hampton Beagle, Alan Miller, Jeannetta Arnette, Paul Willson, Robert Barron, Stan Yale, Cavin Greenfield, John DeMott, H.R. Fox, Shawn Nelson, Jo Ann M. Smith, Manuela Carrillo, Phillip Carr-Foster, Megan Moyer, Mark Smith, Patrick Moyer, Billy Bates, Cynthia Marie, Jacqueline Zambrano, Betsy Lohrsen, Nicholas Love, Steve Traxler, John Moye, Robert Farrell, Suzanne Leggett, John Simon, Scott Littscher, Tom Gildea, Marlene Kisker, Rose Marie

Johnson, Carl Bailey, Michael de Paco, David de Salvo. Dir: Terrell Tannen. Pro: Tom and Megan Moyer. Assoc Pro: Dr. Nilson A. Santos. Screenplay: Tom Moyer, Mike Lammers, Terrell Tannen. Ph: Raoul Lomas. Ed: Denine Rowan, Marion W. Cronin and Daniel Gross. Art: Daniel R. Webster. M: Rick Patterson. (Hill Street Productions–Miracle Films) Rel: floating; first shown London (Classic Haymarket & ABC Edgware Rd) Oct 1983. 93 mins. Cert U.

Young Warriors. A sort of modern crusade against crime led by a High School lad following the raping and subsequent death of his sister. He and his pals set off on their crusade and eventually wipe out the rapist gang – but unfortunately include everyone else who happened to be in the bar at the same time. The ensuing onset of conscience causes the lad to blow himself up, along with his equally unfortunate parents' house. Altogether a pretty wild mess of teenage troubles. Cast: Ernest Borgnine, Richard Roundtree, Lynda Day George, James Van Patten, Anne Lockhart, Tom Reilly, Ed de Stafene, Mike Norris, Dick Shawn, Linnea Quigley, John Alden, Britt Helfer, Don Hepner, April Dawn, Nels Van Patten, Rick Easton, Paul Tanashian, Jimmy Patterson, Berbara Bloomer, Darlene Diangela, George O'Mara Mason, Charles Noriega, Rob Rosen, Charlie Bill, Kip Wing, Gregory Bennett, Michelle Rossi, Randy Woltz, Toni Amber, Nay Dorsey, Michael Green,

Chip Washington, Michael Baron, Doug Ford, John Simmon, Paul Frizler, Rick Matzner, Matt Sisson, Kim Goldman, Ron Gabler, Alice La Deane, Bill Gass, Frank Babbit, Betty Lee, Johnny Pop, Alvin Hurd, Jerry Thomas, Randy Pupul, Daniel Peck, Barry Maultasch, Johnny Quist, Larry Klein, George Woods, Bob Wier, Mika Sosa, Mike Damon, Gene Coreno, Darrell Stripes, Gary Smith, Robin Daubert, Claire Mimier, Lyle Haskell, Lori Zaremba, Matt Kanen, Jordana Merry, Burke Mimier, Ted Hardwick, Wendi Rostan, Jeff Haskell, Eric Gauvin, Beth Merry, Connie Johnson, Teresa Sims, Robin Daubert, Carl Davidson, Jamie Sonne, Renee Richard, Kim Fuller, John Billings, Mark Peleuses, Anthony Godinez, Mike Price, Billy Bates, and 'Casper the Wonder Dog'! Dir and Screenplay: Lawrence D. Foldes. Pro: Victoria Paige Meyerink. Ex Pro: Mark Cohen and George Foldes. Co Pro: Foldes and Russell W. Colgin. Assoc Pro: Joseph R. Milligan and Adam Slater. Ph: Mac Ahlberg. Ed: Ted Nicolaou. Pro Des: Karl Pogany. Art: Richard S. Bylin. M: Rob Walsh. (Star Cinema Production Group–Cannon Film Dist) Rel: 6 Oct 1983. 103 mins. Cert 18.

Zelig. With this film, Woody Allen is almost back to the beginning (circa his 1969 film *Take the Money and Run*) after various experimental excursions into such serious areas as Bergman country. He is at his best in this slyly satirical, witty and highly amusing comedy which, in many ways, is quite an outstanding achievement for all concerned. The film is an account of the life, and death, of Leonard Zelig, whose passion to be loved made him all things to all men and was only finally cured of his curse by the love of his psychiatrist, Mia Farrow. Set in the 20s/30s period the brilliant mixing of silent newsreels and imitation makes it almost impossible to see where one starts and the other ends. Like Beatty in his *Reds* film, there are interpolations – in colour – by real celebrities, such as Saul Bellow, Susan Sontag, and others: unlike *Reds*, though, all adding to the dry humour of the piece. At times, however, beneath all the fun are some serious comments on behaviourism and the way of the (modern) world. Among the many comic gems to savour: Zelig

Woody Allen is back to his comical best in *Zelig*.

causing a rumpus on the Pope's balcony in Rome and putting Hitler off one of his rhetorical diatribes! Rest of cast: John Buckwalter, Marvin Chatinover, Stanley Swerdlow, Paul Nevens, Howard Erskine, George Hamlin, Ralph Bell, Richard Whiting, Will Hussong, Robert Iglesia, Eli Resnick, Edward McPhillips, Gale Hansen, Michael Jeeter, Peter McRobbie, Sol Limita, Marie Louise Wilson, Alice Beardsley, Paula Trueman, Ed Lane, Marianne Tatum, Charles Denney, Michael Kell, Garrett Brown, Sharon Ferrol, Richard Litt, Demitri Vassilopoulos, John Rothman, Stephanie Farrow, Francis Beggins, Jean Trowbridge, Ken Chapin, Gerald Klein, Vincent Jerosa, Deborah Rush, Stanley Simmonds, Robert Berger, Jeanine Jackson, Erma Campbell, Anton Marco, Louise Deitch, Bernice Dowis, John Doumanian, Will Holt, Cole Palen, Pam Barber, Bernie Herold, Susan Sontag, Irving Howe, Saul Bellow, Bricktop, Dr. Bruno Bettelheim, Prof. John Norton Blum, Marshall Coles Sr., Ellen Garrison, Jack Cannon, Theodore R. Smits, Sherman Loud, Elizabeth Rothschild, Kuno Spunholz, Ed Herlihy, Dwight Weist, Gordon Gould, Windy Craig, Jurgen Kuehn. Dir and Screenplay: Woody Allen. Pro: Robert Greenhut. Ex Pro: Charles H.

Joffe. Ph: Gordon Willis. Ed: Susan E. Morse. Assoc Pro: Michael Peyser. Pro Des: Mel Bourne. M: Dick Hyman. Narrator: Patrick Horgan. (Jack Rollins/Charles H. Joffe Production–Orion–Warner) Rel: 16 March 1984. 79 mins. Cert PG.

Ziggy Stardust and the Spiders from Mars. Originally made as an early Video-Cassette experiment and not intended to be released in any form, it took D.A. Pennebaker ten years of persistent efforts to get this recorded concert by David (Ziggy) Bowie and his band into the cinemas – and, as some may well ask, was it all worth it? Bowie fans will obviously say Yes, others as they watch this ghoul-like figure in his flowing, feminine draperies may be less responsive. Performers: Mick Ronson, Trevor Bolder, Mick Woodmansy; with additional musicians Ken Fordham, Brian Wilshaw, Geoffrey MacCormack, John Hutchinson, Mike Garson. Ph: James Desmond, Mike Davis, Nick Doob, Randy Franken, D.A. Pennebaker. Ed: Lorry Whitehead. Dir: D.A. Pennebaker. Pro for him by Edith Van Slyck. Ex Pro: Tony Defries. (Mainman Pro in assoc with Pennebaker Inc & Bewlay Bros. SARL–Mirimax Films–Thorn EMI Classics) Rel: floating; first shown London (Lumiere), Dec 1983. 89 mins. Cert PG.

The Story of the Cinema's Biggest Threat – Video

ANTHONY HAYWOOD

The video industry, which has survived uncertain beginnings and a reputation for being less than honourable, has become the fastest-growing entertainment industry in the Western world, yet it approached 1984 with a feeling of unease, concerned that attempts to ban the so-called video 'nasties' would result in a threat of censorship greater than any entertainment medium had endured since statutory censorship of the theatre ended in the 1960s.

In Britain, Parliament was sending on its way a bill making it compulsory for every video release to be classified by the British Board of Film Censors; any tape without a classification would be illegal. These political moves were, perhaps, ironic, considering that the industry had improved its reputation substantially since its early days, when 'fly-by-night' operators were commonplace and 'respectability' was not con-

Harrison Ford facing the snake in *Raiders of the Lost Ark*, put out by CIC. This was another video blockbuster, and easily one of the best-selling, medium-priced cassettes of the period.

sidered to be a recipe for a profitable business.

Although the video revolution began in the late 1970s, it failed to capture the imagination of the British people until the turn of the decade, when film giants such as Columbia, Warner and CIC entered the market with the release of box-office hits that could normally be seen only occasionally on television after their initial cinema success. Home video had finally come of age. The arrival of the conglomerates gave the new mass medium not only the mark of approval that ensured it had to be taken seriously, but also an air of respectability – so desperately needed after the deluge of blue films ranging from saucy romps to hard porn, on whose back the industry launched itself.

By the end of 1981, so-called adult films accounted for about 45 per cent of the worldwide video-cassette market. In Europe, six out of ten tapes contained this type of material and the figure in Britain had been as high as 75 per cent. *Deep Throat*, the notorious blue movie that put the name of its star, Linda Lovelace, on the tip of every-

one's tongue when it was released in 1972, cost £12,000 to make. In the following ten years, it netted about £12 million, which included revenue from the 300,000 video copies sold but nothing from the estimated 200,000 tapes pirated.

Home video recorders were widely available by 1978, but true video recording began 22 years earlier with Ampex's invention of the Quadruplex recorder. At first, all machines used reel-to-reel tapes and recorded only black-and-white pictures. When colour television became established, cassettes were developed and recorders were designed for domestic use.

Philips became the first company to enter the domestic video market when it launched the now obsolete N1500 recorder. This gave superb picture quality but could record for only an hour at a time and was prone to breakdowns. The company's VCR cassettes were also too expensive to attract enough buyers.

The only cassette system to survive the pioneering days was the Sony U-Matic, introduced in 1970. But the most important innovations were Sony's Betamax format, launched in late 1975, and JVC's VHS system, first marketed early the following year. Betamax quickly became the most popular system in America and Japan, but VHS was adopted more widely throughout the rest of the world, including Britain. Most video-cassettes are now released in both formats.

Philips responded to the dominance of the two Japanese manufacturers by developing, with Grundig, the V2000 system, but failed to regain the ground it had lost when Sony's and JVC's inventions hastened the death of its own VCR format. The launch of the video disc player by Philips in 1982, ten years after being demonstrated in Eindhoven, was also a disappointment. Although the company's Laser Vision system offered the luxury of stereo sound, it could not be used to record and there was a limited number of discs available.

Two other video disc systems followed, one developed jointly by Thorn EMI and JVC, the other launched by RCA, which decided in April 1984 to stop manufacturing its players in America after losing $550 million because of poor sales. RCA continued to market the system in Britain, with special emphasis placed on releasing music videos.

With the two major cassette systems established worldwide, film companies entered the 1980s, and video, with the knowledge that the new medium could add £15,000 to £100,000 to a film's revenue. Just as Americans flocked to the cinema in the Depression of the

Released by Warner Home Video in mid-April, *Rocky III*, starring Sylvester Stallone, was sensationally successful, and according to a survey carried out by CAVIOR was easily the most *watched* video in Great Britain during the year.

1930s, people throughout the Western world – led by Scandinavia, Britain and America – turned to video in the depths of a new economic recession.

Following the major film companies' move into video, the most important change in the British market came with the large-scale shift to renting rather than buying tapes. Retailers in Britain sold feature films on video for about £45, £20 higher than the cost of many similar tapes in America, so it was not surprising that renting had proved more popular with nine out of ten video recorder owners by the end of 1981. The same year saw a boom in other Western countries as well, most notably in Japan and West Germany. And film executives who had seen that box office takings were no longer the way to a fortune, and that video offered another way of exploiting the film medium, will probably reflect that 1981 was the turning-point for this form of entertainment.

Sales of video recorders rose dramatically. At the end of 1980, just 2 per cent of British households had recorders. Three years later, the figure had risen to 26 per cent – 5,800,000 homes. In the same period, the number of pre-

recorded tapes available rose from about 600 to 6,500, although probably 70 per cent of recorder usage is for 'time-shifting', recording directly from the television.

Initially, TV screenings of feature films were the most popular target for people recording at home. Films accounted for 41 per cent of recordings in the last 12 weeks of 1981, according to a survey by Audits of Great Britain, and were overwhelmingly more popular than any type of programme made specifically for television.

Recent research indicates that films no longer feature strongly among the most popular types of recording from TV, and it seems that 'time-shifting' accounts for an increasingly smaller amount of recorder usage, perhaps because the sale and rental of cassettes, on which the British spent £600 million in 1983, has risen dramatically. It is possible to watch a feature film in your own home for less than £1 an evening.

One unexpected result of being able to record television programmes came when, in 1980, ITV screened *Death of a Princess*, a drama-documentary made by award-winning producer-director

The advertisement text reads:

THE WORLD'S NO.1 SELLING MUSICVIDEO FROM THE WORLD'S NO.1 SELLING ARTIST

MARCH RELEASE 1984

£13.91 + VAT
STEREO
60 MINUTES

THE MUSICVIDEO RELEASE YOU'VE BEEN WAITING FOR!

The sensational MICHAEL JACKSON — in the ultimate music movie — "THRILLER".
MICHAEL JACKSON'S Emmy award nominated performance of "Billie Jean" from the "Motown 25" special!
Excerpts of the acclaimed MICHAEL JACKSON musicvideo "Beat It".
A never before released MICHAEL JACKSON video "Can You Feel It"!
A behind-the-scenes look at MICHAEL JACKSON, director JOHN LANDIS (Trading Places, An American Werewolf In London), Academy Award-winning make-up artist RICK BAKER (An American Werewolf In London), and the rest of the all-star team who created "THRILLER" — on location!
AND MUCH, MUCH MORE!

MAKING MICHAEL JACKSON'S THRILLER — THE MUSICVIDEO YOUR CUSTOMERS HAVE BEEN WAITING FOR.
MAKING MICHAEL JACKSON'S THRILLER — THE ULTIMATE MUSIC VIDEOCASSETTE.

VHS: MAH000; BETA: MB11000; V2000: MR11000
RUNNING TIME: 60 minutes. Colour.

Distributed by: Palace, Virgin and Gold Ltd.
69 Flempton Road
London E10 7NL
Tel Number: 01-539 5566

Making Michael Jackson's Thriller, from Vestron Video International, has become the best-selling video ever in the history of the video business, with 800,000 copies sold in the first two months it was on offer, and well on target to sweep past the million mark.

Antony Thomas. Within days, the story of the Saudi Arabian princess being publicly executed for adultery was being seen in the Middle East by Arab families who employed servants in London to record British TV programmes. The Saudi government's protests to Britain were almost certainly a consequence of its inability to stem the flow of illegal video recordings flooding into the country. The power of video was already being seen.

In combination with video 'nasties', illegal recording became one of the two great evils that the British authorities sought to stamp out. Pirating feature films, both those already available on cassette and others that could be seen only in the cinema, had become a multi-million-pound industry and London was its capital. By early 1982, 65 per cent of videos sold in Britain were believed to be pirated copies. With cinema attendances set to fall to a rock-bottom 64 million that year and the film industry claiming that it was losing £100 million annually because of piracy, the Federation Against Copyright Theft (FACT) was formed by the British film and video industries to track down the pirates. By the end of

1983, it had seized almost 30,000 illegal cassettes, including copies of major films not even officially available on video, such as *E.T.*, *The Extraterrestrial*, *Gandhi* and *Tootsie*. FACT also claimed that it had reduced the pirates' share of the video market to 35 per cent.

The legitimate video distributors could now reflect for the first time that they were gaining control of the market. They were also gaining in confidence, perhaps best exemplified by CIC's decision to release a series of film 'blockbusters' on tape for only £19.99, beginning with *Raiders of the Lost Ark* in the autumn of 1983. CIC claimed to have shipped 80,000 copies to dealers in just five weeks, with 30,000 of them being bought rather than rented. Normally, British companies expect to distribute about 25,000 copies of a successful film on video, so CIC had good reason to be happy with the response to *Raiders*. But subsequent low-price releases, including *Flashdance* and *Airplane II*, failed to have the same impact.

Nevertheless, the public's appetite for films on video was undiminished. The most popular among British viewers in 1983 was *Rocky III*, which was watched by 6,800,000 people, according to a survey commissioned by Cinema and Video Industry Audience Research (CAVIAR). The CAVIAR poll also showed that three in every ten people aged seven and over regularly watched films on video. These viewers accounted for almost half of Britain's regular cinemagoers, providing food-for-thought to those in the film business who blame video for falling box office attendances.

But it was a pop music video that became the biggest-selling tape in the world when released in the spring of 1984. *Making Michael Jackson's Thriller* was simply a behind-the-scenes look at the recording of the promotional film which accompanied the American superstar's worldwide No 1 hit single Thriller. In Britain alone, Vestron Video shipped 100,000 copies of the cassette to dealers in its first three days of release.

With the clampdown on pirates and 'nasties' under way, the video industry could look to the future with greater certainty than at any other time in its chequered history. Perhaps, more than anything, it knew there was a future.

Letter from Hollywood

ANTHONY SLIDE

As I write this, a proposal has been made for the redevelopment of the Farmers Market, a popular Los Angeles tourist attraction dating back to the 1920s, a semi-covered marketplace offering fresh fruits and vegetables and all manner of food to be eaten *al fresco* at tables surrounding each of the stalls. Already the Garden Court Apartments, one of the most elegant buildings in Hollywood and the former home of Louis B. Mayer, Mack Sennett and Mae Murray, among others, has been demolished. The Hollywood Roosevelt Hotel, the site of the first Academy Awards presentation and D.W. Griffith's home through much of the 1940s, now stands empty and boarded up.

Los Angeles seems very much a city unable to accept the beauty and the solidity of its past. With wanton abandon, the city has destroyed most of its heritage. The red cars – electric trolley buses – which once provided rapid public transportation throughout the city are long gone, and now Los Angeles debates whether to build an underground railway system to replace the inadequate bus service which replaced the adequate red cars. What matter that we can now fly to the moon when the journey from downtown Los Angeles to Long Beach (home of the *Queen Mary* and Howard Hughes' *Spruce Goose*) takes more than an hour compared to 20 minutes by red car?

As the city says farewell to the magnificence of the Garden Court Apartments, it bids welcome to a hideously ugly new Sheraton Premiere Hotel and an equally vile world headquarters for the Getty Oil Company, two skyscrapers which dominate Universal City, indicating there is probably more money in real estate than in moviemaking – an attitude apparent over at 20th Century-Fox, where plans are still being formulated for the sale of the studio lot and the company's removal to CBS Studios in Studio City (which have formerly been the home of Republic Pictures and before that the new 1928 Mack Sennett Studios).

Hollywood the image survives, but Hollywood the city is slowly dying. Mickey Rooney, starring at the Hollywood Pantages Theatre in *Sugar Babies*, at the end of its triumphal post-Broadway tour (the show opened at the Pantages before going on to New York), pleaded passionately for a clean-up of Hollywood and for an end to the prostitutes and the sex establishments which have become prominent in the city. Everyone paid lip service to Rooney, but no-one seems too concerned with doing anything about it.

One of the more blatantly sleazy aspects of modern Hollywood is its Walk of Fame, with symbolic stars set in the sidewalk in honour of the entertainment world's greats. Many names from the past are missing, but the Hollywood Chamber of Commerce which sponsors the Walk of Fame has little interest in honouring someone who is dead, and instead blithely commemorates new stars to so-called personalities who have been around less than a year and will be gone – hopefully – in the same space of time. Only recently did it come to light that Jane Withers, the best known figure on the Chamber's nominating committee, had resigned some years back over the Chamber's failure to recognize the great names of the past. One still hopes that one day the Chamber will not only clean up its act but also clean up the stars, so that Ernst Lubitsch will no longer appear in the sidewalk as Ernest Lubitsch and Mauritz Stiller as Maurice Diller.

There was much hoopla over the removal of the Jesse L. Lasky/Cecil B. De Mille barn – the site of filming for *The Squaw Man*, Hollywood's first major feature – from a temporary site on Vine Street to a new home on one of the parking lots for the Hollywood Bowl. Presently the building sits there looking like any other decaying wooden structure – and historians might well question whether this is the authentic barn dating back to 1913 or whether it was completely rebuilt at a later date when Paramount began using it as a gymnasium.

Hollywood still has no Hollywood Museum, although there are countless projects afoot, and at least three Hollywood Museums are planned for various sites on Hollywood Boulevard. There is already a Hollywood Hall of Fame, while a Hollywood-Hollywood Hall of Fame has been announced.

One positive step last year was the removal of all the research materials – papers, books, stills, scripts, etc. – which had been donated to the original Hollywood Museum project and had been sitting for years at the former Lincoln Heights Jail near downtown Los Angeles, to new homes at the Academy of Motion Picture Arts and Sciences, the American Film Institute, the University of Southern California, and UCLA. Each of these institutions has signed an agreement with the city to safeguard the materials and make them available to bona fide researchers for an initial period of 20 years.

On a similar note, the Academy of Motion Picture Arts and Sciences recently received the scrapbooks and still photographs of Colleen Moore. Another major gift to the Academy consisted of Edith Head's papers, including costume sketches, still photographs and correspondence.

The Academy was on a major nostalgia 'kick' in 1983. There was considerable excitement at the restoration of George Cukor's 1954 *A Star Is Born* starring Judy Garland and James Mason, with screenings not only in Los Angeles, but also in New York, Oakland and Chicago. James Mason and Lilian Gish were on hand at most of the screenings as were Garland's children, Liza Minnelli, Lorna Luft and Joey Luft. Another noteworthy Academy function was a tribute to Eleanor Powell, at which Esther Williams came out of what seemed a self-imposed exile and proved herself a witty and entertaining speaker.

If Los Angeles displays no respect for its past in terms of its buildings, it resolutely clings to nostalgia for its former stars. There are many gatherings of film buffs and fans, but none is more enduring than the annual clan clave (sic) of the Jeanette MacDonald International Fan Club, now in its 47th year. I was present at the 46th gathering, held in the Versailles ballroom of the Beverly Hilton Hotel, and it was a surprisingly 'fun' evening, hosted by MacDonald's widower Gene Raymond, who could easily gain employment as a stand-up comic. Allan Jones entertained, joined in a duet from *Show Boat* by Kathryn Grayson. Also on hand were Leon Ames, Tom Brown, Constance Towers and others from Hollywood's 'Golden Age'.

The film buff's quest for the past, albeit a little more immediate, was also apparent in the March 1984 auction of memorabilia from Francis Ford Coppola's Zoetrope Studios. More than 1,000 people bid for items used in the production of *One from the Heart*, *Apocalypse Now*, *The Outsiders* and *Rumblefish*. A dirty leather jacket worn by Matt Dillon in *The Outsiders* went for $375, while Dillon's denim jacket from the same film sold for $175. In all, the auction fetched more than $200,000. In view of the film industry's widely publicized crackdown on piracy and its concern over prints of recent films being in private hands, it was surprising to find thirty 35mm prints of Coppola's *The Conversation* on the auction block.

The 1984 Hollywood image – a montage of pornographic advertising to be found in the city.

Judy Garland's children, Joey Luft, Liza Minelli and Lorna Luft at the Los Angeles screening of *A Star is Born*.

For those in the know, a more exciting auction was that held on the premises of the Cinema Mercantile Company, one of the largest prop rental houses in Los Angeles, which went into liquidation. For those who could identify them, there were some exciting finds. The piano at which Dooley Wilson sat to sing 'As Time Goes By' in *Casablanca* sold for $2,500, while one of three pianos used in *Gone with the Wind* went for a similar price. Almost 100 of the chairs from Rick's Café in *Casablanca* were also sold for $30.00 each. Cinema Mercantile had been in business since 1916, and so its auction bore a remarkable resemblance to a gigantic jumble sale with film buffs wandering around clutching stills in their hands and trying to match up the furniture with the items in the stills.

Compared to the past, somehow many of the events of Hollywood's 1983 and 1984 present seemed rather lacklustre. Certainly no exception was Filmex, held from 13 April to 1 May, 1983, which had little to recommend it apart from a tribute to the British Film Institute's 50th Anniversary, including screenings of the silent version of Hitchcock's *Blackmail* and the uncut print of Michael Powell's *The Life and Death of Colonel Blimp*, along with a tribute to James Mason, highlighted by a screening of *Odd Man Out*. The 1983 Filmex was the last festival to be directed by founder Gary Essert, who resigned after a power struggle with various board members. To replace Essert, the board wisely brought in Ken Wlaschin from Britain's National Film Theatre and London Film Festival. It remains to be seen whether he can overcome the petty squabbling and personality clashes which have plagued Filmex through the years.

September saw the Academy of Television Arts and Sciences present its annual Emmy Awards, a show with more awards, it seems, than there are television series. It was as the Los Angeles *Times* headlined 'A Night of

Virginia O'Brien and Esther Williams at the 1983 Academy of Motion Picture Arts and Science's tribute to Eleanor Powell.

119

Lillian Gish, with her co-star Hambone, in her 101st film, *Hambone and Hillie* – coming later in 1984.

Triumph for Cancelled Shows', with Tyne Daley winning Best Lead Actress in a Drama for her role in the recently cancelled (but now temporarily renewed) police series *Cagney and Lacey*, and Judd Hirsch winning Best Lead Actor in a Comedy for his role in the cancelled *Taxi*. Chris Lloyd and Carol

Kane, also in *Taxi*, won Best Supporting Actor and Actress in a Comedy Series. It was also, yet again, a time for nostalgia, with the awards for Best Lead Actress and Best Supporting Actress in a Limited Series going to Barbara Stanwyck and Jean Simmons for their roles in *The Thorn Birds*. As with so many award shows, the host proved more entertaining than the event. In this case co-host Joan Rivers joked about herpes, prostitutes, former Interior Secretary James Watt and homo-

sexuals, and invoked a flood of complaints to NBC, the network airing the show. (In fact, the tape of the show was edited for its later broadcast on the West Coast; it went out live on the East Coast.)

Humour of a similar nature was to be heard at the annual Erotic Film Awards, held in March of 1984, presented to the best porno (or as the Adult Film Association likes to call them 'adult films') features, directors and stars. Al Goldstein, publisher of *Screw* magazine arrived dressed as a vampire, saying 'I wanted to make fun of the living dead, which is what Jerry Falwell symbolizes', a reference to America's answer to Mrs Mary Whitehouse. For the record, the Best Picture Award went to *The Devil in Miss Jones II*, and the Best Actress Award to Kelly Nichols for her part in *In Love*.

On a more serious, and again nostalgic, note, the American Film Institute Life Achievement Award went, in 1984, to Lillian Gish at a gala dinner at the Beverly Hilton, and later aired over CBS. The music to accompany the film clips was quite magnificent, the work of British composer and conductor Carl Davis, the film clips themselves were somewhat disappointing. The sequence from *The Birth of a Nation* showed only one glimpse of Gish, there was nothing from *La Bohème* or *Broken Blossoms*, and nothing from her sound films, excepting *Night of the Hunter*. It seemed ludicrous not to screen anything from, say, *His Double Life* or *A Wedding*. Also depressing was the lack of Lillian Gish's peers and contemporaries, with the honourable exception of Colleen Moore. Those on hand to pay tribute were stars of the present, such as Sally Field, Mary Steenburgen, Sissy Spacek and Lily Tomlin. Douglas Fairbanks Jr was a splendid master of ceremonies, subbing for Carol Burnett, who was in hospital, and the most touching and genuine of tributes came from Robert Mitchum, Gish's co-star in *Night of the Hunter*. Other speakers included Jennifer Jones (looking marvellous), Richard Thomas, Eva Marie Saint, Richard Widmark, John Houseman and last year's AFI Life Achievement Award winner John Huston.

As with all these events, there was a little too much of the American Film Institute's telling the world how wonderful it is. The Institute recently launched a decade of preservation, in-

Hal Roach receives his Honorary Academy Award from Spanky McFarland.

tended to encourage the immediate preservation of this nation's film heritage. So far, there has been much talk and no money. A 1983 dinner hosted by the AFI to launch this decade of preservation was notable for the number of bureaucrats present and that no-one actually involved in film preservation was either invited to speak or invited to attend!

The countdown to the 1984 Academy Awards began in March with the Golden Globe Awards, given each year by the Hollywood Foreign Press Association. Hosted by John Forsythe and Julie Walters, the event was rather dull. Cher won Best Supporting Actress for her role in *Silkwood*; Walters and Michael Caine Best Actress and Actor in a Musical or Comedy, for their work in *Educating Rita*; *Fanny and Alexander* Best Foreign Film; Jack Nicholson, in *Terms of Endearment*, won Best Supporting Actor; and Paul Newman received the Cecil B DeMille Award for his 'outstanding contribution to the entertainment field'. As expected, Best Actress in a Drama Award went to Shirley MacLaine, who announced she deserved it – a remark she repeated at the Academy Awards.

The winners at the Academy Awards were much as one expected, with the one surprise being Linda Hunt who took Best Supporting Actress – particularly for a role in which she played a man! Perhaps equally predictable was the amount of space devoted to nostalgia. For reasons not entirely clear, Shirley Temple was honoured with a considerable number of film clips; Cary Grant (the most sophisticated and intelligent of all personalities on the show)

1984 Academy Award winners for Best Actor and Best Actress – Robert Duvall and Shirley MacLaine.

paid tribute to David Niven; there were clips of the first three songs to win in that category and a nod to Ginger Rogers sitting in the audience; a replacement Oscar was presented to Gene Kelly for the one lost in the disastrous fire at his home. But none of these people was actually winning an Award. There was only one Honorary Award Winner and that was Hal Roach, who

The *Terms of Endearment* Oscar winners – James L. Brooks, Shirley MacLaine and Jack Nicholson.

got short shrift in terms of film clips, a half-hearted standing ovation, and who received his Oscar from Spanky McFarland. It is surprising that someone a little more impressive could not have been found to present an Award to this unique figure in the history of screen comedy.

The final word (almost) was left to Shirley MacLaine, who preceded the embarrassment of the Best Picture presentation by a Frank Capra who obviously was in poor shape. She began a witty and intelligent speech by noting, 'I'm gonna cry because this show has

been as long as my career,' and ended with the remark, 'God bless that potential that we all have for making anything possible if we think we deserve it.'

The potential is there, in Hollywood, to preserve a heritage and to create films in the mould of past productions. This year's Academy Awards seemed to be saying we are not too proud of our present achievements, so we are shoring them up by emphasizing the past. Let us hope that Hollywood's 1985 will have as much to offer as the Hollywood years that are long past.

In Memoriam

Robert Aldrich, who died in his Los Angeles home on 5 December 1983, at the age of 53, made 29 feature films in his 28 years as a director, and in one way or another he had a hand in many more. From a wealthy banking family (his aunt was a Rockefeller), Aldrich persuaded an influential uncle to help him enter the movie business, initially as a production clerk. He soon rose to become production manager and then assistant director, working with such famous names as Renoir, Wellman, Milestone, Ophuls and Chaplin. His directing of episodes of some TV series led to his engagement in 1953 to direct *The Big Leaguer*. The following year he formed his own production company. Among his most successful productions were: *Whatever Happened to Baby Jane?*, *Hush, Hush, Sweet Charlotte*, *The Dirty Dozen* and *Attack*. But after upsetting Columbia's bosses, he was shunned by Hollywood and so made several movies abroad (*The Angry Hills* in Greece; *Ten Seconds to Hell* in West Germany; *The Last Sunset* in Mexico and *Sodom & Gomorrah* in Italy). He had his commercial failures too, like *The Flight of the Phoenix* and *Too Late the Hero*, and in 1973 was forced to sell the studios he had bought and extended in 1968. Aldrich's last film was *The Californian Dolls* (*All the Marbles* in the USA) in which he transmuted some very dubious material about women wrestlers into a very amusing comedy. But it was with violence, the macabre, and the brutal that he excelled, made more effective by his fast-paced direction.

Having suffered from it, he was always ready to say some hard words about Hollywood's business methods, seeing movie-making there as very much of a rat race. He was once reported as saying: 'The stories you hear about us being corrupt and thieves and dirty are all true. It's a swindle; it is corrupt; but if you're tough enough you last and things should get better. It's the system.'

Peter Arne, found murdered in his Knightsbridge flat in London on 1 August 1983, was a popular character actor who, apart from his films, was kept constantly busy by TV work. Born in Malaya in 1922 of an American father and a Swiss-French mother, he became the favourite villain of many

Peter Arne.

casting directors. His first feature film was *Timeslip* in 1953, followed by *The Purple Plain* (1955), *Ice Cold in Alex* (1958), *Chitty Chitty, Bang Bang* (1968), *The Straw Dogs* (1971), *The Return of the Pink Panther* (1975) and, what seems to be his last movie, the French-made *Providence* in 1977. In all, he had well over a score of film appearances to his credit.

Peter Bull, who died in May 1984 at the age of 72, was a very large gentleman indeed, whose massive proportions graced some 22 films, both as straight and comedy actor, beginning with *As You Like It* in 1936 and ending with *Joseph Andrews* in 1977. His other appearances included *Saraband for Dead Lovers*, *The African Queen*, *The Lavender Hill Mob*, *Tom Jones*, *The Old Dark House*, *Dr Strangelove* and *Lady Caroline Lamb*. A journalist before he turned to stage acting in 1933, he was the author of a number of books and famous for his remarkable and unique collection of Teddy Bears!

Luis Buñuel, one of the most important creative figures in the history of the cinema, died from cirrhosis of the liver in Mexico on 29 July 1983, at the age of 83. An admitted atheist, surrealist, and savage social critic, he was often accused of being iconoclastic and subversive. Indeed he was always ready, even anxious, to launch virulent attacks on the Church, the Middle Classes, and the Establishment and its moral code through his work.

He was born in Spain of rich parents on 22 February 1900 and educated by the Jesuits before going on to Madrid University, where he soon became friendly with Salvador Dali, the surrealist artist, and writer Garcia Lorca. An amateur boxer of some class, an amateur actor, a director of a puppet theatre and writer of poetry and highbrow film criticism, Buñuel moved to Paris in 1925, and quickly became deeply involved with movie-making, mostly as an assistant director and cameraman. With money supplied by his mother, he made his first personal film in 1929, the remarkable short *Un Chien Andalou*, on which Dali collaborated with him. It is now a classic of surrealism, notable for a number of shocking sequences, such as the cutting of a woman's eyeball with a razor. Five years later, he produced his even more famous, and first surrealistic feature, again with Dali, *L'Age d'Or*, which was quickly banned because of its scabrous content. This was followed in 1932 by a documentary, *Land Without Bread*, which showed such a horrific view of the plight of the Spanish peasant that it, too, was immediately banned in that country and, later, in France.

During the next few years Buñuel worked on dubbing and other non-production work in Paris, Madrid and Hollywood. After the end of the Spanish Civil War, he moved to Mexico in 1946, where he was to make about 20 commercial and non-provocative films. It was only in 1950 that he returned to what he liked doing best – making a film which showed up the conditions of the poor. This time he exposed the Mexican slums in *Los Olvidados*, which won for him the best direction award at the Cannes Film Festival. The films that followed included *Nazarin*, which took the 1959 Cannes Festival Grand Prix.

Some years after he had left Spain, Buñuel returned to shoot the scabrous subversive *Viridiana*. Initially made with Franco's blessing, it was immediately banned on completion when it was seen to be the subversive picture that it really was. But it was good enough to take the Grand Prix at the 1961 Cannes Film Festival. More Mexican productions followed, and then Buñuel returned to Paris to begin a series of screen classics which showed a mellowing of his former virulence without moving away from his strict moral code that set him against all 'conventional moralities, traditional fantasies and that moral filth which society incorporates into sentimentality'. This period produced some of Buñuel's finest work, such as *Diary of a Chambermaid* in 1964, *Belle de Jour* in 1967, *The Milky Way* in 1969, *Tristana* in 1970, *The Discreet Charm of the Bourgeoisie* in 1972, *Le Fantome de Liberté* in 1974 and, his final work for the screen, *That Obscure Object of Desire* in 1977, since when he lived quietly in Mexico writing his memoirs. Buñuel was never a stylist; indeed, he has been quoted as saying he never wanted to become a professional film director – 'I use it [the film] as a means of expression, but the industry disgusts me.' Even so, during his long and often stormy professional life he made in excess of 30 feature films.

Rod Cameron (real name, Roderick Cox) died after a long illness on 21 December 1983, at the age of 73. He made around a hundred movies in a career spanning nearly 30 years, mostly appearing in Westerns and minor features. Canadian by birth, he went to Los Angeles in the 1930s as a labourer on a tunnel project, and a few years later he broke into films as Buck Jones's stunt double. At the beginning of the 1940s he began to win bit parts and small roles, before starring in a long series of those marvellous old 'B' Westerns. He appeared in *North West Mounted Police*, *The Remarkable Andrew* (playing the Jesse James role), *The Fleet's In*, *The Kansan*, *Dakota Lil*,

Rod Cameron.

Panhandle, *Requiem for a Gunfighter*, *Evel Knievel*, *San Antone* and many more; his last movie seems to have been *Love and the Midnight Auto Supply* in 1978, before he finally retired to his Georgia home. He made a couple of films in Britain (*Passport to Treason* in 1956 and *The Electronic Monster* two years later) and one or two in Spain and Germany, and he appeared in several TV series, including *State Trooper*. In 1960, he made the news headlines by divorcing his wife to marry her mother!

Judy Canova died in Hollywood after a long illness on 5 August 1983, at the age of 66. She came to films via vaudeville and the theatre, and it was after her success in Flo Ziegfeld's *Calling All Stars* on Broadway that she was offered her first film role in *In Caliente* in 1935. She had a quite unique style of hill-billy humour and possessed an extremely powerful and penetrating voice. Some of her other screen appearances were in *Artists and Models* in 1937, *Sleepytime Gal* in 1942, *Louisiana Hayride* in 1944, *Oklahoma Annie* in 1952 and *Carolina Cannonball* in 1955, after which she made no further films until *The Adventures of Huckleberry Finn* in 1960, her final screen appearance. For 12 years she had her own radio show, and she also featured in many other radio productions as well as on TV.

Jackie ('The Kid') **Coogan** died from a heart attack in a Santa Monica hospital on 1 March 1984, after a six-year fight against heart and kidney ailments. He was 69. The son of a couple of vaudevillians, he was already appearing in his parents act by the time he was four. Some six months later, having been seen by Charlie Chaplin, he was signed up for a short film with the maestro, who then gave him the title role in the film which brought both Chaplin and Coogan something approaching immortality – *The Kid*. It was after this triumph that his parents formed a company for him and many of his subsequent films were produced by his father – among them *Peck's Bad Boy*, *Circus Days* and *Oliver Twist*. However, by 1927, he was finding it impossible to get work, and it was only after appearing in a London Palladium variety bill in 1930 that he was offered the starring role in *Tom Sawyer* and *Huckleberry Finn*, both based on novels by Mark Twain. In 1935, in need of money, he found it impossible to get any of the four million dollars supposedly held by his parents for him. In the same year his father was killed in a car accident in which he himself was injured. Two years later, Coogan married Betty Grable, having met her when they were touring in a stage musical. But he was still unable to get hold of the money held by his mother, so he sued her and his manager in a test case which resulted in a change of the law to protect child actors. Divorced from Grable in 1939 (he blamed money troubles for the break-up), he spent the next five years in the US Army, first as a glider instructor and then with the air commandos in Burma. Post-war he appeared in a few movies, usually in 'heavy' roles, but mostly worked successfully in TV. His fourth marriage appears to have been the happiest, lasting 30 years and resulting in two sons.

Roland Culver died from a heart attack at his London home on 29 February 1984, at the age of 83. He divided his career pretty evenly between theatre and films, appearing in more than 40 stage productions and some 50 movies. A RADA graduate, he was a pilot during World War I, and it was not until 1925 that he appeared in his first play (at the Hull Repertory Theatre). Just five years later, he made his London debut in *Dance With No Music*. He made his screen debut in 1931 in *Flat No. 9*, appearing in *77 Park Lane* the following year. Some of his later films included *Quiet Wedding*, *French Without Tears*, *The First of the Few*, *The Life and Death of Colonel Blimp*, *The Emperor Waltz*, *Trio*, *The Ship That Died of Shame*, *The Yellow Rolls Royce*, *Thunderball*, and *Rough Cut*. His very English voice and his expressive face (nobody could raise an eyebrow to greater effect) were two of his great assets.

Marcel Dalio (real name, Israel Moshe Blauschild), who died in Paris on 20 November 1983 at the age of 83, was a familiar supporting actor in French and American films made between 1931 and 1978. After a highly successful series of movies in his native land (including Siodmak's *Mollenard*, Duvivier's *Pepe Le Moko* and Jean Renoir's *La Grande Illusion* and *La Règle Du Jeu*), Dalio fled to the USA during World War II, after his entire family had been murdered by the Nazis. He was soon busy playing the French stereotype in films such as *Casablanca*, *Wilson*, *The Song of Bernadette* and many others – some 70 in all, fairly evenly distributed between those made in Hollywood and those made in France.

With a background of music hall comic and theatrical straight player, Dalio persistently proved his versatility, even if American directors mostly saw him as a bubbling little Gallic comic. About the only time he ever starred in a film was in Pierre Chenal's

Roland Culver.

Jackie Coogan, in Chaplin's The Kid.

William Demarest.

1938 movie *La Maison du Maltais*, playing an Arab poet. In between his films Dalio often returned to the theatre, and he also made a very popular French TV series.

William Demarest died in Palm Springs, Florida, on 27 December 1983 after a long illness. He was 91. In a showbiz career that spanned 70 years, he had appeared in more than 100 movies, as well as being a popular performer on radio, stage and TV. He began his professional career playing in a trio in hotel foyers – he played cello, his brothers piano and violin. From this he moved on to vaudeville, first with one of his brothers, then as a solo act, which was interrupted for two years when he was in the US Army (1917–18). He made his Broadway debut in Olsen and Johnson's *Monkey Business* in 1925, and two years later made his first film, *Finger Prints*, starring Louise Fazenda. In 1933, he moved to Hollywood from New York and started the long run of screen appearances which included *Broadway Melody*, *Diamond*

Jim, *Rebecca of Sunnybrook Farm*, *Mr Smith Goes to Washington*, *The Jolson Story*, *It's a Mad, Mad, Mad World* and, his last film, *Won Ton Ton, The Dog Who Saved Hollywood*. He was a great favourite of director Preston Sturges, appearing in all eight of his productions. Perhaps the notes that Paramount had about Demarest in their casting department give the most apt description of the sort of character he was usually asked to play. According to *Variety* these read: 'When a director is casting an actor to play a loud-mouthed, not-too-bright character his mind automatically turns to William Demarest... He is in a class by himself in such roles as bootleggers, Marine sergeants, dumb cops and racetrack touts.' During the 1930s he took a break from acting to try his hand as an agent and during that period discovered and introduced Ellen Drew and Jane Wyman to the movies.

Diana Dors, a delightful, bubbling personality and reliable actress with the Mae West-ish figure (in later career),

died tragically from cancer in a hospital near her Windsor home on 4 May 1984, at the early age of 52. Born Diana Fluck in Swindon, she graduated from RADA and won her first film role when she was only 14, in *The Shop at Sly Corner*. This was the first of some 35 movies she made including *Holiday Camp*, *Good Time Girl*, *Oliver Twist*, *A Kid for Two Farthings*, *There's a Girl in My Soup*, *Hannie Caulder*, *Steaming* and the 1980 film *Dick Turpin*, which is still on the shelf awaiting release. Diana Dors also appeared on TV, at one time having her own show, *The Innocent*. Throughout her career she fought a weight problem, and her private life was not an easy one. But in public, she always laughed off her troubles and remained cheerful and outgoing. She will be mourned by many, both in and out of showbusiness circles.

Eddie Foy Jr died at a Woodlands Hills, California, nursing home after a long illness on 15 July 1983. He was 78. He started out in show business when he was five, joining his parents' stage act, 'Eddie and the Seven Little Foys' (five sons and two daughters). But the turning point in his career came in 1929 when he made his Broadway stage debut in Flo Ziegfeld's review *Show Girl* and his first movie, *Queen of the Night Clubs*. From then on he continued to divide his time between stage and screen. His very many films included *Present Arms*, *Broadway Through a Keyhole*, *The Pajama Game*, *Dixie*, *30 is a Dangerous Age*, *Cynthia* and four productions in which he played his father, *Frontier Marshall*, *Lillian Russell*, *Wilson* and *Yankee Doodle Dandy*.

Joan Hackett died on 8 October 1983, at the age of 49, after a year-long fight against cancer. Born in Harlem, she became a busy actress who had already impressed on the stage when in 1966 she made her screen debut in *The Group*. Some of her other films included: *The Rivals*, *Support Your Local Sheriff*, *Assignment to Kill* and *Only When I Laugh*, the last bringing her an Oscar nomination. She also appeared on TV, and in 1982 was awarded a Golden Globe credit.

Byron Haskin, who died of lung cancer in Santa Barbara on 16 April 1984 at the age of 84, had a very long and varied career in film production, dating back to the silent era. A naval cadet in World War I, art student, cartoonist and advertising representative, he entered the movie world as a newsreel cameraman for Pathé. In 1919, he went to Hollywood, where after working as first cameraman on a number of films, he directed four movies in 1927. In 1929, he arrived in England and over the following three years worked with Herbert Wilcox on the adaptation of a number of Aldwych stage farces starring Tom Walls. Back in Hollywood, he became the head of Warners' special effects department, a post he held for eight years, earning a number of Oscar nominations for his work. In 1947, he returned to directing with *I Walk Alone*, and continued to direct a string of movies which included *Tarzan's Peril*, *The War of the Worlds*, *His Majesty O'Keefe*, *Conquest of Space*, *Captain Sinbad* and *Robinson Crusoe on Mars*. He also did a lot of television work. His last cinema film was *The Power*, which he directed in 1968. He was at his best when he was in one way or another working on the spectacular, the fantastic and the futuristic, and he brought a professional polish and care too often lacking in this kind of production.

James Hayter, rotund and jolly actor, who was said to have been the perfect Mr Pickwick, was born in India in the April of 1907. He made his acting debut in 1925 and 12 years later the first of his 66 films, *Sensation*, which he followed up with *Big Fella*. He featured in *The Pickwick Papers*, *Nicholas Nickleby* and *David Copperfield*, films based on the books of Charles Dickens, and also had supporting roles in many British movies, among them *Passport to Pimlico*, *The Thirty-Nine Steps* and, in 1971, *The Bawdy Adventures of Tom Jones*.

Sam Jaffe, veteran actor of stage, screen and particularly radio and TV, died from cancer in his Hollywood home on 24 March 1984. He was 93. He started his career as a small boy, appearing with his mother in productions at the New York Yiddish Theatre. His Broadway debut came in 1921 in *The Idle Inn*, but he did not get the opportunity to repeat his stage successes in either *The Jazz Singer* or *Grand Hotel*, when movies were made of them. However, it was his screen test

for the latter which brought him his first film chance, as the Czar of Russia opposite Marlene Dietrich in *The Scarlet Empress*. Some of his best film performances were in *The Asphalt Jungle*, *Ben-Hur* (the 1959 version), *The Day the Earth Stood Still* and *Gentlemen's Agreement*.

Always busily working, Jaffe founded the Equity Library Theatre in New York in 1948, and he was a long-serving member of the Actors' Equity Council; he also negotiated the theatrical managers' agreement to pay actors for rehearsals – not an easy task. He was still working as late as the winter of 1983, with a role in the movie *Nothing Lasts Forever*, which has yet to be screened in Britain.

Carolyn Jones died of cancer at her Hollywood home on 3 August 1983, at the age of ... well, various reference books give different dates for her birth, some saying 1929, others 1933. She was certainly Texas born and started acting at High School, at the same time doing the DJ's job at the local radio station. She graduated from Hollywood's Pasadena Playhouse in 1950 and, signed by Paramount, made her screen debut in *The Turning Point* in 1952. Following this she made four films a year for the next four years, including *Road to Bali*, *The Big Heat*, *House of Wax*, *The Seven Year Itch* and *The Invasion of the Body Snatchers*. Later movies included *The Last Train from Gun Hill*, *How the West Was Won*, *The Bachelor Party* (for which she received the 1957 best supporting actress Oscar nomination) and *Death Trap* (*Eaten Alive*), her final screen appearance, in 1977. She was also a popular and busy stage and television actress.

May McAvoy, who had the distinction of co-starring with Al Jolson in *The Jazz Singer*, died in Sherman Oaks, California, on 26 April 1984, at the age of 82. From a wealthy New York family, she left high school in her first year, against her parents' wishes, in order to begin what she was determined would be an acting career. Being pretty and petite (she was under five foot tall), she soon obtained plenty of model work, and then managed to get an extra's part in *I'll Say So*. After several similar appearances, she won her first leading role in *Hate* in 1917. She was

already a New York star when she went to Hollywood, where she was soon in demand to play the typical wide-eyed heroines so popular during that period. After refusing to appear scantily clad in de Mille's *Adam's Rib*, however, her studio, Paramount, seem to have lost interest in her, so she bought out her contract with them. As a freelance she made a number of highly successful movies, including *The Enchanted Cottage* (with Richard Barthelmass as co-star), *Three Women* and *Lady Windermere's Fan* (both Lubitsch films), the original *Ben-Hur* spectacular and *The Road to Glory* (Howard Hawks' first film as director). After *The Jazz Singer* she married a businessman and retired from the screen, but in 1940 she made a return to the studios, though only as a bit player.

Raymond Massey, screen and stage actor, stage producer and director, died in a Los Angeles hospital following admission with pneumonia on 29 July 1983. He was 86. He will best be remembered for his playing of Abe Lincoln both on the stage and in film, for which he received such tremendous

Raymond Massey.

acclaim, and for his creation of strong roles such as those of fanatics and other villains; comedy roles do not seem to have appealed to him, or perhaps casting directors never saw him as being suitable for such parts. Born in Toronto, Canada, on 30 August 1896, the son of a prosperous businessman, Massey was educated at Oxford, and joined the Canadian Field Artillery in 1915. Although wounded while serving in

France, he remained in the Army and took part in the Canadian Expeditionary Force's Siberian venture in 1918–19. (He re-enlisted in the Canadian Army in 1942, but was again wounded and invalided out within the year.)

It was while staging entertainment for the troops in Russia that he decided to make acting his career, and in 1922 made his London stage debut in a small role in a production of Eugene O'Neill's *In The Zone*. Thereafter, he was kept constantly busy in the theatre, notably with a spell of management of the Everyman Theatre, during which he produced some 13 plays and acted in a dozen. Massey made his New York debut in 1931 in a production of *Hamlet* which was unfavourably received. But three years later, he returned to Broadway in his own production of *The Shining Hour* and won better critical notices. In the interim, he acted in a number of London stage productions and made appearances in several movies including *The Speckled Band* in 1932, playing Sherlock Holmes. Other films of this period included: *The Old Dark House* in the same year, *Things to Come* in 1936, *The Prisoner of Zenda* in 1937, *The Santa Fe Trail* in 1940 and *The 49th Parallel* the following year. Among the other films in which he starred in the 1940s and 1950s were *A Matter of Life and Death* in 1946, *David and Bathsheba* in 1951 and *East of Eden* in 1955. He received an Oscar nomination for his portrayal of the United States President in *Abe Lincoln of Illinois* in 1940, the film of the play Robert Sherwood had written expressly for him. Twenty-two years later he was to play the President again on the screen, but this time for less than a minute, in *How the West Was Won*. His last screen appearance seems to have been in *Mackenna's Gold* in 1969. During the period between 1961 and 1966 he was kept busy portraying Dr Gillespie in the very popular TV series of *Dr Kildare*. More recently, unfortunately, failing health kept him in retirement.

John Le Mesurier, who died aged 71 in a Ramsgate hospital on 15 November 1983, will almost certainly be best remembered for his playing of the long-suffering sergeant in the television series *Dad's Army*. He appeared in more than a hundred movies during his career, generally in small parts, but

John Le Mesurier.

usually with considerable impact, and was one of the most reliable and trusted supporting actors in the business. British films will certainly miss his somewhat lugubrious features and superb professionalism.

David Niven, in UIP's Trail of the Pink Panther.

David Niven, who died from a muscle-wasting disease at his Swiss chalet home on 31 July 1983, at the age of 73, was one of the best loved and most universally popular of all cinema stars of his time.

Born on 1 March 1909, of a family of soldiers (his father was killed during World War I in the Dardenelles campaign), he was educated at Stowe and Sandhurst, where he was commissioned as a 2nd Lieutenant in the Highland Light Infantry. He resigned this commission in 1932 and during the next few years had an odd assortment of jobs, including being a woodcutter, messenger and bartender, before arriving in Hollywood in 1934, where by chance more than design he became an extra. His lack of dramatic training, however, proved no obstacle, and his charm, impeccable English (the first word he ever spoke on the screen was 'Goodbye', in the 1935 film *Without Regret*) and winning personality quickly took him to second, and then first leading

roles, in films like *Splendor* (his first real success), *Thank You Jeeves*, *Dodsworth*, *The Charge of the Light Brigade*, *The Prisoner of Zenda*, *Dawn Patrol* and *Raffles*. Niven was one of the first of the Hollywood stars to enlist at the outbreak of World War II and was commissioned as a 2nd Lieutenant in The Rifle Brigade in the British Army, but soon switched to a Commando unit, where he eventually became a Colonel. Later, with many decorations to his credit, he was made Lieutenant Colonel and became head of the Allied Forces radio network. During his war service the War Office gave him leave to appear in some propaganda films and the two patriotic features *The Way Ahead* and *The First of the Few*.

Discharged from the Army after the war, he starred in Powell and Pressburger's *A Matter of Life and Death* (1946) and thereafter more or less commuted between England and America to appear in a number of films. In 1951, depressed because he felt his career was at a standstill or even failing, he ended his long-term contract with Sam Goldwyn. But his role in *The Moon is Blue* soon after marked an upturn in his fortunes, culminating in his outstanding performance as Phileas Fogg in *Around the World in Eighty Days*, followed by his Oscar and New York Film Critics' Awards for his role as Major Pollack in *Separate Tables* in 1958. It was around this time that with Charles Boyer, Dick Powell and Don Sharpe, he launched the enormously successful TV production company 'Four Stars', which was soon producing a number of top class television series – and making a great deal of money for him. During the 1950s, 1960s and 1970s, Niven appeared in a considerable number of successes, including *The Guns of Navarone*, *The Pink Panther*, *Casino Royale*, *Paper Tiger*, *Death on the Nile*, *Escape to Athens* and many others. His final screen roles were in *Better Late than Never* and the two *Pink Panther* follow-up films.

In all, Niven's screen credits stretch to nearly three figures. Though best remembered for his sophisticated, smooth and urbane comedy parts, he could, and did on occasion, turn in a fine dramatic performance. Yet whatever he did he did well and, it appeared, effortlessly, always remaining delightfully self-deflationary about everything he achieved. Off screen he

Pat O'Brien, in his last film, Milos Forman's Ragtime.

was a witty conversationalist, and was in later years to prove himself a gifted writer with his several books: two novels (*Round the Rugged Rocks* – retitled *Once Over Lightly* for American publication – and *Go Slowly, Come Back Quickly*), his 4-million-selling autobiography *The Moon's a Balloon* and his book of amusing pictures of Hollywood people, *The Empty Horses*. On both sides of the screen David Niven will be greatly missed, and long mourned.

Pat O'Brien, who died from a heart attack at a Santa Monica hospital on 15 October 1983, boasted a stage, radio, television and film career which spanned 60 of his 82 years. Appearing in more than a hundred movies, he will possibly be best remembered for those he made with James Cagney, including *Mayor of Hell*, *Devil Dogs of the Air*, *Boy Meets Girl* and, most memorably, *Angels With Dirty Faces*. And it was with Cagney that he made his last movie, *Ragtime*, in 1981. Possibly his greatest screen success, however, at least in America, was in *Knute Rockne – All American*, in which he asked for, and got, Ronald Reagan as his co-star, playing the famous Notre Dame football player.

Real name William Joseph O'Brien, son of a Milwaukee waitress and a grocer's clerk, O'Brien adopted the name of Pat to commemorate his grand-

father, who was killed in an effort to stop a bar-room brawl. He and his boyhood pal Spencer Tracy (they remained close friends until Tracy's death) enlisted in the US Navy in World War I, and on demobilization both enrolled at the American Academy of Dramatic Art. It was here they met Cagney and began another lifelong, close friendship.

O'Brien made his professional stage debut at the beginning of the 1920s and scored his first big film hit in *The Front Page* in 1931 (ten years after making his first movie, *Shadows of the West*, and the year he married actress Elise Taylor, who survives him). Among the many movies that followed were: *The Irish in Us*, *Public Enemy's Wife*, *San Quentin*, *Riffraff*, *Some Like it Hot*, *The Great O'Malley*, *Escape to Glory*, *The People Against O'Hara*, *Okinawa* and *The Last Hurrah*. During intervals in his film work, O'Brien continually returned to the stage, as late as May 1982 appearing with his wife and daughter in a theatrical production of *On Golden Pond*. He also starred in a number of TV series and shows. Latterly he had been fighting various ailments including arthritis, and he had had a Pacemaker installed. Of these last two disabilities he is quoted as saying: 'I have had arthritis since it first came out; if at my age you don't have it you are either a Communist spy or a pervert.' And of the Pacemaker: 'Every time I cough now the garage doors open.'

Slim Pickens, the actor who 'rode the bomb' in Stanley Kubrick's *Dr Strangelove*, died in California on 8 December 1983, aged 64. Born Louis Bert Lindley on 29 June 1919, he ran away from home to join the rodeo when he was 13, and adopted the name of Pickens. He made his screen debut in *Rocky Mountain* in 1950, the first of an almost continuous string of Westerns in which he appeared. His credits include: *The Sun Shines Bright, One-Eyed Jacks, A Thunder of Guns, Stagecoach, The Ballad of Cable Hogue, The Cowboys, Blazing Saddles, Tom Horn, Beyond the Poseidon Adventure* and *Honeysuckle*

Slim Pickens, in one of his early 'B' Westerns.

Rose. He also appeared in many TV Western series, such as *Wagon Train, Bonanza, Alias Smith & Jones* and *Rawhide*.

William Powell, a golden star of the golden age of Hollywood, died in his Palm Springs home on 5 March 1984, at the age of 91, having retired in 1955 after making some 90 films. Inevitably, he is best recalled as partnering Myrna Loy in the famous 'Thin Man' series of witty detection movies based on Dashiel Hammett stories. Powell, however, started out in the silent days as the villain, and it was only in the 1930s with the advent of sound that his screen image began to change. His roles included many of a detective nature (amusingly in his first film, *Sherlock Holmes* in 1922, he played the despicable Professor Moriarty, long-term opponent to the famous 'tec – played on this occasion by John Barrymore), including that of Van Dine's Private Eye, Philo Vance, in several films. Apart from the 'Thin Man' films Powell topped his career with his performances

William Powell.

in *My Man Godfrey, Life With Father*, and *The Great Ziegfeld*. Some of his other appearances were in *The Road to Singapore, The Key, The Last of Mrs Cheyney, The Treasure of Lost Canyon, How to Marry a Millionaire* and, his last movie, *Mister Roberts* in 1955. Powell first appeared on Broadway in· 1912, and became a matinee idol before he turned to films. But as hero or villain he was always suave, well dressed and witty. Engaged to Jean Harlow at the

time of her death, he subsequently married Carole Lombard (he was divorced from her in 1933) and since 1940 had been married to actress Diana Lewis, who survives him.

Sir Ralph Richardson, who died in London on 10 October 1983, at the age of 80, was without doubt one of the greatest and most individual of classical actors of our time. Although primarily a stage actor, he appeared in more than fifty films, but few allowed him to demonstrate his outstanding talent. He began his acting career in 1920 and became a leading player with the Old Vic company during the 1930s and 1940s. He started to appear in films in 1933, when he made both *The Ghoul* and *Friday the 13th*, and by 1949, he was starring in and directing *Home at Seven*. His movie appearances included: *Things to Come, The Man Who Could Work Miracles, South Riding, The Citadel, The Lion has Wings, Anna Karenina, The Fallen Idol, Outcast of the Islands, Our Man in Havana, Richard III, Smiley, Doctor Zhivago, Oh! What*

Sir Ralph Richardson, in one of his last films, Disney's Dragonslayer.

a Lovely War, Battle of Britain and Charlie Muffin. More recently he was seen in Rollerball, Dragonslayer and Time Bandits, and at the time of his death a further four films were in various stages of completion: Wagner, Invitation to the Wedding, Greystoke and Give My Regards to Broad Street. He also did quite a lot of television work, including a number of marvellous interviews in which his particular style of vagueness and dithering produced some wonderfully funny moments. A notable eccentric, even in old age he still drove a powerful motorbike round London. He had also been an amateur pilot, having served as an instructor in the Fleet Air Arm during World War II, rising to the rank of Lieutenant Commander.

Paul Rotha, who died on 7 March 1984, aged 76, was nothing if not versatile. During a life mainly involved with the cinema, he managed also to paint, design, lecture and write. And among his several books is The Film Till Now, published in 1930, which despite being dated is still accepted by students as a standard reference work on international cinema. But it was as a director and producer of documentaries – The Rising Tide, Shipyard and The Face of Britain – that Rotha was best known. During World War II, he made some fine propaganda films, including World of Plenty and Land of Promise. Yet he made very few feature films, and of these The Silent Raid (1962) was his last work for the cinema. The honours he won included the gold medal at the Venice Festival and two British Film Academy Awards. When president of the New London Film Society, he was made head of the BBC's television documentary department in 1953, a post he held for two years. He was married three times, the last to Irish actress Constance Smith being stormy enough to make the newspaper headlines on more than one occasion.

Jack La Rue, the actor who became type-cast as a gangster, died from a heart attack in Santa Monica, California, on 11 January 1984, aged 82. Born Gaspar Biondolillo, in New York in 1902, he started his acting career in stage plays, appearing as Mae West's leading man in Diamond Lil. Ironically, because he was so tall he lost the leading role in the original Scarface film

Jack La Rue.

in 1929, as he would have made star Paul Muni look too small, so it was not until 1932 in While Paris Sleeps that he made his film debut. He then appeared in films such as The Story of Temple Drake, Trapped by G-Men and Big Town Czar through the 1930s and 1940s, although he did get the occasional chance to play roles other than gangsters, even in comedy. Some of these appearances were in A Farewell to Arms, Christopher Strong, Captains Courageous, Valley of the Giants, Road to Utopia. His last two films were Robin

and the Seven Hoods and For Those Who Think Young made in 1964, after which he retired from the business and opened his own restaurant.

Norma Shearer, after several years of failing health, died of bronchial pneumonia on 12 June 1983, in a Woodland Hills hospital, in California. Though she had neither great physical beauty nor great acting ability, she did have tremendous poise and grace, which gave her screen performances a powerful and impressive character. Ephraim Katz, in his International Film Encyclopaedia, wrote that she 'had a thorough understanding of the nature of motion pictures', and that really says it all.

Norma Shearer was born sometime between 1900 and 1902 (when exactly is open to question) to a well off family living in a suburb of Montreal. Despite being a rather weakly child, she won a beauty contest when she was about 15 and this decided her mother to take her to New York, along with her sister, with the hope of their both becoming Ziegfeld Girls. Ziegfeld turned them down, however, and their first acting jobs were as extras in The Flapper, made in 1920. Sister Athole soon abandoned her acting ambitions and a few

Norma Shearer.

years later met and married film director Howard Hawks. But Norma persisted and won a 'bit' part in Griffith's *Way Down East*. Then, after various modelling jobs, she landed small roles in *Torchy's Millions* and *The Stealers*. For the next couple of years she appeared in a number of minor parts in small films and then won starring roles in two movies. These apparently impressed Louis B. Meyer and Irving Thalberg enough to sign her up on contract. Nursed along by Thalberg, she made a number of pictures before becoming his wife in 1927. Lubitsch's *Student Prince* was the film which lifted her to major stardom. Her first talkie was *The Trial of Mary Dugan*, followed by *The Last of Mrs Cheyney* and *The Hollywood Revue*. In the third year of the Oscar awards (1929–30) she won two nominations for her performances in *Their Own Desire* and *The Divorce* and took the Oscar for the latter. She was to win five more Best Actress nominations during her career, which included such variously successful movies as *Private Lives*, *Strange Interlude*, *Smilin' Through* and *Romeo and Juliet*. It was just after the last had been released that Thalberg died (at the age of 37) leaving her his $5 million fortune. There followed one of her several long breaks from the studios, and though she was yet to make *Marie Antoinette* and *The Women*, and was offered numerous other roles, her career really ended with Thalberg's death. She is credited during this latter period with the 'discovery' of two future film stars, Janet Leigh and Robert Evans who played her late husband in the film *The Man of a Thousand Faces*.

Johnny Weissmuller, 'Me Tarzan, you Jane', died at the age of 79, on 20 January 1984, following something like seven years of intermittent strokes, heart attacks and bouts of pneumonia. Such an end was particularly sad in view of Weissmuller's former athletic prowess. Taking up swimming after being struck down with polio as a child, he went on to set some 67 world records in the sport and won five Olympic gold medals in the games of 1924 and 1928. After seeing him in some sporting short films, and playing a cameo (as himself) in the 1929 film *Glorifying the American Girl*, MGM asked him to play the title role in their *Tarzan the Ape Man*, a film

Johnny Weissmuller.

so successful that more than a dozen more Tarzan films were made, all with the six-and-a-half foot Weissmuller swinging, swimming and grunting his way through them. (Apart from these, further Tarzan films were made with Buster Crabbe and others starring.)

Weissmuller's one effort to break out of the type-casting straight-jacket came in 1946 in *Swamp Fire*, but this proved abortive, so he returned to the jungle for the first of his 'Jungle Jim' films in 1948, repeating this role in a popular TV series later. After his cameo role in *The Phynx* in 1970, he made no further film appearances, and became host at the famous Las Vegas playspot Caesar's Palace in 1973, only relinquishing the job after a disabling heart attack a few years later. His various business enterprises brought him little success and his financial state was not helped by the aftermath of his six marriages and five divorces. At the time of his death negotiations were going on for a film to be based on his life.

Henry (real name Harry) **Wilcoxon**, who played many leading roles in a distinguished stage and film career, died from a heart attack at his Burbank, California, home on 6 March 1984, aged 78. Born in the British West Indies, he began his acting career with the Birmingham Repertory Company in the early 1930s and later appeared in a number of London productions. In 1931, he made his screen debut in *The Perfect Lady*; other films made soon afterwards included *Flying Squad* and *Princess Charming*. Seen by a Paramount talent scout while playing in a London stage production of *The Barretts of Wimpole Street*, he was given a

screen test by that company. But without seeing this Cecil B. de Mille, who was making *Cleopatra* and was suddenly left without a Mark Antony, gave Wilcoxon the role. And so began a friendly and business association which lasted until de Mille's death. Wilcoxon's next film for de Mille was *The Crusades*, in which he was given the role of Richard Coeur de Lion. Some of Wilcoxon's many subsequent films included *Last of the Mohicans*, *Mr Moto*, *Mrs Miniver*, *A Connecticut Yankee at King Arthur's Court*, *Samson and Delilah*, *The Greatest Show on Earth*, a film on which he was also associate producer, and *The Ten Commandments*. In 1959, he produced *The Buccaneer* for Paramount, but did not appear in it.

Other notables who have died include:

Selena Royle, born in New York in 1904, made her stage debut in 1921, 11 years before appearing in her first film, *The Misleading Lady* (1932). Other movies include: *Till the End of Time*, *The Courage of Lassie*, *Joan of Arc*, *The Heiress* and *The Damned Don't Cry*. She was also a popular radio performer.

Sydney Box, who was born in Beckenham on 29 April 1907, collaborated with wife Muriel from 1935 in the writing of a series of successful one-act plays. In 1939, he formed his own film production company and made scores of propaganda and training films for the government. When the war ended he rapidly became one of Britain's busiest and best producers, as well as continuing scriptwriting. And he shared with his wife an Oscar for the script of *Seventh Veil*. His films as co-writer or producer include: *Holiday Camp*, *Quartet*, *Simon and Laura*, *The Passionate Stranger*, *The Truth About Women* and, his last, in 1964, *Rattle of a Simple Man*. He was divorced in 1969.

To complete the period's record **Estelle Winwood**, the delightful British character actress, died on 20 June 1984 at the age of 101, and director **Joseph Losey**, the American director long-based in Britain, died on 22 June 1984 at the age of 75, just after completing his latest production *Steaming*. Fuller, more detailed notes about both will appear in next year's *Film Review*.

The Ten Most Promising Faces of 1984

COMPILED BY JAMES CAMERON-WILSON

Jennifer Beals, with her shapely body, tousled hair and Bambi eyes, is perhaps the most famous actress to emerge recently. The 21-year-old's rise to prominence came while studying at Yale University, when she was offered a holiday job, a part in a small-budget film to be made by an unknown English film-maker. The part was the lead role, the film was *Flashdance*, the director Adrian Lyne and the rest is history. She has been offered well over a million dollars to appear in *Flashdance II*, but has said she wishes to complete her studies at Yale. However, she will be seen with Sting as his co-star in *The Bridge*.

Matthew Broderick, 21-year-old son of the late actor James Broderick, was totally unknown until he was offered a starring role in Neil Simon's Broadway play *Brighton Beach Memoirs* and, at the same time, the role of Marsha Mason's son in Simon's film *Max Dugan Returns*. For the former, Broderick won the Tony Award as Best Featured Actor, and thanks to the latter landed the lead in *War Games*, one of the most successful films of 1983. He will next be seen in *Ladyhawke*, Richard Donner's $21 million medieval fantasy, co-starring Rutger Hauer and Michelle Pfeiffer, and also in *1918*.

Tom Cruise, good-looking, clean-cut New Jersey youngster, scored a hat-trick in 1983 with the hits *The Outsiders*, *Risky Business* and *All the Right Moves*. Can the boy do no wrong? He has appeared in *Endless Love* (his debut), *Taps* and *Losin' It*, and is to play the lead in *Legend*, directed by Ridley Scott.

Rebecca de Mornay, porcelain-featured, but strong-centred American-born, European-raised actress, made a powerful debut as the predatory hooker in Paul Brickman's *Risky Business*. She also won acclaim in the smaller role of a young mother coping with the aftermath of a nuclear holocaust in Lynne Littman's *Testament*. She is next to feature in *The Slugger's Wife*, with Michael O'Keefe.

Rupert Everett, a broody, 24-year-old Heathcliffian British actor (a Terence Stamp for the 'eighties?), made his name in the London stage hit *Another Country*. Recreating his role of the Marxist, homosexual Guy Bennett (based loosely on the young Guy Burgess) in the film version, Everett went on to star in the Oscar-winning short *A Shocking Accident*, Francis Megahy's *Real Life*, *Merlin and the Sword*, and *Dance with A Stranger*, as the boyfriend of murderess Ruth Ellis. He also has a leading role in the TV adaptation of the Judith Krantz best-seller *Princess Daisy*.

Valerie Kaprisky won the coveted role of Monica Poiccard opposite Richard Gere in *Breathless*. The film launched the French actress into the celluloid stratosphere and Valerie Kaprisky became a household body, if not a household name. A sensuous, pouting firebrand, who studied acting in Paris, the 21-year-old beauty, following *Breathless*, quickly secured the lead in Andrew Zulawski's *The Public Woman*, with Lambert Wilson. She also appeared in *Aphrodite* and *Legitimate Violence*. Her next two films are *Camille '85* and *Year of the Madonnas*.

Sean Penn, shrewd talent, adept at playing surly, rebellious youths, caught the attention of Hollywood with his lead roles in *Fast Times* and *Bad Boys*. Before that the 24-year-old made his debut in *Taps*, as a military cadet, and has since appeared in *Crackers* and *Racing with the Moon*. He will next be seen opposite his *Taps* co-star Timothy Hutton in John Schlesinger's *The Falcon and the Snowman*. His younger brother, Christopher Penn, is also doing well, having made memorable contributions to *Rumblefish*, *Footloose* and *All the Right Moves*.

Cynthia Rhodes, who featured in Paramount's hit movies *Flashdance* and *Staying Alive* (playing John Travolta's girlfriend in the latter), last year had the distinction of being signed on an exclusive contract by Paramount – so it is starring roles from now on for this talented, terpsichorean beauty.

Eric Roberts, although highly praised for his work in *King of the Gypsies* (1978) and *Raggedy Man* (1982), unleashed his talent in a colourful portrayal of Paul Snider, the unhinged, jealous husband of playmate Dorothy Stratten in Bob Fosse's *Star 80*. His performance not only won the 28-year-old, RADA-trained actor innumerable accolades, but also the lead in MGM/UA's prestigious, big-budget *Pope of Greenwich Village*. He will next be seen in the Australian *Coca Cola Kid*, with Greta Scacchi.

Helen Slater played the title role of *Supergirl* supported by Faye Dunaway, Peter O'Toole and Mia Farrow, and if the movie does for her what *Superman* did for Christopher Reeve, then she will be yet another superstar. A pretty 20-year-old New Yorker, Slater studied drama at Manhattan's High School of Performing Arts, and despite her film success, her heart is still set on a stage career.

The Continental Film

The films illustrated in this section are those from countries other than the USA, Great Britain, Australia, New Zealand, South Africa and Canada. In most cases the country of origin is included in the caption. A more detailed description of all the films illustrated will be found in 'Films of the Year'.

Chantal Akerman's Franco-Belgian movie *Toute Une Nuit – All Night Long* must be placed high on any list of this year's celluloid curiosities. Owing something to Godard and something to Marguerite Duras, this Other Cinema release consists of a patchwork of apparently non-related incidents taking place during one Brussel's night – fragments with women waiting for men, and vice versa, meetings, partings, mostly without dialogue. Four years back, Chantal Akerman made the fascinating *Les Rendezvous D'Anna* showing promise of outstanding work to come, but on this evidence it still has to be produced.

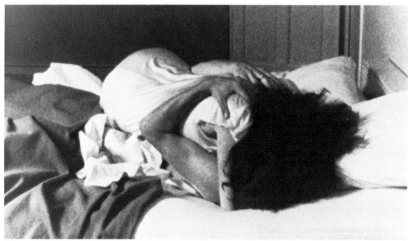

Fellini was at his most imaginative and amusing best in *And The Ship Sailed On* (a Gala Release), which is about a group of opera singers who hire a luxury liner to take the ashes of one of their deceased number back to his birthplace on an Adriatic island. By setting it in July 1914, it gives the maestro the opportunity to inject into all the fun and frolics a serious and threatening undercurrent. The cast includes Fiorenzo Serra, as the plump Archduke, and Philip Locke, as his prime minister.

One likely explanation for writer-director Diane Kury's cinematic success is that all three of her films, including her third, *At First Sight – Coup du Foudre* (a Gala release), are apparently based to a considerable extent on her own and her family's experiences, resulting in her movies having wit, perception and a deep understanding of human nature. In this case, she is concerned with the story of two women (played by Isabelle Huppert and Miou Miou) whose friendship for each other grows mutually more intense until it supplants their hasty, post-war marriages. The husbands are played by Guy Marchand and Jean-Pierre Bacri.

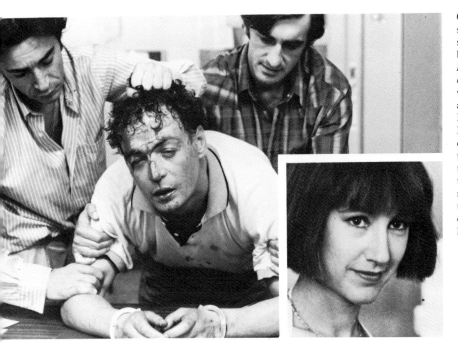

Cops Richard Berry and Philippe Leotard somewhat forcibly try to persuade pimp and small-time gangster Christophe Malavoy to become an informer in *The Balance – La Balance* (a Gala release), a technically first-class but brutal and violent gangster piece which took three of France's premiere César awards for 1983 – Best Film, Best Male Performance (Leotard) and Best Female Performance (Nathalie Baye [inset], as the charming little prostitute). The film is essentially about the war on crime waged by the special police force, the Brigades Territoriales, and it shows them practising methods of brutality linked to a readiness to use guns which would send up a roar of outrage if attempted in obviously more soft-hearted Britain.

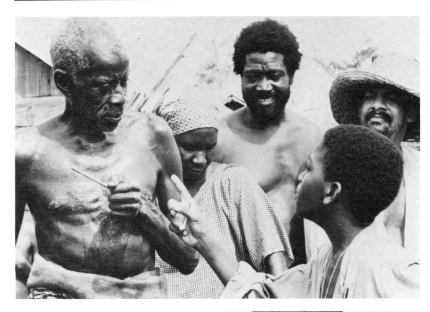

The theme for the Franco-Martinique co-production *Black Shack Alley – Rue Cases Nègres* (an Artificial Eye release) is the oppression of black people under white domination, and the film won director-writer Euzhan Palcy the Silver Lion prize at the Venice Film Festival and also a coveted César award. The film tells of the shocking events that took place in the sugar-cane fields of Martinique in the 1930s, and while it takes a sympathetic standpoint it never becomes tainted by sentimentality.

The Other Cinema's *Blow to the Heart – Colpire al Cuore* explores in some depth the father/son relationship and the effects on it of outside influences, as Jean-Louis Trintignant, the father, becomes embroiled with a terrorist group, much to his young son's disapproval.

Surprisingly for a film from an Iron Curtain country, the Hungarian *Daniel Takes a Train – Szerencsés Daniel* (Cinegate release) is a balanced, unprejudiced chapter of modern history of the country. Set against the background of the 1956 Uprising, it tells the story of two men (played with young conviction by Peter Rudol and Sandol Zsoter) making for the safety of the Austrian border, one seeking his father and the other, a young Jew, in pursuit of a girlfriend, whose fleeing parents do not approve of the romance.

Andrzej Wajda's *Danton* (an Artificial Eye release) is the first film the Polish director has made in French, and also the first he has directed outside his native land. Set against the turmoil of the French Revolution, it tells the true story of the duel between the arrogant, self-indulgent lawyer, with a gift of crowd-swaying oratory – Danton (played with panache by Gérard Dépardieu) – and the bloodily ruthless, but utterly incorruptible, fellow lawyer and revolutionary leader Robespierre (Poland's Wojcieh Pszoniak in a marvellously controlled performance).

Many critics have seen the film as a parallel to present-day events in Poland involving Solidarity, but somewhat understandably Wajda has denied the connection. Nevertheless, even without this implication, *Danton* is a superb example of screencraft – long, wordy, but always absorbing. In this scene, Danton (front) and his friends and supporters, having lost their battle, are trundled to the guillotine.

Swiss-born, BFI graduate Claude Goretta, whose *The Lacemaker* established him as a director of outstanding ability, has continued to show his concern for character and insistence on detail in the Franco-Swiss, Gala release *The Death of Mario Ricci*. The film recounts the story of a crippled TV reporter, assigned to obtain an interview with a distressed and disillusioned scientist hiding away in a small Swiss village, who became involved in a local death and subsequent racial problems. Gian-Maria Volonte, who plays the reporter, won the Best Actor award at the 1983 Cannes Film Festival.

Another impressive Soviet import, this one by Thorn EMI, but of very different calibre, is *Dream Flights – Polioty vo Sne Naiavou*. It is a wry comedy about an irresponsible charmer who behaves outrageously to lovers, family and friends, in fact to all who come into contact with him. But eventually he takes one of his 'jokes' too far and alienates everyone. Here, the joker, played brilliantly by Oleg Yankovsky, rejected and depressed is hiding in a haystack. Beneath the obvious moral point of the inevitable consequences of always taking and not giving in return, many viewers have seen a number of carefully inserted allusions in the film to contemporary Soviet life. Whether they are there or not, the film is still a fascinating view of the USSR today.

The body, the girl (secretary-turned-sleuth, the delectable Fanny Ardant) and the estate agent suspected of murder (Jean-Louis Trintignant) in François Truffaut's *Finally Sunday! – Vivement Dimanche* (an Artificial Eye import) shows the French master of comedy-thriller at his best. Adapting the story from the Charles Williams novel *The Long Saturday Night*, Truffaut shot the film in black-and-white, paying tribute not only to the revered Hitchcock but also to the American 'whodunit' movies of his favourite Bogart era.

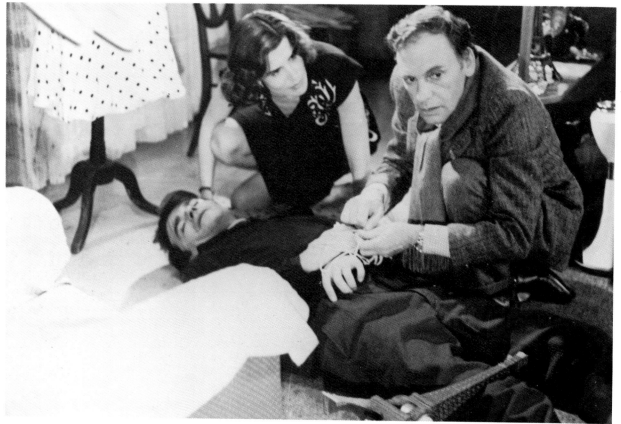

A young policeman comes under the spell of a girl bank-robber, flees with her, but is finally caught by the cops after the girl dies in a new lover's arms. So runs the plot of Jean-Luc Godard's *First name Carmen – Prénom Carmen*. Here the young policeman, Jacques Bonnaffe, forces his pretty prisoner Maruschka Detmers, in a very promising debut, to use the men's toilets so that he can keep his eye on her. It is a typical and rather coarse touch in a film which in style and content is essentially Godard – a disjointed story spaced out by sexual and violent patches, and graced by the occasional touch of humour.

Lover and brother, tailor Miklos B. Szekely measures his sister and mistress, Lili Monori, for the dress which is to be the gift of her brother, Jozsef Toth, in Zsolt Kézdi Kovác's Hungarian film about incest, *Forbidden Relations* (a Cinegate release). This previously taboo screen subject is treated with cool, almost clinical balance in the story about the passion of half-sister for half-brother – started when neither was aware of the relationship – which in spite of every obstacle, including jail sentences, they determinedly continue, flouting the law by producing two children as a result of the affair.

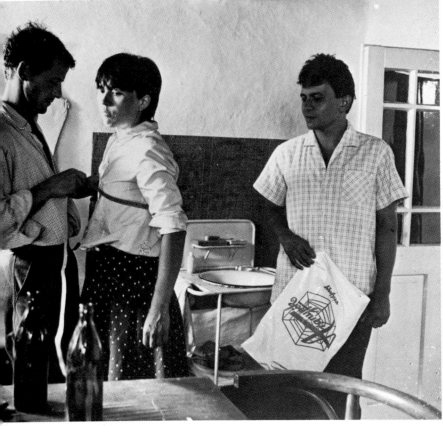

Directed by British ex-film critic Christopher Petit in West Germany, the BFI release *Flight to Berlin* is the perfect 'festival film', with lots of quirky style, fine photography, an almost impenetrable story and players who seem to be acting in a dream – or nightmare. Tusse Silberg (right, with Lisa Kreuzer as her sister and Jean-Francoise Steven as her odd-acting brother-in-law) flies to Berlin after being involved in an accidental killing in the hope of escaping the ensuing British murder case.

Heavily Germanic, feminist orientated, Margarethe von Trotta's story of Berlin intellectuals *Friends and Husbands – Heller Wahn* (a Miracle release) is a study of the friendship between two women, a strong-willed lecturer on German literature (Hanna Schygulla) and the shy, retiring wife of a colleague, whose jealousy spoils the friendship and leads to the wife killing the husband.

Sisters: Or the Balance of Happiness – Die Balance des Glücks (Blue Dolphin release) is also by Margarethe von Trotta and acknowledged to be a superior film to *Friends and Husbands*, with its less Germanic style. It tells the story of two formerly inseparable sisters who grow apart when the elder (played by Gretta Lampe) becomes a very efficient and busily occupied private secretary who begins to be dated by her boss's interested son. As a result, the younger sister (played by Gudrun Gabriel) gradually finds her studies becoming increasingly meaningless, so, largely to punish her sister for what she feels is her neglect, she commits suicide.

(Note: *Sisters* was shown in Britain after Margarethe von Trotta's very successful film *The German Sisters*, but in fact it was made some two years before that movie.)

Set in a small seaside resort near the town in the title, *The Girl from Trieste* tells the tragic story of a sensual and beautiful psychiatric patient (played by Ornella Muti), seen here, bald-headed, studying a book of Braque paintings, watched with some curiosity by her American cartoonist lover (played by Ben Gazzara). Unfortunately, the film never quite achieves the cinematic poetry that it seemed to be aiming for.

Swiss director-writer Alain Tanner used Old Lisbon as the backdrop for *In the White City – Dans la Ville Blanche* (a Contemporary Films import), which was made with Swiss and Portuguese finance. Against this fascinating environment, Tanner tells a very leisurely and rather ambiguous story about a Swiss marine engineer who jumps ship at the port and thereafter drifts idly along without any real motive as he enjoys a passionate love affair with the maid at his hotel and constantly makes home-movies he periodically despatches to his wife with inconclusive letters. A remarkably arduous performance by Bruno Ganza, who is never off screen, is matched by that of Teresa Madruga as the girl.

Typically lean and uncluttered, and beautifully edited to 85 minutes – a refreshing
change to today's unfortunate trend towards
bloated and self-indulgent length – Robert
Bresson's *L'Argent – Money* (an Artificial
Eye import) won, though not without some
controversy, the Grand Prix for 'Outstanding creative cinema' at the 1983 Cannes Film
Festival. The director's background of
philosophic and artistic success in earlier life
is clearly evident in this story of a schoolboy
who cheats a photographer's sales assistant,
an act which leads in logical steps to several
murders.

Helped by two outstanding acting and singing performances by Placido Domingo, as
Alfredo, and Teresa Stratas, as the unfortunate Violetta, Franco Zeffirelli has achieved
what is beyond doubt the finest example of
screened opera yet, *La Traviata* (an ITC
release). Though he did take certain liberties
with the Verdi original – such as starting
with the final scenes as a sort of prelude
(photographed in blue and shadow) before
returning to the opera's usual colourful
opening – the result was stunningly beautiful and successful, making the old familiar
story take on a new and moving dimension.

Compelling performances by two of France's finest players, Philippe Noiret and Simone Signoret, make the otherwise undistinguished *L'Etoile du Nord* (a Gala release) one of the more memorable cinema experiences from across the Channel. Based on a story by Georges Simenon, it tells of an ambling, normally gentle character who in a moment of furious frustration commits a savage and senseless murder, and then wins the heart of the landlady who runs the boarding house where he takes refuge. Inevitably, he is caught and has to pay the price – and Simone Signoret watches sadly as he is shipped off to Devil's Island for the rest of his life.

A major success in its country of origin, Holland, and not doing badly in the USA either, Warner's *The Lift* (dubbed into English for release here), written and directed by Dick Maas, is a horror thriller with some highly effective, blood-curdling scenes. But beneath all the frills and thrills and superficial polish, there is an incredible, and never fully explained, story without any clear motive as to the villainy which causes the elevator to become a killer.

Alan Resnais's films, with their puzzling style and sometimes seemingly wilful ambiguities, have always made him open to accusations of pretentiousness. And that claim is likely to be reinforced by his latest movie *Life is a Bed of Roses – La Vie est un Roman* (an Artificial Eye import). Three quite distinct story threads, set in three different periods, with sudden jumps from one to the other, do not make for easy viewing, more especially as one of the tales is a sort of operatic fairy story (inset) which appears to have little if any connection with the other parts of the movie. The principal roles are played (from left to right) by Fanny Ardant, Geraldine Chaplin and Martine Kelly.

Minema's *Little Ida Growing Up – Liten Ada*, a rare example of a Norwegian film to be shown in this country, is an impressive production, made on a minor scale, but none the worse for that. Ida, brilliantly played by Sunniva Lindekliev, is a child who becomes ostracized by the other local children when during the German Occupation of the country her mother not only consents to work for the hated Germans, but actually welcomes one of them into her bed. With cool and commendable objectivity, the film explores a problem frequently experienced in several countries during the war.

Remarkably topical, being premiered at the time of the siege of the Libyan 'Embassy' in London, Palace Pictures American–Iranian film *The Mission* is a well balanced and impressive movie with a message about the futility of political killings. A dedicated young Moslem from Iran is sent to Britain to murder a fugitive dissident. But to the assassin's discomfort his intended victim befriends him and takes him into his home, where the liberal-minded daughter of the family makes him all the more uneasy by her passionate views about her country's fanaticism. Parviz Sayyad (centre), apart from directing, plays the central role of the victim. The young Moslem student (left) is played by Houshang Tpuzie, and the young woman who confronts him, by Mary Apick.

Made primarily for Italian TV, director-writer Andrei Tarkovsky's 1982 Cannes prize-winner *Nostalgia – Nostalghia* (an Artificial Eye release) has proved to be something of a flawed masterpiece because the impact of superb pictorial images, imaginative action and deep-flowing political and religious undertow is considerably lessened by the slowness of pace and ambiguity of the story. Nevertheless, this, the first of Tarkovsky's six films to be made outside the Soviet Union, is in part memorable and almost certainly destined to become a screen classic.

The ubiquitous Gérard Dépardieu is in early Brando-ish style as the tough, rough stevedore in the Franco-Italian production of *The Moon in the Gutter – La Lune dans la Carniveau*, presented in Britain by Palace Pictures. Set against the shadowy world of the backstreets of a French port, he doggedly searches for the man who raped his sister, which led to her committing suicide. During this search, Dépardieu becomes involved with a lovely upper-class lady (played by Nastassja Kinski) who while slumming is attracted to the labourer's rough masculinity and his muscles. Too consciously striving to be an 'art' film, it is nonetheless often pictorially stunning and harks back in style and atmosphere to the classic French cinema of the 1930s and 1940s. In parts brilliant, in others far less than that, in total it is one of the most collectable movies of the year.

Like Bresson's *L'Argent*, Eric Rohmer's *Pauline at the Beach – Pauline à la Plage* (a Gala release) is also typical of its director's style, and is another of this year's French prize-winners, taking the top award at the 1983 Berlin Film Festival. Little more than an illustrated discussion about love and jealousy among five characters, set against the late summer, sun-drenched beaches of Normandy, it is stylish, witty and almost certainly the most literary movie shown during the year. The cast includes sophisticated seducer Feodore Atkins, nubile schoolgirl Arielle Dombassie (centre) and her elder companion Pauline, Amanda Langlet.

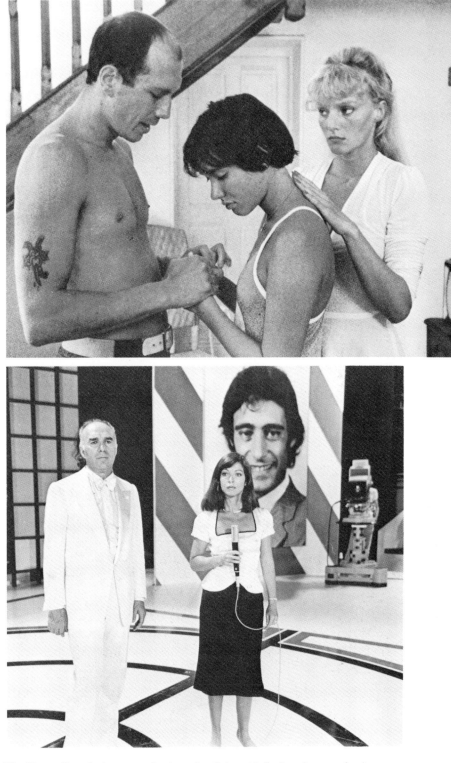

The Franco-Yugoslavian co-production of *The Prize of Peril – Le Prix du Danger*, released by Brent Walker, takes a chilling look at the possible, albeit unlikely way one type of TV programme could develop in the future. Set in France, it depicts a games programme where the contestants hope to gain a mammoth cash prize by literally dicing with death as the prey of a giant man-hunt through Paris. Gérard Lanvin plays the man trying to reach the golden goal with a killer mob on his heels, while back in the studio producer Marie-France Pisier and presenter Michel Picoli, together with the invited audience, watch the deadly – and rigged – game.

Highly stylized, and largely performed against luridly painted backgrounds, *Querelle* (a Palace Pictures release) is the most overtly homosexual of all Rainer Werner Fassbinder's 42 films, this being the last before his death. Based on Jean Genet's 1947 novel, it is the story of explicit male love, lust and accompanying violence, seen against the shadowy, degrading world of Brest's docklands. Among the many strange things in the film is the odd performance by Jeanne Moreau as a sort of Dietrich 'Blue Angel' singer in a nightclub.

Not a particularly charming film, the Dutch-made, Embassy Home Entertainment *Spetters* is aimed rather obviously at the teenager trade and pulls out all the action stops – triple male rape and other explicit sex, motocross races, accidents and a suicide in horrific detail, as well as religious fervour and examples of parental sadism. The best thing about this fast-paced movie is the extremely promising performance by attractive Renee Soutendijk who plays the co-owner of a fish-and-chips stall. Her partner in this venture is her brother, Peter Tuinman, seen here dealing with a particularly awkward customer.

Gérard Dépardieu gave his best screen performance yet as a 16th-century rogue who, for the sake of domestic bliss and financial assets, takes the name and place of a wartime friend, long absent from his village. When suspected by some of the family of being an impostor he faces up with ready wit and confidence to the questioning of the Parliamentary Counsellor (Roger Planchon, a beautiful performance) sent from Toulouse to examine the facts of the case. Only a last minute change of plan by the real Martin Guerre sends the impostor to the gallows. Daniel Vigne's *The Return of Martin Guerre* (Palace Pictures release), was a beautifully photographed, superbly period and finely acted movie based on the Counsellor's own record of the case which has proven the source for so many stories, plays, poems, even an opera.

The normally withdrawn father (Omero Antonutti) dances with his adoring young daughter (Sonsoles Aranguren) in the leisurely and often ambiguous Spanish film *The South – El Sur* (a Contemporary release). After the father's suicide death, the girl, now a teenager, is determined to unravel his past life, and so travels South with just a telephone number as a clue. But the film ends abruptly, leaving many questions unanswered.

For years now, various scripts based on Proust's mammoth literary classic *A la Recherche du Temps Perdu* have been floating around, but the financial backing has not been forthcoming for production to begin. So Volker Schlöndorff's *Swann in Love –Un Amour de Swann* (an Artificial Eye release) based on his own adaptation of a small early part of the work – *Du Côte de Chez Swann* – is a triumph in more ways than one. Though Proust remains virtually impossible to translate into film, Schlöndorff achieves a remarkable near-miss by producing a stunningly visual treat, a finely acted movie with a wonderful recreation of time, atmosphere and place. Jeremy Irons plays the lovesick Swann and Ornella Muti the delicious quarry, Odette.

The Professor and Nobel Prize-winner (Antonio Ferrandis) returns after some thirty-five years teaching in the University of California, to his native town of Gijon to try to pick up some of the threads of his former life in a Civil-War-torn Spain, knowing he has a limited time to live. Winner of the 1983 Best Foreign Film Oscar, Premier Releasing's *To Begin Again – Volver a Empezar*, with its leisurely pace and unashamed sentimentality, was something of a surprise choice.

Made in black-and-white way back in 1953, but never before released in this country, Japanese writer-director Yasujiro Ozu's *Tokyo Story – Tokyo Monogatari* has been resurrected with commendable effort by Cinegate. Yasujiro, who died in 1963, was considered by his countrymen to be the most Japanese of Japanese movie-makers, with a uniquely relaxed style that gave him the time to explore characters and their actions in detail. Nothing much happens in this leisurely, melancholy story about a family's reactions to the Tokyo visit of their provincial mother and father, and then their mother's death. Yet helped by several graceful performances, it is a fascinating experience.

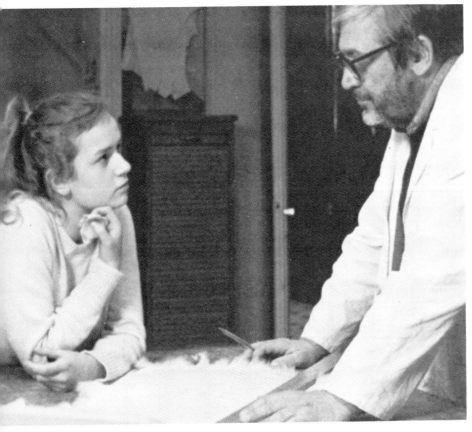

Director-star Maurice Pialat in a scene with Sandrine Bonnaire in Artificial Eye's *To Our Loves – A Nos Amours*, the story of a young girl whose tragedy is that she is emotionally incapable of love, the consciousness of which sends her into a series of unsatisfying love affairs and violent confrontations with her family. The debuting Miss Bonnaire gave an amazingly assured and polished performance.

A marvellous performance by Inna Churikova (left), as the woman who takes over
her husband's large commercial empire, sets
the seal on the excellent Soviet film *Vassa*
(Contemporary Films), a screen adaptation
of the Maxim Gorky play. The politics in the
carefully shaded background of the emergence of the bourgeoisie before the arrival of
communism are subtle and obvious, and
along with the magnificent photography and
the smooth and tender (albeit slow) direction
of Gleb Panfilov, it all helps to create a
remarkably fine period piece.

The delightful Yugoslavian comedy *Who's
Singing Over There – Ko To Tamo Peva*
(imported by Cannon Films) follows the
journey of a shabby old bus and some of its
contrasting passengers who, hoping to get to
Belgrade, are continually thwarted by delays
en route. Set in 1941 (and made in 1980) it
alludes to the end of an era as in the finish, as
the passengers' arguments break into violence, the first bombs begin to fall.

Awards and Festivals

In this section you will find most, if indeed not all of the major, as well as some of the more interesting minor, film prizes of the year, including the awards made at the various annual film festivals. There are, of course, quite a number of minor festivals not mentioned. But in view of the fact these number some two hundred in total, comprehensive coverage would be impractical, and not of great general interest. It is, for instance, highly doubtful if any British readers would wish to be informed about the Big Muddy Festival which takes place at Carbondale, Illinois, or Ostrava-Poruba's Environmental Film event held in Czechoslovakia, or even the Red Cross and Health Film Festival staged by the Bulgarian authorities in Varna. A fairly complete list of all such festivals and similar events is published in *Variety* from time to time, but even that remarkable newspaper does not often cover them in detail.

Some of the most important festivals are, of course, non-competitive, such as those held annually in London and New York, although for a film to be accepted for showing in these festivals brings much sought-after prestige.

Bob Connolly and Robin Anderson, for *First Contact* (Australia); Richard Boutet and Pascal Gelinas, for *La Turlute Des Andées Dures* (Canada).
International Jury's Prix de la Suisse Romande: Grady Watts and Arnold Bennett, for *Books Under Fire* (USA).
Special Gold Sesterce to Jean-Jacques La Grange, for 30 years of documentary productions for Swiss TV.
Certificates of Merit: Mark Rance, for *Death and the Singing Telegram* (USA); Richard Ellison and Stanley Karnow, for *Vietnam – a Television History* (USA); Derk Saver, Jan Blom and Frank Diamand, for *Eduardo Uruguayo* (Holland).

The Second Film Festival of Mediterranean Cultures, Bastia, Corsica, November 1983

Golden Olive Tree Grand Prix Prize: *A Season in Hakkari*, directed by Erden Kiral (Turkey).
Special Jury Prize: *Nesto Izmedu*, directed by Srdan Karanovic (Yugoslavia).
Critics' & Public's Award: *Hector*, directed by Carlos Perez Ferre (Spain).
Best First Film: *Santu Nicoli*, directed by Pierre Cangioni (Corsica).
Best Actor: Pierre Massimi in *Santu Nicoli*.
Best Actress: Danielle Darrieux in *En Haut des Marches*, directed by Paul Vecchiali (France).

The London *Evening Standard* Film Awards for 1983

Best Film: *The Ploughman's Lunch*, directed by Richard Eyre.
Best Actor: Ben Kingsley, in *Gandhi* and *The Betrayal*.
Best Actress: Phyllis Logan, in *Another Time, Another Place*.
The Peter Sellers Award for Best Comedy Performance: Bill Forsyth, in *Local Hero*.
Best Screenplay: Ian McEwan, for *The Ploughman's Lunch*.
Most Promising Newcomer: Neil Jordan, in *Angel*.
Best Technical Achievement: Chris Menges, for *Angel* and *Local Hero*.
Special Award to Richard Attenborough for Services to the British Cinema 1943–83 as actor, director and producer.

The Nyon, Swiss Documentary Festival Awards, October 1983

Gold Sesterce – Grand Prix: Gary Kildea, for *Celso and Cora* (Australia).
Silver Sesterces: Gwynne Dyer and Michael Bryan, for *War* (Canada);

Sitges Fantasy Film Festival, October 1983

Best Film/Best Director: Luc Besson for *Le Dernier Combat – The Last Fight* (France).
Best Actor: (shared) Vincent Price, Christopher Lee, Peter Cushing and John Carradine, in *House of Long Shadows* (Great Britain).
Best Actress: Elizabeth Watt, in *Alone in the Dark* (USA).
Best Cinematography: Jacques Steyn, in *Feuer Und Schwert – Fire and Sword* (Germany).
Best Screenplay: Michael Armstrong, for *House of Long Shadows* (Great Britain).
Best Special Effects: *Return of Captain Invincible* (Australia).
Best Short: Paul Roman, for *Sombras Tragicas – Tragic Shadows* (Spain).
Critics' Award: *The Lost Tribe* (New Zealand).
Special Mention: Luis Ospina, for *Pura Sangre – Pure Blood* (Colombia).

The Utrecht Film Festival Awards, October 1983

(Only Dutch films were in competition).

Best Feature Film: *Life Before Death*, produced by Louis Van Gasteren.

Best Short: *Next Year in Holysloot*, directed by Emiel Van Moerkerken.

Best Documentary: Gerrit Van Elst, for *The Kick*.

Best Actor: Vic Moeremans, in *The Flax Field*.

Best Actress: Carolien Van Den Berg, in *There Was Laughter At The Time*.

Prize to Bert Haanstra for Outstanding Services to Dutch Cinema.

The 25th Annual Australian Film Awards, Sydney, 24 September 1983

Best Film: *Careful, He Might Hear You*.

Best Direction: Carl Schultz, for *Careful, He Might Hear You*.

Best Actress: Wendy Hughes; Best Supporting Actor: John Hargreaves; Best Photography: John Seale; Best Screenplay from another source: Michael Jennings; Best Production Design: John Stoddart; Best Costume Design: Bruce Finlayson. All in *Careful, He Might Hear You*.

Best Actor: Norman Kaye, in *Man of Flowers*.

Best Original Screenplay: John Digwall, for *Buddies*.

Best Supporting Actress: Linda Hunt, in *The Year of Living Dangerously*.

The Venice Film Festival, September 1983

Grand Prix – The Golden Lion: *Prénom Carmen – First Name Carmen*, directed by Jean-Luc Godard (France/ Switzerland).

Special Jury Prize: *Biquefarre – Farrebique: 35 Years Later*, directed by Georges Rouquier (France).

Best Male Performance: (shared) Matthew Modine, Michael Wright, Mitchell Lichtenstein, David Alan Grier, Guy Boyd and George Dzundza, in *Streamers* (USA).

Best Female Performance: Darling Legitimus, in *Rue Cases Nègres – Street of Black Shacks* (France/Martinique).

Most Outstanding Technical Achievement: Raoul Coutard (photography) and François Musy (sound), in *Prénom Carmen*.

The Silver Lion Award for first or second work to *Prénom Carmen*.

Career Award: Michelangelo Antonioni.

Some Unofficial Awards to: Ingmar Bergman's *Fanny and Alexander* (International Critics); *Rue Cases Nègres* (International Catholic Film Office); Juraj Jakubisko's *The 1,000 Year Old Bee* (Czechoslovakia/Italy/ West Germany co-production)

The Golden Phoenix Award for Cinematography: Woody Allen's *Zelig* (Italian Journalists' Award).

The La Coruna, Spanish Film Festival, September 1983

Best Film: Bill Forsyth's *Local Hero* (GB).

Best Direction: (shared) Peter Schamoni, for *Fruehlings Sinfonie – Spring Symphony* (Germany), and Jose Fonseca e Costa, for *Sem Sombra de Pecado – Without a Shade of Sin* (Portugal).

Best Actor: Massimo Troisi, in *Scusate Il Ritardo – Excuse the Delay* (Italy), which he also directed.

Best Actress: Victoria Abril, in *Sem Sombra de Pecado*.

Best Screenplay: (shared) Oldrich Lipskzy, Alexander Lukes and Vladimir Jiranek, for *Srdecny Pozdrav Ze Semekonlke – Best Greetings from Earth* (Czechoslovakia).

Special Mentions: Eugenio Jofra, for his first film *Un Genio En Apuros – A Genius in Trouble* (Spain); and actor Rolf Hoppe, for his performance in *Fruehlings Sinfonie – Spring Symphony* (Germany).

The Montreal, Canadian Film Festival, August 1983

Grand Prix des Amériques: *The Go Masters*, directed by Junya Sato and Duan Jishun (China/Japan co-production).

Special Jury Award: *Benvenuta*, directed by André Delvaux (Belgium/ France co-production).

Jury Award: *Bearn*, or *The Doll's Parlour*, directed by Jaime Chavarri (Spain).

Best Actor: (shared) Gérard Dépardieu and Pszoniak Wojciech, in *Danton* (France).

Best Actress: Yuko Tanaka, in *Amagi Pass* (Japan).

Grand Prix de Montreal (for short film): *La Plante*, directed by Thomas Vamos and Joyce Borenstein (Canada).

Special Award to Norman McLaren for his lifetime achievements.

The Pula, Yugoslavian Film Festival, August 1983

Best Film: Zivojin Pavlovic's *Body Scent*.

Best Direction: Srdjan Karanovic, for *Something In Between*.

Best Actor: Miki Manojlovic, in *Something In Between*.

Best Actress: Ljrljana Medjesi, in *Body Scent*.

Best Photography: Zivko Zalar, for *Something In Between*.

Best Music: Zoran Simjanovic, in *Balkan Express*.

Best Art Direction: Niko Matul, for *Twilight Time*.

The Locarno International Film Festival, August 1983

Golden Leopard: *The Princess*, directed by Pal Erdoss (Hungary).

Silver Leopard: *Hamsin – Hot Wind*, directed by Daniel Wachsmann (Israel).

Bronze Leopard: *Ferestedah – The Mission*, directed by Parviz Sayyad (Iran/ West Germany).

Bronze Leopards for First Films: Spike Lee, for *Joe's Bed-Study Barbershop – We Cut Heads* (USA); Hermano Penna, for *Sargento Getulio* (Brazil).

Critics' Prize: Emile de Antonio's *In the King of Prussia* (USA).

Special Mentions: to *Family Game* (Japan), *The Princess* and *Joe's Bed-Study Barbershop*; to actors Yusaka Matsuda, in *Family Games*, and Siegfried Zimmerschied, in *Grenzenlos* (West Germany); and to cameraman Hughes Ryffel, for *L'Allègement* (Switzerland).

The Odense Film Festival, August 1983

First Prize (Gold): *Once Upon a Time There Was a Dog*, by E. Nazarov (USSR – animated).

Second Prize (Gold): *Fish Team*, by S. Sokolov (USSR – animated).

Third Prize (Gold:) *Oceandra's Armoured Birds*, by Suzanne Maes (Belgium – animated).

Silver Prize: *Clouds in Pants*, by K. Deller (Switzerland – animated).

The Five-Thousand-Dollar Cash Prize: *A Love of Full Stops*, by Jean-Louis Philippon (France – live action).

The Two-Thousand-Five-Hundred-Dollar Prize: *Where Did You Get That Woman?* (USA – documentary).

The Moscow Film Festival, July 1983

First Prizes of Gold Medals: *Vassa*, by Gleb Panifilov (USSR); *Alcino and the Condor*, by Miguel Littin (Nicaragua); and *Amok*, by Souheil Ben Barka (Morocco).

Silver Medals: *Doctor Faustus*, by Franz Seitz (West Germany); *Equilibrium*, by Lyudmil Kirkov (Bulgaria); and *Concrete Pastures*, by Stefan Uher (Czechoslovakia).

Best Actor: shared – Wirgiliusz Gryn, in *Pastorale Heroica*, directed by Henryk Bielski (Poland), and Yoshi Kato, in *Home Village*, directed by Seijiro Koyama (Japan).

Best Actress: shared – Judy Davis, in *Winter of Our Dreams*, directed by John Duigan (Australia), and Jessica Lange, in *Frances*, directed by Graeme Clifford (GB).

International Critics' Prize: *Demons in the Garden*, by Manuel Gutierrez (Spain); and *Without Witness*, by Nikita Mikhalkov (USSR).

The 20th Cracow Festival of Short Film Awards, June 1983

Grand Prix: Bogdan Dziworski's documentary *A Few Stories about Man* (Poland).

Golden Dragons: Bogoslav Marjanovic's documentary *Land Reunion* (Yugoslavia), and O. Rakutko's documentary *Uriengoj* (USSR).

Silver Dragons: Ferenc Czako's animated *Autotortura* (Hungary); Michael Torres's documentary *Chronicles of an Infamy* (Cuba); and Drahomira Vihanova's documentary *Problems of Unmarried Mothers* (Czechoslovakia).

Critics' Prize: Bogoslav Marjanovic's *Land Reunion* (Yugoslavia).

The Annecy Film Festival Prizewinners, June 1983

Grand Prix: *The Possibilities of Dialogue*, directed by Jan Svankmajer (Czechoslovakia).

Special Jury Prizes: 1st, *Dance of Death* by Dennis Tupicoff (Australia); 2nd, *Night Club*, by Jonathan Hodgson (Great Britain); 3rd, *Once Upon a Time There Was a Dog*, by Edouard Nazaron (USSR).

Best Children's Film: *History of the Little Rabbit and the Big Rabbit*, by Johan Hagelback (Sweden).

Best Educational/Scientific Film: *The Blood*, by Jacques Rouzel (France).

Best Commercial Film: *Agis Regression*, by Pierluigi de Mas (Italy).

Best Sponsored Film: *Equality*, by Martti Jannes (Finland).

Best First Film: *Album*, by Kresimir Zimonic (Yugoslavia).

The Special 'Banc-Titre' Critics' Prize: *The Great Cognito*, by Will Vinton (USA).

The Italian David di Donatello Awards announced in Rome, July 1983

Best Film: *Night of the Shooting Stars*, by Paolo and Vittorio Taviani.

Best Direction (the Tavianis), Best Production (Giuliani De Negri), Best Cinematography (Franco di Giacomo) and Best Editing (Robert Perpignani) awards all went to this film.

Best Actor: Francesco Nuti, in *Io, Chiara e Lo Scuro – Light, Darkness and I*.

Best Actress: Giuliana De Sio, in the same film.

Best Supporting Performances: Federica Mastroianni, in *Be Good if You Can*, and Fausto Rossi, in *Strike at the Heart*. Other supporting performance awards to Virna Lisi, in *Scent of the Sea*, Lina Poliyo, in *Excuse Me for Being Late*, and Lello Arena, in the same film.

Best New Director: Francesco Laudadio, for his *Grog*.

The Cannes Film Festival Awards, 30 May 1984

Golden Palm for Best Film: *Paris, Texas*, directed by Wim Wenders (West Germany).

Special Jury Prize: *Naplo*, directed by Marta Meszaros (Hungary).

Best Direction: Bertrand Tavernier, for his *A Sunday in the Country* (France).

Best Actress: Helen Mirren, in *Cal* (Ireland).

Best Actor: (shared) Alfredo Landa and Francisco Rabal, in *The Holy Innocents* (Spain).

Best Artistic Contribution: Peter Biziou, for his photography in *Another Country* (Great Britain).

Best Screenplay: Theo Angelopoulos, Theo Valtinos and Tonino Guerra for *Voyage to Cythera* (Greece).

Special Award for Outstanding Contribution to Cinema: John Huston.

Short Film Golden Palm: *The Iron Horse*, by Gerald Frydman and Pierre Levie (France).

Short Film Jury Prize: *Tchouma*, by David Takaichvili.

International Film Critics' Award: *Paris, Texas* and *Voyage to Cythera*.

The American Academy of Motion Picture Arts and Sciences 1984 (for 1983 movies, etc) Awards announced on 9 April 1984

Best Film: *Terms of Endearment*, directed by James L. Brooks (Paramount-UIP).

Best Direction: James L. Brooks, for *Terms of Endearment*.

Best Actor: Robert Duvall, in *Tender Mercies* (Universal-EMI).

Best Actress: Shirley MacLaine, in *Terms of Endearment*.

Best Supporting Actor: Jack Nicholson, in *Terms of Endearment*.

Best Supporting Actress: Linda Hunt, in *The Year of Living Dangerously* (MGM/UA-UIP).

Best Original Screenplay: Hortin Foote, for *Tender Mercies*.

Best Screenplay Adaptation: James L. Brooks, for *Terms of Endearment*.

Best Cinematography: Sven Nykvist, for Ingmar Bergman's *Fanny and Alexander*.

Best Editing: Glenn Farr, Lisa Fruchtman, Stephen A. Rotter, Douglas Stewart and Tom Rolf, for *The Right Stuff* (Ladd-Warner).

Best Foreign Language Film: Bergman's *Fanny and Alexander*.

Best Original Score: Bill Conti, for *The Right Stuff*.

Best Art Direction: Anna Asp (direction) and Susanne Lingheim (sets), in *Fanny and Alexander*.

Two Oscars in one bed. Shirley MacLaine won this year's premier female acting award of the American Academy of Motion Picture Arts and Sciences for her performance in the Paramount-UIP release *Terms of Endearment*; and for his work in the same film Jack Nicholson was presented with the Best Supporting Actor prize.

Best Sound: Mark Berger, Tom Scott, Randy Thom and David MacMillan, in *The Right Stuff*.

Best Shorts: Animation – Jimmy Picker (producer), *Sunday in New York*; Live Action – Janice L. Platt (producer), *Boys and Girls*.

Best Documentaries: Features – Emile Ardolino (producer), *He Makes Me Feel Like Dancin'*; Shorts – Cynthia Scott and Adam Symansky (producers), *Flamenco at 5.15*.

Honorary Award to Hal Roach 'in recognition of his unparalleled record of contributions to the motion picture art form'.

The Jean Hersholt Humanitarian Award to M.(Mike) J. Frankovich.

The British Academy of Film and Television Arts Awards 1983 announced on 27 March 1984

Best Film: *Educating Rita*, directed by Lewis Gilbert.

Best Direction: Bill Forsyth, for *Local Hero*.

Best Actor: (shared) Michael Caine, in *Educating Rita*, and Dustin Hoffman, in *Tootsie*.

Best Actress: Julie Walters, in *Educating Rita*.

Best Original Screenplay: Paul D. Zimmerman, for *The King of Comedy*.

Best Screenplay Adaptation from a Novel: Ruth Prawer Jhabvala, for *Heat and Dust* (her own novel).

Best Foreign Language Film: *Danton*, directed by Andrzej Wajda.

Best Supporting Actress: Jamie Lee Curtis, in *Trading Places*.

Best Supporting Actor: Denholm Elliott, in *Trading Places*.

Best Newcomer Performance: Phyllis Logan, in *Another Time, Another Place*.

Best Photography: Sven Nykvist, for *Fanny and Alexander*.

Best Art Direction: (shared) Franco Zeffirelli and Gianni Quaranta, for *La Traviata*.

Best Musical Score: Ryuichi Sakamoto, for *Merry Christmas Mr. Lawrence*.

Best Editing: (shared) Bud Smith and Walt Mulconery, for *Flashdance*.

Best Short Film: Ian Emes's *Goodie Two Shoes*.

The results of the French Academy César Awards, announced early March 1984

Best French Film: (shared) *To Our Loves*, directed by Maurice Pialat, and *Le Bal – The Ball*, directed by Ettore Scola.

Best Actor: Coluche, in Claude Berri's *Tchao Pantin*.

Best Actress: Isabelle Adjani, in Jean Becker's *One Deadly Summer*.

Best Director: Ettore Scola, for *Le Bal – The Ball*.

Best Foreign Film: Ingmar Bergman's *Fanny and Alexander*; with Alain Tanner awarded a César for his *In the White City*.

Best Supporting Actor: Richard Anconina, for *Tchao Pantin*.

Best Supporting Actress: Suzanne Flon, in *One Deadly Summer*.

Best First Feature: *Rue Cases Nègres*, directed by Euzhan Palcy.

Shorts Césars were awarded to Agnes Varda (documentary – *Ulysse*), Stephane Drout (fiction – *Star Suburb*) and Jean Manuel Costa (animation – *Le Voyage D'Orphée*).

The Golden Globe Awards – Hollywood, 31 January 1984

Best Picture: *Terms of Endearment*.

Best Actor – Drama: (shared) Robert Duvall, in *Tender Mercies*, and Tom Courtenay, in *The Dresser*.

Best Actress – Drama: Shirley MacLaine, in *Terms of Endearment*.

Best Actor – Comedy: Michael Caine, in *Educating Rita*.

Best Actress – Comedy: Julie Walters, in *Educating Rita*.

Best Supporting Actor: Jack Nicholson, in *Terms of Endearment*.

Best Supporting Actress: Cher, in *Silkwood*.

Best Foreign Film: Ingmar Bergman's *Fanny and Alexander*.

Best Director: Barbra Streisand, for *Yentl*.

Best Screenplay: James L. Brooks, for *Terms of Endearment* (which he also directed).

The Cecil B. de Mille Award: Paul Newman.

Best Original Musical Score: Giorgio Moroder, for *Flashdance*.

The Avoriaz Fantasy Film Festival Awards, France, January 1984

Grand Prix: Dick Maas's *The Lift* (Holland).

Special Jury Prize: Paul Verhoeven's *De Vierde Man – The Fourth Man* (Holland).

Critics' Prize: David Cronenberg's *The Dead Zone* (Canada).

The British Critics' Circle Awards, November 1983

Best Film: *King of Comedy* (Runners up: *E.T.*, *Gandhi*, *Heat and Dust* and *Local Hero*).

Best Film of Foreign Origin: *Yol* (Runners up: *Fanny and Alexander*, *The Leopard*, *Danton* and *L'Argent*).

Best Direction: Andrzej Wajda, for *Danton* (Runners up: Richard Attenborough, for *Gandhi*; Martin Scorsese, for *King of Comedy*; Ingmar Bergman for *Fanny and Alexander*; and Steven Spielberg, for *E.T.*).

Best Screenplay: Ruth Prawer Jhabvala, for *Heat and Dust* (Runners up: Melissa Mathison, for *E.T.*; John Briley, for *Gandhi*; Paul Zimmerman, for *King of Comedy*; and Jean Claude Carriere, for *Danton*).

Special Technical Award: Ben Kingsley, for his performance in *Gandhi*.

Special Non-Technical Award: Artificial Eye distributors for their Quality Programming.

The Mari Kuttna Award: Jonathan Hodgson, for *Night Club*.

The New York Film Critics' Awards for 1983

Best Film: *Terms of Endearment*.

Best Actress: Shirley MacLaine, in *Terms of Endearment*.

Best Actor: Robert Duvall, in *Tender Mercies*.

Best Supporting Actress: Linda Hunt, in *The Year of Living Dangerously*.

Best Supporting Actor: Jack Nicholson, in *Terms of Endearment*.

Best Director: Ingmar Bergman, for *Fanny and Alexander*, which was named as Best Foreign Film.

Best Screenplay: Bill Forsyth, for *Local Hero*.

The American National Society of Film Critics' Awards

Best Film: *Night of the Shooting Stars*.

Best Actress: Debra Winger, in *Terms of Endearment*.

Best Actor: Gérard Dépardieu, in *Danton*.

Best Director: (shared) Paolo and Vittorio Taviani, for *Night of the Shooting Stars*.

Best Screenplay: Bill Forsyth, for *Local Hero*.

Best Supporting Actor: Jack Nicholson, in *Terms of Endearment*.

Best Supporting Actress: Sandra Bernhard, in *The King of Comedy*.

The Berlin Film Festival Awards, February 1984

Golden Bear First Prize: *Love Streams*, directed by John Cassavetes (USA).

Best Director: Ettore Scola, for *Le Bal – The Ball* (Italy).

Best Actor: Albert Finney, in *The Dresser* (Great Britain).

Best Actress: Monica Vitti, in *The Flirt* (Italy); also mentioned Inna Tschurikova, in *Front Romance* (USSR).

Special Jury Prize: *Funny Dirty Little War*, directed by Hector Olivera (Argentina).

Special Mentions: *Class Relations*, by Jean-Marie Straub and Danielle Huillet (Germany).

Various other prizes went to *Rembetico* (Greece), *Struggle Between the Snips and Mussel* (China) and *7 Bicycle Symphony* – short (Denmark).

The First Brussels Fantasy Festival, November 1983

Best Film: Robert Wynne-Simmon's *The Outcasts* (Ireland).

Best Direction: Dusan Vukotic, for his *Gosti iz Galaksije* (Yugoslavia).

Special Jury Prize: *Ritam Zlocina*, directed by Zoran Tadic (Yugoslavia).

The 13th Paris Film Festival of Sci-Fi and Fantasy Films, December 1983

Grand Prix – The Golden Unicorn: *Xtro*, directed by Harry Bromley (Great Britain).

Critics' Jury Prize (and Award for Best Screenplay): *Siege*, directed by Paul Donovan and Maura O'Connel.

Special Jury Prize: *Mausoleum*, directed by Michael Dugan (USA).

The 26th Leipzig Festival of Documentaries, December 1983

Golden Dove (Over 35 mins): *Stand Up and Resist*, directed by Klaus Volkenborn and Johann Feindt (West Berlin).

Golden Dove (Under 35 mins): *Nicaragua: Report from the Front*, directed by Deborah Shaffer and Tom Sigel (USA).

Golden Dove (Animation): (shared) *Black and White* directed by Vaclav Bedrich (Czechoslovakia); and *The Last Newscast*, directed by Nikola Majdak (Yugoslavia).

The Third Damascus International Film Festival, November 1983

The Golden Sword Award: *The Last Gift*, directed by Ghoti Ben Dedoush (Algeria).

The Silver Sword: *Bus Driver*, directed by Atif El-Tayeb (Egypt).

The Bronze Sword: *Red Power*, directed by Lazario Boria (Cuba).

The Fifth Orleans Film Festival, Paris, November 1983

The Grand Prize: *Le Champ de Lin – The Flax Field*, directed and written by Jan Gruyaert (Belgium).

Special Jury Prize: *The Lost Tribe*, directed by John Laing (New Zealand).

Best Male Performance: Fausto Rossi, for *Colpire Al Cuore* (Italy).

Young Auteurs Prize: Robert Salis, for *Lettres d'Amours Perdues* (France). Special Jury Prize in this category to *Peppermint Frieden*, directed by Marianne S.V. Rosenbaum (West Germany).

Difficult Times Down Under

A brief summary of the Australian Cinema, July 1983 to June 1984

FREDERICK DEEPS

Nobody, I fancy, is going to suggest that the year up to July 1984 was anything other than a generally miserable one for both the production and exhibition sides of the Australian Cinema. The brutal truth is that it was the worst period since the crisis sparked by the introduction of television way back in 1956. And the cause of this unhappy state of affairs, as elsewhere, is the increasingly widespread use of the video-cassette. One out of every five homes in Australia now owns or rents a video recorder, and away from the towns and in the outback that figure rises to one in two. The consequences of this are self-evident. While cinema attendance figures have remained fairly steady in the cities and their suburbs, they have declined disastrously in the outback, where it is possible to hire a video-cassette for as little as a dollar a night. In the remote town of Alice Springs, in Northern Territory, for example, both the cinemas have closed down, but no less than 19 video stores have opened up.

The trend is the same throughout the country, if less dramatic. During the year, more than 50 screens were shuttered, and with the news of more closures on the way one of Greater Union circuit's bosses has forecast that of the nation's 750 cinemas, 250 will be shut by the end of 1984. This now looks uncomfortably likely. And there is an equally depressing forecast from Australasian Filmways executive Robert Ward that there will not be a country drive-in cinema left operating come December. The major circuits say that their admissions have dropped, too, by 25 to 30 per cent, and the chairman of the Australian Film Commission is on record as suggesting that the figure is nearer 50 per cent in places.

Yet video cannot be held totally responsible for the demise, and there are other important contributory factors, the rise in admission charges being one of them. High prices – a seat in an urban cinema can cost as much as 7 dollars – are driving people away. Two of the country's main circuits, Hoyts and Village, recognized this and decided last spring that something had to be done to halt the slide. So prices were cut, and paid for by some stringent economies, by dropping all but a few Australian short films as an experiment, and by pruning the programmes so that an extra one could be squeezed in each day.

At the same time the exhibitors united in an effort to procure an agreement for a longer period between the time a new film is premiered in the cinema and the time it is offered on video. The irony here is that two of the

A big success 'down under', somewhat less so in America, Fox's *The Man From Snowy River* has had a chequered career in Britain, surfacing at a few isolated points in 1983 but only getting an even restricted release here in 1984. A mixture of Disney real-life film, *Wilderness Family* type background, and boy-and-horse/boy-and-girl romance, it co-starred Tom Burlinson and Sigrid Thornton (and horses), with Kirk Douglas as a rugged rancher whose opposition to his daughter's choice finally has to give way to approval when the lad proves himself.

159

One of the most completely satisfying artistic films of the year, Paul Cox's *Man of Flowers* is a beautifully told story of a man (magnificently played by Norman Kaye), a recluse because of his Oedipus complex, with a love of flowers and passion for art, whose strange pleasure it is to employ a young girl (Alyson Best) to visit him once a week and strip naked. A film full of subtleties and sensuality, art and music.

major circuits have a considerable interest in the video-cassette business.

But all is not gloom and doom. Big movies, such as *Gandhi*, *Tootsie*, *E.T.* and *Phar Lap* (Australia's most expensive production yet), all took big money at the box office and attracted large audiences wherever they were shown. Significantly, *Phar Lap* took 3 million dollars in Australia, but it will have to make a lot more worldwide to recover its 7 million dollars production cost. And there was a hint of optimism from those who saw the depression as an uncomfortable but passing phase. David Williams, for instance, a senior executive of a large chain, commented: 'This year will see a degree of rationalization in the industry with a lot of cinemas closing. The home-video business will hurt us for at least another

eighteen months. But the sooner it reaches the maximum saturation point of 65 per cent or so the better for us because people will then start to get tired of sitting in their lounges and they'll want to get out and see movies on the big screen.'

If people are to be enticed back to the cinema, then the theatres will have to show the films they want to see. Exhibitors have been claiming that a further reason why audience figures have dropped is that there has been a dearth of good movies, especially Australian ones. In response the movie-makers point an accusing finger at the government. In August 1983, the decision was taken to cut the tax concession for production investment from 150 per cent to 133 per cent. 'That night', says Jane North of the Film and Television

Production Association of Australia, 'investment in film production dried up and only nine months later did it begin to stir back into life.'

Getting a picture into production is still a difficult, some would say impossible task. In February 1984, it was revealed that of some 22 producers trying to get backing for their projects, only three had succeeded in raising enough cash to take their movies into the studio. The financial backing just was not there. Australian Cinema is still too dependent on various government film commissions and it is also hampered by its own internal red tape.

But by the end of June, a more promising picture was emerging, after the Australian Film Commission injected 5 million dollars into the business. And by the beginning of July they were able to announce that in the preceding year 20 productions had been completed and a further 17 were planned for this year.

The gloomier part of this report is all the more sad in that Australia during recent years has been turning out some excellent movies, with fine actors and actresses directed by outstandingly gifted directors. And though some of the best talent has been lured to America and Europe (Gillian Armstrong of *My Brilliant Career* fame working in Canada making *Mrs Soffel* with Diane Keaton; Bruce Beresford – *The Getting of Wisdom*, etc – in Europe making *King David*; and Fred Schepisi – *The Chant of Jimmy Blacksmith* – in the USA making *Iceman*), it appears a wave of promising newcomers is emerging to take their place on the home front.

Last year saw a quintet of Australian movies released in Britain – *The Clinic, Heatwave, Norman Loves Rose, Fighting Back* and *Puberty Blues* – as against the same number this year: *Star Struck, Monkey Grip, We of the Never Never* and Paul Cox's remarkable *Man of Flowers* which managed to look like a million dollars on a tiny quarter-million budget. Among the newcomers to watch are Russell Mulcahy (*Razorback*), George Miller (*Road Warrior*) Simon Wincer (*Phar Lap*), Igor Auzons (*The Coolangatta Gold*) and Michael Pattonson (*Street Gold*). All these films have yet to be seen in Britain, but hopefully they will be released here in due course so we can see this talent for ourselves.

Film Books of the Year

IVAN BUTLER

Cinema audiences may ebb and flow, but the stream of books about the medium continues unabated. Only a proportion of them can be considered here, but it is, I hope, a representative one. Popular biographies continue to flourish in response to an apparently insatiable demand, and works of serious criticism, history and analysis are also well featured. A welcome development in recent years has been the growing number of large-scale reference books often combining entertainment with information, and this year's crop particularly favours the Western and Horror/Science Fiction genres.

Contrary to previous editions of *Film Review*, the division of books into three different categories has now been replaced by a straightforward alphabetical order throughout. The division was always somewhat arbitrary (some biographies, for instance, contain so much documentation as to qualify for inclusion in the reference category, and vice versa); the new arrangement will make any particular title easier to trace. Brief details are given of a number of 'Other Books' which, for one reason or another, it has not been possible to review.

'Best Lists' are always open to question (Best for whom? By what standards?), but it has been suggested that a selection of books which through the year have seemed particularly interesting, entertaining or useful for research might be welcome. Here, therefore, in alphabetical order, is a purely personal choice:

D.W. Griffith and the Birth of Film, Richard Schickel

The Films of Christopher Lee, R.W. Rohle Jr & D.C. Hart, with the participation of Lee

Halliwell's Film and Video Guide (4th edition), Leslie Halliwell

The Illustrated Guide to Film Directors, David Quinlan

The Illustrated Who's Who of the Cinema, Ann Lloyd & Graham Fuller

The Life and Times of the Western Movie, Jay Hyams

The Life of Alfred Hitchcock, Donald Spoto

The Look of Buster Keaton, Robert Benayoun

Roman, Roman Polanski

Science Fiction, Horror and Fantasy – Film and Television Credits (2 vols), Harris M. Lentz

Selected Film Criticism, 1896–1950 (5 vols), Ed Anthony Slide

The Universal Story, Clive Hirschhorn

The Western, Phil Hardy

Special mention for a lightweight but thoroughly entertaining book of anecdotes: *Tales from the Hollywood Raj*, Sheridan Morley

Full details of all the above books will be found in the review section.

Adventures in the Screen Trade, William Goldman, Macdonald & Co, £9.95

This lively, and indeed hilarious, account by a well known scriptwriter of working in recent and contemporary Hollywood is almost at times a light-hearted Guide to the Job; but it is also much more, being full of amusing, sometimes horrific anecdotes, and many a caustic comment on the madness of movie-making. On the 'educational' side, it includes a complete account of the translating of a piece of narrative fiction into a film script, and offers many other hints set out in short, pithy paragraphs. In all a thoroughly enjoyable read – and possibly a warning to aspiring scriptwriters!

The Ages of Gielgud, Ed Ronald Harwood, Hodder & Stoughton, £9.95

To celebrate Sir John Gielgud's 80th birthday, Ronald Harwood has gathered together and usefully annotated 14 specially written brief articles from well known actors, authors and others, such as Alec Guinness, Emlyn Williams, Irene Worth and John Mortimer, in an affectionate, often amusing, but never fulsome tribute to one of the great actors of the past 30 years. Many of the articles range outside their particular subject with interesting and perceptive comments on the dramatic arts in general. There is finally a superb chronology listing every stage, film and TV appearance, in addition to a detailed index. Though mainly concerned with the theatre, this elegant volume cannot fail to be of the greatest interest to any film enthusiast.

Air Force, Ed Lawrence Howard Suid, University of Wisconsin Press (distributed by Academic & University Publishers Group) £10.95 cloth/ £4.20 paper

This further volume in the excellent series of Warner Bros screenplays has as its subject a lesser-known and less starrily cast film than usual – a piece of frank propaganda released in 1943. A long introduction, aptly entitled 'Myth-making for the War Effort', discusses the film and its intentions in relation to World War II. Twenty-four well reproduced frame enlargements, notes, and cast and credit lists follow the usual pattern.

Alec Guinness – A Celebration see under **John Gielgud – A Celebration**

Audrey Hepburn, Ian Woodward, W.H. Allen, £9.95

The first fourteen photographs in this biography follow Miss Hepburn's maternal ancestry back to the year 1572 – one whole page reads somewhat like a John-begat-James chapter from the Bible. She is the daughter of the Dutch Baroness van Heemstra. Her father, a Nazi sympathiser who walked out on the family and disappeared, is not represented. After a traumatic life in war-torn Holland her mother, now penniless, brought her to England where she trained as a dancer under Marie Rambert. From these unusual, and not widely known, beginnings the author traces her career through *Gigi* (one of only two stage appearances listed), to the leap to fame in the film *Roman Holiday*, superstardom and the present day, paying due attention on the way to her personal life, in an occasionally rather fulsome but interesting and enjoyable book, which fills a gap. Well illustrated, with filmography and index.

Ava, Roland Flamini, Robert Hale, £9.95

This is a good, popular showbusiness biography, with invented conversations and the emphasis definitely on Ava Gardner's personal life. With neither filmography (admittedly not very many of the films would merit one) nor index, it is hardly – as described in the blurb – a 'definitive' biography, even allowing for the vagueness of that much overused adjective. But it is a pleasant 'read', nicely produced, illustrated, and treats its subject with warmth and frankness.

Best of British – Cinema and Society 1930–1970, Jeffrey Richards & Anthony Aldgate, Basil Blackwell Publisher, £12.50

In this extremely interesting, important and entertaining book, the authors take ten famous British films (from *Sanders of the River* to *If . . .*) and examine them in considerable detail against their social backgrounds. Their theme is the close-linked relationship between cinema and society, and they have developed it brilliantly. Perhaps the most fascinating chapters are those on Powell's *A Canterbury Tale* and the Ealing comedies (through *The Ladykillers*), but all of them are full of insight and fresh viewpoints – without the undue left-wing bias found in some similar and less convincing studies. The section on *Saturday Night and Sunday Morning* contains some revealing details of the negotiations and compromises between the producer and the BBFC. For both filmgoer and student of modern social history, this attractively produced book (which contains a detailed filmography) is one of the most significant of the year.

Bob Hope, W.R. Faith, Granada, £9.95

Possibly the fullest biography yet of the 80-year-old comedian, dealing in entertaining detail with his many activities from star to 'troops morale-booster'. Illustrated and excellently indexed.

Brigitte Bardot – 'And God Created Woman', Sam Levin, Sidgwick & Jackson, £7.95

A paperback collection of sumptuous large-page studio portraits, in black-and-white and colour, by a famous photographer, plus a selection of film stills, coloured magazine covers and record sleeves. The text – brief biographical paragraphs and film comments – is minimal, but who in these circumstances needs a text?

British Cinema History, Ed James Curran & Vincent Porter, Weidenfeld & Nicolson, £16.50 hardback/ £8.95 paperback

An 'academic' collection of essays on various aspects of the subject, but the approach is in no way 'dusty', the writing in general being lively and the viewpoints often original and fresh. It is somewhat politically biased, but interesting, informative and important, and there is a superb 60-page bibliography – but no index.

Burt Lancaster, Minty Clinch, Arthur Barker, £8.95

This is a very well written, standard showbusiness biography, short on documentation, but painting a credible portrait of Lancaster's career. Enough personal details are given to satisfy most gossip lovers, but the emphasis is mainly on his professional career and on the films themselves, with numerous quotes from contemporary criticisms. Lancaster has a number of notable films to his credit (not forgetting the long underrated *The Swimmer*), and here is a welcome evaluation, as well as a life of a not over-written star. A filmography, or at least a list of movies, would have been welcome, but there is an adequate index.

Cagney, Doug Warren with James Cagney, Robson Books, £8.95

After many years of carefully guarded privacy, Cagney finally consented to co-operate in an 'authorized' biography. He has been fortunate in his choice of Doug Warren, the result being a sound, straightforward, appreciative, yet not unduly adulatory, account of one of the most admired and long lasting of the great Hollywood figures. 'His hope', states the author, 'was to set the record straight on a number of issues, and to tell his entire story.' Cagney's reticence about his personal life being well known, Warren devotes nearly all his eminently readable book (with good effect) to his work and career, including his interest in farming and painting. It is embellished with two full sections of good illustrations and a filmography giving commendably full cast lists.

Chaplin, David Robinson, Secker & Warburg, £9.95 cloth/£6.50 paper

Some years ago, David Robinson wrote one of the very best books on Buster Keaton, and he has now followed this with an equally interesting one on Charlie Chaplin. As indicated by the subtitle – 'The Mirror of Opinion' – the emphasis is on contemporary opinions as expressed both on the comedian's work and on his personality and private life. Also incorporated are the author's own penetrating comments on the films and on the sympathetic relationship of biographical details. The filmography is excellent and original, being set out in tabular form (for, the author claims, the first time), providing at-a-glance filmographies for Chaplin's main assistants, and showing how frequently the same actors appeared in the various productions.

Charles Boyer, Larry Swindell, Weidenfeld & Nicolson, £9.95

It is perhaps surprising to realize that Boyer made as many as 29 European and 47 American films. Many were popular in their time, but apart from a handful – *Mayerling*, *Algiers* (the 'Casbah' film), *Back Street* and *Gaslight* – it is rare they are remembered today: the name has outlasted the titles. Swindell's book is a warm, appreciative portrait of an often underrated actor, who took his own life a few days after his wife's death from cancer. It was a moving, but not depressing finale, as Boyer had been married to the English actress Pat Paterson for 44 years, and the story of their devoted partnership is an inspiring and heart-warming one. The book is well illustrated, with filmography and adequate index.

Clint Eastwood, Gerald Cole & Peter Williams, W.H. Allen, £10.95

Brief but adequate biographical details are given, but the emphasis is on the films themselves (38 of them), which are described and appraised (or reappraised) in depth. This is a useful and attractively produced record of the star's career, with many full page illustrations, a few in colour. There is no index, but the films are listed under each section on the contents page.

D.W. Griffith and the Birth of Film, Richard Schickel, Pavilion (Michael Joseph), £15.00

In his introduction to this immense biography (over 600 pages), the author states that it 'aspires to the definitive', then points out the difficulty of fully 'defining' so complex and elusive a personality. Even so, it is hard to imagine a fuller, more satisfying study of the first master of the cinema. In an easy flowing style he takes us through Griffith's life and work in engrossing detail – and often quite sharp criticism – with long accounts of the making of the major productions, *The Birth of a Nation*, *Intolerance* and *Broken Blossoms*. There is much also on the smaller films, his many associates, and the final years of decline, partly brought about by Griffith himself. With an excellent index, bibliography, and comprehensive film checklist, only the illustrations are somewhat disappointing, being poorly reproduced by modern standards and with several stills (including the famous *Intolerance* spectacular) badly split by a double-page spread.

Undoubtedly one of the most important biographies of the year, once taken up, it is, despite its weight, almost impossible to put down.

Elsa Lanchester – Herself, Elsa Lanchester, Michael Joseph, £10.95

As much a biography of Charles Laughton as an autobiography, Elsa Lanchester's book provides a lively – at times caustic – picture of the showbusiness world, starting with her night-club and music-hall period of the 1920s. Most famous in the cinema for her unforgettable bride in the second Karloff *Frankenstein* film, she also writes interestingly on *Rembrandt* and *The Vessel of Wrath* (titled *The Beachcomber* in the USA) – both with Laughton – and others. And Laughton's tragic final years are movingly described. For the rest, she sails through her entertaining story with cheerful disregard for minor inaccuracies – for example, her close associate Lloyd Wright, son of the famous architect, is spelt thus in the first couple of references and the index, and then at least 40 times appears, oddly, as Loyd.

The Epic Film, Derek Elley, Routledge & Keegan Paul, £14.95

In this very welcome addition to the 'Cinema and Society' series, the author considers the epic film, from the early Italian spectaculars to the present day, against the social and political background of the periods in which they were made. After a gallant attempt to define the word 'epic' as applied to film, he divides his survey into several sections, biblical, mythical and historical Greece and Rome, Norsemen, Anglo-Saxon (King Arthur), with a final chapter on what might be called fringe exploits. Incorporated in each section is a full and fascinating account of the various basic myths and legends themselves. His book is, in fact, scholarly in both history and film, pretentious in neither, and thoroughly entertaining in both. While in no way uncritical, he takes his subject seriously, and conveys his enjoyment of the epic cinema with infectious enthusiasm. The book is illustrated with dozens of fine stills, and contains a huge and invaluable list of mainly European films set in eras up to the end of the Dark Ages.

Fellini's Road, Donald P. Costello, University of Notre Dame Press, distributed by Academic & University Publishers, £7.50

A deep and detailed study of four major films: *La Strada*, *La Dolce Vita*, *8½*, and *Juliet of the Spirits*. Required reading for anyone interested in the art of film in general as well as Fellini in particular. Well illustrated.

The Films of Christopher Lee, R.W. Rohle Jr & D.C. Hart, Scarecrow, distributed by Bailey Bros & Swinfen, £29.25

This is a magnificent collection of reviews, comprehensive – if occasionally erratic – cast and credit lists, and a superb section of illustrations, together with often lengthy comments on individual films from Lee himself. A handsome volume and a definitive record, essential for all devotees.

Four Thrillers, Cornell Woolrich, Zomba Books, £5.95 paperback

Fiction is rarely covered in this section, but the recent Zomba series is of particular interest to the film viewer as in several cases they consist of collections of past classics from which movies have been adapted, in this instance by a doyen of *film noir* writers – *Phantom Lady* (directed by Siodmak), *Rear Window* (Hitchcock), *The Bride Wore Black* and *Waltz into Darkness* (Truffaut). A collection by W.R. Burnett is scheduled for appearance shortly. Well printed and stoutly bound, the paperback edition (the books are available in hardback also) is very good value for money.

Fred Astaire, Michael Freedland, W.H. Allen, £10.95

Yet another life of Astaire, but with the emphasis on his work – and above all the 'work' that goes into his work – and on the illustrations, which are lavish, many of them full page and rare. This is, in fact, a pictorial biography, but with a fuller text than usual, by an experienced showbusiness writer. Of particular interest, both in photographs and text, is the attention given to the earlier years.

Grand Illusions, Richard Lawton, Columbus Books, £9.95

This superb collection of photographs of Hollywood stars from the Golden Years was highly recommended on its first appearance, in hardback, in the 1975/6 *Film Review*. Now reissued in stout paperback, the illustrations have lost none of their remarkable quality of reproduction. Mainly studio portraits, but including a number of stills, each has been chosen for its artistic merit, and the result is a stunning conglomeration of glamour – male and female – from 'The Twenties and Before' to 'The Forties'. The early years get an unusually good showing, and many of the photographs are exceedingly rare. Hugo Lecky provides an enjoyably nostalgic text, and altogether this is a unique record of what, to many millions, 'going to the movies' was all about.

The Great Book of Movie Monsters, Jan Stacy & Ryder Syvertsen, Columbus Books, £7.95

Not just another horror book. Happily, one cannot be serious all the time and this Who's Who of monsters is a well sustained joke which also contains a good deal of useful reference material. Apart from one or two interestingly unusual people, such as Carrie and Norman (*Psycho*) Bates, dull ordinary human beings are in general excluded. In fact, the few exceptions to this (Lon Chaney and Christopher Lee) are to be regretted as they slightly dispel the illusion. Otherwise, only directors and technicians are mentioned. Each monster is provided with a photograph (of variable quality), a history and a number of very entertaining details, such as height, occupation, food, habits and – best of all – 'What To Do If You Meet'. Amusing, often witty, and recommended to every horror buff. (Note: Some name misspellings have crept in – Richard Dreyfus, Fredrick March.)

Halliwell's Film and Video Guide, (4th Edition), Leslie Halliwell, Granada, £15.00

The new edition of this massive and essential reference book should need no recommendation to the discerning filmgoer. A new three-column layout enables no fewer than 2,000 extra entries to be compressed comfortably into its 900 pages. The sections on silent and foreign films have been enlarged, as has the number of shorts. There are three comprehensive lists of alternative titles and an interesting section (very useful for TV viewers) on comparative screen sizes and shapes, together with some 250 good illustrations, mainly stills. Critical comments are, of course, individual, but mainly fair – and one does not *have* to agree with all of them!

Hollywood Hunks, Jacqueline Nicholson, Columbus Books, £3.95

This somewhat unfortunately titled paperback devotes two or three pages of photographs and gossipy details to each of 38 so-called he-men of the screen, from Gable onwards. They are grouped under headings such as Heroes of the American Heartland, Anti-Heroes and the Big Four (Eastwood, Redford, Newman and Reynolds), although some might query this last category. Essentially for light reading, or dipping in to, the claim of 'wonderful insight' on the back cover is flying a little high.

The Illustrated Guide to Film Directors, David Quinlan, Batsford, £14.95

This is a companion volume to the same author's *Directory of Film Stars*. With fewer names to cover (570), the author has space for fuller commentaries on each director, and these are both concise and detailed. Filmographies are as complete as possible and include TV movies as well as shorts. Some 250 good photographs round off a handsome and useful addition to the reference shelf.

The Illustrated Who's Who of the Cinema, Ed Ann Lloyd & Graham Fuller, Orbis, £12.50

This large-scale reference book is particularly notable for its wide scope. Apart from stars and directors, it includes writers, composers, cameramen, producers, distributors and others, both English-speaking and foreign. The time scale extends from the early silents (generously treated) to the present day. Filmographies are only selective, but this is inevitable if the book is to be kept within reasonable length. The 450 four-column pages also contain hundreds of excellent illustrations, many in colour. Well written, and entertaining as well as informative, it is highly recommended for quick and easy reference.

In My Mind's Eye, Michael Redgrave, Weidenfeld & Nicolson, £9.95

Though primarily devoted to the theatre, and almost unwillingly led into films, Michael Redgrave eventually left the cinema richer by a number of unforgettable performances – *The Browning Version*, *Dead of Night* and *The Way to the Stars*, to mention but three. All are represented (though perhaps not as fully as the filmgoer might have wished) in this autobiography. The pages are full of witty and perceptive comments on his work; he is disarmingly frank about his fluctuating political opinions, and movingly objective in describing the tragic onset of the Parkinson's disease which brought his career to a premature close. Nobody who remembers his many screen and stage performances should miss this book – well illustrated and excellently indexed – by one of the most sensitive and haunting actors of our time.

International Film Guide 1984, Ed Peter Cowie, Tantivy, £6.50
International TV & Video Guide 1984, Ed Tuomola, Tantivy, £6.40

With this issue the *Film Guide* reaches its 21st birthday, as reliable and all-embracing as ever, combining coverage of world cinema from Argentina to Yugoslavia (and in due course, no doubt, Zimbabwe may join the company), together with ancillary activities from festivals to film magazines. There is a rich section on animation.

The *TV Guide*, now two years old, follows a similar formula and should surely prove as valuable. Particularly useful are the long lists of TV plays and films for Britain (from 1980) and the USA (from 1982–3), providing at least some kind of record of a very transient medium. Both books contain a large number of illustrations.

The James Bond Films, Steven Jay Rubin, Columbus Books, £7.95

Steven Rubin describes and analyzes the making of every Bond film in detail, from *Dr No* to *Never Say Never Again*, explaining how many of the effects and stunts were worked, and how various other problems were solved. An introductory chapter goes back to the source – Ian Fleming himself – and also provides a glimpse of the very first James

Bond, Barry Nelson, in the 1954 live television screening of *Casino Royale*. The facetious 'jokey' chapter headings are irritating when one is leafing through to find a particular film, otherwise this is a useful addition to the Bond literature.

Jazz Baby, David Houston, Robson Books, £8.50

The subtitle, 'The Shocking Story of Joan Crawford's Tormented Childhood', in fact promises (or threatens) more than it delivers. Presumably an attempt to excuse, or at least explain, her lurid later domestic life, this is a short account, told with much imaginary dialogue, of the events up to the point when Billie Cassin became, via Lucille LeSueur, Joan Crawford. Perhaps the subject may now be regarded as being sufficiently covered.

Joan Crawford – The Ultimate Star, Alexander Walker, Weidenfeld & Nicolson, £12.50

A companion volume to the same author's beautifully produced book on Garbo, this equally handsome biography is described as 'authorized by Metro-Goldwyn-Mayer', signifying that here also Alexander Walker has had access to the files of the great studio. The result is both an engrossing and a highly entertaining text accompanied by a lavish collection of illustrations, all excellently reproduced.

It is a warmly appreciative but frank account: for instance, it puts into proper perspective the sensations and scandals in the years following the star's death. And because of the author's freedom of the files, it is also packed with fascinating details not to be found elsewhere.

There is a generally concise and usefully annotated filmography, and also a note of the dollar-sterling exchange rate variations over the years, which is essential for a true understanding of earnings and profits.

John Gielgud – A Celebration, Gyles Brandreth, Pavilion (Michael Joseph), £12.95
Alex Guinness – A Celebration, John Russell Taylor, Pavilion (Michael Joseph), £12.95

These two beautifully produced volumes each celebrate a birthday – in the first case of 80 years, in the second of 70 – and most worthy tributes they are. Fairly brief, but perfectly adequate, accounts of two of the most illustrious careers in contemporary theatre and cinema are accompanied by a dazzling array of excellent photographs, many of them rare, all reproduced with crystal clarity. The books conclude with comprehensive chronologies of stage, screen and television appearances, and good indexes. Each is a decoration to any theatrical bookshelf, and also a most useful work of reference.

Kino, Jay Leyda, George Allen & Unwin, £7.95

This reprint in paperback of the famous, mammoth *History of the Russian and Soviet Film* (1960) will be welcome to all students of the USSR cinema. New material includes a survey of Soviet productions since the end of World War II and a 60-page select list of titles from 1907 to 1982, yet even at this length the list contains only about one in 20 of the films actually produced. Sixty-four pages of stills and copious notes round off an authoritative, well researched and documented study.

Kubrick, Michael Ciment, Collins, £13.95

This superbly illustrated book consists of a brief biographical section, a survey and analysis of Kubrick's work, chapters on two specific films (*2001, A Space Odyssey* and *The Shining*), four interviews with colleagues and – to crown the volume – three rare interviews with the director himself, on *A Clockwork Orange, Barrie Lyndon* and *The Shining*. A detailed bibliography and filmography complete the collection. The author, an experienced film critic and historian, brings to his subject enthusiasm, authority and perception in equal proportions and has been lucidly translated by Gilbert Adair.

Lana, Lana Turner, New English Library, £8.95

An odd mixture that reads something like an 'intimate confessions' article in a popular magazine, and at others as a true and at times moving story of an eventful life, with quite sharply etched portraits of the people and places concerned – notably Golden Hollywood. The horrifying central episode of the killing of gangster Johnny Stompanato is narrated with courageous frankness. Lana Turner states that her purpose in writing the book is 'to tell it all' – and it appears that indeed she has.

The Life and Times of the Western Movie, Jay Hyams, Columbus Books, £9.95

The Western, despite its current so-called decline, is inexhaustible: so it seems are the books that can be written about it. This is a straightforward history, divided into decades, and very pleasant and easy to read. The author obviously knows and loves his subject and has the knack of conveying his enthusiasm to his reader. Some 400 films are discussed and brought enjoyably to the memory. Though, justifiably, the greater coverage is given to 1950 onwards, it is good to find reasonable space given to the often neglected silents. Particular care has been taken over the stills, some full-page and in colour. By no means an exhaustive treatment and without reference material except for what can be found in the text, this is a modest, unpretentious, well indexed and attractively produced survey.

The Life of Alfred Hitchcock, Donald Spoto, Collins, £12.95

It is probable that more has been written about Hitchcock than any other director, but it is questionable whether the springs of his inspiration have yet been as thoroughly investigated than in this immense study (nearly 600 pages) aptly subtitled 'The Dark Side of Genius'. Despite the 'courteous refusal' of Hitchcock's family to co-operate actively or contribute to the book, following his wishes, the author has delved as deeply as possible in order to lay special stress on the autobiographical elements in the films. Whether one agrees or not with all the conclusions drawn, the result is engrossing reading, and the book is based on personal memories, years of study, and interviews with a great many friends and associates.

Spoto's study is very well documented, with full notes (not cluttering the pages of the text but gathered together at the end), an excellent filmography, a list of television films and a first-rate index, in addition to interestingly unhackneyed illustrations. This is an important addition to Hitchcockian literature.

Liza! Liza!, Alan W. Petrucelli, Columbus Books, £8.95

A large paperback, 'unauthorized' biography of Liza Minelli, popular in approach but well researched and documented with a filmography and lists of theatrical and TV appearances. Plenty also about mother Judy. The book is somewhat awkward to handle, but easy to read and embellished with a large number of excellent illustrations, many full page, including enchanting glimpses of Liza as a small child.

The Look of Buster Keaton, Robert Benayoun, Pavilion (Michael Joseph), £15.00

At first glance this super-coffee-table book, with its comparisons of Keaton to painters such as Picabia, Derain, Chirico and Magritte, and to Dadaism and Surrealism, etc, might arouse fears that it enters the higher reaches of critical preciosity. In fact, it turns out to be a most original and stimulating study of his films, appearance and personality, guaranteed to increase any enthusiast's appreciation of the great comedian of the silent cinema. The text is lucid, unpretentious, affectionate and penetrating; the copious illustrations are apt, often rare and superbly reproduced. An ingeniously combined filmography and biographical section round off a most useful and enjoyable tribute. (Note: The still on page 148 shows George K. Arthur (L), not Jack Haley.)

Mae West, George Eells & Stanley Musgrove, Robson Books, £9.95

'The Lies, The Legends and The Truth' is the challenging subtitle of this biography by two close friends. It is certainly detailed, and certainly frank. Mae West's films have not worn well, and it may be difficult nowadays to appreciate the furore she caused (and also in the theatre, of course) when they first appeared. It is all told here, in what may well come to be regarded as the definitive study of her life. A useful bonus to this readable book is the very full coverage of stage and screen cast lists. The illustrations are interesting, if rather smudgy: one may question the caption 'The Many Faces of Mae West' – on the contrary it has been noted before that she seems to have at most only two expressions, at any rate for the still camera. The index is patchy and at times careless – no fewer than eight or nine errors in the first few pages, for instance.

Margaret Rutherford – A Blithe Spirit, Dawn Langley Simmons, Arthur Barker, £8.95

After a somewhat uncertain (and confusing) opening section in which it seems the authoress is anxious to tell us more of her own not uneventful life than that of her subject, the book continues as a fairly straightforward biography. It is an intensely personal record, with the writer (Margaret Rutherford's adopted daughter) sharing a good deal of the limelight – and also, it may be considered, a fair share of the not very generous photographic section – but on the whole there is a lot about the great character actress's life and work. Despite an occasionally fulsome style, it is a warm and appreciative portrait, only occasionally mawkish, of an obviously lovable, highly talented and original personality.

McQueen, William F. Nolan, Arthur Barker, £8.95

Steve McQueen was known for his dislike, especially in his later years, of giving interviews. However, he planned to collaborate with his friend, the present author, and authorized him to continue the book after his death. The result is an intimate memoir by an experienced writer which rates a high place among biographies of the year. Each chapter is prefaced with a note relevant to the following pages, and much of the story is told in McQueen's own words. The final chapter, covering the tragedy of his cancer, his courage, his acceptance of unorthodox treatment and the controversy this caused in medical circles, is moving and engrossing reading. Filmography, index, and a generous section of illustrations.

The MGM Girls, P.H. & P.A. Brown, Harrap, £8.95

Though this account of the triumphs, disasters and battles of the stars against the Metro-Goldwyn-Mayer establishment covers much familiar ground, it is lively, entertaining and very well illustrated. Modestly disclaiming any attempt to be a film history, it is well researched and sets a few records straight, in addition to supplying numerous extra nuggets of gossip from the seemingly bottomless Metro mine. Among the many names included, from L.B. Mayer down (or up), are Garland, Garbo, Shearer, Harlow, Maclaine, Davies (Marion), Murray (Mae), Lamarr and Elizabeth Taylor – the only star, according to the authors 'to buck successfully the MGM system'.

(Note: Many senior filmgoers, with fond memories of the enchanting Renee Adoree, will be up in arms at seeing her described as a 'sickly, melancholy circus performer'.)

Moraldo in the City & A Journey with Anita, Federico Fellini, University of Illinois Press (distributed by Academic & University Publishers), £11.00

Two early, unfilmed screenplays by Fellini (1954 and 1957 respectively) are very attractively presented in this neat volume. The first was to have been a sequel to *I Vitelloni*, and both – edited and translated for the first time into English by John C. Stubbs – are written in the form of present-tense novelettes, which makes for very easy reading.

In view of the unique autobiographical content of all Fellini's screenplays, these two (one concerned with youth, the other with maturity) are obviously of the greatest interest to serious students of the great director's career; but they can equally well be read and enjoyed simply as first-class, subtle, often amusing and moving stories. An important appendix lists sections of both scripts which provided material for use in his later films such as *La Dolce Vita* and *Amarcord*.

My Hollywood, Sheilah Graham, Michael Joseph, £10.95

Though at times resembling a sort of knitting together of gossip column extracts, this is on the whole an entertaining if somewhat scrappy collection of anecdotes, memories and opinions by the ex-Cochran Young Lady who became one of the leading chroniclers of the Golden Era. Among the dozens of names dropping all around are Scott Fitzgerald (prominent, as might be expected in view of her close relationship with him), Louella and Hedda, the dreadful duo who could 'make or break' in their newspaper columns, and almost every well known star of the period. There is a rather charming chapter on Ronald Reagan, and a slightly sad 'then-and-now' section. Miss Graham's approach is in the main kindly – her claws are generally sheathed. However, her style is sometimes clumsy ('Eisenhower was, and Ford is, two of his golf partners'), and on page 155 there is a most unfortunate confusion of 'infer' with 'imply'. Nevertheless it is a very enjoyable nostalgic gallimaufry.

My Last Breath, Luis Buñuel, Jonathan Cape, £8.95

A lively, urbane and often very amusing combination of memoirs and opinions by one of the greatest – if sometimes infuriatingly tantalizing – of directors. With wit and charm, he writes of his repressive Jesuitical schooldays, the Spanish Civil War, Dali and *Un Chien Andalou*, his later struggles and poverty, and the final great flowering in Mexico. He also airs his views on a multitude of subjects, from religion to dwarves to newspaper reporters, his hatred of the use of 'gutter words' by modern writers and the pretentious jargon of some forms of film 'scholarship'. This fascinating autobiography is without an index – a pity.

Napoleon, Kevin Brownlow, Jonathan Cape, £10.95

Kevin Brownlow's brilliantly successful recovery and reassembly of Abel Gance's epic film (first shown in Paris in 1927) is a major event in the history of cinema. The full story, climaxing in the triumphant screening at the Empire Theatre, London, in 1980, with full orchestral accompaniment, is told in this important and fascinating book. Packed with stills and production photographs, a 20-page synopsis, enormous cast and credit lists and a fine index, it is as exciting and tense to read as any detective thriller – which indeed it at times resembles – and is a worthy monument to the author's 35 years of devotion to the five-hour masterpiece.

Niven's Hollywood, Tom Hutchinson, Macmillan, £10.95

In this affectionate tribute to his friend, the author skilfully combines an appreciation of David Niven and his work with what might be called a potted survey of Hollywood, past and present. He is greatly aided by the illustrations (very well captioned), a fascinating and wide ranging collection of frequently offbeat informal photographs of people and places from the silent days of the cinema to the present. Nostalgic and amusing.

Oscar, Thomas Simonet & Editors of Associated Press, Columbus Books, £6.95

The outstanding qualities of this pictorial history of the Academy Awards are first its completeness and secondly its illustrations. In addition to the obvious main classes – actors, cameramen, directors and best picture, etc – there are *full* lists, including nominations where relevant, of awards for editing, scientific and technical work, documentaries, shorts and honorary awards, etc. All are arranged by category, each of which is prefaced by an introductory note. Every award in the main categories is accompanied by a photograph, and dozens of others are scattered through the remaining sections. The book is rounded off with a medley of comparisons, oddities, jinxes and a large index. The approach and writing style are sometimes rather casual and chatty, but the serious reference value is very high. Indeed with the amount of handling the book will probably get, a hardback edition (the above is a stout paperback) would be useful.

A Passion for Films – Henri Langlois and the Cinémathèque Française, Richard Roud, Secker & Warburg, £9.95

This is a timely and important biography-cum-tribute to the famous French archivist – founder (with Georges Franju) and director of the great film library which is as essential to the cinema in France as the British Film Institute is to Britain. The author, well known critic, director of the London Film Festival for nine years and of the New York Film Festival since its inception in 1963, has written a detailed account of Langlois's life and work, guiding the reader through sometimes complicated events with commendable conciseness and lucidity. There is a full account of the notorious '*affaire Langlois*'. A brief section of interesting illustrations includes two charming portraits of the young and the older Louise Brooks who, as she says herself, 'owes her rediscovery' to Langlois.

The Private Cary Grant, William C. McIntosh & William Weaver, Sidgwick & Jackson, £8.95

As the title suggests, this is a 'personal' life, based on the experiences and recollections of Grant's secretary/companion/bodyguard/chauffeur, William Weaver, over about 20 years. Grant's early career is briefly treated, but the main part of the book covers the years after his last film in 1966 – his marriage to Dyan Cannon and the unhappy legal wrangles over his young daughter, his activities as businessman and traveller, his horror of publicity and ceremony, and his numerous strange foibles. Affectionate but by no means adulatory, and often very amusing, the portrait presented may considerably surprise the thousands who know only the elegant, confident, drily humorous star of over 70 films. All in all, a thoroughly enjoyable read.

A Private View, Irene Mayer Selznick, Weidenfeld & Nicolson, £9.95

An autobiography by a daughter of L.B. Mayer and the wife of David Selznick could hardly fail to arouse great expectations. Though one might (unreasonably, in view of the title) wish for more of the inside story of MGM and less of the domestic details, there is plenty to grip the attention of anyone interested in the most famous studio of them all – the Harlow/Paul Bern tragedy, first impressions of Katharine Hepburn, and yet another view of the making of *G.W.T.W.* After leaving Hollywood and husband, Irene Mayer became a notable producer herself in the theatre (*A Streetcar Named Desire, The Chalk Garden*), yet the final section of the book, though far from the cinema, still contains many references to film personalities. One black mark: the book cries out for an index – but does not get one.

Richard Attenborough – A Pictorial Film Biography, David Castell, The Bodley Head, £12.50 hardback/ £7.95 paperback

This follows more or less the same formula as the long-running 'Films of...' series from various sources, ie, lengthy biographical and analytical introduction (particularly interesting in this case), full coverage of all films, as actor and/or director, with several stills in each instance, critical comments, filmography and index. It is a very good example of this useful type of reference book, and a worthy tribute to one of the most notable and likeable figures in British cinema.

Rita – The Life of Rita Hayworth, Edward Z. Epstein & Joseph Morella, W.H. Allen, £9.95

Messrs Epstein and Morella are well known practitioners of popular show-business biographies, with the emphasis on the personal lives of their subjects. Here there is much attention to Orson Welles, Prince Aly Khan and others closely associated with the star, less about her films – though Harry Cohn, notorious movie mogul of Columbia ('a sadist who, in the end, was intent on destroying her') receives plenty of attention. All this is recounted with suitable regard for dramatic highlights, but also with sympathy, in particular to the tragedy of her later alcoholism and contraction of the frightful Alzheimer's disease at the age of 62. Good index; no filmography but in this instance it is hardly called for.

Roman, Roman Polanski, Heinemann, £12.95

From a precarious and later ghastly childhood under first the Nazi then the Soviet occupation of Poland (including a vicious physical assault which almost killed him), Polanski passed through years of struggle to prove his skill as a film maker. His successes with *Repulsion*, *Cul-de-Sac* and *Rosemary's Baby* proved he was a brilliant director, with a penchant for the macabre. Success

also brought a reputation for trendy living. An assured position in the contemporary cinema and a truly happy marriage were brutally shattered by the terrible murder of his wife, Sharon Tate. Later, after recovering enough to make his most esteemed film, *Chinatown*, a charge of raping a 13-year-old girl (reduced, on his plea of guilty, to 'unlawful sexual intercourse') led to his leaving the USA for good. After making the beautiful version of Hardy's *Tess* in France, he returned to his early love, the theatre, with a highly successful production of Peter Shaffer's *Amadeus*, in which he also played Mozart.

All this is recounted in this autobiography (dictated to and brilliantly written out by Edward Behr), partly to set matters straight after years of misrepresentation in the press. The more lurid events are treated frankly, but without sensationalism, self-exoneration or self-pity. Most importantly, the circumstances and problems in the making of all the films are recorded in fascinating detail. Well illustrated, engrossing reading, but regrettably no index: with several blank pages, this should surely have been included.

(Note: In a reference to a projected but unmade film, the title is given as *The Dinner Party*. As it dealt with the tragic, true history of the unhappy Donner Party who were driven to cannibalism in their trek across America in 1846 this is a most unfortunate misspelling.)

The Samurai Film, Alain Silver, Columbus Books, £14.95

This is a revised and updated edition of the book originally published in 1977. In the 1978/9 *Film Review*, I commended it for the lucidity with which the author explains many of the mysteries of the subject – one of the stranger film genres. A historical description of the Samurai is followed by a study of the 'warrior retained in the service of a clan' (see glossary provided) in fiction and film, and the work of various directors, led by Akira Kurosawa. A massive reference section, in which the author is joined by James Ursini, includes a detailed series of filmographies and an excellent index. This handsomely produced volume, fully illustrated with stills and frame enlargements, is a most welcome reissue.

Science Fiction, Horror & Fantasy – Film and Television Credits (2 vols), Harris M. Lentz III, McFarland (distributed by Bailey Bros & Swinfen), £69.95 the set

This gargantuan reference work, almost 4,000 pages, without doubt provides the most comprehensive coverage of the three film categories yet published. About 600 pages are devoted to the film and television credits of thousands of players, while 130 pages are given to directors, writers and producers, etc. The second volume contains director and casts of an almost equal number of film and television productions. The range is vast – in time, from the early silents to 1982, in subject from the obvious to such as *Jane Eyre, Laugh, Clown, Laugh* and *Rasputin* (five titles). Though the work is American based, British television is well represented, even in cases where the productions have not been screened in the USA. Many series are included in detail – Alfred Hitchcock and Dr Who fill 12 pages each, *The Prisoner* (the recently revived cult series of the 1960s) is covered in full. Though it would be miraculous if such a massive undertaking was completely free of errors, it is obvious that scrupulous efforts have been made to achieve accuracy. The two stout, attractive volumes are indispensable for libraries – public and private.

The Science Fiction Image, Gene Wright, Columbus Books, £9.95

An illustrated encyclopedia which has the advantage over similar reference books of covering not only cinema but also television, radio and theatre. The first, however, has predominance, a large number of sci-fi films being provided with an informative commentary, brief cast list and technical credits. Directors, writers, technicians, fictional characters and others have individual entries, and a large number of explanatory paragraphs on technical terms and procedures, such as dolby, laser, holography and introvision (with diagram), form a particularly useful addition. There is the occasional odd omission (for example, John Wyndham, when room is found for Lewis Carroll), but with over 1,000 entries the genre as a whole is generously covered. The illustrations, which include colour sections, are unhackneyed and of good quality. A useful handbook, which fills a number of gaps.

Screen World 1983, John Willis, Muller, £12.95

All the usual features of the 33 preceding volumes are to be found in this coverage of the American film year: no comments or criticism, but very comprehensive cast lists, several stills on each film, technical credits, obituaries, biographical data, etc, and an enormous index. A complete on-going American reference work – earlier volumes are collector's pieces.

Seeing Is Believing, Peter Biskind, Pluto Press, £6.95

The author takes some 30 films of the 1950s, such as *Twelve Angry Men, High Noon, From Here to Eternity, Invasion of the Body Snatchers, Giant* and *I Was a Teenage Werewolf,* and analyzes them in relation to the politics and social attitudes of the period in America. Some of his analogies may seen rather strained, but he writes lucidly, unpretentiously and often with humour, a welcome rarity in such analytical undertakings. A quality paperback, well indexed and illustrated with stills.

Selected Film Criticism (1896–1950), Ed Anthony Slide, Scarecrow (distributed by Baily Bros & Swinfen) £9.35–£16.65

Five handsome volumes of contemporary criticisms of hundreds of American-produced films, taken from various sources, many of them rare. This invaluable collection compiled by a well known historian and archivist is highly recommended for all enthusiasts, students and researchers.

Skywalking – The Life and Films of George Lucas, Dale Pollock, Elm Tree Books, £9.95

A full-scale, serious and solid (in no pejorative sense) study of one of the most remarkable leaps to fame – and fortune – in the cinema. With only a handful of shorts, three features as director (*THX 1138, American Graffiti* and *Star Wars*) and four as executive producer/part writer to cover, the author is able to go into great detail with each production – *Star Wars,* understandably, taking pride of place. The ambivalent relationship with Francis Ford Coppola is also given due prominence. Cast and credit lists are dauntingly comprehensive. Lucas himself has given full co-operation to this well written 'unauthorized' biography, and the result is an engrossing picture of the 'agony and ecstasy' of film making.

Stars!, Daphne Davis, Columbus Books, £14.95

Large glossy photograph albums of film stars are not hard to find. Where this one scores is in its range (from Mary Pickford to E.T.) and in the reference material supplied – for example, the full filmographies, such as that of Mary Pickford, which starts from 1909, make a formidable list. Nearly 50 names are represented, including directors Steven Spielberg and George Lucas; there are also 'group' sections such as Tracy/Hepburn and the *Godfather* family. Daphne Davis provides brief commentaries and an unusually interesting introduction, though her style, for some reason, becomes progressively slangy as she approaches the present day, with some rather dreadful non-words such as 'prophesizes'. However, this is more than just a glamour portfolio, it can also be used as a reference book. The illustrations themselves are superb and reproduced with crystal clarity.

The Steven Spielberg Story, Tony Crawley, Zomba Books, £4.50

This, to my knowledge, is the first full-length study of Spielberg's work. With blockbusters such as *Jaws* (the original), *Close Encounters . . .*, *Raiders of the Lost Ark* and *E.T.* to his credit, it is certainly time that one should appear. Much of the contents was dictated by Spielberg himself, the rest is written in a lively, if occasionally scrappy, style which nevertheless makes for easy reading. Stoutly made and very well illustrated, this paperback is a useful and reasonably priced introduction.

Tales from the Hollywood Raj, Sheridan Morley, Weidenfeld & Nicolson, £10.95

A very entertaining account of the 'British Colony' in Hollywood, chiefly in the 1930s, led by such stalwarts as actors Aubrey Smith and Ronald Colman, and writers Hugh Walpole and R.C. Sherriff. The book sparkles with anecdotes, some familiar, others new, and with long, often hilarious memoirs from the people concerned. On occasion the comments are stimulatingly caustic. A less pleasant chapter recounts the snide jeers from Michael Balcon and some magazine journalists on the outbreak of war. Interesting details of less widely known players such as Reginald Denny and John Loder are included. All in all, this is a vivid picture of the sheer dottiness at times of the famous Golden Era of movie-making.

(Note: Sheridan Morley makes an odd slip in calling Ida Lupino the daughter of Lupino Lane; her father was Stanley Lupino.)

The Universal Story, Clive Hirschhorn, Octopus, £12.95

Another in the massive 'Complete Studio Story' series (following MGM, RKO and Warner), covering over 2,600 feature films from 1913 to 1982, together with brief history outline, lists of associated productions and releases (foreign, Hammer and documentary, etc) and an enormous double index of titles and personnel. The mass of films produced during the early years (over 900 silents alone) has necessitated curtailing details of the less important movies during this period, but all are listed. With these exceptions, every film is given a critical commentary, main cast and credits and a still, this ranging from miniature to full-page, but all excellently reproduced and many, especially in early years, extremely rare. From Lon Chaney to E.T. this is a veritable storehouse of delight for the nostalgic buff and of useful information for the serious researcher.

(Note: An odd omission is the strange and haunting 1947 film *The Lost Moment,* based on Henry James's *The Aspern Papers,* directed by Martin Gabel and one of Susan Hayward's best.)

The Warner Brothers, Michael Freedland, Harrap, £8.95

Apart from Jack Warner's autobiography of 1965, this is the first full study of the brothers (as apart their Studio) to come my way. Michael Freedland deals very skilfully in a fairly brief book with the complications of coping with four brothers and the manifold ramifications of their careers. Moving fairly quickly to their famous break into sound movies with *The Jazz Singer* (though some enjoyable if minor films were made in the silent period), the book then deals with the great years of the gangster, 'sociological', musical and prestige productions, the internal battles – including, of course, the legal wrangle with Bette Davis – and then the later decades up to the death of Jack in 1978, the year of *Superman*. It is well researched and, above all, eminently entertaining.

(Note: May Robson could hardly be described as 'an old *silent* screen actress' (page 120); and Margaret Sullavan and James Stewart appeared in *The Mortal Storm*, not the 'International' one.)

The Western, Phil Hardy, Aurum Press, £14.95

This is the first volume in an important new series of major reference books: future titles, scheduled to appear about once a year, include (2) Science Fiction and (3) Horror, with others to follow. In 400 pages the Western film is covered from 1929 to the present in ten-year sections. Over 1,600 films (from B features to spectaculars) are given a brief synopsis and history, leading plays, directors, etc, and technical details. Eight useful appendices include 'Most Successful Westerns' (inflation adjusted) and a complete record, with brief details, of all sound Westerns not included in the main text. The book is lavishly illustrated with stills (from the Kobal collection), well indexed and handsomely presented. A valuable addition to any reference collection.

Who's Who on the Screen, John Walter Skinner, Madeleine Productions, £6.95

For yet another Who's Who to be justified, it must have a new approach – which can fairly be said to apply in the case of this attractively neat and fact-packed book. To start with, all its 830 entries are living at the time of publication. This means that, with no Garbo, Gable, Swanson, Wayne and other towering, but profusely covered, giants to deal with, space can be given to very many other players for whom the researcher may hunt in vain – James Cossins, Talia Shira, Bert Kwouk, Victoria Principal, to pick but a tiny handful at random. All are given carefully checked biographical and personal details together with selected films, including TV movies and series, in addition to relevant book titles. Every name is accompanied by a photograph. Strongly recommended as both useful and – for a hardback – reasonably priced.

Other Books

The Man You Loved to Hate – Erich von Stroheim and Hollywood, Richard Koszarski, OUP, £7.95

Cary Grant, Richard Schickel, Pavilion Books (Michael Joseph), £10.95

Peter O'Toole, Nicholas Wapshott, New English Library, £8.95

Duke – A Love Story, Pat Stacey, Souvenir Press, £8.95

Cary Grant – Haunted Idol, Geoffrey Wansell, Collins, £8.95

Golden Boy – the Untold Story of William Holden, Bob Thomas, Weidenfeld & Nicolson, £8.95

Judy and Liza, James Spada, Sidgwick & Jackson, £9.95

Sean Connery, Kenneth Passingham, Sidgwick & Jackson, £7.95

The Films of Dustin Hoffman, Douglas Brodie, Citadel, £14.95

The Last Sitting (Marilyn Monroe), Bert Stern, Orbis, £12.50

Heartbreaker – Two Months with Judy, John Meyer, W.H. Allen, £8.95

Elstree, Patricia Warren, Elm Tree Books, £9.95

Gotta Sing Gotta Dance, John Kobal, Hamlyn, £9.50

Index